Mark Twain and Youth

D1520154

Also available from Bloomsbury

Melville: Fashioning in Modernity, Stephen Matterson
Poe and the Subversion of American Literature: Satire, Fantasy, Critique,
Robert T. Tally Jr.
Toni Morrison and Literary Tradition: The Invention of an Aesthetic,
Justine Baillie

Clemens family on the porch of their Hartford home in 1884. From left to right: Clara, Sam, Jean, Livy, and Susy.

Mark Twain and Youth

Studies in His Life and Writings

Edited by
Kevin Mac Donnell and R. Kent Rasmussen

Foreword by Hal Holbrook

Bloomsbury Academic
An imprint of Bloomsbury Publishing Plc

B L O O M S B U R Y
LONDON · OXFORD · NEW YORK · NEW DELHI · SYDNEY

Bloomsbury Academic

An Imprint of Bloomsbury Publishing Plc

50 Bedford Square	1385 Broadway
London	New York
WC1B 3DP	NY 10018
UK	USA

www.bloomsbury.com

**BLOOMSBURY and the Diana logo are trademarks of
Bloomsbury Publishing Plc**

First published 2016
Reprinted 2016

© Kevin Mac Donnell, R. Kent Rasmussen, and contributors, 2016

Kevin Mac Donnell and R. Kent Rasmussen have asserted their right under the Copyright,
Designs, and Patents Act, 1988, to be identified as Editors of this work.

British Library Cataloguing-in-Publication Data
A catalogue record for this book is available from the British Library.

ISBN: HB: 978-1-4742-2312-6
PB: 978-1-4742-2538-0
ePDF: 978-1-4742-2313-3
ePub: 978-1-4742-2311-9

Library of Congress Cataloging-in-Publication Data
A catalog record for this book is available from the Library of Congress.

The cover image of the young Sam Clemens gazing at the muddy Mississippi River
from above Hannibal, Mo., was drawn by Edmund Franklin Ward for the serialization of
Albert Bigelow Paine's "The Boys' Life of Mark Twain" in the November 1915 issue of
St. Nicholas. Its color was added by R. Kent Rasmussen.

Typeset by Deanta Global Publishing Services, Chennai, India
Printed and bound in the United States of America

To the memory of
Albert E. Stone (1924–2012),
whose pioneering work helped inspire this book,
and
Thomas A. Tenney (1931–2012),
whose unflagging energy and generous support
of Mark Twain studies inspired everyone

Contents

Foreword

Hal Holbrook

He was a boy raised on a river.

"I used to be drowned in that river every summer and then be fished out and drained out and set going again by some chance enemy of the human race."

You've got the whole man right there. His boyhood launching pad was the river, then the twinge of a satiric mind, the outrider with his eye on us and it's going to be salty. He was raised that way. "People born to be hanged are safe in water," said his mother. This is not a long stretch from Mark Twain's grown-up observation, *"I wonder if God invented Man because he was disappointed in the monkey."*

You think that's a joke? Think again. Look in the mirror. His welcome to the twentieth century is an echo: *"Give her soap and a towel but spare the looking glass."*

The century I was born into was not funny. Mark Twain died in its tenth year, but the wave of our country's future had been rolling in and the getting or losing of money would define it. Nor was my boyhood funny. I was raised by my grandfather down near the ancestral landing on the way to Cape Cod, along with my two sisters, because our Mom and Dad had left us in the playpen and hit the road. Never came back. Nobody wanted us so Grandpa took on the job. He was our hero. Strict. Hair combed at breakfast and speak when spoken to. Survive on your own, that was the New England game and I wandered by myself through the blueberry patch out back and made my own Kentucky long rifle out of the branch of a tree when I was Dan'l Boone, and all that stuff Tom Sawyer did was part of me, except I did it alone and I never heard of Sawyer.

Books? There were no books. Only one shelf in the small bookcase to the right of the fireplace, about the genealogy of New England. Never read that, but my Grandfather gave me two books in the Rover Boy series. *The Will to Win* and *Do or Dare*. They prepared me for suicide. Never heard of Twain. That was much later, twenty-nine years old was my age then and I'd been out on the road for four years with my first wife, Ruby, trying to make a living with a little two-person show we put together in college to tour schools, and Mark Twain was in one of the sketches we did. Suddenly we had a baby and the show was history. Do you know what it's like walking the hot cement sidewalks of New York looking for a job as an actor when nobody's heard of you and nobody cares two cents how desperate you are? "Join the club" is the answer to that.

I turned around one day and went up to the office of a tough old bird who knew Twain because his father booked Mark Twain's lecture tours. "Why don't you do a solo?"

"What??"

"Twain."

"Go out on the stage alone?"

"I think you could get bookings," said Bim Pond. He didn't smile.

I walked out on 45th Street and looked at the people and the taxis going by and felt as hopeless as I would ever feel again. I walked up to 59th Street to the old Argosy Book Store. "Where's Mark Twain?"

"Upstairs to the left. At the end."

This guy wrote a lot of books. *Tom Sawyer*. Heard of him and took it home. By page three I started feeling better. I don't know why. Maybe it took me back to the blueberry patch and the long rifle. At Argosy, I got some more. *Roughing It*, *Huckleberry Finn*, and a book called *Mark Twain Social Critic*. Social critic? I thought he wrote books for kids!

That was sixty-two years ago. Yes, he was a social critic and yes he used children to write his books, but maybe that's where the subversive part comes in. That wry country kid in the guise of Huck Finn describing his Pap thus: "*Whenever his liquor begun to work, he most always went for the government.*"

> Call this a guvment! Just look at it and see what it's like! Why, looky here. There was a free nigger over there from Ohio—a mulatter. . . . And what do you think? Why, they said he was a p'fessor in a college, and could talk all kind a languages, and knowed everything. . . . And that ain't the wust! They said he could vote when he was at home. Well, that let me out! Thinks I, what's this country a'coming to? Why, it was 'lection day and I was just about to go and vote myself if I warn't too drunk to get there; but when they told me they was a state in this country where they'd let that nigger vote, I drawed out. . . . The country may rot for all of me.

The world he observed turned him into a subversive because some of it was not nice. The salty grin concealed it. Maybe he used children as a disguise. The boy on the raft going down river with a runaway slave, from him he learns about loyalty and friendship—On the raft, not from his father. In *Tom Sawyer* the great Judge Thatcher visits the Sunday school and praises the dear children for reading their Bible so diligently and asks Tom the names of the first two disciples. His teacher freezes. It is impossible this boy can come up with the answer. "*David and Goliath*," says Tom.

Twain was taking an uppercut at the hypocrisy of the frontier Calvinism he'd been enslaved under in Hannibal. American literature of the later 1800s began to release the pent up passion to escape religious hypocrisy's stranglehold on America's conscience. Lawrence Berkove writes about it eloquently in this book and the boy from Hannibal began to preach. But his sermons were disguised. Children did the preaching. Huck Finn, the Prince and the Pauper, Joan of Arc, and Sandy in *A Connecticut Yankee*. Lots of people didn't get it. *Adventures of Huckleberry Finn* was pulled out of the libraries over a hundred years ago because it wasn't proper reading for young minds. What a joke! It wasn't proper reading for the racist nation called America that was busy lynching Negroes.

Maybe Mark Twain used the young generation to express his commentary on the hypocrisies of his world until they overwhelmed him. Was *Joan of Arc* a hymn to the daughter he loved and lost, Susy? The world began to break apart then. The larger world and the personal one surrounding him. He'd seen the Devil at play in America's corporate front yard and in our nation's grab in the Philippines and he knew it by the back and gave up hiding behind children. "*I am against the eagle putting its talons on any other land.*"

But it was in this disguised but darker world of Twain that Hollywood has failed our great American chronicler. Mark Dawidziak pursues that humbling fact through his account of the films about Twain and his books where Hollywood has dropped the ball. Why? No guts. They are afraid of anything that rises above the level of box office perfume and that has killed more good stuff in our literature-to-film agenda than anything else. When I met Fredric March after playing Twain in Hollywood in 1959, he said, "Tell me, didn't you feel this guy was a horse's ass? That white suit and all?' I said I didn't look at it that way. "Well, you understand him." March was a hero actor for me in film and on stage, and he did a good job in *The Adventures of Mark Twain*, but that was because March was one hell of an actor. The dialogue smelled Hollywood, but he surmounted it. Mostly. Whenever the film business has got hold of Mark Twain, they detour around the gut and soul of him. His satiric, subversive view of us all does not suit a money machine. The greatest crime the motion picture business has committed in my particular view is to have allowed *Huckleberry Finn* to be turned into Hollywood mendacity instead of what it should be: the great American film. They lack the courage. Look at John Ford's *The Grapes of Wrath* and think what Huck could have been.

I read Steinbeck's book on a troop ship in the North Atlantic. Kept me from getting seasick. It changed my focus on my country, stuff I knew nothing about, the desperate plight of the Dust Bowl Okies in the fruit-picking farms of central California, desperate for pennies to buy milk and flour, starved and preyed upon by the same corporate farms which took their homes from them in Oklahoma. I had seen those ragged survivors on Route 66 when Grandma drove me west to see my father in '39. I saw the shaky homemade trucks sagging down with whole families hanging on, pans and farm implements dangling off their sides. This was America?

Mark Twain came on the scene at the end of the Civil War when a slow but urgent change in the moral strictures of American society was challenging the church for the source of truth. The Presbyterian heaven was losing its attraction. Wars will do that. Clemens had got himself to the Nevada silver mines where the skeptical culture of life and journalism in Virginia City and San Francisco was producing a bunch of irreverent writers whose opinions were not subject to the shadow of the pulpit. They were shaping a new kind of journalism. Sassy and bold. "We had a political editor who was already excellent and needed only a term or two in the penitentiary to be perfect." It was reporting with a devil's eye that toyed with truth like a boy torturing a cat and sometimes yanking its tail to make it screech. Mark Twain's subversive nature responded, it fit the frontier style of Missouri. A humorist could find his style with Artemus Ward in town. Twain would find a deeper use for it.

Writing about his experiences in Hawaii in *Roughing It*, he spread broad strokes of burlesque over the missionaries' corruption of the native culture by the introduction of Christian values. Watching the native ladies swimming, Twain wrote, "I went down and sat on their clothes." On Sundays, their attempt to dress themselves for churchgoing in a bizarre arrangement of mismatched styles to satisfy the Christian preachers, one native dame strides in with a top hat on. Then Twain's payoff: "How sad it is to think of the multitudes who went to their graves on that beautiful island and never knew there was a hell."

The subversive urge grows and spreads as the 1880 decade arrives with the assassinations of Czar Alexander and President Garfield in America. *The Prince and the Pauper* is written, then *Huckleberry Finn*, and it closes out with *A Connecticut Yankee*. He reaches into English history to find a cutting edge. The story ain't cute. Speaking to students in Zagreb in 1960 behind the Iron Curtain, a young communist youth said, "Mr. Holbrook. In *The Connecticut Yankee*, was Mark Twain writing about England or America?"

Smart, those communists. "Good question," I said. "When the book was published, only one London reviewer wrote about it. It was considered a slam at England. It was no more a slam at England than America. Remember those slaves in chains in *Yankee*? That has happened everywhere. Not just England. Even here." Silence. Subversive at work.

Do people get it? Do they want to get it? When the hypocrisies we protect ourselves with are exposed, do we get it? When we dress up nice for church and sit in the pews and sing those hymns about Jesus and how we love him and how he loved the poor folks, do we get it? Look in the mirror. Ask ourselves, Why did he write *The Mysterious Stranger*? "Oh, he got depressed in his old age. His daughter died and his wife was sick and he went bankrupt and had to work real hard to pay back . . . well, he was old." Right. So, "The War Prayer" has nothing to do with us?

In Sam Clemens's time people read books. Not the cute ones splashed with cartoon color they hawk to kids and mommas today. Books. Today the young minds being trained-up to run the Western world are nose deep in cell phones communicating with other young geniuses about girls and football and trying to understand Pink Floyd's message in "The Wall." The surge from Dickens to Harry Potter has been huge. There's a difference. In Dickens, you get a history lesson. In Dreiser, you get a history lesson. In Steinbeck . . . . Yes, I have just opened myself to a frontal attack, but I am not trying to defend cell phones and Harry Potter. Who was Abraham Lincoln? Answer me that.

What we get from Alan Gribben in his essay here is an understanding of how those old-fashioned pioneers without cars and television entertained themselves 150 years ago. Poor buggers. Read books. To each other. For entertainment. Emerson and Wordsworth. Walt Whitman and Poe. There may be a truth out there, waiting to upset everything: the more we reach for the stars, the less we know about each other and the more trouble we get the world into. In *Tom Sawyer Abroad*, Tom and Huck are "*disputing about a subject rather too large for them.*" Tom is saying how discouraging it is "*to see the days and the years slipping away and him getting older and no wars breaking out,*" where he can make a name for himself and get a reputation. Then he strikes an idea. He will go on a Crusade.

"*What's a Crusade?*" *says Huck.*

"*Is it possible that you don't know what a Crusade is?*"

"*No I don't and I don't care. I have lived my life to this time without knowing and I have my health, and if you don't wish to tell me, I'd as soon I didn't know. What's a Crusade? Is there any money in it?*"

"*No! A crusade is war! War against the heathen cannibals to reclaim the Holy Land.*"

"*Which holy land is that?*"

"*There is only one Holy Land! You think there's a million?*"

"*How did we come to let them get it?*"

"*We did not come to let them get hold of it. They always had it!*"

"*Oh. Then it belongs to them.*"

"*Certainly.*"

"*I understand it now. If I had a farm and it was my farm and another fellow wanted it, would it be right for him to take it? If they own anything at all it's the land. As for the holiness, they can have that if they want it.*"

"*You don't get the hang of it at all! It has nothing to do with farming! It's on a higher plane. It's religious!*"

"*What? Religious to take a man's land away from him?*"

"*Of course! It's always been so!*"

A question enters my mind—Did Twain and some of those thoughtful reading folks see this religious war in the Middle East coming at us now, including ISIS, over one hundred years ago?

The second question might be, What started it? The cell phone? It is surprising the amount of historical thinking one might find buried in literature.

Shelley Fisher Fishkin is someone I've known for some time and her essay here about Hannibal and the environment where Mark Twain grew up gives us the foundation under him. Missouri was a slave state then and Sam Clemens's father owned slaves. The historical remnants of Hannibal's slave town character were hidden for decades in deference to protecting the legends where Tom painted the fence and got lost in the cave with Becky, and nearly every store and gas station hung out his name. Things are changing. A new respect for the tortures that our black population in America has endured for well over three hundred years is urging the change upon Hannibal and that is a good thing. Truth is the best trail through any forest of deception and I have to dearly believe that Twain would have it so.

Shelley's history of the slaves' lives in Hannibal will surprise you. I won't intrude upon her telling of it except to say that there was more going on than you and I have dreamed about and the story of belief in one's self when those about you don't share it is the heart blood of the American dream. We say we believe in courage. It was in hiding here. But what it says about Mark Twain is also revealing. Because he says very little about his feelings for the Civil War and his allegiance during it. He cut out. Went west with his brother and quit the war.

Why? Depends on which cage your brain is in. Let's see. He loved his job as a riverboat pilot on the Mississippi: "*I loved that profession far better than any*

I've followed since. . . . I hoped to follow the river the rest of my days and die at the wheel when my mission was over. But by and by the War came and commerce on the river ceased and my occupation was gone. I joined the Confederacy, served for two weeks, deserted and the Confederacy fell."

There you get it again, twinge of the satiric mind. What he is not telling us is: His father owned slaves, his home was a slave town, he hated losing the pilot house job on the Mississippi that he loved because a war started and blew it away. It's safe to say those were his strong feelings about it. The cause of the war, why it was fought, these were issues he was not ready to face because his feelings were stirred by the pilot house memories and summers on his uncle's farm, playing with young black and white kids and listening to Uncle Dan'l tell ghost stories. The slave who became Jim in *Huckleberry Finn* was Dan'l. His sympathies were uncertain about the cause of the war. He finally joined friends in a hometown Confederate militia that called themselves the Marion Rangers, served for two weeks, decided he did not feel good trying to kill people, quit soldiering, and joined his brother Orion who was going west to the Nevada Territory to serve in the territorial government. It must have been a deeply disturbing decision. His mind about the issue of slavery had not been made up? How interesting—twenty years later he would write *Huckleberry Finn*. And then *A Connecticut Yankee*. And then *Pudd'nhead Wilson*.

On the streets of San Francisco, he watched a policeman laughing while a Chinese person coming home from work was being stoned by children. I can remember when we made fun of the Chinks. The Jews, too. Cripples. All kinds of folks. It was the American way. The young man from the slave state Missouri was a journalist, and he wrote about the cop laughing at the Chinese guy being stoned. The police chief got wind of the story and warned him not to send it to the editor again. Sam Clemens did, the editor refused to print it and Clemens quit the paper and left town. He went up into the mountains of Calaveras County with the Gillis brothers, stayed through the winter in a cabin on Jackass Hill and heard a story in the bar quite a walk away, about a jumping frog. He wrote it. Took the suggestion to send it east to a publication and suddenly he had a career.

This is where Mark Twain began to be Twain. Cruelty angered him. When he sailed to the Hawaiian Islands and saw the Christian religion re-clothing the honest native traditions with Presbyterian hypocrisy, that angered him. When he worked in Washington for the senator from Nevada in Congress, political corruption angered him and he quit. The throat-hold the Calvinist religion had on him since a child and had on the people of his country as he spoke to them on lecture tours, that angered him. He tried to suppress it and be nice. Then the chance came to join a pilgrimage to the Holy Land with a boatload of Christians. He made the deal to go and wrote a book. *The Innocents Abroad*. Big hit. He was freed up. After *Roughing It* he wrote The *Gilded Age*, a book that so sliced open the guts of political corruption in Washington that its name was given to the historical decade. Mark Twain's satiric glint had found its target, the one he couldn't find ten years before.

I have pondered this. I don't think we know the direction we're taking until we decide what it is. He was like many people in the heartland of our country. They move slow. Have to think about it. When the War Between the States began, he was not sure about slavery. He had to find out. Twenty years later he wrote *Huckleberry Finn*.

Fate has placed us in a questioning time. Now the borders of our decisions are raging with dangers and we are unsure. We did not understand the enemy before and we have been walked into a trap by the ignorance of politicians and of history. We were playing politics and looking at cell phones, and our people have been killed. Now it's too late. We are in a religious war. They do not end. ISIS knows this. Do we?

Fools are abroad. The boy who became Mark Twain had so much to learn. He learned how deep the wounds of slavery had scarred his country. Too late. The scars opened into bleeding wounds and we know them now, but do we know ourselves? Do we get *Huckleberry Finn*? Is it a book about America's curse of slavery and the racism lodged in our souls or is it "a racist book"? How can we do the job staring in our face if we do not know ourselves? The punishment of slavery is now ours. In 2008 we made Abe Lincoln proud. We elected a black man president with the largest number of votes ever given to an elected president. His electoral vote margin was 365 to 173. A near landslide. The same day the leader of the losing party in our democracy declared for all to hear that their goal in the next four years was to defeat him. Since his election, more guns have been sold to white men than ever before.

Is this the end of democracy? Are you laughing?

Introduction

Concepts of youth

Among major American writers of the nineteenth century, no name is more closely associated with concepts of youth than that of Mark Twain. Born Samuel L. Clemens in 1835, Twain is incontestably most famous as creator of two of the most iconic children in literature—Tom Sawyer and Huckleberry Finn. During his lifetime, both critics and readers saw him as a champion of an idyllic American childhood—an author who wrote nostalgic books "for young people of all ages"—as the subtitle of his 1882 novel *The Prince and the Pauper* proclaimed. Moreover, his public persona always projected youthful energy, even if there were moments when his private remarks belied that public image, as when writing on May 24, 1905 to decline an invitation to travel to Nevada and relive his early western years. He waxed nostalgic, and then concluded,

> Those were the days! . . . They will come no more. Youth will come no more. They were so full to the brim with the wine of life. There have been no others like them. It chokes me up to think of them. Would you like me to come out there and cry?

He ended that letter with a heartfelt benediction: "Goodbye . . . and take an old man's blessing." However, youth prevailed, and shortly after he died in 1910, his intimate friend William Dean Howells published *My Mark Twain*, a memoir in which he said of him, "He was a youth to the end of his days, the heart of a boy with the head of a sage; the heart of a good boy, or a bad boy, but always a wilful boy, and wilfulest to show himself out at every time for just the boy he was" (5). Two decades later, Twain's daughter Clara Clemens expressed a similar sentiment in her own memoir—which added a single word to Howells's title—*My Father, Mark Twain*:

> He was fundamentally young to the day of his death and would in no way have been marked by the increase of years had not sorrow clutched at the vitals of his heart. I remember thinking, when I saw him lightly running up and down the stairs on the day that a large banquet was to be given in honor of his seventieth birthday, "Father is younger now than I have ever felt." (258)

In the public mind, Twain is most closely associated with youth in the context of his writings. While during his own time, *The Prince and the Pauper* was commonly regarded as his most appropriate work for prim and proper children, questions about whether children should read *The Adventures of Tom Sawyer* and *Adventures of Huckleberry Finn* were—and still are—debated. Not long after publication it was banned from the shelves of the public library in Concord, Massachusetts, because it was deemed morally repugnant. One Concord school board member dismissed the book as "the veriest trash, suitable only for the slums." Despite such harsh condemnation, there was no debate about the Tom and Huck novels being primarily books for children—especially boys. Meanwhile, Twain's dark social satires and indictments of slavery and religion were long virtually ignored.

The importance of Twain's own childhood as an inspiration for his writings has long been widely recognized, and his own ever-youthful appearance and outlook attracted frequent comment. Again, however, such observations were usually made in the context of Twain's being a writer of books for children. Even after his death, as critical works on his writings began appearing in steadily growing numbers, the function of youth in his other works did not receive much attention. Indeed, his writings were typically seen as falling into distinctly separate, neat categories, including books for children, political satires, social satires, comic aphorisms, jolly travel writings, and his late pessimistic writings. Any notions that youth might have served as a way to convey his satire by seeing the world through the innocent eyes of the young, or that his darker views of humanity could be found not only in his later works but also in his earlier writings, or that youth was a recurring motif to be found in most of his writings throughout his life were slow to take hold.

By 1961, when Yale professor Albert E. Stone, Jr., published *The Innocent Eye: Childhood in Mark Twain's Imagination*, perceptions of Mark Twain had begun to change. Critics such as Philip S. Foner were paying more attention to his social satire. Twain's earlier writings were coming to light and attracting study by scholars such as Edgar M. Branch, and the cynical underpinnings of his outlook were becoming visible as previously unpublished works appeared in print from time to time. Around the same time, however, Twain's only surviving daughter, Clara, was still living and refusing to allow certain of her father's manuscripts to be published. The revealing diaries of Twain's secretary Isabel Lyon were not yet available to scholars; his own massive, so-called Ashcroft-Lyon Manuscript remained to be discovered; the illuminating first half of his original manuscript of *Huckleberry Finn* was still thought to be irretrievably lost; only a modest—and heavily edited—volume of extracts from his fifty notebooks had been published; documentation of his own library and reading habits was fragmentary and scattered; as much as half of his autobiographical writings and many other manuscripts still awaited publication.

An excellent overview of Twain's youth-themed writings, Stone's study extended well beyond the familiar works traditionally regarded as written for children. Stone lacked access to the materials outlined above but made masterful use of the published resources available before 1961, as well as several then-unpublished manuscripts—notably "Villagers of 1840-3" and "Record of the Small Foolishnesses of Susie and 'Bay' Clemens (Infants)." Stone presented children as Twain's deliberate agents of his satire and touched on social themes such as race to explain the literary context from which Twain's own literature sprang. At the same time, he acknowledged the grimmer aspects of Twain's youth writings and explored Sam's boyhood for additional clues. The main focus of his study, however, was the role and depiction of childhood within Twain's work—not those broader themes.

In the more than a half-century since Stone's landmark volume was published, a wealth of primary sources and fresh biographical information has come to light, while the body of critical works about Twain has grown at least twenty-fold. Several important Twain works have been published for the first time; definitive scholarly editions of his major youth-oriented writings have appeared; and thousands of letters written by him, his family, and his associates have been found. The result has been that critical insights into Twain's writings and biography have followed paths that could not even have been imagined during the mid-twentieth century. Nevertheless, although numerous articles about the youthful aspects of Twain's life and literature have been published, and many books about him have included chapters on youth-related themes, the present volume is the first new book exploring the full breadth of Twain and youth to appear since Stone's 1961 book.

Written by many of today's leading Mark Twain scholars, the essays in this volume inevitably cover some of the same ground explored by Stone. However, our end-of-volume "Works Cited" list should reveal the obvious: The essays rely heavily on primary sources discovered since 1961 and critical works published since that year. Moreover, the essays greatly expand the scope of the work pioneered by Stone so long ago. It should not be surprising, therefore, that they reflect fresh critical insights and abundant new details about Twain's life and works. It should also not be surprising that they do not all agree with one another or speak with a single voice—calling to mind *Huckleberry Finn*'s "Explanatory" note stating it was no accident Twain's characters spoke in different voices. Twain did not want readers to suppose his "characters were trying to talk alike and not succeeding." Essayists in this volume—the characters in our own drama—also speak in different voices, and not by accident. We called upon them to offer their insights as researchers and literary critics to provide biographical background and social contexts and to share their personal experiences teaching Mark Twain. They could no more accomplish all those goals in one voice than one voice could have sustained Twain's great American novel.

The Table of Contents should explain our book's overall approach. Essays examine Sam's childhood, the family and friends of his youth, his youthful and adult reading habits and their influence on his writings, his own children and their parenting, how he portrayed youth in his early writings and in his books built around youthful characters, how he retained his youthful outlook throughout his life and coped with aging, and how themes and concepts of youth figured into his writings on such issues as race relations, gender roles, aging, and healthcare. Finally, our essays conclude with modern depictions of Twain's works in film and personal narratives of how he is taught today and perceived by today's youth.

While not all the book's essays fit in neat categories, we have tried to arrange them in broadly relevant sections. Essays in the first section, collected under the prosaic heading "Overviews," survey two broad themes—Twain's lifelong attitudes toward youth and aging and the place of his writings in the broader context of the literature of his time. Holger Kersten begins the discussion by describing how Twain, his family and acquaintances, and his public coped with his growing old, and what that tells us about our own views of youth. Lawrence Berkove then explores how Twain's darker view of humanity and countertheology extended to his conceptions of youth. Consideration of Twain's place in nineteenth-century children's literature begins with Lucy Rollin's survey of that literature and how Twain's writings figure into it. Alan Gribben then discusses what is known about Twain's own youthful reading and lifelong familiarity with children's literature.

The next section, "The Clemens Family," opens with Henry Sweets's examination of the young Sam's boyhood family with particular attention to his relationships with his siblings and how those relationships influenced his later writings, laying a solid biographical foundation for the rest of the book. John Bird then examines the surprisingly modern parenting techniques the adult Sam and his wife, Livy, applied to their own children, who are then discussed—in order of their births—in the essays that follow.

The life of Twain's first child, Langdon Clemens, was so tragically brief that the boy is typically almost forgotten in discussions of Twain's children. Joseph Csicsila's essay on Langdon makes a convincing case that Twain wrote

The Adventures of Tom Sawyer in response to his grief over losing his only ؛
Similarly tragic was the early death of Twain's second child and first daughter,
Susy Clemens. James Golden offers a vivid portrait of the girl whose youthful
demise has tended to define her place in the Twain narrative. The story of Clara,
Mark Twain's second daughter and only child to outlive her parents, was much
different. Cindy Lovell's essay on her provides a balanced view of the child who
would go on to play an important role in shaping her father's public image. The
story of Twain's youngest child, Jean Clemens, is yet another kind of tragedy.
Karen Lystra narrates the misfortunes of Jean, separated from her parents by
illness and later from her father by his private secretary, only to have her joyful
reunion with him cut short by her untimely death.

Essays in the third section in the book, "Sam Clemens's Life Experiences,"
examine broad aspects of Twain's life. It opens, appropriately with a discussion
of how Twain dealt with the memories of his youth in the autobiographical
writings he composed during the last years of his life. Written in the novel form
of a dialogue between an Old Editor and a Young Editor who have devoted years
working on the autobiography at The Bancroft Library's Mark Twain Papers and
Project, it was composed by two of the Project's veteran editors, Vic Fischer and
Benjamin Griffin—who insist that they themselves are not necessarily the Old
Editor and Young Editor of their dialogue.

Here, it should be explained that we originally asked Henry Sweets to write his
essay on Twain's youthful friends and siblings. After seeing how much he had to
say about both subjects, we decided it would be better to split his essay into two
parts. The part on friends is thus the logical second essay in this section of the
book. Next, the resident physician of Mark Twain studies, Dr. K. Patrick Ober,
documents the poor state of healthcare and astonishingly high mortality rates of
children in Twain's day and goes on to show how those dismal conditions cast
a lifelong shadow over his childhood, parenting, and writings. Barbara Schmidt
then examines the motivations behind Twain's "adoption" of young "angelfish"
girls as surrogate grandchildren during his last years, as he coped with aging and
loneliness.

Twain's most notable writings on youthful themes provide the subject of the
book's next section, in which they are explored in chronological order of their
publication. David E. E. Sloane traces Twain's radical departure from Victorian
norms—first back to his earliest Western writings and then forward to his later
works. Peter Messent illustrates how the theme of youth is present throughout
Twain's first solo novel, *Tom Sawyer*, along with the twin themes of nostalgia
and nightmare visions of childhood. Hugh Davis next shows how *The Prince*

and Pauper shares some of the darker aspects of youth that are more often associated with the childhoods of Tom and Huck and also looks at how Twain's genteel historical novel has been adapted into modern popular culture. Making innovative use of Twain's recently published *A Family Sketch and Other Private Writings*, Andrew Levy demonstrates that *Huckleberry Finn* is just as much a stinging rebuke of American childhood as it is of slavery, and that viewing the novel as a light-hearted portrayal of childhood is unrealistic. Debra Ann MacComb then documents how nurture trumps nature in *Pudd'nhead Wilson*, and shows how Twain indicts a social system that exerts self-serving and absolute power over the powerless—children and slaves alike. Ronald Jenn rounds out this section, describing how *Personal Recollections of Joan of Arc*, from Twain's conception of the work to its critical reception, is clearly linked to childhood, youth, gender, feminism, and sainthood.

The final essays in this section explore two themes pervading Twain's writings. Linda Morris takes a close look at the extent to which Twain role-played with gender identity in his works, and why he used youthful characters more often than adults to do that. Finally, Wendelinus Wurth shows how a surprisingly large number of Twain's characters—both youths and adults—are orphans and how they see the world differently from a position of isolation, and even disaffection and nihilism.

Perhaps the logical conclusion to the book is its section on "Modern Perspectives." Shelley Fisher Fishkin offers a penetrating discussion of Hannibal's black and white youth that begins by tracing the lives of two children born in northeastern Missouri in 1835—one free and white, the other black and enslaved. She then continues their story and its aftermath up to the present day. The remaining essays examine Mark Twain's reception in modern times. Mark Dawidziak reviews a selection of notable films based on Twain's works and their seminal influence on shaping modern popular images of the role of children in Twain's works. Jocelyn Chadwick explains how different generations of young readers, most recently Generations "X" and "Z," have responded to Twain's writings and argues why these young people are the key to Twain's future. John Pascal concludes the book with vivid eye-witness testimony of how his young students respond to Twain in his classrooms.

We believe that a new book on Twain and youth has <u>long</u> been overdue and, as its editors, hope another half-century does not pass before the next book appears on this subject. Youth was at the core of Twain's writings; his own youth the prism through which he framed his narratives, and his narratives the prism through which his readers view not only American culture but all of humanity in our most tragic and comic moments. We hope these essays refract all the colors of these prisms.

Kevin Mac Donnell
R. Kent Rasmussen

Note on Citations

In the interest of conserving space and streamlining citations, we have reduced all but a handful of footnotes and endnotes to truncated or abbreviated parenthetical citations. These are keyed to the lists of Works Cited on pages 269–85. The first list contains Mark Twain's own writings, virtually all of which have been reduced to abbreviations, such as "*AMT1*" for volume 1 of the recent University of California Press (UCP) edition of *Autobiography of Mark Twain*. Note, incidentally, that because the UCP edition is now complete, we have converted all references to other editions of the autobiography to *AMT1*, *AMT2*, or *AMT3* citations. Also, because readers are likely to use different editions of Mark Twain's books, we have converted most page references to his books to chapter references, which should be of broader use than page references to specific editions. Exceptions include editions such as the 1996 Oxford University Press (OUP) volumes that contain special editorial content. Because some of Mark Twain's shorter works appeared as both magazine pieces and individual books, their titles may appear both in italics and inside quote marks.

The second Works Cited list contains books, articles, correspondence, and interviews of other authors. Parenthetical citations for these sources vary. Most simply contain author names, such as "Cox," for the only James Cox title in the list, *Mark Twain: The Fate of Humor*; or author names followed by truncated titles in cases of authors with multiple titles listed.

If any mistakes have found their way into the citations, they are more likely to be the fault of the editors than that of the contributors.

Part One

Overviews

Mark Twain on Youth and Aging

Holger Kersten

One of the curious things in America's reaction toward Mark Twain is that even as the nation watched the famous author grow old, it continued to associate him with the attributes of youth. Despite the fact that newspaper readers in the first decade of the twentieth century were used to photographs showing Twain in almost iconic fashion as an elderly gentleman with the trademark shock of wavy hair, bushy eyebrows, and a heavy mustache, verbal descriptions of him often drew attention to what journalists highlighted as youthful features. A. E. Thomas of the *New York Times*, for example, described him at the age of seventy as "straight and spare as a New England pine" with a "face unlined and his cheeks touched with a ruddy glow. . . . Nobody who saw him thus," observed Thomas, "could ever possibly think of Mark Twain as old" (Thomas). The *New York Sunday World* remarked that "the surprising thing about him is the absence of an appearance of age" (*CI* 521), and because "his youth remains in his sparkling eyes," the *Seattle Star* felt it appropriate to call Clemens "70 years young" (*CI* 525).

Similarly, people who were close to Clemens emphasized that he showed no signs of being an old man. In 1908, Isabel Lyon referred to him at the age of seventy-two as "young and vigorous . . . as a youth would have been" (Hoffmann 120). A year later, Albert Bigelow Paine, Twain's official biographer, wrote that Clemens was "the embodiment of eternal youth, with youth's eternal charm" (Scharnhorst, *Twain* 302). Shortly after Clemens's death, American realist author and literary critic William Dean Howells called his friend "a youth to the end of his days" (*MMT* 5).

Outside Twain's circle of friends and acquaintances, another Twain biographer, Archibald Henderson credited the writer with the supreme literary energy that "typified the youth of America" and found "the spirit of eternal youth" to be his "outstanding, omnipresent and eternally ineradicable" quality (Henderson 75–76). That quality fit into a general atmosphere that elevated "youth" into a national characteristic. At a time when American culture was still struggling with the problem of how to define the specific character of a distinctive national literature, the English writer D. H. Lawrence saw the country's movement "from old age to golden youth" as "the true myth of America" (Lawrence). In Lawrence's wake, Henry Seidel Canby identified "youth" as "the most important" and "the most determining characteristic" feature of America's literary tradition in a 1940 article (Canby 16), and a generation later, Leslie Fiedler's cultural analysis came to the conclusion that America was the place where "everyone is young" and "where youth is indefinitely extended" (Fiedler 19–20).

In a cultural climate in which "youth" came to be a central concern, old age was regarded "only too commonly [as] a hateful and even ghastly thing." Consequently, there were few old men who did "not seek to seem to others younger than their real physiological age," according to psychologist G. Stanley Hall (195). Shortly before his sixtieth birthday, Samuel Clemens, too, declared his aversion to aging: "I have detested old age from my infancy" (*MTSpk* 301).

It was not the first time that Clemens had run up against what he would call "the wanton insult of Old Age" in "The Five Boons of Life" in 1902 (*CTSS2* 526). The first known indication that Clemens became aware of his advancing years appeared in the aftermath of his forty-third birthday. He apparently realized that his youth was over as he was writing to his mother-in-law and signed his letter "Your now middle-aged son, Saml." (SLC to Olivia Lewis Langdon, 2 Dec. 1878, *UCCL* 01611). In a letter to his own mother and sister he wrote a day earlier, he went even further when he wrote, "I broke the back of life yesterday & started down-hill toward old age" (SLC to JLC and PAM, 1 Dec. 1878, *UCCL* 0160).

Viewing the forties as a period of a fundamental change in a person's life course was not exceptional at the time Clemens reached that age. His contemporaries were familiar with the notion that the "battle with old age [begins] before we are fifty" (H. Paine 3). In *The Autocrat of the Breakfast-Table* (1858), a book with which Clemens was very familiar (*MTLR* 317–18), the American author Oliver Wendell Holmes wrote, "Old age begins at forty-six years, according to the common opinion" (Holmes 183). It was a reflex of the classic opinion advanced in Cicero's *De Senectute*, an ancient Roman treatise on aging well known in late nineteenth-century America.

Despite Clemens's rather dramatic word choices, it was not until his fiftieth birthday in 1885 that he saw himself confronted much more intensively with a recognizable landmark in his life. Although there was no official celebration, the literary journal *The Critic* printed a few birthday letters from friends and fellow writers and thus created publicity for the event. Despite the fact that Clemens was "very much pleased" with the congratulatory messages received from prominent writers, these "letters of condolence" (*AMT2* 259)—as the journal jokingly introduced them—also hit a sore spot.

Soon after that event, newspapers reported that Twain seemed offended by the large number of congratulations he received for his fiftieth birthday. In a tone of mock seriousness, he complained about the rudeness of his "many enemies"— an attitude that implied that turning fifty was a matter that should better not be mentioned since it had a devastating effect on the person concerned. He had "shot at people in the dark" when he had "something unusual against them," he said in a comment on the occasion, but had "never congratulated a person on being fifty years of age," according to the Palo Pinto, Texas, *Star* of January 29, 1886.

While this response was tailored to meet the public demand for yet another amusing quote from Twain, Clemens's private papers show that being "half-a-hundred years old" (*AMT2* 259) was not a joke for him. In his thank-you note to Joel Chandler Harris, he spoke about the "affront" of the fiftieth birthday (*AMT2* 577). In a letter to Holmes, who had contributed a birthday poem to *The Critic*, he went even further and confided that he had enjoyed Holmes's lines above all for their soothing effect: They had "drawn the sting of my fiftieth year; taken away the pain of it, the grief of it, the somehow *shame* of it" (*AMT2* 577). Twenty years later, Clemens was still convinced that any person crossing "his fiftieth parallel" would invariably experience the same emotional distress he had encountered. "When a man reaches fifty," he wrote in his autobiographical dictation for October 30, 1906, "age seems to suddenly descend upon him like a black cloud. He feels immeasurably old" (*AMT2* 265).

During the next decade of Clemens's life, the shock of having crossed the threshold of old age lost some of its intensity and urgency. Clemens seemed to take solace in the observation that the time-induced transformations in his aging body were slow, gradual and all but imperceptible. "How stunning are the changes which age makes in a man while he sleeps," he wrote to Howells in 1887 (SLC to William Dean Howells, 22 Aug. 1887, *UCCL* 02670). Because of the incremental nature of the aging process, Clemens noted a mismatch between his chronological age and his felt age. "I am old," he admitted in a 1905 letter, "I recognize it but I don't realize it. I wonder if a person ever really ceases to feel young—I mean, for a whole day at a time" (*MTL2* 789). Shortly before his seventy-first birthday he repeated that he had never felt "so young as I am now, in spirit, since I was fourteen" (*AMT2* 266). This sense of discrepancy was not limited to Clemens's feelings about himself. On one occasion, he stated that his friend and financial advisor Henry Huttleston Rogers was "sixty-seven years old by the almanac, but otherwise only twenty-five, and is as lively and companionable as any other youth of his age" (*AMT2* 161). Modern psychologists have found that for elderly people to see themselves "as considerably younger than their chronological age" was not a singular phenomenon but a common experience (Barak and Schifman 603). Unaware of the frequency of such a self-perception, Clemens resigned himself to the mystery of the aging process and concluded that "age has no age," and that the "word has no definite meaning" (*CI* 690).

As has been noted in other contexts, it is hardly possible to pin down Clemens to an unequivocal position. Since he simply "did not feel obliged to reconcile the inconsistencies in his opinions" (Andrews 237), his attitude toward old age was subject to changes according to the specific circumstances in which they appeared. It thus appears that despite his insistence that he felt young, he also admitted that he actively suppressed any awareness of his advancing years: "Anything that removes from me even for a few moments the consciousness that I am old is gratifying to me," he told an Australian audience in 1895 (*MTSpk* 301).

One way for Clemens to distract himself from the inevitability of growing older was to indulge in a fantasy of rejuvenation in which human life culminated in youth, not in old age. According to Paine, it was one of his "favorite fancies" that "life should begin with old age . . . to end at last with pampered and beloved babyhood" (*MTL2* 709). Such a reversal of the life course was Clemens's response to what he saw as an unfair distribution of life benefits, a problem that he blamed on a fundamental flaw in the original design of human life. The first half of life, Clemens complained in a 1901 letter, "consists of the capacity to enjoy without the chance; the last half consists of the chance without the capacity" (*MTL2* 709). Several years later, he illustrated this abstract observation with a reference to male sex life. In "Letters from the Earth," he wrote that "man is competent from the age of sixteen or seventeen thenceforward for thirty-five years. After 50 his performance is of poor quality, the intervals are wide, and its satisfactions of no great value to either party" ("Letters from the Earth" 439). To remedy this situation, Clemens suggested an improvement for God's creation. It would have been much better, Clemens explained, to

> start human beings with old age . . . and have all the bitterness and blindness of age in the beginning! One would not mind then if he were looking forward to a joyful youth. Think of the joyous prospect of growing young instead of old! Think of looking forward to eighteen instead of eighty! (*MTB* 1440–41)

As humorously ingenious as Clemens's vision may sound, he was not the only writer to entertain such ideas. In the February 1892 issue of *Harper's New Monthly Magazine*, Clemens's friend and former Hartford neighbor Charles Dudley Warner observed that "our life is wrong end first." "Youth is delightful," Warner stated, "but we are always getting away from it." A reversal of the normal developmental direction would bring "a charming descent, without struggle, and with only the lessening infirmities that belong to decreasing age!"

The conviction that youthful existence is to be preferred over whatever privileges maturity might offer is also encapsulated in the motto that Clemens used repeatedly after his seventieth birthday. Originally invented as an epigraph for chapter 8 in *Pudd'nhead Wilson* (1894), "It is better to be a young June-bug than an old bird of paradise" gained popularity in 1907 after American newspapers gave it wide circulation (Kersten). The underlying attitude is in keeping with the jocular advice he gave to one of his correspondents in 1906, when he wrote "Don't get any older" to Gertrude Natkin, a girl of fifteen, adding "Stay always just as you are—youth is the golden time" (*MTAq* 21).

While Twain's June-bug motto suggested that it was preferable to be young rather than old, the difficulty lay in finding a way to preserve youth. At one point, he playfully advertised the powers of Lake Tahoe as a "Fountain of Youth" (*L1* 245) but his later encounter with the "Well of Long Life," at Briddhkal Temple in India, only triggered a satirical attack on the fountain-of-youth effects attributed to this "shallow pool of stagnant sewage" (*FE* 486–89). Not that he would have completely denied the healing potential of water. From his childhood days in Hannibal to the time when he and his family visited European spas in search of relief for various ailments, Clemens at least partially entertained the belief that the application of water had therapeutic effects (Ober 98; 115). At one time, he even attempted to pass himself off as "a solid believer in the precepts of hydrotherapy" (Ober 112). When he ultimately rejected the notion that the water cure qualified as an effective medical treatment (Ober 117), Clemens did not abandon the belief in alternate forms of medical intervention altogether. According to biographer Michael Shelden, "Miracle cures appealed to his imagination" (Shelden 70), and several incidents in his biography show that he could "muster up the will to believe in the therapeutic powers of most any unconventional treatment" (Quirk 29).

An unconventional treatment of a different kind was based on the belief that contact with young people would counteract the effects of old age. On a psychological level, interaction with young children provided the elderly with a sense that, even if their professional life had ended, they still had a purpose in life. A "sympathetic interest in youth," wrote the English physician Caleb W. Saleeby, would allow an old man to live "again in his children and grandchildren" (Saleeby 186). According to his own testimony, Clemens "had reached the grandpapa stage of life" and felt deprived of what he called "a treasure palace of little people" (*MTAq* 21). Spending time with children would not only alleviate feelings of solitude but also change the way he felt about himself. "When I am in the company of very young people," he wrote shortly before his seventy-first birthday, "I always feel that I am one of them" (*AMT2* 266).

For Clemens, these young people were exclusively female, a group of ultimately twelve girls, aged between ten and sixteen, whom he referred to as his "angelfish" (*MTAq* 94). When asked why he liked "the ladies very much, especially the young ladies," he explained publicly that they "make one feel young again to be with them" (*CI* 680). Although attitudes expressed by Clemens's daughter Clara and, later, Twain scholar Hamlin Hill have led to discussions about the propriety of the relationship between the elderly Clemens and the girls of his "Aquarium Club," such a constellation was not as unconventional as it might at first appear. Christopher W. Hufeland's *Art of Prolonging Life*—a book reprinted at least five times in America between 1854 and 1880—mentioned the longstanding belief that the body of an old person could gain "new strength and vigor" when it was brought in contact with "the effluvia of fresh and blooming youth" (Hufeland 16). Citing biblical and medieval precedent, Saleeby declared in 1907, "There was a sound psychological truth symbolized in the old notion that the company of a young girl was the best means for the rejuvenescence of an old man" (Saleeby 186).

According to Clemens's own account, his self-prescribed rejuvenation therapy did have the intended effect. When he had passed the seventy-year-mark, he variously told his interviewers that he felt "only 14 years old" (*CI* 617), or twenty-five "at 8 in the morning, when I'm shaving" (*CI* 639). Less than one year before his death, he referred to himself as "a young buck" (*CI* 583) and "a boy" and predicted that he wouldn't die until he was "at least 100 years old, or possibly older" (*CI* 686).

Despite the evidence assembled here that Sam Clemens saw youth as "the golden time" (*MTAq* 21), a time "so full to the brim with the wine of life" (*MTL2* 773), it remains doubtful if, given the chance, he would have returned to youthful state of existence. A scene in *Captain Stormfield's Visit to Heaven* illustrates that all the advantages youth appears to offer turn out to be less desirable than expected. Seventy-two-year-old angel Sandy McWilliams, who once had taken the option to return to a younger age, quickly reversed his decision when he realized that joining young people at picnics, dances, and parties, turned out to be a bore. He complained that "the deepest subjects those young folks could strike was only *a-b-c* to me." He decided that he preferred "to sit quiet, and smoke and think—not tear around with a parcel of giddy young kids" (*ECS* 48).

Clemens had a similar vision for what he wanted to do at the age of seventy. At his seventieth birthday banquet, he told the more than 160 guests that he "would nestle in the chimney corner, and smoke my pipe, and read my book, and take my rest" (*MTSpk* 467). Judging from the ideas he entertained at that pivotal moment in his life, he felt no desire to return to a youthful existence. Although his speech is mainly remembered for its humorous catalog of forbidden pleasures and its overall tone of serenity, it ended on a note of finality and irreversibility, advising the guests, "When you . . . arrive at pier No. 70 you may step aboard your waiting ship with a reconciled spirit, and lay your course toward the sinking sun with a contented heart" (*MTSpk* 467). Drawing on the familiar metaphor of the journey into the sunset, Clemens's concluding words signaled a sense of ultimate composure, creating a moment of intense emotionality that brought his listeners to "the verge of tears," according to the *New News Daily Press*'s December 10, 1905, account of the event. According to the account in the Bryan, Texas, *Morning Eagle* of December 14, however, Clemens found the right language to keep his illustrious audience from falling into a mournful mood by conjuring up "a sweet and tender pathos in which there is no note of despair."

In private, however, Clemens harbored more somber thoughts about the stage of life he had reached in 1905. Shortly after his emotional public moment, Clemens revised the official version of his birthday speech and abandoned the sentimental and sugarcoated representation of the journey of life for a far less appealing image: In "Old Age," a short manuscript he left unpublished during his lifetime, the gentle sea voyage on the golden-lit ocean is replaced by a "long trek" "across the world's continents behind oxen," and the destination is no longer the mythical place where the sun sets but "the ice-summit" (*FM* 441). In contrast to Henry Wadsworth Longfellow, who had described his own seventieth birthday also as an arrival on "a snow-crowned summit," Clemens could neither see before him "other summits higher and whiter" nor agree with the poet's conclusion "that life is opportunity" (Hilen 230). Surveying the various stages of his previous life from this exposed location, the weary speaker in Clemens's text finds himself alone and entirely disillusioned, "the temple empty, the idols broken, the worshippers in their graves," with only one question remaining, "'Would you do it again if you had the chance?'" (*FM* 442). The manuscript ends there, but it is tempting to supply the missing answer from the words that Clemens chose for a passage in *Letters from the Earth*, written less than six months before his death, that "there has never been an intelligent person of the age of sixty who would consent to live his life over again. His or anyone else's" (*WIM?* 428).

Viewed in their entirety, Clemens's comments on old age show him caught up in the paradoxes of later life. Immersed in a culture that celebrated "youth" as the most desirable state of being, he struggled to define his older self among the contradictory experiences of what medical humanist Thomas R. Cole called the "wisdom and suffering, spiritual growth and physical decline, honor and vulnerability" (Cole xxv). Although Clemens never tried to hide his chronological age, he often expressed his inability to grasp the meaning of being "old."

good
sum -

From a shock of recognition in his early forties that he had "started down-hill toward old age," through a fifteen-year period of alternating feelings after his fiftieth birthday, to the publicly displayed acceptance of old age on his seventieth birthday, Clemens's reactions cover a broad spectrum. It would be too simple to claim that this process followed a straight linear development. The documentary record shows that, depending on the circumstances, his attitude was subject to change. At times of psychological distress, he felt tired and old and was ready to die; in brighter moments, he was happy to proclaim that he felt young, healthy, and energetic. Additionally, one might suspect that he tailored his responses to match the specific situation he found himself in: In an interview with the press, he might express himself differently than in a private letter, and in a public speech, he might offer his audience a diluted version of the provocative ideas he held in private.

It seems too much to expect a person to hold a coherent position with regard to such a thoroughly existential problem. Ultimately, however, it is apparent that Clemens, who "detested old age," who said he felt like a young man even when he had entered into the sixth decade of his life, and who was depicted by others as a symbol of youth throughout his career, felt no desire to celebrate youth as a superior period of life. In the end, the question for Clemens was not so much if youth was preferable to old age, it was enough to realize that youth was a part of human life—and that life was not worth living: "Life was not a valuable gift, but death was" and if there was a "blessed refuge" (*WIM?* 442–43) it was the grave and not "pampered and beloved babyhood."

Mark Twain surrounded by children aboard the SS *Minneapolis*, on which he sailed home from England after receiving his honorary University of Oxford degree in 1907.

P. Richards [Richard Pichler], *Zeichner und "Gezeichnete"* (1912).

2

"Same Damned Fools": Mark Twain and the Deceptive Promise of Youth

Lawrence Berkove

The subject of Mark Twain and youth is complicated by assumptions brought to readings of his writings, especially his novels. Well into the middle of the twentieth century, Twain was commonly regarded as an author who nostalgically celebrated an idyllic period of innocence in American history, and his novels, especially *The Adventures of Tom Sawyer* (1876) and *Adventures of Huckleberry Finn* (1885), were read as masterpieces of boys' literature. While that view of *Huckleberry Finn* has long since been displaced among academically trained readers by a view that treats the book as a serious novel, Twain is still generally associated with a happy view of childhood. Current scholarship, however, is weighing new information that advances the position that Twain's view of human life was fundamentally tragic, that the human race was damned, and that youth was included in the bleakness of his vision (see Berkove and Csicsila). The most convincing evidence of this understanding is to be found in his response to the context of his historical era and in straightforward readings of his novels of boyhood.

Twain's disillusionment with youth had many precedents, including William Wordsworth's "Intimations of Immortality" (1802–06), with which, according to Alan Gribben, he was familiar (*MTLR* 786). That poem might be supposed to be the very center of a youth-affirming outlook, with its lines "But trailing clouds of glory do we come/ From God, who is our home." But the poet later accepts that this splendid vision inevitably dies and fades away and is replaced by "Shades of the prison house," and that the directly experienced happiness of childhood years is replaced by the cold comfort of the "philosophical mind." Ultimately, the poem concedes a disparity between the joyousness of youth and the gloom that follows it, a recurring lament in both British and American nineteenth-century literature.

The nineteenth century was a period of great changes and profound and extensive turmoil and its influence can be seen in Twain's writing. Although England's Victorian era is often regarded as a time of a somewhat stuffy but benevolently regulated society that fostered reasonably happy family life—and it undoubtedly sometimes worked out that way—British literature abundantly supplies serious evidence of a more somber view. England was in the midst of the Industrial Revolution, and the demands of imperialism and capitalism often took precedence over social welfare concerns. The novels of Charles Dickens, one of England's greatest writers—such as *Oliver Twist* (1838), *David Copperfield* (1850), *Hard Times* (1854), and *Great Expectations* (1860-61)—are openly shocking indictments of the damage done to youth in the name of progress. Thomas Hardy's novels, especially *Jude the Obscure* (1895), are often bleak and fatalistic works of social criticism and character development in which young people suffer blighted lives. Still later, A. E. Housman's *A Shropshire Lad* (1896) poignantly portrays youth as a time of frustration and tragedy even in an idyllic setting, and Samuel Butler's bitter *The Way of All Flesh* (1903) describes first the building up of the religious illusions of young Ernest Pontifex and then the slow and painful process of his disillusionment. Twain read widely in Dickens, some in Butler, and considerably in Hardy. His authorized biographer, Albert Bigelow Paine, reported that *Jude the Obscure* was the last book Twain read in its entirety, ten days before he died. Twain owned a copy of Housman's *A Shropshire Lad*, and while ownership of a book does not prove influence, his familiarity with these writers argues for his awareness of these literary trends (see *MTLR*).

The works of America's romantic writers also provide ample evidence for the view that youth was often an unhappy experience, and in this field, too, Twain was an avid reader. In Nathaniel Hawthorne's novels, for example, both *The Scarlet Letter* (1850) and *The Blithedale Romance* (1852), depict love and idealism—the most sublime emotions of youth—as blighted by human nature and heartbreak. And in such tales as "The Gentle Boy" (1831), "My Kinsman, Major Molineux" (1832), "The May-Pole of Merry Mount" (1835), and "Young Goodman Brown" (1835), Hawthorne depicts the vulnerabilities and traumas of youth.

In 1859, Emily Dickinson composed "These are the days when birds come back" (Dickinson 63), one of her most tender and moving poems, from the aspect of youthful credulity. The poignancy of the poem largely derives from the longing of an adult narrator to believe with the naïve simplicity of a child in something that is not true—in this case that a few spring-like autumnal days (or life experiences) mean that time and age will reverse. In the poem, the real seasons of spring or early summer are denounced by the speaker as "sophistries" and "fraud," because they make one wish they would last instead of being remorselessly transient. The narrator's wish to be a naïve child again is paired with a knowingly futile wish for time and age to go back and remain forever at a delightful place. Insofar as it is understood by implication that Nature follows God's pattern for it, the poem anticipates but does not equal Twain's own criticism of God for making youth a time of credulity, vulnerable to God's hoaxes.

Between Dickinson's and Twain's view is that of Ambrose Bierce. In the lyrical elegy that concludes his autobiographical memoir of the Battle of Shiloh, Bierce laments his loss of the magical delusion of youth to override the ugliness of life, specifically the horror of war:

> Ah, Youth, there is no such wizard as thou! Give me but one touch of thine artist hand upon the dull canvas of the Present; gild for but one moment the drear and somber scenes of to-day, and I will willingly surrender another life than the one that I should have thrown away at Shiloh. (Bierce 24–25)[1]

Herman Melville also grimly comments on youth's susceptibility to the appeal of war in his Civil War poems: "Youth must its ignorant impulse lend -/ Age finds place in the rear./ All wars are boyish, and are fought by boys,/ The champions and enthusiasts of the state:" ("The March into Virginia" (1861)).[2]

Between 1886 and 1891, William D. Howells, a close friend of Twain and a leading supporter of literary realism made a claim—intended as a compliment—that American novelists typically concerned themselves with "the more smiling aspects of life" (Howells ch. 21). That assertion is usually cited as a notorious example of how wrong Howells was; it certainly was inaccurate in regard to Twain. But Edwin Cady argues that Howells's claim has been misconstrued and that not even the bulk of Howells's fiction conforms to his theory. Certainly, his best-known short story, "Editha" (1905), did not find youth a smiling time; it satirized a young woman whose romantic jingoism encourages her lover to enlist in the Spanish-American War, in which he is killed.

Any list of authors in the Victorian period of British and American literature, especially those in the modes of realism and naturalism, who were skeptical of youth as a time of joy can be easily extended, but there still remains a large division between them and Twain. Even before 1872, with the composition of the novelistic *Roughing It*, Twain wrote out of a heretical religious position he had amalgamated for himself from the frontier Calvinism in which he had been indoctrinated from childhood, the Deism of Tom Paine, which had undermined his belief in Christianity, and the subjection of religion to the technique of the hoax, which his fellow writers of Nevada's Sagebrush School used frequently and polished into literary art. This somber creed affected almost all of his writing, including works presenting his views of youth.

Twain's statements to the effect that the human race was damned used to be dismissed as colorful hyperbole. But since scholarship has studied the writings of Twain's late period, both unpublished and published but not widely circulated, it has become increasingly recognized that he literally meant what he said. The heretical version of Calvinism that exists at the core of most of his major and many of his minor works has been summarized as a nine-point "countertheology." Briefly, it affirms a belief in a god, but one who is malevolently inclined toward humanity; one whose created world is only an illusion, a dream of life; one who has cursed humanity with a "Moral Sense," whose only office is to enable humanity to do wrong; one who has caused all humanity to be born with the guilt of original sin that has corrupted human nature so thoroughly that all humans deserve damnation; one who has made salvation impossible except by God's mysterious grace; one who has predestined *everything* since before creation, therefore precluding freedom to all human beings; one who has predestined all humans to hell except for a small number of elect; one whose predestinations are immutable both in scheme and detail; and one who has implanted conscience in all human beings in order to irritate them and keep them uncomfortable (Berkove and Csicsila 14–17).

In addition, Twain illustrates how God has sown life thickly with hoaxes that take advantage of corrupt human nature's inclination to misinterpret sins as virtues and virtues as folly. Twain personally would have hated each point in this statement of his countertheology, but he maintained them because he believed them empirically true; they described life as he saw it. Although Twain's criticism of racism and classism in his works affects major segments of the population, his countertheology applies to *all* human beings. Thus, although black slaves in his fiction are obviously without freedom, everybody, including their white masters, is more subtly but equally effectively manipulated to act out predestined roles. And especially so are all youths, who are in fact the most vulnerable human beings because of their naiveté, credulity, impractical idealism, and passions ungoverned by seasoned wisdom. This can be seen in three of Twain's best-known books.

Roughing It (1872), far from being the unclassifiable potpourri of entertaining vignettes that it is usually regarded as, is instead a masterful book whose novelistic character and structure are brilliantly disguised as artlessness. Its central theme is stated in chapter 36: "It is a pity that Adam could not have gone straight out of Eden into a quartz mill, in order to understand the full force of his doom to 'earn his bread by the sweat of his brow'" (*RI 1993* 233). The biblical quotation emphasizes God's authority behind a destiny that cannot be evaded. Accordingly, the Western US portion of the book is largely devoted to the mostly futile attempt to become rich without working, and the Hawaiian portion is devoted to the mostly futile attempt to find another Eden where work is not necessary. The book's protagonist is an incredibly naïve young man for whom life is a romantic adventure until point by point, incident by incident, he learns the rough way that his expectations are grandiosely unrealistic. In Nevada, an entire wave of emigrants is shown to have succumbed to the seductive sickness of "silver fever" and unwittingly doomed themselves to waste their youth on mostly unproductive hard labor, reckless drinking and gambling, solitary existence, and vain hopes. If the few who atypically did get rich were ignorant before, their riches did not buy them wisdom, and a profligate lifestyle soon dissipated their wealth. In Hawaii, there were noxious insects, scorpions, hellish volcanoes, and a native history of repressive priestcraft and human sacrifice that were "providentially" replaced by a severe missionary Christianity that taught how easy it was to go to hell (*RI 1993* 440, 498). An alter ego, the narrator's older and wiser self, intrudes periodically with the voice of experience contrasting with the youth's high hopes. In the book's last chapter the youthful optimist is no more; he has been replaced by the older, disillusioned pessimist he became. What started out to be a three-month wealth-garnering revel in a new, rich, and unspoiled Eden turns out to be "seven years of vicissitudes" among scenes of ruin reminiscent of hell that left the protagonist with no gains. He did not escape God's curse; in retrospect he realizes that he would have done better in the long run to have stayed at home and worked at a conventional job (*RI 1993* 542).

Although many generations of readers have enjoyed *Tom Sawyer* as a quintessential boy's book, scholarship reveals that it has a dark side and adult themes that connect to *Huckleberry Finn*. In the novel, Tom grows up in St. Petersburg, a narrow-minded town of many violent biases, expressed at church, home, and school. The town minister is a fundamentalist Calvinist who sets the moral tone by preaching worship of a God who deals out eternal damnation generously but salvation to a minuscule few. At home, Tom is whipped for misdemeanors he did not commit as well as for those he did. Though his Aunt Polly loves him she is guided by the biblical adage "spare the rod and spoil the child." The martinet schoolmaster hypocritically hides diagrams of nudes in his desk but punishes his pupils mercilessly for minor infractions. The town doctor robs graves for corpses to dissect. The townspeople are ready to tar-and-feather, or even lynch without a trial, individuals they only suspect of being malefactors. This, of course, intimidates the slaves and someone like Injun Joe, who is "guilty" of being a half-breed. St. Petersburg is the first of the small towns Twain satirizes in his books, and is thus part of the "revolt from the village" movement in American literature. Small wonder that Tom finds relief in romantic novels, in playing hooky from school, and in escaping to the woods or Jackson's Island where he can sublimate his resentments playing games in which he and his chums are rebels, pirates, or robbers. Nevertheless, by chapter 18 Tom's character changes. It can be interpreted as his beginning to grow up, but it involves his accepting the status quo and internalizing the town's questionable morality. By the final two chapters of the novel, Tom has become "civilized," an extension of the budding con man earlier glimpsed in the fence-painting episode, a boy who now identifies with society and who will deceive Huck and Jim and exploit them for his own enjoyment in *Huckleberry Finn*.

The strongest expression of Twain's view of youth occurs in *Huckleberry Finn*. Starting with the eleven-or-twelve-year-old, marginally educated, semi-outcast boy, the son of the town drunkard and ne'er-do-well, Twain devotes the novel to a moving and brilliantly subtle depiction of how personal growth and freedom are dangled before Huck seemingly encouragingly but actually seductively, and how he is manipulated throughout and deceived at the end to forfeit all of his gains, including the noblest purpose of his life. This may seem a revolutionary way of looking at the novel, but only because readers have for many years been persuaded by Leo Marx and others to misread the story as a paradox in which the farther south Huck and Jim drift (up to the "evasion" chapters), the freer they become (see Marx).

A simpler, more direct way of interpreting the novel that is more consonant with biographical as well as textual evidence is as a work that *denies* the possibility of human freedom. The Calvinism of Twain's youth, which he could not shake off, even later in his life when he flirted with determinism, maintained that everything was predestined, every word, thought, and feeling as well as every act, whether it is seen as such or not. The power to predestine is a logical attribute of a God who is omniscient and omnipotent, for God's power to *know* the future means that what God knows will perforce occur (see Bible, especially *Romans* 8:29–30 and *Ephesians* 1:5, 11). Huck's life, therefore, as well as the lives of Jim and everyone else in the novel, is predestined, and they are not meant by a malevolent and deceptive deity to be free. This can be seen in a number of ways in the novel.

First, the decision to escape to freedom by floating down the river on a raft is chancy at best. A raft has no power of its own but is passively swept along by the current. The current, moreover, is flowing south, the wrong direction for freedom. Every adventure Huck and Jim have on the river is potentially threatening and increasingly dangerous. Once the two reach Cairo (the name ominously recalls Egypt, a place biblically associated with slavery) a fog "coincidentally" occurs, and they are unintentionally carried past the junction of the Ohio River. This not only effectively ends their plan to catch a steamer north to Cincinnati and connections to the underground railway, but it means that from now on their raft will take them ever nearer to New Orleans, where the main slave market exists.

In Arkansas, where they end up, they "coincidentally" become entangled with members of Tom Sawyer's family who misidentify Huck as Tom, which, in turn, causes Huck to relax his guard. Then Tom himself—in this novel the antithesis of Huck—"coincidentally" meets up with Huck and persuades him to impersonate Tom while Tom impersonates his brother Sid, continues the ruse, and directs events. Tom knows what Huck and Jim do not, that Miss Watson manumitted Jim, and he sees an opportunity to indulge his love of play acting and involve Huck and Jim, who believe that he is helping them free Jim. As Pascal Covici points out, however, anyone who believes that Tom would go against society and really help a slave to escape does not know Tom and is hoaxed (Covici, *Mark Twain's Humor* 160–61).

The main hoax in *Huckleberry Finn*, however, does not occur until chapter 42 when Tom's plan goes awry and he is shot and caught. When Tom learns that Jim has been recaptured, he cries out, "Turn him loose! he ain't no slave; he's as free as any cretur that walks this earth!" (*HF 2003* 356). This statement is the crux of the novel and a function of Twain's countertheology. It is true that Jim is no slave, but it is *not* true that he is literally free. He has been "freed" in the loose sense that he was manumitted, but manumitted slaves were, technically, f.m.c.—"free men of color"—and they were not free as whites were. Although no longer having legal masters, they had almost none of the rights of whites and none of the protections of slaves; the worst of both worlds (Berkove and Csicsila ch. 4). Hank Morgan in chapter 13 of *A Connecticut Yankee in King Arthur's Court* (1889) referred to the medieval English equivalent of f.m.c. status as "a sarcasm of law and phrase" (*CY 1979* 109). In point of fact, Jim would have few options on returning to St. Petersburg other than working like a slave at a pitiful wage to buy his wife's freedom—if her master would sell her—and then working again with his wife to buy their deaf and dumb daughter from her master—if he would sell her. This empty category of freedom reveals the central hoax of the novel. Twain by implication extended it to all humans by the irony of "he's as free as any cretur that walks this earth!" Every creature is as free as Jim—*but Jim is not free.* Obeying Tom's silly romantic whims during the "evasion" chapter tragically reverses the free and equal relationship of both Huck and Jim to what they were at the beginning except that now Jim mistakenly thinks he's free. Huck still intends to "light out for the Territory" (*HF 2003* 362). What this romantic fantasy about the territory would entail in reality is suggested in "Huck Finn and Tom Sawyer Among the Indians" (1884), Twain's unfinished sequel consisting of violent disasters.

Huck's journey down the river is ultimately made useless; nothing is gained from it. Like the narrator of *Roughing It*, if he had stayed at home in St. Petersburg, everything that made him flee in the first place—his wishes to escape Pap and to help Jim—would have been accomplished. It was unnecessary to put himself and Jim at risk on the raft trip. Readers can see, moreover, that the character developments that occur on the trip become illusions and vanish at the end.

Twain's wife Livy called him "Youth," an endearing compliment for it conveyed all the good associations of youth: vigor, high spirits, happiness, love, optimism, and idealism. It helps explain his comment in a February 23, 1897, letter to W. D. Howells that youth was "the only thing that was worth giving to the race" (*UCCL* 05505). But in all other regards this statement is at odds with what he more typically believed of youth. That can be found in "The Five Boons of Life" (1902). In it, a fairy appears in the morning of life to a youth and offers him a choice of gifts: Fame, Love, Riches, Pleasure, and Death, advising him that only one was valuable. The youth eagerly chose Pleasure. Once he attained it, however, he found it "short-lived and disappointing, vain and empty." The youth becomes a man and the fairy returns to him, offering fewer choices but with the same advice. After he chooses all but Death and eventually regrets each one, he understands that Death is the "inestimable one, that dear and sweet and kindly one that steeps in dreamless and enduring sleep the pains that persecute the body, and the shames and griefs that eat the mind and heart." But that last gift is withheld; all that is left him is "the wanton insult of Old Age" (*WIM?* 98–100). Youth, in other words, is a time of myopic folly that may be enjoyed while one possesses it, but is short-lasting. This is borne in upon Twain in 1902 when he revisited Hannibal. Among the crowd at the railway station, his boyhood chum Tom Nash bellowed at him, "Same damned fools, Sam" (*AMT1* 353). To Twain, it was a verdict on youth as well as on age: His youthful friends had aged but not become wiser or better. When his younger choices turned out to be painful disappointments, he came around to believe oblivion the best choice. Twain reaffirmed this position in the tender and moving "Death of Jean" (1911): "In her loss I am almost bankrupt, and my life is a bitterness, but I am content: for she has been enriched with the most precious of all gifts—that gift which makes all other gifts mean and poor—death" (*DJ* 349).

Twain was very much an author of his time, yet unique in his ideas as well as his art. From the time he reached manhood, his bleak and bitter countertheology formed the deep core of almost all his important works. Beneath the "smiling aspects" of the surfaces of life and his representations of it, life to him was a damned illusion created by a controlling and cruel deity, and youth, a phase of life, was not exempt from its transience, deceptions, and ultimate disappointments and griefs.

Notes

1   See elsewhere in *A Sole Survivor*, pp. 1–86, *passim*. Bierce's "Killed at Resaca" (1887) and "A Son of the Gods" (1888) emphasize the relationship between youth and fatal emotionalism. "Chickamauga" (1889) is a tragic commentary on the famous battle from the viewpoint of a six-year-old deaf mute boy, the victim alike of war, upbringing, and nature. The relationship of Bierce and Twain is explored in Berkove's "Kindred Rivals."

2   Melville's war poems deplore the tragic "martyr-passion" of "the Boy." See also "Apathy and Enthusiasm" (1860–61), "Ball's Bluff" (1861), "The College Colonel," and "At the Cannon's Mouth" (1864).

3

Children's Literature in the Nineteenth Century

Lucy E. Rollin

Although Mark Twain is typically associated with nineteenth-century American literature for children, he never wrote books exclusively for young readers. However, the three famous books *about* children he published between 1875 and 1885 reflect themes resonating in and around children's books since the beginning of the nineteenth century.

In the early nineteenth century, as Americans recovered from a war of independence, they knew they must soon turn over the responsibilities of democracy to their children. How could children be prepared for their responsibilities as the world watched this new country? How could they be *useful* in this crucial moment in American history? With these challenges, writers dedicated to the improvement of the younger generation began to prepare children for the future.

During the early nineteenth century, Americans relied on British imports for most of their literature, including books for children. Isaac Watts's *Divine Songs* (1715), for example, remained popular well into the century. Maria Edgeworth's *Early Lessons* (1801) offered short stories depicting children learning moral behavior; her lively but gentle prose set a standard for balancing a good story with a moral. Her most popular tale, "The Purple Jar," remains a perfect example of a lesson in *usefulness* as Rosamond suffers the consequences of choosing a purple jar over a pair of shoes. Ann and Jane Taylor wrote poetry for children that still resonates today in "Twinkle, Twinkle, Little Star," but most of their poems were gentle moral lessons, such as "The Little Husbandman"—who says, "I've been useful all the day: I'd rather be a plough-boy than/ A useless little gentleman." Their most popular (and most parodied) verse "My Mother," ends with a warning: "For God who lives above the skies,/ Would look with vengeance in his eyes,/ If I should ever dare despise—My Mother" (Hunt 5–9). In their *Original Poems for Infant Minds,* published in Philadelphia in 1829, the Taylors underscore the need for good behavior *now,* to protect the future: "To waste precious time we can never recal [sic], Is waste of the wickedest kind" (12). A boy pulling weeds is cautioned, "You are yourself a bud, my blooming boy,/ Weigh well the consequences ere you destroy,/ Lest for the present paltry sport, you kill a future joy" (78).

The work of Anna Letitia Barbauld, another turn-of-the-century English writer, also remained popular in America throughout the nineteenth century. Believing that children "should be kept from reading verse til they are able to relish good verse," Barbauld created *Hymns in Prose for Children* in 1781 to impress upon them "the full force of the idea of God" (vi). Though these vignettes tout the usual morals and cautions, some are surprisingly evocative and liberal in their themes. In one "hymn," Barbauld describes a household settling down for the night: "As the mother moveth about the house with her finger on her lips, and stilleth every little noise that her infant be not disturbed . . . God draweth the curtains of darkness around us; so He maketh all things to be hushed and still, that his large family may sleep in peace" (24). In another, Barbauld explores "God's family," with images and text about an Eskimo, a Spaniard, an Egyptian, and a "Negro" woman. The Negro woman is pictured in shabby surroundings, holding her infant and gazing up at a high moonlit window; the hymn addresses her, "who sittest pining in captivity, and weepest over thy sick child: though no one seeth thee, God seeth thee . . . raise thy voice, forlorn and abandoned one . . . assuredly He will hear thee" (48).

√   Toward mid-century, as American writers for children took the reins, emphasis on moral perfection increased, for the world was watching this new country dealing with its tensions. American-produced catechisms, school books, and tracts poured forth, continually emphasizing usefulness and Christian morality. Catechisms like those in Puritan days—question-and-answer books about religious matters—remained fundamental reading for American children. Thomas Baldwin, DD, wrote *Catechism or Compendium of Christian Doctrine and Practice* in 1817. The following year, "A Lady of New Jersey" wrote *A Plain and Easy Catechism for Children of a Tender Age.* One of the most interesting efforts in this vein was that of Bronson Alcott, who taught a catechism class to a group of children in his Temple school. He had a scribe record word-for-word all the meetings and published the entire script in 1836 as *Conversations About the Gospels.* His approach caused some consternation at the time, since among other things he asked the children questions about what *conceive* means and how Mary's baby got to the barn.

In schools, McGuffey's readers and spellers took every opportunity to promote moral and religious behavior. A lesson in the 1846 *McGuffey's Eclectic Spelling Book* introduces James, a model boy who is very kind to his sick mother. He sings hymns with her, "can read quite well, and feels glad that he has learned so much. His friends love him, because he is a good boy. . . . When he lies down at night, he asks God to bless him; for James loves God, and prays to him every day" (67). For Sunday schools, the American Sunday School Union produced such highly successful tracts as "The Fiery Furnace," "Rosa the Work Girl," "Children of the Bible," "Paris, Ancient and Modern," and "The Origin and Progress of Language." In her preface to an 1859 Sunday School Union tract titled *Georgy Lee; Or, the Boy Who Became a Great Artist*, Mrs. O. A. S. Beale reminded readers, "These stories are not 'fancy sketches.' When truth is strange, imagination can have little to supply. Let my youthful readers never forget that no path is safe aside from that of duty."

Individual books adopted a similar tone. Lydia Sigourney, a popular American poet, created the gloomy story *Olive Buds* (1836) to warn young readers of the horrors of war and the emotional scars a war leaves. She speaks directly to children in her introduction: "You are yourselves buds, my dear children, buds of hope not yet unfolded, but beautiful to the eye of those who love you." Lydia Maria Child focused her attention on girls; in her introduction to her 1833 *Girls' Own Book*, she warns, "in this land of precarious fortunes, every girl should know how to be *useful*." Some admonishments were less than graceful. The 1845 anonymously written *Infant Primer* captions a picture of a crying child, "Come little girl, you must not cry because your little bird is dead; we must all die, girls, boys, and birds, and every living thing must die; get up and go play with your little playmates."

Samuel Clemens, like other mid-nineteenth-century American boys, enjoyed popular versions of Daniel Defoe's 1719 novel *Robinson Crusoe* and the Robin Hood myth, along with lively contemporary adventure tales by Ned Buntline (Colonel E. Z. C. Judson). But also like other boys, he knew the didactic literature very well indeed, as Twain's hilarious evocations of Tom Sawyer's church, Sunday school, and school experiences demonstrate. Yet his Sunday school book-learning also haunted him in ways that were not funny. In Hannibal, he witnessed deaths, duels, and lynchings. He gave matches to a prisoner who asked for them, only to have the jail catch fire and the prisoner burn to death. He saw his own dead father stretched out on the kitchen table for an autopsy. These images tortured his youthful Presbyterian conscience (as he called it), especially at night:

> My teaching and training enabled me to see deeper into these tragedies than an ignorant person could have done. I knew what they were for. I tried to disguise it from myself, but down in the secret deeps of my troubled heart I knew—and I knew I knew. They were inventions of Providence to beguile me to a better life. It sounds curiously innocent and conceited, now, but to me there was nothing strange about it; it was quite in accordance with the thoughtful and judicious ways of Providence as I understood them. (*AMT1* 158–59)

Even later, when he was dictating his autobiography, Clemens was haunted by "creatures of fear and darkness" and added, "in my age, as in my youth night brings me many a deep remorse" (*AMT1* 159). Other children surely shared these feelings, given the ubiquity of such literature and its infusions of guilt about not living usefully.

No wonder, then, when the children's writer Peter Parley began his first book in 1827 with a hearty "Here I am!," children could cheer up. To them, Parley was a gouty old gentleman who had traveled the world and seen everything and loved to tell about it in ways they could appreciate. To the American publishing business, however, he was Samuel Goodrich—in actuality an energetic man in his early thirties with experience in the book trade, who began a series of children's books bursting with energy and information. Some of the books were ghost-written, but he was both prolific and extremely popular. Moral lessons were very much a part of his books, but he never preached, preferring straightforward prose to tell a straightforward story:

> I am now going to tell you the story of a cabin boy. His name was George Gordon. His mother was a widow, who lived at Marblehead in Massachusetts. George was her only child. His father, who was a sailor, had not been heard of for several years. ("The Story of a Cabin Boy," in *Peter Parley's Tales of the Sea*, 1839)

Peter Parley's information about history, geography, and science was sometimes questionable, but Goodrich made young readers eager to know about their world and about faraway places. Goodrich himself was thoroughly American, and eager to publish American authors such as Nathaniel Hawthorne. "It is with Goodrich that the mainstream of English and American writing for children divides," says Gillian Avery, an English scholar of children's literature. England at that time was experiencing "gentrification," while "America was in the grip of facts. Knowledge was the key to prosperity and would open up the future.

[Goodrich] brought color and interest into children's lives . . . opening windows for many young Americans" (Avery 81).

During the 1830s, Jacob Abbott also began opening windows, eventually surpassing Goodrich in the number of his publications. His most popular books were his twenty-eight volumes about the boy Rollo. His little stories of Rollo learning to read, trying to avoid bedtime, and undertaking other mundane matters, emphasize *cheerful* obedience to kind and thoughtful authority, with usefulness the ultimate goal. Twain owned the entire Rollo series and read them to his children (*MTLR* 4–5). His library, however, apparently lacked five other Abbott stories of unusual interest: the "Rainbow" series, which went out of print in 1868 after two printings only. The "Rainbow" of these tales is a nickname for "a highly intelligent and exceedingly honest and altruistic fourteen-year-old free black male" who lives outside Boston just before the Civil War (Lessels and Sterling 84). The books follow Rainbow as he encounters a wide range of racist attitudes while having adventures and helping others in distress. A life-long New Englander who had once been a Congregational minister, Abbott used these books to undermine the stereotypes purveyed by northern and southern prejudice, as he *showed*, rather than told, how racial injustice harms individuals and society. These stories allowed young people to empathize with a person of color—a rare opportunity, in life and in children's books, but one that evidently did not take root at the time.

By mid-century, writing for children had become a lucrative occupation, especially in periodicals. Between 1830 and 1870, more than 130 such journals were in print; the number grew to 150 up to 1900 (Avery 146). Magazines such as *Our Young Folks*, *Oliver Optic's Magazine*, Samuel Goodrich's *Merry's Museum*, and the influential and successful *St. Nicholas* provided entertainment, a high moral tone, and literary excellence to a wide range of readers. Twain contributed to *St. Nicholas*, and such distinguished writers as Mary Mapes Dodge, Louisa May Alcott, and Harriet Beecher Stowe made their living writing and editing for such periodicals. The editor of *The Youth's Companion*, published from 1827 to 1929, proudly announced the purpose of his periodical: "Our children are born to higher destinies than their fathers. . . . Let their minds be formed, their hearts prepared, and their character moulded for the scenes and duties of a brighter day" (Avery 83). *The Juvenile Miscellany*, begun in 1826, offered more variety of purpose and was highly successful but its efforts at education seem chilling today. For example, an 1835 article entitled "Varieties of the Human Race" proclaimed: "What a difference between the delicate skin, blended with the rose and the lily, which distinguishes the European race, and the coarse skin and greasy blackness of the African negro!" By 1852, however, as a serialized *Uncle Tom's Cabin* closed its final chapter, Harriet Beecher Stowe spoke directly to young readers of the *National Era*: "When you grow up, we hope that the foolish and unchristian prejudice against people, merely on account of their complexion, will be done away with" (Lessels and Sterling 99).

During the Civil War, periodicals for youth played a central role in the North by introducing the issues surrounding slavery and racial prejudice—topics they previously had been avoiding. Through stories and essays, the periodicals helped children understand the reasons for and impact of the war, though the approach was frequently over-simplified, for example, by promoting the idea that "the South had gone to war at the instigation and in the best interests of only a few aristocratic slaveholders" (Marten 41). The popular and prolific "Oliver Optic" (William P. Adams) contributed biographies about Union soldiers and their heroism. The Confederacy, in contrast, lacked the luxury of magazines. It struggled merely to maintain its schools, and its presses produced textbooks—with surprising success under the circumstances, printing "nearly 100 schoolbooks for patriotic and economic reasons" (Marten 54).

Some young people in the North created periodicals for themselves, such as *The Athenaeum* at Newark High School. Its young editors and scholars wrote about the war with insights of their own. James Marten estimates that "untold thousands of northern boys and girls read the periodical literature and novels inspired by the Civil War"—works that no longer threatened or overtly preached, but acknowledged that young people's intelligence, enterprise, and yes, usefulness, had readied them for more mature reading (Marten 50).

Meanwhile, however, a few periodicals appealed to young people's playful sides and anticipated modern promotional strategies. The cover of *Demorest's Young America* (1866–75), for example, trumpeted "The Entertaining! The Useful! and the Beautiful! A Well-Spring of Pleasure in the Home Circle." It offered premiums for subscribing—microscopes, pocketknives, paints and brushes, and paper dolls—and printed fan letters it received from its readers around the country.

The American children's book most associated with this period is Louisa May Alcott's *Little Women*. Published in 1868, it marked a significant change in literature for young readers, as well as the height of Alcott's long writing career. Based on her own family (tidied up), the novel offered an image of real life at the time, with the Civil War as backdrop while ordinary people coped at home. Alcott avoids preaching and lugubrious warnings, while her story's four girls and their mother go about their lives energetically, loving each other without being soppy. An immediate success with adults and youth, the book remains a watershed in literature for young readers.

Where was Twain while the Civil War and "Oliver Optic" forged on? He lit out. The war ended his plan to become a steamboat pilot, and after a brief, disorganized stint in the Missouri militia, he joined his brother Orion heading west to Nevada Territory. From there, he kept moving, prospecting for silver, writing for newspapers, and narrowly escaping a couple of duels. But those years became his watershed. Among other things, he wrote what would become his breakout work: the variously titled jumping frog story. He also took revenge on his Sunday-school experiences by publishing "Advice for Good Little Girls" and "Advice for Good Little Boys" (1865)—parodies for adult readers of the moral drivel he loathed. The popularity of these pieces testifies to the pervasiveness of the originals.

Post-Civil War literature for children was marked first by a new infusion of children's books from Great Britain. Beginning with Lewis Carroll's *Alice in Wonderland* in 1865, American readers, both children and adults, enjoyed the tales of faerie and royalty that crossed the Atlantic. Second, and more importantly, the stern morality that had dominated prewar American children's reading began to soften and with it, distinctions between adults' and children's books in America. *Little Women* was one of the first examples, followed by what would become the defining trend of postwar American literature: the boy book. Marcia Jacobson suggests that boy books were a response to the dramatic social change the country was enduring, offering escapism along with social criticism; moreover, theories about boyhood were fueled during the 1880s and 1890s by pioneering psychologist G. Stanley Hall's identification of adolescence in boys as a phase and as an echo of savagery (Jacobson 7–13).

The "bad boy," of course, had long been a staple of prewar moral tales. Now, instead of a symbol of pernicious carelessness, he became a lens through which male authors could revisit their own boyhoods. George W. Peck's *Peck's Bad Boy* and Horatio Alger's tales of enterprising poor boys represented commercial versions of the trend, but several well-known authors engaged seriously with their own boyhood memories. Albert E. Stone identifies ten such books published between 1869 and 1899, all aimed at a readership of adults and youth (*IE* 62). Thomas Bailey Aldrich's *The Story of a Bad Boy* (1869) was the first to appear. A popular success, its tone was wise and wry—that of an adult shaking his head in wonder at his youthful escapades—and touched but lightly on moral issues.

Although professing only mild interest in Aldrich's book, Twain recognized the possibilities. Drawing on memories of his boyhood, he drafted *The Adventures of Tom Sawyer* and showed it to his friend William Dean Howells, insisting that it was for adults. Howells, however, persuaded him that it would succeed as a boy book that grown-ups would enjoy as well, so he capitulated and said it was for boys and girls. Reviewers immediately recognized its unique appeal: "a boy's adventure tale on one level, an adult work on another" (*IE* 61). In Stone's brilliant and sensitive analysis, *Tom Sawyer* is a "full-dress study of personality, community, and the anatomy of social evil" while dramatizing "something fundamental in the emotional relations of children and grown-ups" (*IE* 63, 83). In an 1883 letter to Twain, a nine-year-old girl offered her opinion: "I think Tom is just perfect" (*DMT* 99).

Twain ventured into the boy-book arena twice more. Intrigued by the story of Edward Tudor, the son of England's King Henry VIII who ascended the throne as a boy, Twain created his own version of this event in *The Prince and the Pauper* (1881). The two-boy plot had been a staple in literature for children since Thomas Day's *History of Sandford and Merton* (1783–89), the episodic story of a haughty rich boy and the generous poor boy hired to improve the rich boy's attitude. Reprinted many times during the nineteenth century (an edition appeared as late as 1887), *Sandford and Merton* provided a template for moral tales. In *The Prince and the Pauper*, Prince Edward accidentally changes places with poor boy Tom Canty and learns about poverty at first hand, while Tom tries to fit into the role of king. Both ponder the moral issues that arise from the situation. Published in 1881, it became one of Twain's most popular works. Although it wore the trappings of a historical novel (for all ages, Twain insisted), it was in some ways a boy book, resembling *Tom Sawyer* and later *Huckleberry Finn*, as well as a lively story that lent itself to stage adaptations (see *MTAZ* 363–70).

And what about *Huckleberry Finn* (1885), that triumph of the late nineteenth century that some call a book for children while others insist it is appropriate only for adult readers? All the issues surrounding it cannot be addressed here, but at the time, considering the efforts to suppress it, *Huckleberry Finn* seemed to upset adult readers more than children. In 1888, Twain received a letter addressed directly to Huck: The young male correspondent wrote, "I wish you would write another book and tell us if Aunt Sally 'civilized' you. How old are you? I am thirteen" (*DMT* 138). In 1902, a twelve-year-old girl wrote that she had read the novel "about fifty times" and believed it was "the best book ever written" (*DMT* 200). *Huckleberry Finn* continues to elude classification. Andrew Levy—one of the latest scholars to explore it—observes, "Like the truancy and anti-social behavior it celebrates, *Huck Finn* was designed to lie outside the system" (Levy 169).

While he was writing *Huckleberry Finn*, Twain was cultivating a friendship with Joel Chandler Harris, the author of the Uncle Remus stories. Also a journalist, Harris wrote for the Atlanta *Constitution*, in which he first published Uncle Remus's "Brer Rabbit" tales that made him a celebrity, especially with children. Harris's poor-boy background and his newspaper work created a personal bond with Twain, who had published two dialect pieces himself in 1874 ("A True Story" and "Sociable Jimmy") and was in the process of creating the character of Jim for *Huckleberry Finn*. Twain admired Harris's ability to reproduce southern black dialect in print. Although frustrated by Harris's shyness and reluctance to perform in public, he remained his friend until Harris's death in 1908. The "Brer Rabbit" stories live on and, like *Huckleberry Finn*, continue to cause discomfort and delight among readers of all ages.

An unusual nineteenth-century European book attracted not just children but Twain as well. *Struwwelpeter* ("Shock-headed Peter," also known as "Slovenly Peter"), written in German by Heinrich Hoffman, was first published in 1835. It quickly became popular in Europe and was soon translated into English. In a series of hilarious poems accompanied by gruesome illustrations, it depicted the actions of bad children and the dreadful punishments that ensue. American children loved its send-up of the preaching that infused their assigned reading. Twain and his daughters discovered *Struwwelpeter* in Germany. In 1891, Twain wrote his own translation of the book's 1845 edition and presented it to his daughters as a gift. It was an irreverent thumbing of his nose at all the moral tales he and countless other children had endured while growing up.

Mark Twain's impact on children's books continues today. Writing for children *and* adults, he changed the game for both: He treated didactic morality lightly, created characters who were real, engaged his child characters with adult issues, and made his readers—adults and children—laugh together. His equal has not yet appeared.

4

Mark Twain's Lifelong Reading

Alan Gribben

As the author of two indelible novels featuring boy characters, Mark Twain is, of course, associated in the public mind and in critical commentary with books for and about children. However, his connections with juvenile literature were much earlier, deeper, and long-lasting than many readers might suppose. His acquaintance with writings for young people spanned almost his entire lifetime and merged with the impressively broad range of works for older readers he is known to have owned or read.

Before considering the trajectory of his lifetime reading, we should recognize how much more elastic were the classifications of literature in his day. Our contemporary bookstores, libraries, and online distributors are eager to assign labels such as "Toddler Picture Books," "Juvenile," "Young Adult Fiction," "Historical Romances," "Adult Novels," and so forth to every publication. For the purchasers of nineteenth-century literature, these notions were far more fluid and shifting; adults were as happy to read Lewis Carroll's *Alice in Wonderland* (1865) and Twain's *The Adventures of Tom Sawyer* (1876) as were the children in their families. Today, one generally encounters *Tom Sawyer* quarantined in the "Teen" sections of public libraries and retail bookstores, with *Adventures of Huckleberry Finn* (1885) privileged to sit on the "Adult" shelves. A century and a half ago this kind of rigid demarcation was vastly different from how literature was generally approached. Shared reading experiences were more commonly the norm. Those who can recall the excitement generated by J. K. Rowling's *Harry Potter* installments and their resulting films—with both parents and their progeny lining up alike at the Barnes & Noble outlets and movie theaters—can sense how flexible was the division between "children" and "adult" publications in an earlier era. Many parents and other relatives got their introductions to juvenile fiction and poetry by reading to younger family members, and for that matter children were often encouraged to read aloud to adults when extended families gathered around domestic hearths in the evenings. So in contemplating the "children's" literature that Clemens knew, it is advisable to suspend any patronizing preconceptions about the supposed inferiority or limitations of writings aimed at young readers. Everyone of any age was just as apt to have dipped into those publications, and there was no attitude of condescension when opening their pages.

What Samuel Clemens read as a boy in Hannibal is a tantalizing but essentially unanswerable question. Only a few hints in his later writings suggest the types of books to which he was first attracted. Minnie M. Brashear attempted to compensate for this vacuum of evidence by producing, in 1934, an educated guess at the reading material available to, and sought by, the citizens of northeastern Missouri in the 1840s and 1850s, though there is no corroborating proof that Clemens himself read these same publications (*MTSM* 77, 143–44, 201–02, 205–07). Nonetheless, her survey is valuable for establishing the literary milieu in the region. She found that despite the relative isolation of Hannibal, young Clemens had access to a town library, four bookstores, several private libraries, and his brother Orion's newspaper exchanges (*MTSM* 209). Indeed, she concluded, "Hannibal had a more distinctly literary atmosphere than towns in Missouri have today," and literary allusions in local newspapers and speeches were prevalent (*MTSM* 143). Dixon Wecter's *Sam Clemens of Hannibal* (1952) cautioned, however, that the collection of the town library was "modest" and its resources were "slowly collapsing"; moreover, the impoverished Clemens family had little to spare for literary luxuries in the retail bookstores. In fact, concludes Wecter, "the town offered few contacts with what the world called literature," and he argued that "the real Hannibal was neither the total cultural desert imagined by Van Wyck Brooks in *The Ordeal of Mark Twain* (1920, 1933) nor the seat of the muses patriotically conceived by Minnie Brashear in *Mark Twain: Son of Missouri*" (*SCOH* 208–09).

Clemens himself supplied a couple of murky clues to his boyhood literary activities. He made it obvious, for example, that the Bible (especially the New Testament) and Sunday-school stories were among his earliest literary impressions. In an autobiographical dictation, he recalled reciting New Testament verses in order to win the three blue tickets that entitled a child to borrow one book for a week from the Sunday-school bookcase: "They were pretty dreary books, for there was not a bad boy in the entire bookcase. They were *all* good boys and good girls and drearily uninteresting, but they were better society than none, and I was glad to have their company and disapprove of it" (*AMT1* 418). We also have the almost-too-perfect anecdote of his finding, at the age of thirteen, a leaf from a book about Joan of Arc, though Albert E. Stone (Stone, "Mark Twain's Joan" 1n.1; *IE* 202n.1) raised a quizzical eyebrow over Twain's omission of this alleged event from his "The Turning-Point of My Life" (1910), and Dixon Wecter took note of the variations discernible in Twain's several accounts of the supposedly influential occurrence (*SCOH* 211, 309n.23).

If Clemens subsequently sought a *Joan of Arc* volume among the books his father and mother owned, he was disappointed. The appraisal of John Marshall Clemens's personal property on May 21, 1847 shows that he owned only twenty-five or thirty books, and they were strictly utilitarian and religious—law books, a geography, a six-volume encyclopedia, a dictionary, a New Testament, a large Bible, and two small Bibles. Not a single work of *belles-lettres* appears in the list, unless one counts the Bibles. (Young Clemens probably made use of his father's set of Nicholson's *Encyclopedia*, for he particularly requested these volumes and his mother's Bible from Mollie Clemens's executor in 1904.) (McDermott 198; OC to "Miss Woods," 3 Oct. 1858, *UCCL* 46942). This meager library was supplemented by the Hannibal Library Institute, which Clemens's father helped found in 1844 but which declined after his death in 1847 and was no longer operating by 1853. Unfortunately, no record of its holdings appears to have survived, but a newspaper article in 1854 reported that at its peak the town library contained "between four and five hundred volumes" (Hannibal *Missouri Courier*, 22 June 1854).

Clemens's brothers might have encouraged him to make use of his reading opportunities. The family did manage to subscribe to the leading children's periodical, *Parley's Magazine*. Albert Bigelow Paine was told that Henry Clemens "read everything obtainable" (*MTB* 14, 65) and Henry's eldest brother, Orion, remembered Henry as a "quiet, observing, thoughtful" youth who "devoted much of his leisure hours to reading" (OC to "Miss Woods," 3 Oct. 1858, *UCCL* 46942). Orion evidently relished good books as well: When Minnie Brashear analyzed the "fillers" that Orion employed in the columns of his Hannibal *Journal* during the early 1850s, she found quotations from William Makepeace Thackeray and from Charles Dickens's *Pickwick Papers* (1836–37), as well as references to Captain Frederick Marryat, Nathaniel Hawthorne, Harriet Beecher Stowe, Daniel Webster, Edward Bulwer-Lytton, Thomas Macaulay, and Frances Trollope. James Boswell's *Life of Samuel Johnson* (1791) was a favorite source of anecdotes, and there were allusions to other eighteenth-century authors, including Oliver Goldsmith, Alexander Pope, Robert Burns, Hannah More, Edward Young, Thomas Gray, William Cowper, and Benjamin Franklin (the most often-cited source). Orion also worked in tales from Greek mythology and referred to Cicero and Demosthenes (*MTSM* 142–43; see Fanning). He undoubtedly had garnered some of these allusions from his reading in St. Louis, Missouri, during his years there as a printer following his father's death in 1847. Presumably, Twain intended Stanchfield Garvey, a character in "The Refuge of the Derelicts" (written 1905–06) notoriously prone to fads, to resemble his brother. As a young printer's apprentice Garvey looked "into the first chapter of every useful book in the Mechanic's Library, but never any further than that in any instance. And so, whereas he picked up a slight smattering of many breeds of knowledge, his accumulation was valueless and unusable, it was a mere helter-skelter scrap-heap" (*FM* 240). According to Paine's biography, Clemens was content to let his brothers accomplish the bulk of reading in their family; as a young apprentice printer in Hannibal "he cared little for reading, himself, beyond a few exciting tales" (*MTB* 80).

There are reasons for supposing that Tom Sawyer's penchant for romance-reading was a trait Twain remembered—apparently with chagrin—from his own youth. He recalled, for example, that around 1850 he threatened the school bully "with a dark and murderous scowl on my face, copied from a pirate romance" (*AMT2* 299). Laura Hawkins of *The Gilded Age* (1873) had been affected by similar books in rustic Hawkeye, Missouri:

> There was another world opened to her—a world of books. But it was not the best world of that sort, for the small libraries she had access to in Hawkeye were decidedly miscellaneous, and largely made up of romances and fictions which fed her imagination with the most exaggerated notions of life, and showed her men and women in a very false sort of heroism. (*GA* ch. 18)

The distortions of reality cultivated by "romances," particularly for inexperienced and susceptible youth, became a lifelong preoccupation of Twain, and a certain ambivalence about them informed and motivated the satire in Tom's chronic misinterpretations of his beloved literary "authorities" about what constitutes "adventures." One of many examples is Tom's misconstruing of a combat scene he recites by heart from Joseph Cundall's *Robin Hood and His Merry Foresters* (1841), when he and Joe Harper are fighting with wooden lath swords on Cardiff Hill in chapter 8 of *Tom Sawyer* (see Gribben, "How Tom Sawyer," 201–04). In his childhood, Twain would recall, the tale of Robin Hood "paled the interest of all other books & made them tame & colorless" (SLC to Jervis Langdon II, 19 Dec. 1883, *UCCL* 02867). It can hardly be coincidental that Clemens displayed in adulthood a strong sense that the books of his boyhood had altogether betrayed him, that they failed to prepare him for the real world as he later found it.

But like Samuel Clemens in Hannibal, Laura Hawkins found reading matter in Hawkeye besides romances: "There were also other books—histories, biographies of distinguished people, travels in far lands, poems, especially those of Byron, Scott and Shelley and Moore, which she eagerly absorbed" (*GA* ch. 18; see Leisy 446). Twain remembered his "youthful readings" about the north central United States depicting it as "a Great Lone Land, a gaunt, hungry, forbidding desert" (*MTNB 35* 18). He similarly recalled the sensation that resulted when "Eugene Sue's 'Wandering Jew' [published in 1844–1845] appeared, and made great talk for a while" (*FE* ch. 46). He lamented to his wife Olivia that "in boyhood" he had failed to appreciate the satire in Jonathan Swift's *Gulliver's Travels* (1726), and "only gloated over its prodigies & its marvels" (*LL* 76). However, he would also recall reading "the *Walpole Letters* when I was a boy. I absorbed them, gathered in their grace, wit, and humor, and put them away to be used by and by" (*MTSpk* 323). Asked in 1887 to recommend some of the best books for young people to read, Clemens explained that he was away from home, but nevertheless "on the wing" he advised boys to read "Macaulay; Plutarch; Grant's Memoirs [which Clemens's firm had published two years earlier]; Crusoe; Arabian Nights; Gulliver." He suggested "the same for the girl, after striking Crusoe & substituting Tennyson" (PH in CU-MARK).

Throughout his life Clemens seemed to associate the novels of Alexandre Dumas and the marvels of *The Arabian Nights* with childhood, so it appears fairly certain that he made their acquaintance in Hannibal. Much later in life, he designated "Aladdin and the Wonderful Lamp" and "Ali Baba and the Forty Thieves" as his favorite tales for inclusion in *Favorite Fairy Tales*, an anthology published by Harper Brothers in 1907. There is incontrovertible proof that as a youth Clemens was thoroughly familiar with William Harrison Ainsworth's lurid crime novel, *Jack Sheppard: A Romance* (1839), which was based on the life of a famous London thief, robber, and escape artist who was hanged in 1724 (*MTLR* 13–14). Ned Buntline's hair-raising dime novels were another source of entertainment for him back then (Valentine 29–48). When Tom Sawyer conflates and enacts adventures based on these readings in antebellum Missouri, however, the result is a burlesque of his sources; this mixture of esteem and scorn for romances that feed one's imagination with "exaggerated notions of life" permeates Twain's fiction.

In "Villagers of 1840-3" (written in 1897), Twain scoffed at the literature with which he grew up: "Literature. Byron, Scott, Cooper, Marryatt [*sic*], [Dickens's]

Boz. Pirates and Knights preferred to other society. Songs tended to regrets for bygone days and vanished joys." Four of these writers—but especially Walter Scott and James Fenimore Cooper—were favorite targets for his derision as he matured. He seemed to blame them for "all that sentimentality and romance among young folk" that was "puerile" as well as "soft, sappy, melancholy" (*HH&T* 34–35). One is reminded of his celebrated letter to Will Bowen in 1876 (DeVoto, *Portable Mark Twain* 751), which denounced Bowen's sentimentality about former Hannibal days—another gesture, it might be, toward rejecting a viewpoint Clemens himself had once ardently shared. Walter Scott came to typify for Clemens everything he detested about his own youthful notions, and his caustic reaction against Scott (though amusing) was far from rational. It is noteworthy that in one of his assaults on Scott's reputation, a letter condemning Scott's novels written to Brander Matthews on May 4, 1903, Clemens conceded that readers might reasonably have preferred to read Scott "in his day—an era of sentimentality & sloppy romantics—but land! can a body do it to-day?" (*UCCL* 06644). Yet Scott's "day" carried over into Clemens's youth, and this contemptuous dismissal could stand for Clemens's later attitude toward his first phase as a developing reader.

Undoubtedly the books Clemens read as an adolescent contributed to his decision to leave Hannibal in 1853 for several years of wandering that took him to St. Louis, New York City, Washington, DC, and Philadelphia before his return to St. Louis and (later) his move to Keokuk to assist Orion in establishing his printing shop. In 1868 Twain began writing a story about a mysterious balloon aeronaut whose autobiographical recollections suggest the writer's own motivations for travel: "I read a good deal, especially books of travel & adventure," explains Jean Pierre Marteau to the astonished farmers of the Illinois prairie where his balloon descended. "It is a thing which other boys have done. I grew restless & discontented. I longed to go to sea—to visit strange lands—to have adventures of my own" (*N&J1* 514).

Young Clemens's experiences as a roving apprentice printer were far more prosaic, but they did stimulate him to continue reading. At Mrs. Pavey's boardinghouse in St. Louis in 1853 he became acquainted with Jacob H. Burrough, a youth slightly older than himself, who "was fond of Dickens, Thackeray, Scott & [Benjamin] Disraeli, & was the only reading-man in the establishment, & the only one equipped with fine literary appreciations & a sound & competent judgment. He & I were comrades & close friends" (SLC to Frank E. Burrough, 15 Dec. 1900, Southeast Missouri State College). Clemens would later criticize three of these literary giants, but at the age of seventeen, he apparently still shared an affection for their novels. In New York City, of course, his opportunities for reading were immensely expanded. He assured his mother on August 31, 1853, that he generally spent his evenings at the free printers' libraries in New York City (*L1* 10). One of these contained more than four thousand volumes, he informed his sister Pamela (*L1* 14). Clemens wrote to his brother Orion on October 26, 1853, from Philadelphia, describing a recent sightseeing excursion, "Geo. Lippard, in his 'Legends of Washington and His Generals,' has rendered the Wissahickon sacred in my eyes" (Lippard; see *MTB* 100; see *L1* 21–22). It seems relevant that in chapter 5 of *Huckleberry Finn*, this same book ("about Washington and the wars") is the volume Huck Finn selects to read aloud when his father demands proof that he is now literate. Thereupon Pap Finn angrily knocks this book "across the house." After such extensive contact with books Clemens was naturally amused, in traveling through Missouri on family errands in July 1855, to note that the so-called reading room of the sole hotel in Paris, Missouri, contained only two books (*N&J1* 37).

In "The Turning Point of My Life" (1910), Twain recalled how William L. Herndon's published accounts of the Amazon motivated him to start down the Mississippi River toward fortune-hunting in South America, and his letter of August 6, 1856 to his brother Henry corroborates this version (*L1* 66). He would never actually reach the Amazon region, but his reading inclinations remained intact after he met a steamboat pilot named Horace Bixby and took up a new career. Minnie Brashear determined that by 1861, when he left river piloting for other adventures in the Far West, Clemens had at least sampled the writings of Dickens, Edgar Allan Poe, Miguel de Cervantes, Thomas Hood, Oliver Goldsmith, John Milton, and William Shakespeare, as well as Horace Walpole's letters and the Bible (*MTSM* 223). Shakespeare would remain a venerated staple of his mental reservoir for quotation throughout the years, as would the narratives and cadences of the King James Bible. Edgar M. Branch added Thomas Paine and Voltaire to Brashear's list, along with the observation that "his fellow pilots thought of him as a great reader" (Branch 25). Twain himself later claimed that he was virtually deprived of reading privileges during his tenure as a cub pilot. In 1876, he told Mrs. James T. Fields that when a senior pilot discovered him behind a barrel reading Walter Scott's *The Fortunes of Nigel* (1822), he received a lecture on the ruinous effects of reading on one's memory. Twain was clearly jokingly exaggerating this prohibition, however, for he concluded by asserting that the deprivation left him only able to read "the Encyclopedia nowadays" (Howe 345).

As a pilot Twain remained extremely conscious of his acquaintances' literary tastes, which became (as in the earlier case of Jacob Burrough in St. Louis) a prominent feature of their remembered characters. After a twenty-year interval, when he recalled Laura Wright, a young Missouri girl for whom he formed an attachment while piloting, he thought of her as having "a wise head, a great appetite for books, a good mental digestion, with grave ways, & inclined to introspection—an unusual girl" (Covici, "Dear Master Bowser" 108).

Clemens's western period is relatively barren of literary allusions compared to his later writings, but his references to literature suggest that he remained aware of audience-levels and popular appeal. His column in the March 18, 1865 issue of the *Californian* reported that "in most of those little [mining] camps they have no libraries, and no books to speak of, except now and then a patent-office report, or a prayer-book, or literature of that kind . . . but as for novels, they pass them around and wear them out in a week or two" (*SkS* 158–65). In his own notebook he recorded seeing in a miner's cabin at Jackass Hill "Byron[,] Shakspeare, Bacon[,] Dickens, & every kinds of only first class Literature" (*N&J1* 70). Years afterward, he would recall the books generally visible on a typical parlor table in Honolulu when he visited the port in 1866: "[Richard Allestree's] The Whole Duty of Man, [Richard] Baxter's Saints' Rest, [John] Fox[e]'s [Book of] Martyrs, [Martin] Tupper's Proverbial Philosophy, bound copies of The Missionary Herald and of Father Damon's Seaman's [*sic*] Friend" (*FE* ch. 3).

The zest with which Clemens devoured books during ocean voyages was apparent by January 3, 1867, when he looked up from reading aboard the *San Francisco*, en route to New York City, and found himself amazed at the hour of night—"been sitting here reading so long" (*N&J1* 213). Among other sightseeing in New York in May 1867, he visited August Brentano's bookshop and newspaper store (*N&J1* 326).

As "Mark Twain," Clemens instituted his lifelong campaign against the "romantic" notions of the world fostered by one's childhood reading in a letter of August 31, 1867, to the *New York Tribune*, gleefully contrasting the tawdry realities he encountered on his *Quaker City* travels with the idealized, "untruthful" fictions he had absorbed earlier. "The books of travel have shamefully deceived me all these years," he declared. "The Narghili, the dervishes, the aromatic coffee, the Turkish bath—these are the things I have accepted and believed in, with simple, unquestioning faith, from boyhood; and, behold, they are the poorest, sickest, wretchedest humbugs the world can furnish. Wonders, forsooth!" (McKeithan 132). He also found much to complain about in the library assembled by the *Quaker City* pilgrims for their journey. In the second act of an unfinished play based upon his experiences, "The *Quaker City* Holy Land Excursion," written in 1867, he listed its contents as he recalled them: William Prime's *Tent Life in the Holy Land*, John Bunyan's *Pilgrim's Progress*, Hannah More's *The Shepherd of Salisbury Plain*, Richard Allestree's *The Whole Duty of Man*, and a collection of Mother Goose rhymes set to music (SLC, MS at CU-MARK). As he remarked laconically in Notebook 8, "Library will be furnished by Young Men's Chr. Assn" (*N&J1* 324). Probably he had no need to exaggerate the deficiencies; another *Quaker City* passenger, Dr. Abraham R. Jackson, reported that "with the exception of the books furnished by the passengers themselves," the ship's library "consisted of a score and a half of the 'Plymouth Collection' and two volumes of *Harper's Weekly*" (New York *Herald*, 21 Nov. 1867). When *The Innocents Abroad* issued in 1869, therefore, Twain had already discovered, experimented with, and successfully mastered various possibilities for exploiting humor in simple lists of reading materials. The genesis of these satires probably lay in his brief notation in 1855 about the paucity of reading matter in that Paris, Missouri, hotel, but he had benefited from much close observation of universal reading habits and tastes since then. Later, when he entered the Athenaeum Club in London in June 1873, his first impressions centered on the reading advantages enjoyed by its members in its "dim religious light. All manner of books—tables full of them. Luxurious chairs. Huge reading room. Very few people there" (*N&J1* 533).

Clemens valued uninterrupted leisure for reading, and he truly believed that such a splendid luxury, like Cervantes's imprisonment while writing *Don Quixote* (1605, 1615), was worth its enormous price. The bridegroom hero of Twain's fragmentary "The Mysterious Chamber," probably written in 1875, was to have been confined in isolation for fifteen to twenty years; during that period he "finds old books in the haunted chamber, and a Bible, and becomes learned and religious" (SLC, MS, DV 56 at CU-MARK). Clemens was justifiably proud of the prodigious amounts of reading he often accomplished himself without such an advantage, setting aside a few hours each day to investigate his new library shelves in the Hartford house. "I cannot quite say I have read *nothing*," he wrote to Mary Fairbanks from Elmira on August 6, 1877, and then proceeded to give an impressively lengthy, detailed description of his current reading—much of it related to the French Revolution (*MTTF* 207). During this same decade he created an enduring character to represent and dramatize the dichotomy he had long sensed between "romances" (i.e., illusion) and the empirical, factual world (reality): an orphaned boy in a river village, Tom Sawyer. In Tom's wide-ranging but usually misunderstood reading, Twain was able to satirize the effects of overreliance on fanciful narratives, and Huck came to be the perfect foil for highlighting the aberrations of Tom's fictional derangement.

Twain's systematic reading in English history for *The Prince and the Pauper* (1882) was followed by a reading program in American humor that surely had ramifications in his subsequent fiction. The purpose was the compilation of a large one-volume collection of sketches representing the foremost native humorists in American literary history, and under the arrangement agreed upon early in 1882, Twain read selections submitted by Charles H. Clark and William Dean Howells for inclusion in their joint venture. The volume would not be published until 1888, when it appeared as *Mark Twain's Library of Humor* without credit to the coeditors, but in the early 1880s, Twain read avidly in hopes of issuing the book straightaway (*MTHL* 396). Though the anthology of humor soon fell behind his optimistic schedule, Clemens's notebooks between 1880 and 1888 record his enthusiastic search for suitable material in what was certainly one of the most significant and sustained reading projects he ever undertook.

Clemens's other study program during the 1880s is better known—the event he announced with awe to Mary Fairbanks on November 16, 1886: "Think of it!—I've been elected Reader to a [Robert] Browning class—I who have never of my own inclination, read a poem in my life" (see Gribben, "A Splendor . . ." 87–103). The exaggeration about his lack of credentials, like so many of his statements in correspondence with intimate friends, was for heightened effect, but he did sense and seem to enjoy the anomaly of the best-known American humorist leading these study sessions of a richly complex Victorian poet for female aesthetes in Hartford. Perhaps these seeming contradictions gave him the impetus to continue those readings for nearly a year. Another enthusiasm that he picked up in the 1870s was his loyalty to Edward FitzGerald's version of the *Rubáiyát of Omar Khayyám* (1859). As he remarked in 1907, "No poem had ever given me so much pleasure before, and none has given me so much pleasure since; it is the only poem I have ever carried about with me" (*AMT3* 159; see *MTR*; Gribben, "Bond Slave . . ." 245–62). Yet Clemens's friends hardly found him bookish in manner, for all his impulsive reading campaigns. As Grace King noted when Clemens entertained her with his talk at parties in the autumn of 1888, "He does not mow from books, but from his own life, his absurd, grotesque Mark Twain mind—takes what the eye brings it—and turns out fun. His fun is so personal; it is autobiographical" (Bush 39–40). Much of his reading, it would appear, was performed largely on the basis of constantly shifting, rapturous excitements, and these infatuations merely supplied ancillary material for his skill as a raconteur.

During the decade between 1884 and 1894 Clemens had the only regular long-term obligation to review literature in his lifetime—his duties as president and chief stockholder of Charles L. Webster & Company. There is no way of determining how many of the roughly eighty books on the house list of Clemens's publishing firm he personally read and approved before the firm collapsed in 1894, but his correspondence with Webster and his successor Fred J. Hall suggests that the number was considerable. Of course, he also read and rejected many manuscripts that his firm declined to accept, of which quite a few were subsequently brought out by other publishers. Toward the end of Clemens's efforts to sustain his firm, as Hamlin Hill has observed, his expatriation to Europe noticeably and deplorably affected the quality of books that bore the Webster imprint (*MTLP* 300).

Aside from the necessity to investigate particular subjects for special purposes, Clemens received little apparent outside influence on his reading. Mrs. Fairbanks hazarded a few suggestions, but in 1870 she got a letter back from Clemens disparaging the second half of a novel she had recommended, George MacDonald's *Robert Falconer* (1868) (*L4* 187–89). William Dean Howells, however, frequently passed along book titles that came to his attention as a professional reviewer and critic. The two men often but not always agreed on the merits of these works. Jane Austen was one point of contention among the older authors Howells admired, and he and Clemens had their differences regarding the Georgia novelist Will Harben in the last year of Clemens's life. Clemens's admiration for Howells's novels, stories, essays, and plays, on the other hand, approached outright worship, and he owned and devotedly read copies of virtually everything Howells published. Where Clemens's other close friends were concerned, proximity could outweigh his critical judgment. He had a far higher regard for the writings of several Nook Farm neighbors than seems warranted today; he gushed over the poetry and fiction of Thomas Bailey Aldrich and warmly praised Charles Dudley Warner's now-neglected essays. Their publications prominently and permanently occupied several shelves in his personal library.

In the role of father to three daughters Clemens inevitably came in contact with a large number of children's books that otherwise might not have come to his attention. He and Olivia made their children familiar with Jacob Abbott's Franconia Series and the girls became even better acquainted with his numerous Rollo books. George MacDonald's *Sir Gibbie* (1879) and *At the Back of the North Wind* (1871) became staples of bedtime reading. Of the latter book Clemens declared that his daughters "have read and re-read their own copy so many times that it looks as if it had been through the wars." Later he would recall, "Oh, what happy days they were when that book was read, and how Susy loved it!" Charles Kingsley's poignant *The Water-Babies: A Fairy Tale for a Land-Baby*

(1863) presumably held the children in thrall as it did in so many homes of that era. Dozens upon dozens of other works for juveniles entertained the family, including children's history books by Charles Dickens and Charlotte Yonge. *St. Nicholas: A Magazine for Boys and Girls* made its regular appearances in the mail.

After the girls grew up, Clemens continued to make reading recommendations and personally gave gifts of books for their edification. Indications are that the Clemens family members cultivated their literary tastes well beyond the point of conformity with prevailing levels in their Hartford society, even though that city's intellectual standard surpassed those of most other communities. Jean Clemens seems to have preferred practical handbooks, particularly volumes on birds and animal husbandry, but others explored numerous subjects in the humanities. Clemens felt a special connection with Susy owing to her urge to devour literature of all types. Clara's commonplace book, undated except for a reference to 1888 and another to 1904, contains quotations from standard authors of the nineteenth century—Bulwer-Lytton, Hawthorne, Robert Louis Stevenson, Christina Rossetti, Paul Bourget, George Eliot, Heinrich Heine, Johann Wolfgang von Goethe, Louis de Rouvory, *duc de* Saint-Simon, Dickens, Shakespeare, Victor Hugo, and Robert Browning (Paine 150, CU-MARK). Clara's mother Olivia made the effort to read noteworthy fiction and biographies, such as James Cabot's *Emerson* (1887) and George Eliot's novels, along with *George Eliot's Life as Related in Her Letters and Journals* (1885) (OLC, *Diary* 1610). She followed her husband's lead in reading Hippolyte Taine's *Ancient Régime* (1876), as well as Taine's *History of English Literature* (1871), but in 1887 George Meredith's *Diana of the Crossroads* (1885) proved to be one of the dividing lines in taste for the couple (*MTB* 847).

The Clemens family's many summer sojourns at Quarry Farm outside Elmira, New York, opened up the ample book collection of Theodore and Susan Crane to Clemens's perusal. In the indulgent Cranes' household, Clemens luxuriated in easy access to a copy of Richard Henry Dana's *Two Years Before the Mast* (1840) (*MTB* 511) together with works by Thomas Carlyle, W. E. H. Lecky, Thomas Macaulay, Dickens, and many others. The marginalia he left behind in that Quarry Farm library confirm his repeated readings of scores of volumes he found there (Fulton *passim*).

In 1893, Clemens commenced for business reasons a friendship that had a stultifying effect on his reading, inasmuch as his relationship with Henry Huttleston Rogers, a vice president of Standard Oil, consumed large amounts of time and energy and partially set the tone of his thought and work until Rogers's death in 1909. The two men rarely discussed or even mentioned literature in their long and voluminous correspondence, beyond occasional references to the poetry of Rudyard Kipling and James Whitcomb Riley. (Clemens had discovered and revered Riley's verse in the 1880s and had begun to quote Kipling frequently in the 1890s.) Though Rogers salvaged Clemens's financial security in the final decades of his life, he and his Wall Street and Washington cronies with whom Clemens fraternized hardly resembled Clemens's earlier friends—such as Howells, Joseph Twichell, Warner, Aldrich, and Mrs. Fairbanks. Clemens seemed embarrassed to bring up literary works with which Rogers was unacquainted; in fact, he was reluctant to give the impression to Rogers of being "literary" at all. For instance, his satire about Paul Bourget, he assured Rogers, was designed to laugh "at some of our oracular owls who find them 'important.' What the hell makes them important, I should like to know!" (*HHR* 80).

Rogers, for his part, began their correspondence on December 19, 1893, with a self-conscious gesture toward literary allusion—likening the African-American boxer Frank "Coffee-Cooler" Craig to "a malignant and turbaned Turk" (a line from Shakespeare's *Othello*, act 5) (*HHR* 28), but he soon dropped this attempt at embellishing letters to his author-friend. Thereafter, the two men wrote mainly of business, publishing contracts, lecture itineraries, personal associates, yachts, boxing, billiards, and vacation journeys. Clemens did send Rogers a copy of Sarah P. McLean Green's *Flood-Tide* (1901), inasmuch as its coastal Maine character sketches were written by an author known for her Cape Cod stories, and Rogers politely responded that he "enjoyed it" (*HHR* 529). But Rogers's high school education in Fairhaven, Massachusetts, had not prepared him for extensive literary discussions, nor did his serious business affairs allow him leisure to cultivate such refinements. Clemens made certain that Rogers found this no barrier between them, and as a consequence their correspondence filled 666 pages when it was published in 1969 (*HHR*).

Yet despite all hindrances and discouraging circumstances—just as Clemens persevered in spite of the small library resources in Hannibal, his lack of formal education, his frequent moves and changes of career—he managed somehow to continue reading diversely. "London dailies discuss notable new books in leading articles," he noted in October 1896, during his bereavement over Susy's death (*MTNB 39* 11). And when his household dwindled pathetically during his final decade, he found his secretary Isabel Lyon willing to direct and share much of his reading (*MTGF*; Trombley, *Mark Twain's Other Woman*; Shelden, *Mark Twain: Man in White*). Like Olivia, for whom she became an intellectual surrogate, Lyon was allowed to suggest Clemens's reading materials, but he was no more hesitant in rejecting her opinions (of Friedrich Nietzsche, for example) than he had been in rejecting his wife's.

As an intrepid autodidact, Clemens overcame his own handicaps of background and education so completely in developing as a voracious reader that it seems self-contradictory in *Is Shakespeare Dead?* (1909) for him to reject the probability of Shakespeare's authorship partly on the grounds that his humble birth and education in Stratford could not have prepared the poet adequately for composing the works with which he is credited. Clemens's self-education as a reader, like Shakespeare's great dramatic achievements, is a victory for human will over circumstance and likelihood, a refusal to accept the normal course of events, and a moving example of intellectual quest and resolve.

Part Two

The Clemens Family

5

Sam and His Siblings

Henry Sweets

As Sam Clemens was growing up in mid-nineteenth-century Missouri, frontier life was rugged and often filled with heartbreak. The Hannibal *Gazette* of June 3, 1847, reported that "one quarter of the children born die before they are one year old; one half die before they are 21" (Hannibal *Gazette*, 3 June 1847). Sam's own nine-member family found death a frequent companion; indeed, it lost three young children and a fourth at age twenty. The remaining three children lived into adulthood, closely reflecting the grim statistic of the Hannibal newspaper.

Sam's father, John Marshall Clemens, finished his law studies in Columbia, Kentucky, was admitted to the bar, and married Jane Lampton in 1823. The newlyweds then moved to Tennessee, where Clemens started a series of business adventures—from practicing law to serving as postmaster and running general stores. Always looking to better his family's condition, he moved the family several times as it grew. The first of John and Jane's five Tennessee children, Orion, was born on July 17, 1825. The first girl, Pamela Ann, arrived on September 13, 1827, and the first casualty, a boy, Pleasant Hannibal (named for two uncles), lived but three months in 1828 or 1829. Two more children followed: Margaret on May 31, 1830 and Benjamin on June 8, 1832. Looking for financial improvement, and encouraged by Jane's sister and brother-in law, Patsy and John Quarles, the growing family moved to Florida, Missouri, in late summer 1835 to seek their fortune. Sam was born on November 30, 1835, and the family's seventh child, Henry, on July 13, 1838.

Sam was not yet four years old when the family left Florida for Hannibal, so his memories of his first home are scant. They include a family story of a sleepwalking episode that found him at the bedside of Margaret, who was sick with bilious fever, and tugging at her coverlet (*MTB* 22). Superstition held that this behavior signaled impending death, and when young Margaret succumbed to her illness on August 17, 1839, it was thought Sam had prophetic powers. It was also one of the first of a long series of family experiences that would be etched in his mind, and it haunted him through the rest of his life.

John never prospered in Florida, and his eye soon turned toward nearby Hannibal, on the banks of the Mississippi, as a more fertile environment to better his life. Margaret's death hastened his family's desire to relocate there in November, 1839. Sam then spent his next thirteen and one-half years in Hannibal as the town swelled from a population of 800 in 1839 to more than 3,000 in 1853. Likewise, the family's dynamics changed drastically in those years.

The Clemens household makeup was as variable as John's fortunes. He began in Hannibal with the purchase of a full lot of downtown property that included the Virginia House where he ensconced his family while starting another general store. As the store faltered, he sold most of his properties and moved his family into what is now known as the Mark Twain Boyhood Home on Hill Street some time before early 1844. He was elected justice of the peace and ran court sessions, but prosperity eluded him, and in late 1846 his family suffered the indignities of having its possessions sold at a sheriff's auction and moving in with Dr. Grant's family. While a candidate for clerk of the county court, John died on March 24, 1847, and Jane Clemens moved the family back into the Boyhood Home and persevered. These circumstances took a toll on young Sam and his siblings.

Known by his family as O´ri-on (accented like Flor´-ee-an), Orion was fourteen years old when the family arrived in Hannibal and ten years Sam's elder (*MTBM* 9). Soon after the family store opened, he was positioned as a clerk "in a new suit of clothes" (*MTB* 27). His absent-mindedness was not an asset, and when the store began to fail, he was apprenticed to the Hannibal *Journal* at his father's insistence. Orion learned the printing trade fairly quickly and by 1842 was off to Ustick's Steam Printing House in St. Louis to begin earning a living. Sam left few recollections of Orion from these years, when Benjamin and Henry were his playmates. Orion was consigned to the adult world, far from the interests of the young, mischievous boy enjoying his freedom.

Pamela (known as Pa-mee´la by the family) was eight years older than Sam and helped raise the boys (*MTBM* 5). Only five years apart, Benjamin, Sam, and Henry were a handful. Pamela's overseeing of the boys would later be Sam's inspiration for Tom's cousin Mary in *The Adventures of Tom Sawyer* (1876). Pamela took an early interest in religion and joined the Presbyterian Church along with her mother in February 1841 (Sweets 17). Sam had earlier attended the Methodist Sunday school but was brought to the Presbyterian school and church services. Shortly after arriving in Hannibal, Pamela and Benjamin had started school under the tutelage of Elizabeth Horr. Pamela once received a note of commendation from Mrs. Horr that read, "Miss Pamela Clemens has won the love of her teacher and schoolmates by her amiable deportment and faithful application to her various studies. E. Horr, Teacher" (*MTB* 39).

Pamela was a musician who accomplished enough on piano and guitar to give lessons. Young Sam learned to play both from her instruction and used his piano ability to entertain company later in life. Following the death of John in 1847, Pamela traveled to Paris and Florida, Missouri to provide music instruction. This work enabled her to send money back to support the family. After returning to Hannibal, she was given a piano by Joe Buchanan, the owner of the Hannibal *Journal* newspaper who was heading to California in 1850, when he was caught up with gold fever. Later, Orion would buy the *Journal* to merge it with his *Western Union*.

After John's death, Jane Clemens took on boarders to supplement the family's meager income. One boarder was a boy, Jim Wolf, whose shyness and Pamela's circle of friends afforded Sam the opportunity for a major prank. "Jim Wolf and the Cats" recounts how Pamela was having a winter candy-pull. Sam described enticing Jim, dressed in only his nightshirt, to climb out onto the icy roof, from which he slid off and onto the plates of steaming candy amid the startled girls. Pamela became Sam's second sibling to leave Hannibal. In the summer of 1851, she traveled to Kentucky to visit relatives. There she encountered William Anderson Moffett, also of Hannibal. After marrying on September 20, the couple headed to St. Louis, ending Pamela's Hannibal days and her close association with Sam.

Sam left few memories of his other older brothers, Pleasant Hannibal and Benjamin. Pleasant, whom he never mentioned, died before he was born. In spring, 1842, when he was six, Ben suddenly became the family's third casualty after a sudden illness, dying on May 12. His mother's reaction to his death was engrained in Sam's memory. In 1897, he wrote that his mother had "made the children feel the cheek of the dead boy, and tried to make them understand the calamity that had befallen" (*HH&T* 39). Sam believed that somehow he was responsible for Ben's death. Though he was in no way responsible, this incident also haunted Sam the rest of his days. It may be significant that the few recollections Sam left of Margaret and Benjamin dealt with their deaths and his perceived guilt instead of happier childhood experiences.

When John became seriously ill in 1847, Orion briefly returned home to help. Following John's death, Orion returned to St. Louis and sent regular monetary contributions to the family. In 1850, the family dynamic again changed when Orion came back to Hannibal, purchased printing equipment, and launched his *Western Union* newspaper. Soon thereafter he purchased Joe Buchanan's Hannibal *Journal*, beginning a series of name changes for his newspapers. Orion's return reunited the family and prompted major changes in the lives of his brothers. Now twenty-five and in the business world, Orion served as breadwinner for the family and assumed a father's role for his brothers that had been missing during the formative years of Sam's life. Sam had already been taken from school and apprenticed to Hannibal papers, and within a year of Orion's return, Sam, and later Henry, were to switch to their brother's paper.

Working for Orion provided both instruction and disappointment for Sam. Orion was a strict taskmaster who appreciated Sam's literary abilities. Orion had developed good editing skills and his oversight of Sam pushed the young aspiring journalist to improve his abilities and venture into print. Sam was turned loose with a "Local" column reporting Hannibal news, and on several occasions he had control of the paper when Orion was away on business. He made the most of those opportunities, stirring up local interest with his vivid imagination. Orion's return always meant a return to the usual dullness of the paper. One of these absences in late spring 1853 inspired Sam to run a series of comic articles berating another newspaper editor. Sam's characterization of the ineptitude of the man, who even failed at suicide, led to a quick apology by Orion upon his return, increasing Sam's desire to leave Hannibal and the supervision of his brother.

Sam used noms de plume for the first time in Orion's paper. Those he included were "W. Ephaminondas Adrastus Blab," "A Dog-be-deviled Citizen," and "Rambler." His dabbling with pen names would continue until he settled on "Mark Twain" in his Nevada days. Sam was a fairly good typesetter. Orion later said, "I was tyrannical and unjust to Sam. He was as swift and as clean as a good journeyman. I gave him tasks, and if he got through well I begrudged him the time and made him work more. He set a clean proof, and Henry a very dirty one" (*MTB* 85).

The younger brothers played pranks on each other similar to those Tom and Sid would play on each other in *Tom Sawyer*. For example, Sam once described dropping a half-eaten watermelon on Henry's head from a second-story window. Henry got his revenge several days later by landing a cobblestone against the side of Sam's head (*AMT1* 458).

Sam shared a room with Henry and remained close to his playmate and confidant, admiring Henry's studious nature and absorption of facts. Henry's closeness in years meant many shared escapades with Sam, as when both joined the Cadets of Temperance when that organization was founded. Sam later recalled

> My mother had a great deal of trouble with me, but I think she enjoyed it. She had none at all with my brother, Henry, who was two years younger than I, and I think that the unbroken monotony of his goodness and truthfulness and obedience would have been a burden to her but for the relief and variety which I furnished in the other direction. I was a tonic. I was valuable to her. I never thought of it before, but now I see it. I never knew Henry to do a vicious thing toward me, or toward anyone else—but he frequently did righteous ones that cost me as heavily. It was his duty to report me, when I needed reporting and neglected to do it myself, and he was faithful in discharging that duty. (*AMT1* 350)

Sam's confidence grew while working under his brother's editorship, and he came to admire Orion's honesty and integrity. However, Orion's dreary editorial policy, heavy-handedness, and promises of cash salaries that never materialized prompted Sam to follow his sister's lead by leaving Hannibal in May of 1853. Later the same year, Henry accompanied Orion and their mother to Muscatine, Iowa and then to Keokuk, Iowa. Sam would later return to Orion's employ in Keokuk and again share a room with his beloved Henry. His departure from Hannibal at age seventeen ended his childhood association with his siblings. Thereafter, he considered himself an adult, ready to tackle the world. However, the family ties that were formed during the Hannibal days remained strong throughout his life, reflected by joyful reunions after separations and a constant exchange of letters among the family members.

While later piloting steamboats on the river, Sam found Henry a job on the *Pennsylvania*, inadvertently setting the stage for a tragedy. Henry was scalded when that steamboat's boilers exploded. He died in Memphis, Tennessee, on June 21, 1858, shortly after Sam rushed to be at his side (*LM* ch. 20). Sam had left the *Pennsylvania* just days earlier and felt responsible for Henry's death—a guilt that followed him the rest of his life. Before the accident, he dreamed that he saw Henry in a metal coffin in another of his prophetic episodes.

Pamela and her husband William Moffett were living in St. Louis at the time Sam left Hannibal. He stayed with them and borrowed a portion of the money needed for his piloting lessons from William. While piloting on the river, he used his sister's home as his St. Louis apartment. After William died in 1865, he regularly sent checks to Pamela to help support her family. Later, he suggested Pamela move her family to Fredonia, New York, and assisted in that move.

Meanwhile, both Pamela and Orion helped Sam by scrapbooking clippings he sent to them that he would later use to help write his books and stories. Surviving correspondence shows busy lines of communication among the three surviving Clemens siblings.

Sam and Orion became closer in adulthood after Sam started working in Orion's Iowa print shop. With the advent of the Civil War and the curtailment of steamboat commerce on the Mississippi River in 1861, Sam's piloting days abruptly ended. Orion was appointed secretary of the new Nevada territorial government, and Sam soon accompanied his brother west, paying for the trip with his piloting earnings. Orion's notes and his recollections of the brothers' western adventures would also later prove invaluable when Sam was writing *Roughing It* (1872). Orion also kept scrapbooks and later wrote an autobiography that would trigger fresh memories in Sam's own autobiographical dictations. Orion's stint as secretary and occasional acting governor of Nevada Territory would prove the pinnacle of his career. He had studied law and even been admitted to the bar but never established a firm practice, instead struggling to stay gainfully employed. Gradually, Sam took the mantle of family head from Orion as he was the more financially successful. Sam lobbied for a job for Orion in the United States Patent Office and later helped him gain work with his publisher in Hartford, Connecticut. Nevertheless, Orion remained financially needy, and Sam helped support him and his wife, Mollie, the rest of their days.

Two of Sam's siblings and his mother are depicted in *Tom Sawyer* in Aunt Polly's household. Jane Clemens inspired Aunt Polly, Pamela appears as cousin Mary, and Henry as Tom's half-brother, Sid, thus altering the real-life kinship connections substantially. Sam also coauthored the earlier novel *The Gilded Age* (1873), in which he modeled one character on Orion, but *Tom Sawyer* was his first solo attempt at long fiction. When he wrote it, he had not yet learned the character development he would perfect in *Adventures of Huckleberry Finn* (1885) and other writings. In Pamela's case, he did not have a well-developed character in mind when he introduced cousin Mary in *Tom Sawyer*, and Sid is far from the real Henry Clemens. Sam later noted that Henry "is 'Sid' in 'Tom Sawyer.' But Sid was not Henry. Henry was a very much finer and better boy than ever Sid was" (*AMT1* 350).

By portraying his own mother as Tom Sawyer's Aunt Polly, Sam allowed Tom to escape remorse for most of his actions that a mother figure would have evoked. This is hinted at in chapter 18 with Tom's sorrowfulness for not reporting news of the boys' safety when they are feared dead and Aunt Polly is grieving. Similarly, Mary's being a "cousin" allowed her to be a relatively insignificant character who makes only a few appearances in the story, much as Pamela seemed to do in Sam's real life. As a half-brother, Sid could get Tom into trouble in ways that Sam's real brother Henry did not. Sam had strong ties to his family members, but always on his own terms. By helping Jane Clemens and Pamela and her family move to Fredonia, New York, while he lived in Hartford, Sam kept them at a comfortable distance. After Orion's brief employments in Vermont and Hartford ended, Sam encouraged him to move back to Keokuk.

Sam never took his wife, Livy, and children to his boyhood home of Hannibal. Was he ashamed of his background? Was he embarrassed by the lack of success of his siblings Pamela and Orion? Or, might closer associations with them have brought on deep feelings of debts he may have felt he owed them? He clouds answers to these questions in his recorded memories, which often betray his true appreciation for his siblings. Sam frequently held Orion up to ridicule in letters to family and friends, but the correspondence between them shows that Sam often valued Orion's opinion and certainly used Orion's memory as a resource in his writings. He also drew on Orion's editorial and research skills to perform tasks he thought boring or beneath him. For example, Orion was the researcher for the little booklet of facts that accompanied Mark Twain's Memory-Builder game (*MTBM* 218).

What we know about Sam and Orion's relationship has generally been taken from Sam's writings since Orion's own autobiography is lost. A study of the two brothers can lead to a different conclusion. In *Mark Twain: Son of Missouri* (1934), Minnie Brashear suggested that it was "probably not an exaggeration to say that the greatest single influence in Mark Twain's life was his older brother, lasting through the publication of *Roughing It*" (*MTSM* 105–06). In *Mark Twain and Orion Clemens* (2003), Philip Fanning examines Sam and Orion's long-strained relationship. From chafing under his brother's heavy-handed treatment in the Hannibal print shop through his experiences in Nevada and later, when Orion admonished him about his deportment in business and public situations, Sam nursed resentments toward his brother. Fanning cites numerous examples of strains and suggests, "Perhaps the most important pattern that owes something to Orion is that of the pariah who turns out to be right" (Fanning 220). Despite all his condescending remarks, Sam made a revealing comment in his autobiography that indicates what he liked about Orion, while perhaps recognizing his own failings: "He was a most strange creature—but in spite of his eccentricities he was beloved, all his life, in whatever community he lived. And he was held in high esteem, for at the bottom he was a sterling man" (*AMT2* 26).

Sam's family always remained at the fore of his consciousness, and his perceived role of family head spurred him to financially support his brother and sister, as well as his mother, Jane, who lived alternately with Pamela and Orion. Sam's family bonds, rooted in his Hannibal years, endured throughout their lives.

6

Sam and Livy as Parents

John Bird

"We are a very happy family," thirteen-year-old Susy Clemens wrote as she began a biography of her famous father, known to the world as Mark Twain, but to his three daughters as "Papa" (*AMT1* 339). Samuel and Olivia Clemens had four children: Langdon, who died in infancy, Susy, Clara, and Jean. In her memoir about her father, Clara, the only daughter who outlived him, wrote these words twenty years after his death:

> When my thoughts return to childhood, I see figures of romance moving in the atmosphere of fairyland, kings and queens in the world of dreams. I wish that words could give a true picture of those long-vanished, unforgettable days— days filled with joy, sorrow, humor, fun, work, and always sparkling interest. How sad it is that children take kindnesses from their parents so utterly for granted. (*MFMT* 1–2)

While romanticized and tinged with nostalgia, Clara's focus on "joy, sorrow, humor, fun, and always sparkling interest" captures what life must have been like in Hartford, Elmira, Europe, and other places in which these children under the parenting of their famous father and caring, loving mother.

Parenting, of course, is both an inexact science and highly individualized, developed in partnership, relying on the experience of each parent's upbringing, practiced mostly in private, but also reacting to the pressures and attitudes of society at large, and very much an evolving, adaptive, and improvisational process. Sam was the product of a strict Calvinist upbringing, with a stern, distant father who died when Sam was eleven, and a lively, loving, and witty mother. Olivia was the product of a liberal and affluent upbringing, the daughter of a wealthy coal merchant and his devoted wife, a family that supported abolition and full education for women. In the late nineteenth century, when Sam and

Livy became parents, societal attitudes toward children and childrearing were changing. As Peter W. Stearns argues in *Anxious Parents: A History of Modern Childrearing in America* (2003), the move from viewing children as sinful to innocent but vulnerable had a big effect on parents, especially on mothers, who almost always took the lead role and bore the most responsibility for children (Stearns 17). He goes on: "As beliefs in original sin declined, a dominant image of children's innocence emerged in the 19th century. Children were seen as fundamentally good, and, though they could be led astray, if not corrupted by bad example they would grow naturally into their great potential" (Stearns 21). This description fits the Clemens household well, and it applies especially well to the raising of three daughters, who were presumed good but in need of strong moral examples and sound moral instruction, as well as protection from the outside world.

For Livy Clemens, like most American women of her time, the domestic life of the household and the children were her primary responsibility. Although as the wife in a wealthy household—the wealth coming as much from her inheritance as from her husband's substantial earning as a writer—Livy had the support of servants, nurses, and governesses. She was in charge of the children's health, their education, their religious and moral instruction, and their discipline, as well as running the household and entertaining constantly. Twain's writing career kept him busy during the day when he was at work on his next book, and often required travel and business engagements that kept him away from home. But when he was with the family, mornings and evenings mainly, he was an attentive and doting father who took a keen interest in his daughters' activities and upbringing. He entertained them with inventive storytelling, and he enthusiastically encouraged their play and creativity, often joining in and leading their games.

Through most of their childhood years, Susy, Clara, and Jean were home-schooled, with a succession of governesses as teachers, but with Livy taking a prominent role. Livy had received a strong liberal education from the age of five in Miss Thurston's seminary, then the preparatory division of Elmira Female College, studying science and mathematics in addition to the traditional subjects of grammar, literature, and the Bible. Despite her schooling being interrupted in her teenage years because of serious illness, she studied at home with Elmira College professors, who taught her physical science, astronomy, French, and Shakespeare (F. Kaplan 230–33). Her broad formal, liberal education stood in stark contrast to that of her husband, who was forced to leave school upon his father's death, but who attained broad and deep knowledge on a variety of subjects through voracious reading and an ever-curious mind. Although Livy took the lead in the children's education, their father was active and interested in their educational progress.

From 1874 to 1883, the family employed a German-American maid, Rosina Hay, and her instruction, along with travel to Germany in 1878, instituted a lifelong study of the German language by the children and both their parents (Courtney 79). Young Jean became especially fluent in German, becoming essentially bilingual. In what would now be called language immersion, the children's schoolroom was dubbed "the German room" with only German allowed to be spoken within the room, and with all subjects, including arithmetic, taught in German. Somewhat competent in the language, but frustrated at having to converse with his daughters, Twain would sometimes begin a sentence in German inside the room then step outside the door to finish his thought in English.

In her biography of her father, Susy delineated a typical day in 1885, showing Livy's deep involvement in the girls' schooling: teaching Jean German from 9 a.m. to 10 a.m., reading German with Susy from 10 a.m. to 11 a.m., reading English history to Susy and Jean while the girls sewed, until lunch, followed by more reading aloud to her daughters in the afternoon (*AMT2* 210). The most enduring of a procession of governesses was Lilly Foote, who took over instruction as the children grew older. Livy describes examinations when Clara and Susy were eleven and thirteen:

> Clara passed a most excellent examination in her Geography. Susy told the story of Cupid and Psyche in Latin, Miss Foote asking her questions. Susy gave what I think without partiality was a brilliant recitation in Ancient History. She talked for fully an hour. . . . Occasionally she would say well Miss Foote, the book says so and so, but it seems to me in this way, stating something quite different. (Courtney 84)

The girls' father encouraged their learning by quizzing them on their reading and on history, his favorite subject. He established a rule that each member of the family must bring a fact to breakfast every day—"a fact drawn from a book or from any other source; any fact would answer" (*AMT2* 330). The children were further educated by their exposure to an endless succession of dazzling house guests, including writers, clergymen, doctors, politicians, editors, businessmen, and their wives. Twain's letters to his friends and associates, especially William Dean Howells, are full of stories about his children. Twain was especially proud of Susy's writing ability, and he praised all of his daughters for their deep, critical thinking.

Children's health was of special concern to parents in the nineteenth century, given that infant mortality rates in 1880 were over 20 percent, 214.8 deaths per 1,000 births (Haines). For Sam and Livy, the death of their son Langdon at eighteen months from diphtheria was an ever-present reminder of the fragility of life for small children. Clemens mistakenly blamed himself for his son's death, thinking that he had left him exposed to the cold in his carriage (*MTAZ* 79). In addition, Livy had the memory of her long convalescence in her teen years. Sam, too, had the reminder of his own frail early childhood, as well as his memory of his own dead siblings: Pleasant, Margaret, and Benjamin. Sam and Livy had the advantage for their daughters of being able to afford nurses and the best doctors. The girls had the usual childhood diseases with no lasting effects, the most serious being Jean's scarlet fever in her second year. Clara was especially accident prone, including having her finger badly cut by the metal canopy of her baby stroller, nearly being burned when a croup kettle lit the curtains on fire in the nursery, and crashing into a tree while riding a toboggan (*MFMT* 4–6). The nature of their childhood illnesses changed as the children grew older. Jean may have had her first epileptic seizure in her tenth year, but it wasn't until she was sixteen that she was diagnosed with the disease, which led the family on a search of Europe and America for a cure. She died on Christmas Eve, 1909, five years after her mother's death and several months before her father's death (*MTAZ* 78). Susy died in 1896, after a sudden bout of spinal meningitis (*MTAZ* 84). Clara then became the only surviving member of what Susy had called "a very happy family."

Discipline of children in many nineteenth-century households was often the province of the father, but in the Clemens household, Livy took full responsibility. Susy described the process at length: When the nurse caught Susy and Clara being naughty, she would call Livy, who would appear suddenly and look at her daughters with clear displeasure, which the girls found to be punishment in itself. Then Livy would simply say, "Clara" or "Susy, what do you mean by this?" At times, she resorted to placing the offender in solitary confinement, although Clara was so inventive that she enjoyed the solitude of even a dark closet. More common was consulting the daughter and asking her what she thought the punishment should be. As a last resort, and only in the worst cases, the child was taken into the bathroom and whipped with a paper cutter—akin to a letter opener. But first, Livy would make the child understand that the punishment was for the child's sake, and that her mother loved her so much that she could not allow the child to do wrong. However, she always waited before administering any corporal punishment until she was perfectly calm, never punishing in anger. Afterward, she held the offending child and talked to her to make her understand why she had been whipped, not letting the child go until the daughter was, as Susy wrote, "perfectly happy" (*AMT2* 327).

Discipline is almost always a private family matter, but Sam made his wife's methods quite public in 1885 after Livy had shown him an article in the *Christian Union*, "What Ought He to Have Done?," in which a mother wrote about the stern discipline of her husband on their young son. Twain wrote a reply to the magazine that contrasted his wife's reasoned and humane discipline with that of the man in question, "John Senior." Livy was not overly pleased to see their private life made public, and even less pleased at the negative letters Twain subsequently received, including an especially nasty one, whose pseudonymous author, "Thomas Twain" writes of his wish to confine Clemens's wife to a room, tie her hands, and beat her harshly. Twain assumed the writer was "John Senior" of the original article, and despite his inclinations, he did not reply. The majority of the letters they received were very positive, approving of Livy's disciplinary methods (*DMT* 115–19).

Livy also assumed responsibility for the children's religious training, reading the girls Bible stories, supervising their prayers at night, and taking them to Asylum Hill Congregationalist Church in Hartford. Their father accompanied them to the family pew, and although one of his best friends was the church's pastor, Joseph Twichell, he maintained skepticism about Christian orthodoxy. He also expressed delight at his children's growing philosophical questioning. At age seven, Susy began questioning the mysteries of human life and death, asking, "Mamma, what is it all for?" (*AMT2* 325–26). A year later, after she had begun to learn about the religion of the Indians, she proclaimed that she could no longer pray to God in the same way, telling her mother, "Well, mamma, the Indians believed they knew, but now we know they were wrong. By and by it can turn out that we are wrong. So now I only pray that there may be a God and a heaven—or something better" (*AMT2* 326). Her father was to write years later, "Its untaught grace and simplicity are a child's, but the wisdom and the pathos of it are all the ages that have come and gone since the race of man has lived, and longed, and hoped, and feared, and doubted" (*AMT2* 326).

Sam's biggest role in his children's upbringing was in the area of storytelling, sports, games, entertainment, music, and his example as a writer. He took time from his work to spend quality time with his daughters, notably telling them bedtime stories. A nightly ritual was to gather in the ornate library of the Hartford house, where he had to improvise a story based on the knickknacks, sculptures, and pictures that lined the walls and the mantel. The story had to be different every time, and he must not change the order of the items that underlay the plot of the story. As Twain wrote in his autobiography, "Those bric-a-bracs were never allowed a peaceful day, a reposeful day, a restful Sabbath. In their lives there was no Sabbath; in their lives there was no peace; they knew no existence but a monotonous career of violence and bloodshed. In the course of time the bric-a-brac and the pictures showed wear" (Courtney 20). Clara remembered the stories many years later: "Passing from picture to picture, his power of invention led us into countries and among human figures that held us spellbound. He treated a Medusa head according to his own individual method, the snakes being sometimes changed to laurel leaves that tickled joy in Medusa's hair and inspired thoughts of victory" (*MFMT* 2). Storytelling was ingrained into the house itself, with ceramic tiles and the wallpaper in the nursery depicting nursery rhymes (Courtney 79).

Sam was active with his daughters in playing games such as tennis and croquet, and in winter activities such as ice skating and sledding. The children of Nook Farm, including the Warner and Twichell children, provided a wealth of playmates. In the early 1880s, their father combined game-playing with education by developing "Mark Twain's Memory Builder," a game for remembering dates, which he tried out with his children before manufacturing for sale a board game. Charades provided amusement many nights that combined fun and education for the girls. From an early age, the children composed and acted out their own plays, which both Sam and Livy encouraged. In 1884, as a surprise for her husband, who was away on his lecture tour with George Washington Cable, Livy wrote a stage adaptation of *The Prince and the Pauper*, which was staged with elaborate costumes and scenery, the girls and their neighborhood friends playing the major roles. The play was such a success that it was repeated for friends and the neighborhood several times over the next few years, with Twain taking on the role of Miles Hendon (*AMT2* 165–66).

Music was a constant in the family home, with the girls all studying piano and voice. Clara's musical talents led her to serious study of the piano and then voice in Europe in her early twenties, with hopes of a musical career that never were fully realized. Their father loved to sit down at the piano and raucously play and sing Negro spirituals. An elaborate music box that sat in the entry hall, purchased in Geneva during their 1878–79 trip, provided nightly entertainment as the family dined (Courtney 40).

The Clemens family had a constant menagerie of pets, numerous cats and dogs, often with colorful names: Sour Mash, Pestilence, Famine, and Damnation, for example. Notable was a donkey named Cadichon, which the children pronounced as "Kiditchin." It provided endless hours of entertainment as the children tried to ride it (*AMT2* 217). These pets instilled in the children a deep love of animals. That love was strongest in Jean, who later in life devoted herself to the causes of antivivisection and prevention of cruelty to animals—causes her father took up and wrote about in stories like "A Dog's Tale" (1903) and "A Horse's Tale" (1906).

Sam and Livy's love for their children can best be seen in private manuscripts Sam wrote to document the girls' sayings and actions: "A Record of the Small Foolishness of Susie and 'Bay' Clemens (Infants)," "A Family Sketch," and "At the Farm" (*FSk*). In these private writings, we can see the depth of love and family bonds that lay at the heart of the domestic scene for this mostly happy family. The short entries in "A Record of Small Foolishnesses" span the years 1876–85, focusing mainly on Susy and Clara, but eventually including Jean. Although the anecdotes were never meant for anyone but their parents to read and treasure, they give us one of the clearest pictures of the children's personalities and their parents' childrearing. "At the Farm," written in the summer of 1884 at Quarry Farm in Elmira, could be considered a part of or an extension of "A Record of Small Foolishness," with a special focus on young Jean and her love of animals, especially the cows, which she had to visit daily. "A Family Sketch," dictated in the last decade of Twain's life, begins with memories of the children, but expands to describe the wider family circle of servants, one of the best accounts we have of that integral part of the household.

Parenting and domestic life run throughout Twain's fiction, with mixed depictions. The McWilliams stories are thinly veiled comic exaggerations of Sam and Livy, with "Experiences of the McWilliamses with Membranous Croup" (1875) the one most focused on parenting. This comic rendering of an over-solicitous mother in the face of the dreaded membranous croup exaggerates the family's experience with childhood diseases.

In his two greatest novels about childhood, *The Adventures of Tom Sawyer* (1876) and *Adventures of Huckleberry Finn* (1885), family life and parenting are portrayed very differently. Tom Sawyer is an orphan, raised by his Aunt Polly, who is modeled on Twain's mother, Jane Lampton Clemens. Aunt Polly administers discipline (and patent medicine), but with clear love and affection for her mischievous nephew. Tom is tormented by religion and education, but he is free to play and let his imagination run wild in a novel Twain called "a hymn to boyhood." The situation in the novel's sequel is quite different. Huck Finn's mother is dead, and his father is an abusive alcoholic. Pap Finn is mostly absent, but Huck is worse off when Pap is present. Twain portrays here a brutal, hellish depiction of parenting; Pap Finn is surely one of the worst fathers in literature. He berates his son, demands money from him, kidnaps and imprisons him, beats him mercilessly, and, in a drunken rage, threatens to kill him. Huck's adventures are set in motion by his need to escape his father's abusive parenting. In his escape, he finds a surrogate father in the runaway slave Jim, who, even though he is cut off from his own family by slavery, shows himself to be a caring and loving parent. Huck's realization that Jim deeply loves his wife and children is a key moment in his ultimate decision to help Jim achieve freedom.

Although *A Connecticut Yankee in King Arthur's Court* (1889) is predominantly a comic satire of both Arthurian England and nineteenth-century America, Hank Morgan, his wife Sandy, and their child, Hello-Central, constitute a loving and affectionate family. Parenting is only an undercurrent in the novel, and the happy family is destroyed by Hank's return to the nineteenth century, the novel ending with the sadness of their eternal separation. *Pudd'nhead Wilson* (1894) depicts parenting as it has been inverted by the evils of slavery: A product of miscegenation, Roxy switches her 1/32nd black baby with the master's baby, allowing her true son to be raised by the rich white master. The false Tom Driscoll is then spoiled by both his surrogate father and his true mother, resulting in a wayward child, an arrogant young man, and eventually, a murderer and thief.

In Twain's late, mostly unpublished fragments, family life has become a tragic, nightmarish horror, as in "The Great Dark" (1898), in which a father takes his family into great peril on a sea voyage through a microscopic drop of water, perhaps a symbolic rendering of the travails of the Clemens family after their mostly idyllic halcyon days of the 1870s and 1880s. The story beings on March 19, the real Susy's birthday, and the mother opens the narrative by saying, "We were a happy family," a clear echo of the opening of Susy's biography of her father.

"We are a very happy family," Susy had proclaimed in 1885, but the happiness largely unraveled in the last two decades of Twain's life: bankruptcy, illness, and death. As his daughters grew into young women, he had trouble letting go their innocent younger days. There were disagreements with Susy over her female friendships as she briefly attended Bryn Mawr, and her death in 1896 of spinal meningitis plunged the family into a despair from which neither Sam nor Livy ever fully recovered. Jean's epilepsy worsened, and Clara increasingly exerted her independence. After Livy's death in 1904, Sam was left nearly alone, Jean being confined because of her illness and Clara in Europe pursuing a musical career. Twain's formation of a group of admiring young girls, his "angelfish," was an attempt at recapturing the glory days of his daughters' youth. He reunited with Jean in his last years, but that reunion was cut short by her tragic death by drowning in 1909. When Sam died a few months later in April 1910, he was probably unaware that Clara, his only surviving daughter, was about to bring him his only grandchild.

But the happy days from the two decades of the girls' childhood show Sam and Olivia as parents who were devoted to their children, with family life at the center of their marriage, and with an approach to parenting that shares more with the latter part of the twentieth century than the latter part of the nineteenth century.

7

Langdon Clemens and *The Adventures of Tom Sawyer*

Joseph Csicsila

The Adventures of Tom Sawyer (1876) has long been appreciated as a fictionalized reminiscence of Mark Twain's youth in Hannibal, Missouri. The current critical view is that the composition of the novel, which Twain is believed to have begun sometime between December 1872 and early January 1873, has its origins in the short burlesques of Sunday-school literature Twain wrote in the 1860s and the unpublished story he composed sometime between 1868 and 1870, known as "A Boy's Manuscript." It is also believed to have been generally inspired by letters Twain exchanged with his childhood friend Will Bowen, in which he rehashed his adolescent experiences nearly three years earlier, in February 1870. New evidence, however, including freshly uncovered information from the holograph manuscript of *Tom Sawyer* itself, challenges the scholarly consensus regarding both the dates of composition and the sources of Twain's first foray into what has been called the "Matter of Hannibal," revealing that Twain actually began writing *Tom Sawyer* significantly earlier than has been thought—specifically during the summer months of 1872, within weeks of the death of his eighteen-month-old son, Langdon. *Tom Sawyer* may actually represent much more than simply a nostalgic look back at Twain's childhood. *Tom Sawyer* might very well be about Twain grieving the loss of Langdon.

The death of Langdon has long been a curious gap in discussions of Twain's life. Typically, biographers scarcely devote more than a paragraph or two to the incident, and a review of the scholarly record reveals just one article taking up the subject of Langdon's passing and the shattering effect it had on his parents—Barbara Snedecor's 2012 essay, "'He Was So Rarely Beautiful': Langdon Clemens." The oversight seems all the more conspicuous, given the considerable attention critics have paid to Twain's responses, literary and otherwise, to the deaths of his wife and daughters and even to his brother Henry's fatal accident in 1858. At least part of the reason scholarship has neglected the subject would seem to lie with Twain himself. He simply does not appear to have left much behind to indicate that he pondered Langdon's loss to any considerable extent. However, Langdon was Twain's firstborn child and only son. A closer look reveals that the boy's death actually affected Twain deeply and that he grieved the loss for decades after. In 1906, for example, after some thirty-four years of silence on the subject, Twain made the well-known disclosure in his autobiographical dictations that he had always felt responsible for Langdon's death for having allowed a blanket to slip off his son during a carriage ride on a particularly chilly morning a month or two before the infant died. In view of the fact that Twain clearly dwelt on the subject for so long, it seems strange that Langdon would not figure more prominently in his literary imagination. The reality is, however, that Twain did respond to Langdon's death in ways reminiscent of those following the deaths of Livy, Susy, and Jean. And that response, as it turns out, has been hiding in plain sight now for nearly a century and a half.

Langdon was born on November 7, 1870, a month premature, weighing just four and a half pounds. Nobody, including Twain, expected the infant to live. Langdon survived his initial critical weeks but for much of the following year, he was a sickly child. Prone to coughs and colds, he required constant attention from his parents and nurses. He also reportedly cried incessantly. In 2001, Victor Doyno speculated that Langdon's symptoms and features of his physical appearance were consistent with what modern pediatric neurologists identify as "'a bossed forehead,' indicative of a hydrocephalic condition" (Kiskis and Trombley 34). Whether because of continual illness or some undetected disability, Langdon's growth and development were slow. As late as the end of 1872, none of Langdon's teeth had yet come in and he was still not walking or talking. At the age of fifteen months, however, he began to exhibit signs that he was at last gaining his health. In February 1872, Twain described Langdon as "flourishing wonderfully": "He is white as snow, but seems entirely healthy, & is very fat & chubby, & always cheerful & happy-hearted" (*L5* 44). During the course of that spring, however, Langdon's newfound vitality gradually began to fail. He developed a severe cough in early May and his condition worsened steadily over the next week or two. At the end of the month, doctors diagnosed him with diphtheria. Langdon died just a few days later on June 2, 1872, in Hartford, Connecticut.

Neither Twain nor his wife accompanied the child's body to Elmira, New York, for burial. Livy, severely depressed, was too ill to travel and Twain would not leave her, so the couple remained in Hartford with their two-month-old daughter, Susy. Surviving letters and accounts of neighbors suggest that in the days immediately following Langdon's death Twain was profoundly somber. But by mid-June, just a week or two later, flashes of levity suddenly began appearing in his correspondence with close acquaintances. On July 5, 1872, about a month after Langdon's death, Twain took Livy and Susy for the summer to Fenwick Hall, a newly built seaside resort in New Saybrook, Connecticut, about 50 miles south of Hartford. Livy, still mourning, remained close to her room for much of their stay. Twain, on the other hand, threw himself into the social milieu of New Saybrook and became "a very visible participant in the daily activities," often playing billiards and ten-pins in the resort's main hall by day and entertaining guests in the hotel's parlor by night (*L5* 113). The Hartford Courant even reported that summer that Twain was "a great favorite with the ladies, really the lion of the house" (*L5* 113). Outwardly, Twain seemed his characteristic demonstrative self. Inwardly, it is nearly impossible to believe that he, like Livy, was not still grieving at New Saybrook, appearing to cope with Langdon's death through modes of avoidance.[1]

By the end of July 1872, Twain would seek out a more tried-and-true way of distracting himself—travel. While vacationing at New Saybrook, he decided to journey to England for a few months, ostensibly to gather material for a new book. He left his wife and infant daughter behind at Fenwick Hall with family and friends and sailed from New York alone on August 21, 1872. While he was away, Livy, perhaps sensing her husband's pain despite appearances to the contrary, confided in a letter to Mary Mason Fairbanks, "I am contented to have him away because I think it is just the work he should be at now" (*MTMF* 164). And just as he had that summer at New Saybrook, Twain immersed himself that fall in London's social life. "Too much company—too much dining—too much sociability," he protested, if a little facetiously, in a letter to Livy just a week or two after his arrival (*L5* 155). But such remonstrations were too frequent during the London trip not to have been constructed at least in part for Livy's consumption, even if they were an accurate reflection of Twain's busy schedule. She would sorely miss her husband while he was away, objecting repeatedly that he hadn't written her often enough or that he continuously seemed to be rushing off to one event or another: "Livy darling, got yours of 8th tonight, & was amused to see how you always complain of being 'sleepy & stupid' when you write, & I am always 'in haste—dinner ready'" (*L5* 178–79). Throughout much of September and October, as Twain regularly wrote home with stories of attending elaborate banquets with England's elites and delivering speeches to large adoring audiences, he also unfailingly expressed love and affection to his wife and daughter. Only once during that trip, however—in a letter dated September 11—did Twain seemingly refer to Langdon and then only by way of a possible Freudian slip, "I send all my love to you & our dear babies" (*L5* 155). Twain at last returned to Hartford the final week of November, but evidently only after Livy pleaded with him to come home.

From the end of November, through December, and into early January, Twain remained in Hartford writing, entertaining guests, and celebrating the holidays with his family. It is during this seven- or eight-week period that textual scholars have thought Twain began writing *Tom Sawyer*. The manuscript of *Tom Sawyer* shows that he drafted as many as 118 pages in that first stint, taking the story from chapter 1 roughly through the middle of chapter 5, to the point where Tom plays with a pinch-bug during a minister's sermon. Editors at the Mark Twain Project (MTP) offer up evidence from paper and ink as they date the manuscript,[2] as well as from a notation Twain made at the top of MS p. 23, the first page of chapter 2, to a snowstorm that hit Hartford in early January 1873. The reference, dated January 9, 1873, in Twain's hand, was undoubtedly written after he began chapter two in the manuscript. The next ninety-five pages are written on the same brand of paper and in the same ink, so it is conjectured that they, too, were composed between December 1872 and January 9, 1873.

There is, however, another likely possibility. In a letter written in 1934, Isabel Lyon, Twain's private secretary from 1904 to 1909, recalled that Twain had told her years before that he began writing *Tom Sawyer* while vacationing at New Saybrook in 1872:

> He spoke with tenderness of the boy and the playmates and the pranks which inspired *Tom Sawyer*. . . . He said that during all the years between boyhood and a summer spent in Saybrook, Connecticut—"about 1872"—when he definitely began to write a book about those boys, he had "never lost sight of the magic and freedom and careless young life on the river." (*L5* 114)

Lyon's striking revelation is too precise and the details too specific not to be taken seriously. That Twain would recall the composition of the novel in this way so many years later bears considerably on discussions of the subject of him processing Langdon's death and its relationship to the composition of *Tom Sawyer*. As for the quality of Lyon's memory, biographer Laura Trombley says that "in her few available after-the-fact statements and letters it appears that she was very much on target with an enviable recall of distant events" (Trombley, Email). The manuscript of *Tom Sawyer* offers further corroboration that Lyon's statement is accurate, and that Twain actually began writing the novel during the summer of 1872 in the weeks following Langdon's death.

In 1980, as editors at the MTP at the University of California, Berkeley, prepared the first authoritative scholarly edition of *Tom Sawyer* for publication, Twain scholar Paul Baender included the following description in the "Textual Notes" appendix to the volume:

On the verso of MS p. 22, which concludes chapter 1, Mark Twain inscribed several numbers in pencil—multiplications, divisions, etc. They evidently have no bearing on the text (*TS 1980* 518).

Baender was mistaken. The page, which was reproduced in the facsimile edition of the holograph manuscript of *Tom Sawyer* in 1982, discloses an enormous amount about Twain's novel. To a simple glance at the manuscript leaf, it does in fact appear to be only a piece of scratch paper filled with seemingly random calculations, as Baender claims. However, turned on its side, the verso of MS p. 22 reveals itself to be a sketch of the Farmington Avenue lot in Hartford, Connecticut, that Twain and his wife would come to purchase and where they would eventually build their Nook Farm home. Twain's drawing and his computations offer important clues about the time line for the composition of the manuscript, ultimately calling into question the assertion that Twain began writing *Tom Sawyer* in Hartford between December 1872 and January 1873.

Twain purchased the Farmington Avenue property from Franklin Chamberlin on January 16, 1873, for $10,000. The subdivided parcel was essentially the west half of Chamberlin's Nook Farm lot. Chamberlin's home was located at the southeast corner of the property. This residence, 1 Forest Street, is the house Harriet Beecher Stowe purchased from Chamberlin in 1873 and which she and her family would live in for the next two decades—but, more on that in a moment. Chamberlin subdivided his plot of land, ultimately keeping a section at the corner of Farmington and Forest for himself and parceling off for Twain an irregularly shaped lot that measured 544 feet on the north and 320 feet along the east. The North Branch of the Park River wound its way along the southwestern edge of Twain's property, which was bordered by neighbors' lots directly to the west on one side and the south on another. The sketch on the verso of MS p. 22 shows all of these features, including all of the measurements—except two. And they are key. These missing measurements confirm that Twain's drawing had to have been made several weeks before the January 16 purchase date. If true, then it follows that Twain began writing the manuscript of *Tom Sawyer* even before that.

Twain's sketch shows Chamberlin's entire 894 feet of frontage along Farmington Avenue with its distinctive northeast angle divided into five strips, moving west to east, measured in feet: 269, 100, 175, 200, and 150. The property along Forest Street is measured in two sections, again in feet, 270 and 150. The calculations spread about the page are all related in one way or another to these measurements. Studied closely, the calculations reveal several attempts over a period of time to weigh options. Twain, it would seem, was unsure how much land to buy, where the most desirable parcel within the piece of property lies, or where he might place his home once he began to build. Clearly this is not a drawing made days or even a week or two before closing. There are at least two, possibly three sets of pencil markings presumably made at different times, indicating that this was a drawing Twain went back to repeatedly before the purchase.

Chamberlin's home is unmistakably marked on the sketch. Twain, however, seemed to be playing with placing his own house in different locations on the property. One such placement is near where Twain eventually built the house, but the structure is shown seemingly turned 90-degrees so that its familiar length stretches west-to-east rather than in the north-to-south direction in which it is eventually constructed. In addition, the placement clearly overlaps the property line Twain eventually agreed to on January 16, 1873, revealing, again, that at the time he made the drawing, he had not decided which part of Chamberlin's property to buy.[3] There is also the suggestion that Twain was toying with the idea of building his home in the location along the ridge where he eventually placed his carriage house. At first glance this part of the drawing looks like Twain is simply considering different locations for the carriage house itself. But a closer look indicates that it is possible he might actually have been thinking about that location for his residence. The three rectangles there (each representing placement at a slightly different angle), for example, are all the same size as the rectangle marking the other location as well as the one for Chamberlin's house.

The lightest pencil markings appear to be the first drawings and calculations Twain made on the verso of MS p. 22. They include the map outline of Chamberlin's entire property, several lines subdividing the lot into strips, at least one attempt to place Twain's house near where the carriage house was eventually built, and a handful of calculations. The darker pencil markings, presumably made at a later date, add the five measurements along Farmington Avenue (269, 100, 175, 200, and 150), two vertical lines through the property, rectangles representing Chamberlin's house and Twain's eventual building site, and several more calculations. The two darker vertical lines are placed 350 feet from the corner of Farmington and Forest, which would later become Twain's eastern border, and 625 feet from that same corner. There is also a darker curving line approximating the southwest edge of the lot. Finally, Twain inserted the measurement "544" near this curve. This figure of 544 feet is one of the two measurement dimensions of the lot Twain purchased from Chamberlin on January 16, 1873. However, the other measurement, 320, appears nowhere on the sketch. Its absence suggests that Twain had not yet reached the point of deciding to purchase the 544' × 320' section of Chamberlin's property when he made the drawing. How long before the purchase date, then, does that put this sketch? Several weeks? A month? More than a month? The second missing measurement offers a clue.

On January 7, 1873, just nine days before Twain purchased his Farmington Avenue property, Franklin Chamberlin sold his home at 1 Forest Street to Harriet Beecher Stowe for $15,000.[4] The lot Chamberlin included with the sale of his home to Stowe measured 150' × 75'. These dimensions do not appear on Twain's sketch either. In fact, there is absolutely no indication anywhere in Twain's drawing that he was then even aware of Stowe's transaction with Chamberlin. Interestingly enough, Stowe announced that she had agreed to purchase the Chamberlin home in a surviving letter to her daughters dated December 23, 1872—a date roughly two weeks before the purchase date of January 7, 1873. Information about the impending move would presumably have become public knowledge soon after. Nook Farm was an intimate neighborhood whose residents (many of whom were related to Stowe) socialized frequently with each other. Additionally, Chamberlin was a respected lawyer within this community with an especially strong reputation for integrity. For these reasons and others, it is unlikely Twain would not have been aware of Chamberlin's discussions with Stowe in the weeks leading up to his own transaction with Chamberlin. Twain's sketch, then, had to have been started at least before December 23, 1872. His drawing shows that he was thinking about numerous options with different sections of Chamberlin's lot over a period of time, and letters indicate that Twain and Livy had been visiting the property throughout 1872, and fairly frequently in the weeks leading up to the sale. It would seem, therefore, that the very latest the sketch on the verso of MS p. 22 could have been drawn would have been the first week or two of December. The presence of multiple sets of pencil markings in Twain's drawing suggesting several returns to the sketch arguably pushes that date back even further—conceivably even to before Twain's return home from abroad in November 1872.

There is, additionally, the very practical question of whether or not Twain even had the time to write the first 118 pages of *Tom Sawyer* in Hartford between December 1872 and early January 1873. In a letter to his mother-in-law dated December 3, 1872, for instance, Twain reported, "I went to work on my English book yesterday & turned out 36 pages of on satisfactory manuscript" (*L5* 235). He would continue to write material related to his trip to England over the next few weeks, as well as a handful of lengthy letters to newspapers about matters ranging from the ailing health of sea captain Ned Wakeman to criticism of Mayor Abraham Hall of New York. In total, editors at the MTP speculate that there are five or six pieces of writing Twain might have been working on in December 1872. The MTP also believes it is likely that both Twain and Charles Dudley Warner were already at work on *The Gilded Age* (1873) by the end of the month: "All accounts agree that the authors conceived of the project soon after Clemens's return from England. By late December or early January, Clemens had begun writing the opening chapters" (*L5* 259). With Twain at work on the England book at the beginning of December, *The Gilded Age* by the end of December, and writing various other shorter pieces in between, it seems as if there would have been very little time to compose the first five chapters of *Tom Sawyer* during the December 1872–January 1873 period. And all of this is to say nothing of the time he would have spent celebrating the Christmas holiday with his family or presumably preparing for the purchase of the Farmington Avenue property in January 1873.

Ultimately, all available evidence appears to lead to the conclusion that Twain began writing *Tom Sawyer* not in Hartford in December 1872 but months earlier at New Saybrook in the summer of 1872, as Lyon reported in 1934. The implications of these findings are far reaching. Most importantly, they place Langdon's death and Twain's composition of *Tom Sawyer* in immediate proximity to each other. Coincidence simply cannot adequately account for Twain suddenly reflecting on his boyhood within a few short weeks of his eighteen-month-old son's passing. The work of American social psychologist James Pennebaker, a pioneer of writing therapy, for example, has brought to light in recent years connections between authorship and recovering from trauma. Indeed, scholarship for decades now has recognized the ways in which Twain dealt with loss during the course of his life through his writing. Whether Twain sought to avoid his pain by immersing himself in a reminiscence of his own boyhood or whether the passing of his young son triggered extensive memories of his own youth, mourning Langdon's death was the catalyst for Twain's discovery of the river and the town that lie at the center of his most enduring work as an American literary artist. As such,

Tom Sawyer emerges not from a place of nostalgia but instead from Twain's grief and is fundamentally about him processing the loss of his son.

Some years after the publication of *Tom Sawyer*, Mark Twain remarked that the novel was "simply a hymn, put into prose form to give it a worldly air" (SLC to W. R. Ward, 8 Sept. 1887, *UCCL* 03773). Commentators over time have taken Twain's description to signify any number of things, but most have read his use of the term "hymn" to mean a sort of tribute or homage. Bernard DeVoto reflected this sentiment when he memorialized *Tom Sawyer* in 1934 as "the supreme American idyll" (DeVoto, *Mark Twain's America* 304). Since then, others have similarly styled the book as "a paean to innocent boyhood, a nostalgic celebration" (Scharnhorst, *Critical Essays* 10). But hymns are not tributes or idylls or celebrations or even paeans. The term, particularly as Twain uses it, is much more solemn, much more ambiguous. In his description, Twain creates a juxtaposition between the idea of the "hymn" and its expression, "put

Death mask of Langdon Clemens.

Courtesy Mark Twain Museum, Hannibal, Missouri

into prose form to give it worldly air." For Twain, the essential subject of his "hymn" is deeply and spiritually personal, something practically inexpressible; the "prose form to give it a worldly air," or the novel itself, became its symbol. *Tom Sawyer* represents something profound in Twain's imagination, very likely unconscious, but all tied back to the anguish of June 2, 1872, and somehow the reminiscence of his youth emerged as its articulation. But the two are not the same. Scholarship has focused almost exclusively on the symbol, the nostalgic look back to Twain's boyhood. Mark Twain, however, was coming to grips with something much deeper during that summer in 1872. In this sense, then, *Tom Sawyer* is as much about the lost childhood of Langdon as it is about its author's own youth.

Notes

1 Noted grief expert Elizabeth Kübler-Ross, M.D., described in her groundbreaking book *On Death and Dying* (1969) five stages of grief common to all who experience significant loss: denial, anger, bargaining, depression, and acceptance. These stages are often misunderstood as prescribed stops on a linear grieving time line, but Cobbler-Ross and coauthor David Kessler explain in their 2005 study *On Grief and Grieving* that not everyone experiences all of these reactions or goes through them in a specific order. Twain's avoidance and distraction (denial) and Livy's deep depression make it clear that they experienced and expressed grief in fundamentally different ways.

2 The paper Twain used for the first 119 pages of the manuscript for *Tom Sawyer* is identified by editors at the MTP as "E.H. MFG. Co." because of its embossment, which reads: E.H. MFG. Co. It was a type of paper that Twain used briefly in August and October of 1868 and then again, according to MTP editors, between September 1872 and May 1874. Nothing was known about the source or the producer of this stock. However, I have found two nineteenth-century Connecticut business directories that list a firm identified as "East Hartford Manufacturing Company" located on Burnside Avenue in East Hartford, Connecticut, that is described as a producer of "Writing paper" (*New England Directory and Gazetteer* 1587 and "The American Stationer" 25). The East Hartford Manufacturing Company was producing and selling writing paper during the 1868 to 1874 period when Twain was using "E.H. MFG. Co." stock.

   The break between the 1868 usage and September 1872 when Twain is known to have begun writing with it again is probably explained by the fact that Twain visited Hartford in August 1868 to work with his publisher on *The Innocents*

Abroad (1869). He undoubtedly borrowed the few sheets of E.H. MFG. Co. paper he used in 1868 during that trip. Twain then moved to Hartford permanently in October 1871 but was lecturing throughout the East and Midwest between October 1871 and March 1872. He likely purchased more E.H. MFG. Co. paper during the summer of 1872 because he had the paper with him in England during the following fall.

3 Between March 1873 and March 1881 he would make five additional purchases of land bordering his lot, increasing the total size of his Farmington Avenue property considerably.

4 All information regarding Harriet Beecher Stowe's purchase of the Franklin Chamberlin home is taken from the "Historic Structures Report, The Harriet Beecher Stowe House, prepared for the Harriet Beecher Stowe Center, Hartford, CT" by Myron O. Stachiw, Thomas Paske, and Susan L. Buck, December 2001, available at the Harriet Beecher Stowe Center in Hartford, Connecticut. A very special thanks to Elizabeth Giard Burgess, Collections Manager at the Harriet Beecher Stowe Center, for her invaluable assistance with these other related materials.

8

Susy Clemens: Defined by Her Death

James Golden

Olivia Susan "Susy" Clemens (1872–96) is a youth defined by her death. The oldest daughter of Samuel and Olivia Clemens, she is often defined by her tragic early death from spinal meningitis, and the impact this had on her father's writing. Emotionally, Clemens never recovered from losing her when she was only twenty-four. He was in England and she in Hartford, Connecticut, when she died; her mother and sister were on a ship on the Atlantic, hoping to make it home in time to help care for her. They arrived too late, and the news of Susy's death reached them while their ship was moored in New York Harbor. Sam, alone in the town of Guildford, Surrey, received a telegram, and marveled that he was able to survive the news (*AMT1* 323–24).

Susy's death can be seen as one of the chief reasons Clemens's later work was so dominated by pessimism and a dismal and bleak view of human nature. His cynical, incisive, and impatient later works are rejoinders to the happiness of his earlier writing: If Mark Twain is only known as the author of authentically American and authentically youthful works, as (simply) the ultimate boys' adventure writer, then the full emotional power of his writing is nullified into kitsch. The arc from *The Adventures of Tom Sawyer* (1876) to *The War Prayer* (1905), *What Is Man?* (1906), and *Letters from the Earth* (written in 1909) is one of the most compelling aspects of Twain's canon. Obviously his early work, with its disruptive humor, would always stand as one of the great achievements of American literature—but his bleak later years make his early writing all the more beautiful.

In the traditional view of Clemens's life, his literary descent into jagged (yet insightful) melancholy came from the combination of the "thunder-stroke" of Susy's death and his financial troubles in the 1890s, what biographer Ron Powers described as producing "a literature of grief for Susy that would spill from

Samuel Clemens for the rest of his life" (Powers, *Mark Twain* 579). Susy's final moments were fraught—wandering the elegant rooms of the mansion at 351 Farmington Avenue in Hartford, deliriously writing in a stream of fevered half-consciousness. It is distorting that the defining image of Susy's clear, intelligent life is her muddled, confused death. Furthermore, while it may be ironic that her life is defined by her early death, it is even more ironic that the great frustration of her life—being known primarily as Twain's daughter—is magnified by the way her private tragedy is telescoped into its impact on Twain's writing.

How does the tender and sustaining father-daughter relationship that Sam and Susy shared change our understanding of the father's life, work, and cultural legacy? Inasmuch as Clemens's grief following Susy's death prompted (or at least expedited) a shift in his literary focus, his delight in her life and the companionship she provided was a creative prompt and an instrumental part of the domestic "fairyland" in Hartford that was the context of his most successful work. The material for his great literature came from his boyhood and early, wandering years, from his perpetual need to travel and explore the wilds of the pre-railroad American West. Yet, he translated these experiences into nation-defining prose from the comfort of a red, smoke-filled billiard room perched at the top of a large New England house, and an octagonal gazebo overlooking Elmira, New York, farmland and river valley, thinking of the Mississippi flowing through the heart of the continent while gazing at Hartford's Park and Elmira's Chemung rivers. The life of the houses in Nook Farm and Quarry Farm was playful and wordy, a succession of dinner parties, storytelling games, and charades. Susy herself noted the main occupations of Quarry Farm summers as playing whist, games of tennis, donkey riding, and reading German books (*FSk* 124–25). Twain, famous for creating Tom Sawyer and Huckleberry Finn, the most authentic boys of American literature, wrote those works within an environment of intellectually curious daughters. These girls grew up while he wrote his lasting books. Indeed, Laura Skandera Trombley argued that "the first sign that his creative voice was ebbing coincided with the maturation of his daughters" (Trombley, *Mark Twain* 155). Their influence on him, and their importance to his life, is significant.

Sam and Olivia lived in the Nook Farm neighborhood of Hartford for twenty years, 1871–91. During seventeen of those years they lived in their purpose-built home at 351 Farmington Avenue, constructed between 1873 and 1874, then expanded and extensively decorated in 1881 by the Associated Artists Company. The years spent between Hartford and Elmira saw the publication of the bulk of Twain's enduring, influential, and beloved work, including

Roughing It (1872), *The Gilded Age: A Tale of Today* (1873), *The Adventures of Tom Sawyer* (1876), *A Tramp Abroad* (1880), *The Prince and the Pauper* (1882), *Life on the Mississippi* (1883), *Adventures of Huckleberry Finn* (1885), and *A Connecticut Yankee in King Arthur's Court* (1889). Sam's domestic tranquility and familial expansion directly coincided with Twain's literary flourishing. The particular cultures of Quarry Farm near Elmira and Nook Farm in Hartford were the contexts for one of the greatest outputs in American literary history. Obviously, Twain produced important work before and after Susy's life. However, their shared life in Hartford and Elmira coincided with the sustained run of books, essays, lectures, and stories that defined American identity at a critical moment in the industrializing, urbanizing nation's history. However, a sketch of Susy's own life, seen from her perspective, and not through her father's, is of a rather more ordinary American world. No less true than the glimpses of her that we normally see through the respectable curtains of her father's fame, her biography makes Twain normal.

Olivia Susan Clemens was born on March 19, 1872, in Elmira, New York, in the home of her uncle and aunt, Theodore and Susan Crane. Baptized on March 26, she grew up in Hartford, the leafy, wealthy capital city of Connecticut. Her unruly hair earned her the nickname of the "Modoc" when she was a baby, after a warlike California tribe, and she entered a family of two parents separated by a decade of age, disparate origins (Missouri and New York), education, and religious inclination, but united by genuine love. When Susy was born she had an older brother, Langdon, who died when he was only nineteen months old, and she herself was a mere two months old. Susy later recorded intimate, tender details of Langdon's toddler habits—such as carrying a pencil as a toy and holding his hands palms inward, indicating the sustained sense that, despite his early death Susy considered him part of the family eternally (*FSk* 111).

When Susy was two years old, another baby joined the family—Clara Langdon Clemens, who was herself given the nickname of the "Bay," from Susy's inability to pronounce the word "baby." The immediate neighborhood she and Clara shared as children was one of large gothic-influenced mansions and Italianate villas standing on shaded lawns, with a small creek running behind her own home. A straight avenue led east past more square, upright brick homes of square, upright New England burghers to the haphazard downtown, a compact jumble of brownstone storefronts in a colonial cityscape that gave way to the seedy streets fronting the broad silver-blue ribbon of the Connecticut River. North and south of downtown trim brick row houses, bay-windowed and substantial, provided housing for the thousands who worked in Hartford's booming factories. To the west the small Park River kept the land open and rambling for the girls to explore. In 1880, when Susy was eight, a third girl joined the family: Jane Lampton Clemens, always known as Jean.

Like so many of her friends' and playmates' parents, Susy's own parents combined business, intellect, and politics. Her father was a writer, lecturer, publisher, and investor who fit in with a neighborhood of editors, novelists, journalists, lawyers, and politicians. Her well-educated mother organized a regular stream of dinner parties in their fashionable, Asian-decorated dining room. This was a house of constant visitors, the leading cultural figures passing through that elegant house. One such visitor noted of her visits that the "three children were not, at that time, old enough to assert themselves as different personalities. They were like tree branches—individual enough to add to the beauty of the parent stock, but not so pronounced as to have their horizontal tendencies count as divergencies" (Wheeler 324–25). Yet clearly their branches were key to the parent plant.

Early on, Sam displayed a distinctively un-Victorian attitude to his children, being a relatively active hands-on parent at a time when this was not expected of the middle class, and especially not of middle-class men. While traveling in Cleveland, he wrote a letter ostensibly addressed to two-month-old Susy that included the lines "Many's the night I've lain awake till 2 o'clock in the morning reading Dumas & drinking beer, listening for the slightest sound you might make, my daughter, & suffering as only a father can suffer, with anxiety for his child. Some day you will thank me for this" (SLC to OSC, 9 May 1872, *UCCL* 00746). His other letters to her, when she was a young child, are suffused with whimsy. Once, from New York City, he told her "if you have a very fine sunset, put a blanket over it & keep it till I come" (SLC to OSC, 16 July 1877, *UCCL* 01451). When Susy was a toddler she accompanied her parents on a trip through Great Britain, where she was photographed in Edinburgh in the lap of her mother's close friend Clara Spaulding. At the age of six she and her sister again accompanied her parents abroad, for an extended trip through Germany, Switzerland, Italy, and France. The family stayed in Heidelberg, Baden-Baden, Geneva, Venice, Munich, and Paris. This experience gave her an excellent foundation in the European languages that were to be important for her education, notably German. The education was begun under her mother and shaped by a series of governesses who prepared her for the neo-gothic majesty of Hartford Public High School and then, in 1890, Bryn Mawr, on Philadelphia's Main Line.

Susy entered the college when she was nineteen. Founded five years earlier, it was a Quaker institution whose purpose was to create an intellectually challenging environment for women, a female college dedicated to academic achievement. Although Susy's father had left school at a young age, her mother had benefited from higher education, attending Elmira Female College. While at Bryn Mawr, Susy tried to distance herself from her childhood, using her full given name of Olivia, never used at home in Hartford. However, home and Hartford came to visit her, when Samuel Clemens traveled to speak to her class. It is this moment, one of the most infamous incidents of Mark Twain's public speaking career, that crystallized not only the dichotomy of Mark Twain/Samuel Clemens, but how his family life consistently tested that dichotomy.

In March of 1891, Sam traveled down to Bryn Mawr to address Susy's class. She had apparently "begged" him not to tell one of his favorite stories, "The Golden Arm" about a man who buries his deceased wife, only to disinter her to retrieve her solid-gold arm. He is then haunted by her voice, creeping ever closer, wailing "W-h-o—g-o-t—m-y—g-o-l-d-e-n—a-r-m?" This was a kind of ur-story for Twain, a definitive template of American oral culture. First learned as a child from Uncle Dan'l, one of his uncle's slaves, the power of the story lay in the telling of it. When told correctly, the audience jumped. It united several themes for Twain: the power of African-American dialect, the need to master the way a story was told and not just the content (see *HTTS*), the danger of lusting after wealth, and the constant presence of the death of family members. It was, however, ultimately merely a ghost story, and Susy, it seems, did not want Twain to tell the story because it would not be sophisticated enough for the intellectually serious quietude of Bryn Mawr. When his speech began with the story's familiar opening, she ran from the lecture hall, weeping. Indeed, she had long been unhappy with the story. At thirteen, she had been present when Twain read the story at Vassar. Susy accompanied her father to a public reading and they stayed in the college. Although scared by the story, she was impressed with her father's command over the room at making everybody jump (*FSk* 119). Justin Kaplan has suggested that Susy's discomfort with the tale surpassed any snobbishness about the subject about what was originally a story gleaned from enslaved people. He points out that the story's focus on the death of a wife was too close a subject for Susy's comfort, given her mother's chronically bad health (J. Kaplan 309–10). More recently, Ann M. Ryan posited a more complex racial strand to Susy's frustration about the story: In personifying the voice of the deceased wife "Twain promises to be a good white father, and instead, he becomes an angry and haunting black woman" (Kiskis and Trombley 176). All of these interpretations are based in the contrast between the public and private personas, between Twain and Clemens.

Susy wanted Bryn Mawr to meet the version of her father that she saw: the businessman-writer of Nook Farm, at ease within the intellectual elites of New England, hopping on trains to Boston or New York for the intertwined worlds of business and politics. Instead, he presented himself as Mark Twain, a repository of American humor and wisdom gathered in a childhood and youth spent in Missouri, Illinois, and Iowa, from travels up and down the Mississippi, and young-adult years in Nevada and California. He was, of course, both iterations, and both sat relatively comfortably within his own understanding of his self. However, observing Twain through the eyes of Susy makes clear how not everybody close to him felt the same way.

The space between Mark Twain and Samuel Clemens, the disparities of identity, public role, and common perception were very much a concern of Susy in adolescence, as she began to explore how her private father was a public figure as well. The only lasting piece of her writing was her biography of her father, begun at age thirteen, much of which Twain used as framing excerpts in his rambling autobiography. Her family essay begins "We are a very happy family! we consist of papa, mamma, Jean Clara and me. It is papa I am writing about, and I shall have no trouble in not knowing what to say about him as he is a very striking character" (*FSk* 105). At thirteen, she already had strong opinions about not only her father's work, but also about his public reception. She noted that

> it trobles me to have so few people know papa, I mean realy to know him, they think of Mark Twain as a humorist joking at everything. . . . I have wanted papa to write a book that would reveal something of his kind sympathetic nature, and the "Prince and Pauper" partly does it. The book is full of lovely charming ideas, and oh the language! it is perfect, I think. (*FSk* 108)

Susy, notably, performed in a private theatrical version of that book, playing the prince to her friend Margaret (Daisy) Warner's pauper, Tom Canty. Twain noted the first time the play was performed it was actually in the home of George Warner, Daisy's father and brother of Charles Dudley Warner, Twain's coauthor on *The Gilded Age*. The performance was a surprise upon Twain's return from an exhausting lecture tour (*AMT1* 335).

Amateur dramatics were an important part of Nook Farm culture. While an early teenager, Susy herself wrote plays and cast her younger sisters, Clara and Jean, along with the neighborhood children. Several of these early works survive, notably a notebook containing the titles "Held by the French," "Loves Labor Won," and "The Tanglewood Mystery." The same cast of sisters and neighborhood friends performed a fourth play of Susy's, entitled "A Love-Chase" (OSC, "Notebook"). Susy was not only following the family business, but the neighborhood business as well: One of her neighbors was the influential actor William Gillette. This grounding in theater prepared her well for Bryn Mawr, where she was cast in the role of Phyllis in the W. S. Gilbert and Arthur Sullivan operetta *Iolanthe; Or, The Peer and the Peri* (1882). While at Bryn Mawr, Susy formed an intense friendship with another student, Louise Sheffield Brownell, who was older than Susy and already several years into a college career. Susy's extended correspondence to Brownell survives (Hamilton College Library, Saunders Family Papers Collection): It documents the ardor of her affection for Brownell, and suggests levels of physical intimacy beyond the norm of the seemingly romantic language that suffused much of Victorian women's writing. Linda Morris considered this relationship in the light of nineteenth-century female college culture (Morris 11–20); Peter Stoneley discussed it in the context of Twain's writing (Stoneley 99–101); Charles Neider quoted from the letters and explored the possibility that Susy left Bryn Mawr at least in part because of the nature of her relationship with Louise Brownell (OSC, *Papa* 10–31). Ultimately, there is no definitive evidence for why Susy left Bryn Mawr early. Given her early death, and her noted moodiness and emotional turmoil (Trombley 162–64), this passionate relationship was certainly a central experience of her life. Many of the letters Susy wrote to Brownell were composed during a pained period of separation and exile abroad, following her departure.

In 1891, Susy again left for Europe with her family, as they closed the Hartford house, never to live there again as a family. Unlike their 1878–79 jaunt, this trip was forced on them by financial reversals of her father's: investments in new technology which failed, during a generally difficult time in the American economy. It was cheaper to live abroad than to maintain the expected lavishness of their Hartford lifestyle. After a brief stop in Paris, Susy, her sisters, her aunt Susan Crane, and family servant Katy Leary stayed in Geneva, while her rheumatic parents established themselves in the spa town of Aix-les-Bains. Their next substantial stop was Bayreuth, where they indulged in weeks of Richard Wagner music. A bust of Wagner had adorned the piano in Susy's beloved playroom-cum-classroom that adjoined the children's Hartford nursery. Livy's musical tastes ran to opera, rather than the spirituals and camp songs beloved by Sam. Indeed, on their previous European trip of 1878–79, one of the highlight purchases of an extended European shopping spree was a Swiss music box containing songs from at least three different Wagner operas. As Kerry Driscoll has argued in "Mark Twain's Music Box," this box and its customized playlist was a distinctive example of the Clemens's desire, early in their marriage and Nook Farm years, to establish a cultural credibility through European travel, and specifically, European furnishings for their home, displaying not just wealth but erudition and taste (Ryan and McCullough 140–88). Now, driven back to Europe through financial difficulties, Livy's indulging in Wagner came from a deep love of the music itself.

The family traveled through Lausanne and Marienbad, before Susy accompanied her mother and aunt to Berlin in advance of Clara and her father. The family was reunited in the bustling, beautiful, and culturally charged Wilhelmine capital in the winter of 1892. American popular opinion invariably places Twain in the South or Wild West, not in Connecticut, and certainly not in a Berlin of Prussian helmets and Otto von Bismarck. Twain belongs on the Mississippi River, not Germany's Spree. Yet the Clemens daughters spoke German and performed German music. As early as their first continental trip in 1878, Susy wrote to her grandmother in German (OLC and OSC to Olivia Langdon, 8 Dec. 1878, *UCCL* 01612). Sam himself wrote to Susy and Clara in German, addressing the letters to "Mein liebes Tochterchen" (SLC to CC, 14 Dec. 1884, *UCCL* 03058; SLC to OSC, 14 Dec. 1884, *UCCL* 03059). Their Hartford house contained significant amounts of European furniture and paintings. Much of it had been purchased years earlier in Florence, including some of the pieces most important to the Clemens girls' childhoods: the Daniele Ranzoni painting they named "Emmeline," which closed their evening storytelling game, and their parents famous "Angel Bed," where they rested when sick and whose detachable cherubs they bathed as dolls (see *MFMT*).

The Clemenses next journeyed to Rome and Florence, and through the summer of 1892 alternated, primarily between the spa town of Bad Nauheim and Florence. Susy was coming of age in *fin-de-siècle* Europe, not America. While her father wrote his most specifically pointed work on American race relations and the Missouri of his pre-Civil War youth—*Pudd'nhead Wilson* (1894)—Susy brooded around Europe in the decades before World War I. She finally returned to her aunt's home in Elmira in 1895, uninterested in following her family on a round-the-world lecture tour of her father's—the trip that would produce *Following the Equator* (1897). However, while visiting friends in Hartford in August, 1896, she contracted the meningitis that killed her, and defined her forever by her death's effect on her father's work. She was surrounded by people who loved her, including the Reverend Joseph Twichell, who had officiated at her parents' marriage. Her parents were unable to return home before she died, and the house that had been the center of a family's happiness became a memorial to her death. Susy's father noted her serious mind, writing,

> The summer seasons of Susy's childhood were spent at Quarry Farm on the hills east of Elmira, New York, the other seasons of the year at the home in Hartford. Like other children, she was blithe and happy, fond of play, *un*like the other average of children she was at times much given to retiring within herself and trying to search out the hidden meanings of the deep things that make the puzzle and pathos of human existence, and in all the ages have baffled the inquirer and mocked him. (*AMT1* 325)

Like many fathers, Clemens was proud of his child's intellectual precocity and depth. But this passage followed an account of her premature death, and its continuation makes all too clear how the pain of losing Susy prompted Twain into his own spiral of melancholic reflection:

> A myriad of men are born; they labor and sweat and struggle for bread; they squabble and scold and fight; they scramble for little mean advantages over each other; age creeps upon them; infirmities follow; shames and humiliations bring down their prides and their vanities; those they love are taken from them, and the joy of life is turned to aching grief. The burden of pain, care, misery, grows heavier year by year; at length ambition is dead; pride is dead; vanity is dead; longing for release is in their place. It comes at last—the only unpoisoned gift earth ever had for them—and they vanish from a world where they were of no consequence; where they achieved nothing; where they were a mistake and a failure and a foolishness; where they have left no sign that they have existed—a world which will lament them a day and forget them forever. Then another myriad takes their place, and copies all they did, and goes along the same profitless road, and vanishes as they vanished—to make room for another and another and a million other myriads to follow the same arid path through the same desert and accomplish what the first myriad, and all the myriads that came after it accomplished—nothing!

"Mamma, what is it all for?" asked Susy, preliminarily stating the above details in her own halting language, after long brooding over them alone in the privacy of the nursery (*AMT1* 325–26). Clemens dictated that gloomy passage in 1906, ten years after Susy had died. In the same period of his life, he published *What Is Man?*, in which he posited that people were essentially machines wound up by a brutal God.

In her youth, Susy provided Samuel Clemens with a chance for playfulness, for frivolity and silliness. Hers was a world of pets and games and laughter, which he indulged and even sustained. As a young woman, her world was distinctively European, a reminder to acknowledge the importance of Continental culture to the most distinctively American writer of the nineteenth century. Her tragedy is that she remained a young woman always, never to grow old, never to grow into a steward of her father's legacy, like her sister Clara. Instead, her father became the guardian of her memory. In so many accounts of her personality, she is moody, fragile, elegant, intellectual, and emotional. While her tragedy was never growing up fully, her father's tragedy was that he did.

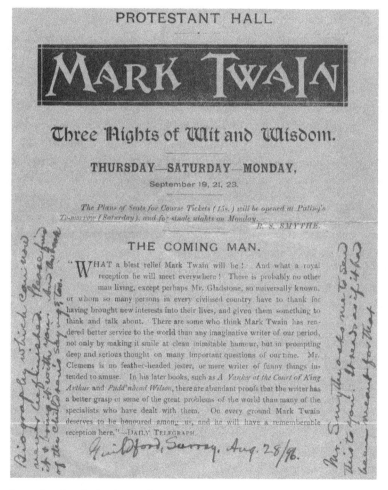

Ten days after Susy's death, Mark Twain asked his wife to bring Susy's unfinished biography of him, along with a manuscript about the children that would be posthumously published as "A Record of the Small Foolishnesses of Susie and 'Bay' Clemens (Infants)" in *A Family Sketch* (2014).

Courtesy Kevin Mac Donnell, Austin, Texas

9

Clara Clemens: The "Bay"

Cindy Lovell

Clara Clemens, Mark Twain's second daughter, is the progeny whom scholars love to hate. They have been privy to, and even participated in, some admittedly derisive conversations and speculations about the only one of Sam and Olivia Clemens's children to survive both parents. They have chastised her for including her first husband's image on the Elmira grave marker shared by her father. They have disdained her romantic choices and have shaken their fists at her second husband's gambling addiction, whose gambling debts hastened Clara's dispersal of her father's estate. And, they have played armchair psychologist with wry insights about her "middle child" complex. They have done all this judging of Clara while Susy (sometimes spelled "Susie"), Jean, and Langdon (Sam's little "cub")—who all died in their youth remained tragic and beloved figures. Clara, in contrast, lived on, made questionable decisions, suppressed her father's most controversial writings, and made a fool of herself as a seventy-year-old bride.

But long before she became Clara Langdon Clemens Gabrilowitsch Samossoud, she was first dubbed "the Bay" thanks to big sister Susy's mispronunciation of "the baby" and shortly thereafter was also nicknamed "Clara Langdon Lewis O'Day Botheker McAleer McLaughlin Clemens" after the wet nurses who fed her.

Clara was born on a Monday morning, June 8, 1874, at her maternal aunt Susan Crane's Quarry Farm in Elmira, New York. She was the third of the Clemens children. Rachel Brooks Gleason, her mother's physician, had been summoned to Quarry Farm the day before. Her father reported that the doctor spent the night so as to be on hand when Clara made her appearance (*L6* 155–56). In a letter to their friends, Joe and Harmony Twichell, he boasted of Livy's stoicism: "She waltzed through this ordeal, walking the floor & sewing baby clothes in the bravest possible way," and he later reported that the doctor was not summoned from her sleep until fifteen minutes before Clara's birth (*L6* 157–58).

Three months prior to Clara's arrival, Livy had come close to miscarrying. In a letter to friends, Sam worriedly wrote that Livy experienced labor pains in their rented Hartford home and had been confined to bed (*L6* 77). In fact, the doctor cautioned the couple that Livy should arrive in Elmira the first week of April if at all possible to avoid traveling at the end of her pregnancy. At seven and one-half pounds, Clara was the couple's largest baby, more than double the weight of Langdon and almost double Susy's weight, accounting for Sam's calling her "the great American Giantess" in his letter to the Twichells (*L6* 157).

Although Sam and Livy named the newborn after family friend Clara Spaulding (*L6* 156n.2), two-year-old Susy christened Clara with her first nickname when she met her new sister an hour after her birth. Sam noted Susy's admiration in the family record: "She said, in her imperfect way, 'Lat bay (baby) got boofu hair'—so Clara has been commonly called 'Bay' to this day, but will take up her right name in time" (*FSk* 53).

In his letter written to the Twichells when Clara was just three days old, Sam said, "it is an admirable child, though, & has intellect. It puts its fingers against its brow & thinks. It was born with a caul, & so of course possesses the gift of second sight" (*L6* 158). Clemens's typically skeptical "of course" suggests his dismissal of the old superstition that claimed a baby born with the fetal membrane covering its head was the beneficiary of unusual good luck.

Clemens was known to cast himself in the role of the guilty party with regard to family tragedies, such as the deaths of his brother Henry and infant son Langdon. He narrowly avoided a similar tragedy when Clara was one week old. Unaware the newborn was sleeping on a pillow placed on a rocking chair, Clemens wound up a mechanical toy and set it on the parlor floor. When headed toward the rocking chair, he kicked the rocker out of its path. "The Bay lit on the floor with a thump, her head within two inches of the iron fender of the grate, but with the pillow undermost. So she came within 3 inches of an obituary" (*FSk* 53). The strapping infant survived that close call and would go on to survive many more.

And so the infant Clara started life at Quarry Farm, a beloved setting to the entire family. The farm offered respite and escape where Sam could work uninterrupted. During the summer after Clara's birth, Sam's thoughtful sister-in-law oversaw the construction of an octagonal study on the nearby hill, where Sam could write in peace. Each evening he would rejoin family, guests, and servants on the porch of the house to read from his day's work, tell stories, and enjoy conversation.

If the farm offered the security of a family home, Hartford would soon offer the same if at a slightly more frantic pace. Sam and Livy had been renting a Nook Farm house from Isabella Beecher Hooker just a stone's throw from where their own family home was being built. On the rainy Saturday afternoon of September 19, 1874, they moved with infant Clara, two-year-old Susy, and nursemaid Rosina Hay into rooms on the second floor of their still under-construction house at 351 Farmington Avenue. They would reside there seventeen years.

From the day of her birth, the Bay could not abide cow's milk, and Livy was unable to furnish breast milk. A long line of wet nurses were employed to satisfy the hungry infant. Mary Lewis, wife of John Lewis, fed Clara the first few weeks. Then Maggie O'Day from Elmira divided her milk between Clara and her own blind infant, but this proved insufficient for both babies. The Clemenses next hired Lizzie Botheker, paying her "worthless husband" (according to Sam) sixty dollars to permit her merely to come, in addition to five dollars a week in wages. After Botheker came Mary McAleer, the wife of Patrick McAleer, the family's coachman. All was still not bliss, however. Finally, they hired Maria McLaughlin who nursed Clara for a year until she was weaned.

> Maria chewed, smoked, (swore, used obscene language in the kitchen) stole the beer from the cellar an got drunk every now and then, and was a hard lot in every possible way—but the bay throve on her vices, right along. So the Bay's name in full is Clara Langdon Lewis O'Day Botheker McAleer McLaughlin Clemens. (*FSk* 54)

The lengthy nickname stuck, and Clara would soon learn to recite it. In 1879, while the family was living in Paris, Clara dictated a few lines to include in a letter to Grandma Clemens: "I had a hard pinch in my finger: that I was looking in the looking-glass door & Rosa closed the looking glass; & sometimes Susie plays with my things & I get a-fighting at her. That's all, now, that I can write. And that all my names is Clara Lewis O'Day Botheker McAleer McLachlin Bay Clemens" (CC to JLC and PAM, 30 Mar. 1879, *UCCL* 12755).

Of all the wet nurses, Maria McLaughlin was the most colorful of characters:

> Maria arrived home about 11 o'clock that night, as full as an egg and as unsteady on end. But the Bay was as empty as she was full; so after a steady pull of 20 minutes the Bay's person was level full of milk punch constructed of lager beer, cheap whisky, rum and wretched brandy, flavored with chewing tobacco, cigar smoke and profanity, and the pair were regally "sprung" and serenely happy.

The Bay never throve so robustly on any nurse's milk as she did on Maria's, for no other milk had so much substance to it. (*FSk* 54)

Eventually, there would be seven full-time servants employed at the Hartford house. When Clara was one year old, the tip of her middle finger was nearly cut off in an accident. The bleeding was severe, but Patrick McAleer, their quick-thinking coachman, bound the injury with tobacco until a doctor could properly stitch and bandage the wound (SLC to PAM, 28 June 1875, *L6* 501). As an adult, Clara would recall having been the most accident-prone member of the family:

> Once I was nearly drowned; another time, when ill with croup, I was snatched from a blazing crib with my hair on fire; at the age of four I was discovered on the sixth story, crawling around the inside of the banister of a hotel corridor, with a marble floor far below. After other narrow escapes I added to the list a dreadful experience with a horse.

Livy, who had witnessed the accident, exclaimed, "Really, it is miraculous how Clara always escapes with her life!" to which Sam replied, "Yes, I don't believe God cares much about meeting her" (*MFMT* 6).

Clara also recalled a toboggan accident in Hartford: "I was the only one hurt, but my damages were severe. One leg was bent around into the shape of a half-moon, and after the gardener and coachman had carried me into the house, my shoe had to be cut off the crooked foot" (*MFMT* 5). Sam and Livy had planned a large dinner party for the evening, and the accident had occurred too late for them to call it off. Anxious about Clara's condition, they took turns visiting her throughout their meal. Although her leg worsened and there was talk of possible amputation, Clara recovered. Her father was understandably upset, and during Clara's convalescence came up with various ways to cheer her: "Among other pleasant surprises, he arranged to have one hundred valentines sent to me on St. Valentine's Day. It was one of the biggest events of my entire childhood!" (*MFMT* 6).

Clara may have been the most accident-prone member of the family, but Livy suffered almost chronic poor health. Six months after Clara's birth, Livy wrote to her sister-in-law, "I have been quite miserable and we have not felt like doing a great deal for Christmas" (OC & SLC to MEC, 27 Dec. 1874, *L6* 332). Livy's condition was likely complicated by post-partum problems. By the following year, the combination of poor health and an especially hot Hartford summer convinced her that time at the seaside would be beneficial to all, so the family headed to Bateman's Point near Newport, Rhode Island (*AMT2* 385).

After two weeks Sam confessed to his sister in a letter that they were miserably homesick, but the children were "in superb condition" (*L6* 524). Sam wrote that "the children used to sleep a couple of hours every day under umbrellas on the rocks within six feet of the wash of the waves, and that made them strong and hearty" (*FSk* 55).

In their family record book the following summer, Sam commented on Clara's development. "The Bay learned to walk early enough, but now at 2 years and 2 months she cannot say ten words, but understands the entire language" (*FSk* 55). "She can only say a few words; is very fond of rocking and singing—to no tune" (*FSk* 62). Experts today say an average two-year-old has around one hundred words in her vocabulary, but older siblings frequently communicate on behalf of younger children (Brooks and Kempe). By all accounts, Clara was downright adorable. She was feisty, naughty, beautiful, intelligent, curious, brave, and indomitable. The girls grew up in a privileged environment with the benefit of tutors and travel, living abroad for long periods, learning foreign languages, reading great literature, and learning to perform musically. While living in Munich, Papa—as Clemens's daughters called him—noted on February 25, 1879, "Bay finished her little First German Reader, yesterday, and came in with the triumphant announcement: 'I'm through, papa! I can read any German book that ever was, now!'" (*FSk* 66). The following May, the girls were required to converse with their German nursemaid solely in German for one week. Bay complained to her namesake, saying, "Aunt Clara, I *wish* God had made Rose in English" (*FSk* 67). The girls were taught to read in German, not English, so when Clara accidentally got hold of an English version of a children's poetry book, her father was impressed with how quickly she taught herself to read in her native tongue without any assistance. In ten days, she read English with "astounding facility" (*FSk* 80). Perhaps Clara's gift for language inspired a similar trait in the character Forty-four in Mark Twain's 1898 story, "Schoolhouse Hill."

"Bay is a sturdy little character; very practical, precious little sentiment, no nonsense" (*FSk* 75). Sam admired the "pluck and fortitude" of her character at such a young age and was proud of her physical courage, which even Susy, two years older than Clara, lacked. When a painful boil on her hand had to be lanced, Clara only winced. When Livy and Susy both praised her courage, a proud Bay told them, "*There ain't anybody braver but* God!" (*FSk* 76).

This portrait of a fearless adventurer might suggest the reason twenty-one-year-old Clara was the only daughter who elected to accompany Sam and Livy when they left on their thirteen-month world lecture tour in 1895. From the time she was a child, it was her nature to embrace adventure. As a small girl, her attitude could get her into all sorts of situations. For instance, although she and Susy were both given candy for not quarreling, only Clara was paid specifically *not* to quarrel—at a rate of three cents a day (*FSk* 80–81). Clara did seem determined to behave. At Quarry Farm, Livy found a scrap of paper in Clara's Bible indicating such determination, a note little Clara had scrawled as a self-reminder:

> Be good to Susy, be not rude, overbearing, cross or pick her. . . . Be as sweet and
> generous to Jean as Susy is and even more so, and be not selfish with the donkey
> but think how much you like to ride her and Jean enjoys it just about as much.
> Be sweet to Mamma and when you see that she is tired you ought to ask her as
> few questions as you can not to bother her. Be not cross and unmannerly to Julie
> even if you do think her queer, perhaps she thinks you queer. Be good always.
> (*FSk* 102)

Sister Jean's birth in 1880 brought a new dynamic to the family. Just as Susy had bestowed Clara with her first nickname, Jean's mispronunciation of "Bay" as "Ben" led to another nickname for Clara, with Papa noting, "We have dropped 'Bay' and adopted 'Ben,' in consequence." In 1882 he wrote, "Ben had a birthday party of 67 children" (*FSk* 85). On Clara's following birthday (her ninth), he recorded an incident inspired by his own habit of writing marginalia inside books. Clemens had penciled, "A poor slovenly book; a mess of sappy drivel and bad grammar" on the fly-leaf of *Daniel Boone* by John S. C. Abbott. Upon reading her father's review, Clara remarked, "Oh, that must be lovely!" and hurried off to read it (*FSk* 88).

Clara and her sisters savored their summers with their cousins in Elmira, where Aunt Sue tellingly referred to her Quarry Farm home as "Do as you Please Hall" (*MFMT* 59). But they appeared equally to treasure their time in Hartford with family, friends, and playmates. Papa's storytelling legacy is legendary, nestled with the family in the Hartford library after dinners, telling fresh new stories incorporating the family's knickknacks into all sorts of romances. These were some of the fondest shared memories of the girls' childhood. Papa and George Griffin, the family's butler, often provided horseback rides to the girls as they "hunted tigers" in the conservatory. As they grew older, the girls performed plays to the delight of the adults, with their friends joining casts as needed and even with Papa stepping in to play Miles Hendon in *The Prince and the Pauper*. Children and adults played charades together, and Papa blew smoke into soap bubbles to delight the girls.

Among Clara's favorite visitors to the Clemens household was her father's writer/editor friend William Dean Howells. "He always brought sunshine and cheer into the house as no one else could. Everyone loved him and wanted him to stay a long time" (*MFMT* 43). They played songs on a music box Sam bought in New York when Clara was about five. She remembered the "Pilgrim's Chorus" from Richard Wagner's opera *Tannhauser* and the "Lohengrin Wedding Marcher" as favorites (*MFMT* 31). Papa and Mamma allowed the girls to remove the wooden cherubs from the four posts of their bed, bathing them in a tub as though they were dolls. During dinner parties, Susy and Clara frequently eavesdropped from the stairs, from which they could gauge how far the dinner had progressed by whatever story Papa was telling. From all accounts, it appeared to be a charmed existence from the perspective of the children.

Christmases tended toward the sublime. As Clara reminisced, "I shall never forget the royal preparations for Christmastide in our home" (*MFMT* 35). She described her mother's thorough preparations, wrapping gifts in the mahogany room, hanging stockings, and preparing and delivering baskets to the poor on Christmas Eve. The girls got to accompany coachman Patrick McAleer on these deliveries. "Great baskets with the feet of turkey protruding below blankets of flowers and fruits. Wrapped up in mufflers and snugly tucked in a fur robe, we children drove far out into the country in an open sleigh, tingling with delight at the sound of the bells" (*MFMT* 40).

The entire family loved their animals, not just the menagerie of dogs, cats, squirrels, and turtles but also the farm animals. In Hartford, Clara's favorite was Jumbo the calf. Patrick convinced her that if she curried the calf each morning and trained him with a saddle and bridle he would grow into a horse. "The idea seemed marvelous to me and I was always ready to believe in miracles, even at the age of six," she wrote in 1931 (*MFMT* 28). Clara had one dress just for barn time and fondly remembered the smell of the barn as a source of happy memories. She recalled one of the servants giving her a piece of green billiard-cloth that she draped over Jumbo's back. Clara and Patrick promenaded Jumbo on Farmington Avenue to the delight of passers-by. When Patrick placed a saddle and bridle on the "steed," Clara was promptly ejected. She was not discouraged, however, and returned the next morning to try again only to learn that Patrick had sold Jumbo. "I raised such a hullaballoo," she later wrote

that my screams reached even my father's study. . . . When he discovered the cause of my misery, he . . . told Patrick he would have to buy the calf back immediately; which was done that very day. (*MFMT* 29)

Clara recorded her memories of childhood twenty-one years after her father's death.

I wish that words could give a true picture of those long-vanished, unforgettable days—days filled with joy, sorrow, humor, fun work, and always sparkling interest. How sad it is that children take kindnesses from their parents so utterly for granted. (*MFMT* 1–2)

Among the girls' favorite books, Clara named *At the Back of the North Wind*, *The Days of Bruce*, *The Children of the New Forest*, *Robinson Crusoe*, and *The Prince and the Pauper* (*MFMT* 25). She remembered evenings when the family had no company and Papa read to them during dinner from *Gulliver's Travels* or *The Arabian Nights*. And she recalled Papa's fascination with the beautiful ice-covered branches in the winter months, touched by tears she saw "come to his eyes, for great beauty overwhelmed and moved him" (*MFMT* 44). There was an abundance of love and imagination in the household.

The three daughters were primarily schooled at home. Lilly Gillette Foote became the girls' governess in 1880. Fidelia Bridges served as governess in 1882–83, while Foote was traveling abroad (Salsbury 153). However, Susy and Clara did attend Hartford Public High School, albeit briefly. The family traveled and lived abroad so frequently that regular attendance in a public school was difficult. Ledgers in the Hartford high school's archive show that during Clara's attendance there from January 28 to February 22, 1889, she studied mathematics, modern languages, Latin, and reading. During this short stint, her grades were above average, although she managed to accrue two excused absences, one unexcused absence, one "lateness," and one demerit in conduct, resulting in a score of 7.8 out of 10 for "Rank in Attendance and Deportment."

Clara's greatest interest was in music. As a young adult she took singing lessons for several years. In Vienna, Austria, she met her future husband, Ossip Gabrilowitsch, while both were studying piano under the gifted Polish teacher Theodor Leschetizky. Clara later sang professionally, making her debut in Florence and appearing in London and Paris, but she remained financially dependent upon her father. Her relationship with Gabrilowitsch was tumultuous. She was also romantically connected to Charles "Will" Wark, her accompanist, who was already married. Clara married Gabrilowitsch in 1909, with her approving father in attendance. (*AMT3* 611)

In *My Father Mark Twain* (1931), Clara titled her third chapter, "The Clemens Temper." In a diplomatic fashion, the then fifty-seven-year-old daughter, who was continuing to polish her father's halo, spoke of her father's temper in endearing terms. She opened the chapter writing, "Every member of our family was provided with a healthy temper, but none of us possessed one comparable to the regal proportions of Father's," and explained, "Father's temper shone with the light of his genius. Being angry or irritable in the ordinary way is merely bad management of a good thing, the soul. But the consuming rage of a temper such as Father's has its roots in heaven" (*MFMT* 24). Clemens's temper is well documented, and one might speculate an entire career in academia as to the effects such a temper has on those within its range.

Clara's account, however, does not quite square with the guilt Sam himself described in a letter he wrote to William Dean Howells in 1886, when Clara was twelve: "I found that all their lives my children have been afraid of me! have stood all their days in uneasy dread of my sharp tongue and uncertain temper" (SLC to WDH, 12 Dec. 1886, *UCCL* 43132). It is likely that neither Clara's nor her father's description of the effects of his temper is completely true.

Clara's temperament as a strong-willed and confident child revealed itself in her adult life and throughout her relationship with her equally strong-willed

Clara Clemens Samossoud in 1950, on the eve of an auction at her Hollywood, California, home at which she sold her father's books and possessions to raise money to pay off her second husband's gambling debts. The resulting dispersal of those materials would be a serious blow to future scholarship. (The bust on her mantel represents Joan of Arc, whom Clara had portrayed in a dramatic adaptation of her father's novel about the French national hero during the 1920s.)

Courtesy Mark Twain House & Museum, Hartford, Connecticut

father. Susy's untimely death in 1896 sent the family into years of constant grief. This sustained mourning strained both Clara and Jean, who should have naturally focused on moving forward in life despite the tragic death of a sibling. Clara sought independence and found escape in her musical studies. After her mother's death in 1904, she suffered from nervous exhaustion, in part due to the strain of enduring the ravages of her father's extreme grief. Clara again sought respite in her musical career. She kept herself busy and away, only fully engaging when she suspected her father's secretary of misappropriating funds. She also disapproved of his "angelfish" girls, the adopted "granddaughters" on whom he doted. When Jean died in 1909, Sam appeared to lose the will to live, and he himself died only four months later. In the end, all that remained of the Clemens clan was the "Bay."

Clara died in 1962 at the age of eighty-eight. Her life story was well documented by the press, her secretary, and herself. During the 1930s, she published books about her father and her first husband. Her relationship with her only child, Nina, was fraught with conflict. Clara bought a house for Nina and established a trust to provide for her, but she left the bulk of her estate, which included the royalties from her father's works, to her second husband, Jacques Samossoud.

The scrappy middle child of the Clemens family shared the strongest physical resemblance to her father. And despite the obvious favoritism shown by Sam toward Susy, his steadfast admiration of Clara's "pluck and fortitude" was sincere. Perhaps, in Clara, Sam recognized a bit of himself: "I have to put the Bay to sleep every night, because she won't mind anybody else—wants to be rocked or sung to, & we can't allow that" (SLC to JLC and PAM, 22 June 1876, *UCCL* 12738).

10

Jean Clemens: A Family Reclaimed

Karen Lystra

Mark Twain's beloved wife, Livy, had a pet name for her charming husband: She called him "Youth." And indeed, he lived up to his nickname in all sorts of ways. None was more striking than the game of charades he played with his daughter Jean and her friends in Dublin, New Hampshire, in 1906. Dublin beckoned American artists, writers, and intellectuals to a summer of good weather, camaraderie, and concentrated work. His wife had died in Italy in 1904, and for two years after her death Twain chose Dublin as his summer retreat. It proved to be a place of healing for him as well as his youngest daughter, Jean. By far the most athletic member of the family, Jean relished horseback riding, walking, birding, and hiking up Monadnock, a local mountain. But the most precious gift that Dublin bestowed on Jean was friends.

Though their members were often eight to ten years younger than Clemens's twenty-six-year-old daughter, the Dublin junior set accepted Jean into their inner circle. Jean and her father were often invited to play charades with the local children. Clemens and the other adult participant, George de Forest Brush, an accomplished painter, each led a team. On one memorable evening, Clemens's team acted out the word "Champagne." "Sham" was dramatized as a kitten imitating a lion and scaring a brave warrior. In staging the next syllable, the curtain opened, Jean remembered, "exposing Father lying on the bench in a baby-cap and long white robe with a bottle in his mouth, asleep." Jean described two nurses who entered and began discussing the sleeping baby, saying they were afraid to take his bottle away for fear he would start to cry. As if on cue, Clemens began to wail. A doctor was called in who examined the "still violently yelling" patient and prescribed a warm bath. After a tiny footbath was brought in, Twain, then aged seventy, rolled off the bench onto the ridiculous prop. Jean reported that everyone was "nearly sick" from laughing so hard. That summer

Clemens also played a roaring Irish drunk, a doctor pumping a baby's stomach with a pair of fire bellows, and a lover trying to coax his desperately shy fiancée into a kiss (Jean Clemens, *Diaries* [hereafter *JCD*], 22 June, 1 and 8 Aug. 1906).

The truth of Livy's nickname "Youth" is nowhere better illustrated than by the playfulness that Clemens exhibited with Jean and her friends. "I have worked pretty steadily for 65 years," he wrote the same year to his friend Thomas Bailey Aldrich, a well-known writer, "and don't care what I do with the 2 or 3 that remain to me so that I get pleasure out of them" (SLC to Aldrich, 2 Oct. 1906, *UCCL* 07534). One obstacle made it difficult to achieve the fun-loving, self-indulgence Clemens longed for in old age. His youngest daughter, Jean, suffered from epilepsy, incurable at the time and viciously stigmatized as the cause of everything from criminal behavior to a nasty temperament.

Jean had her first major seizure while at school in February 1896 (Dr. Moses Allen Starr to Susan Langdon Crane, 29 Feb., 19 Mar., 16 Apr., 26 May 1896, *UCCL* 48921, 48920, 48919, 48918). She was staying with her aunt at Quarry Farm in Elmira, New York, while her parents, with their middle daughter Clara in tow, went on an around-the-world lecture tour to clear Twain's bankruptcy debts. Jean suffered generalized convulsive seizures, with loss of consciousness and involuntary shaking of the arms and legs, and non-convulsive seizures (petit mal), with brief lapses of consciousness. She had been taking a daily dose of bromide since her first generalized seizure and her attacks had stopped several months before she was reunited with her mother and sister Clara. They had rushed back to America in August to see Jean's other sister, Susy, who was reported to be ill. Susy died of spinal meningitis shortly before they landed, so the reunion was not a happy one (*MFMT* 64, 179).

During the rest of 1896, the family grieved Susy's death in England, where Jean gave her parents hope that a cure for her epilepsy had been achieved. Dr. Starr, the first in a procession of physicians who treated Jean, offered Livy a tantalizing possibility—that if her daughter's convulsions could be staved off for a year, they might never reappear. In the summer of 1897, three months past the doctor's bellwether mark for recovery, Jean suffered two generalized convulsive seizures.

After relocating to Vienna at the end of September, Sam and Livy redoubled their efforts to prevent Jean's seizures with new medical instructions to administer increasing doses of bromide upon the first signs of an impending attack. Compelled to treat their adolescent daughter with clinical objectivity, they subjected the poor girl to unceasing scrutiny and themselves to unwavering vigilance. Bromide was a sedative with a depressive effect on the central nervous system but was a poison if taken in high enough doses. A Viennese doctor doubled Jean's daily dose, prescribing three to six doses for "extraordinary emergencies." "It was like watching a house that was forever catching fire," Twain reflected, "& promised to burn down if you ever closed an eye" (SLC, "Jean's Illness." CU-MARK). The toll on Jean and her parents was great. Jean was never able to twitch without being intimately scrutinized for signs of an impending attack. As a consequence, she virtually became her disease in the eyes of parents who strove to save her from what they could not. On March 19, 1899, after fourteen and a half months of tracking the smallest changes in her behavior, she had a generalized convulsive seizure. In her father's revealing metaphor, the house burned down and his record keeping ceased (SLC, "Jean's Illness." CU-MARK).

As long as her mother was alive, Jean had a loving protector and diligent advocate. And Clemens acted the part of the dutiful father. But Livy's death cut him loose from his lifelong moral compass and his youngest daughter's illness weighed heavily on his urge to be free of onerous responsibilities. He saw her—and often treated her—as a child, even when she was in her mid-twenties. For her part, Jean remained noticeably youthful and immature. She joined friends eight to ten years her junior in Dublin for games of tag and gleefully recorded a memorable food fight in her diary (JCD, 8 July and 15 Sept. 1906). However, while she sometimes acted like a child, Jean yearned for the independence and autonomy that would come from earning her own income. She hoped her hobby, wood carving, would earn her "a little something" so that she could buy "a small plot of ground" in Dublin (JCD, 4 June and 5 Oct. 1906).

Jean's "felt stigma"—avoidance of full disclosure about her epilepsy for fear of a damaging or hurtful response—weakened during her second summer in Dublin, and she told friends for the first time about her disease (JCD, 7 May, 16 June, and 22 July 1906; see also Whitman and Hermann 250). However, she continued to worry about her mental capacities and the effect of her "petit mal" on her memory. Reassured by a friend that people did not think she was stupid, Jean nonetheless felt an aching sense of inferiority and incompetence. She yearned for a boyfriend but despaired of her chances. "Why must I long so for the love and companionship that only a man can give, and that man a husband," she asked in her diary, "Am I never to know what love means, because I am an epileptic and shouldn't marry if I had the chance?" (JCD, 4 July 1906). Her doctor, along with many physicians and psychologist at the time, would have answered affirmatively. The idea of transmitting so-called degenerate heredity was of great concern to scientists and social science professionals, who urged a variety of remedies, including institutionalization and sterilization. Jean resisted these conclusions, as did most people who were on intimate terms with sufferers from this disease (Rosenberg and Golden 248–70).

Nonetheless, Jean was isolated by her own fears of rejection as well as the prejudice she recognized in others. "Will I have to go on indefinitely leading this empty, cheerless life without aim or real interest?" she asked herself. Aware of her own vulnerability, she observed that "every time I see a young man that I like I begin to hope that he may before long do more than like me. Even when they are younger, as is generally the case, than I am, I cannot help wishing, wishing, wishing, that some day they may overlook my age my stupidities and especially my disease" (*JCD*, 4 July 1906). Hers was a heartbreaking lament.

Jean found little to counter her sense of inferiority from her immediate family. Her father treated her like a child. His secretary, Isabel Lyon, extravagantly praised Jean's older sister, Clara, of whom she wrote in her journal, "You who make a shrine of any house you inhabit—you who are a gift to every one who falls under your sweet thrall" (IVL, *Journal*, 1903–04, 30 Mar. 1905). Jean's father and his secretary agreed that Jean should never be left unsupervised, even in a house full of servants who actually cared for her during her attacks. Clara made a point of absenting herself from her father's household as much as possible after her mother's death. Clemens felt free to roam, assigning Jean's supervision to Lyon after he became bored with Dublin that second summer. Lyon saw herself as Prometheus, chained to Jean and unable to be with "the ones with whom I would willingly be," and in her journal she dramatically bemoaned the fact that "daily my soul is torn out of me—no—*not* my soul—*not* my soul" (IVL, *Daily Reminder*, 5 July 1906).

In the summer of 1906, Lyon was able to break the chains that bound her to Twain's youngest daughter. She persuaded Jean and her father, with the strong support of the physician in charge of Jean's case, Dr. Peterson, that Jean might restore her health by spending the winter in a sanitarium (*JCD*, 26–27 Sept. 1906). Jean had not been separated from her family for ten years and found it "desperately hard to leave Father and Clara in order to come out to a totally strange place." At her departure, Clara wept bitterly; Clemens was depressed; and Jean remarked that "the whole business was perfectly *horrible* to me" (*JCD*, 25 Oct. 1906).

Soon after she left, Twain agreed to a plan, concocted by Lyon, to save him from anxiety and worry about his youngest daughter. Lyon suggested that Jean's letters would contain unreasonable requests, imaginary complaints, and projects that he would be compelled to refuse. She offered to read the letters

Jean wrote from the sanitarium and tell him only what he needed to know. He would write a draft response, based on Lyon's account, let her edit the result, then rewrite "the vacuum," as he later characterized the outcome, and return it to the secretary for mailing. This pitiable compact, he admitted later, in the last major segment of his autobiography, was a monumental betrayal of Jean (Ashcroft-Lyon MS. [hereafter *AL-AMT3*] 341–42, 435). Each time a letter arrived, Twain reenacted this ritual of betrayal, not only of his daughter but also of himself, abdicating his role as parent and protector to save himself anxiety and distress.

At first Jean freely acquiesced to the regimen of sanitarium life, enjoying the four to five hours of outdoor exercise that was medically mandated during her stay. Her dietary treatment was less salutary, however, as salt was forbidden, and meals at Katonah, the location of her sanitarium in New York, were sparse and sometimes inedible. She was regularly ordering four to six pounds of chocolate to supplement her meager dinners (*JCD*, 1, 3, 27 Nov.; 11, 23 Dec. 1906). The sincere, if futile, hope of some doctors was that following a tightly controlled regimen of diet and exercise might actually cure a patient's epilepsy.

As the days warmed, Jean longed for Dublin, but most of all, she missed her father. "My voice refused [to] come and my thoughts all fled," she wrote about a phone call from her father after he returned from England in mid-1907, "it was beautiful to know you were really back again & yet so *horrible* too, when I couldn't actually get to you." Jean missed her father with growing desperation, and she expressed her loneliness in letters he did not read. "I don't want you to tire yourself, dear little Herr Doktar," she wrote thoughtfully, referring to his honorary degree from Oxford, "but when you do feel up to a hard trip, *please* come out here & give me a squeeze. I sometimes feel as though I could not endure it much longer to stay away from you" (JC to SLC, 23 July 1907, *UCCL* 11552). By summer's end, Jean was desperate to leave Katonah and wrote her father, begging him to let her come home. "Until the doctors have discussed, it is useless for him to mention the matter," Jean summarized his mechanical reply, "No word of regret about my unhappiness—nothing" (*JCED*, 26, 30 Sept. 1907). Of course she could never imagine the reason.

Twain's secretary was not only reading Jean's letters for her boss, she was the only member of the household consulting Dr. Peterson. Lyon wrote in her diary that Peterson said "Jean must never live with her father again." But events would prove that this was the secretary's dictum, not the doctor's. What she "didn't tell the King"—her revealing appellation for her boss—was that Jean's "affection might easily turn into a violent and insane hatred and she could slay, just by the sudden and terrible and ungovernable revulsion of feeling" (IVL, *Stenographic Notebook #4*, 5 Oct. 1907). Certainly Clemens saw no halo around his youngest daughter's head, but he never detected any proclivity to violence. On the basis of hundreds of patient case files, letters to doctors, and family questionnaires filled out in the early decades of the twentieth century, a leading authority in the field has concluded that family members, including those closest to the person with epilepsy, normally dismissed the stereotypes of violence and criminality. However, Lyon maintained—or returned to—the attitudes of a stranger toward Jean (see Dwyer 408; Rosenberg and Golden 260–61).

Twain later characterized himself as having been "peacefully asleep" through Jean's enforced confinement to the sanitarium (*AL-AMT3* 331). While he eventually understood how he had been manipulated by his secretary, he never recognized the role his own attitude toward epilepsy played in giving her the upper hand. He, too, often reduced Jean's personality to a disease, and routinely discounted her feelings (when he was informed of them), blaming her "epileptic temperament." He seemed to doubt that his daughter could be happy anywhere, believing that her epilepsy condemned her to continuous dissatisfaction and discontent. To the extent he was aware of Jean's pleas to leave Katonah; he was able to dismiss them as byproducts of her disease.

As the New Year of 1908 approached, Jean finally received much-hoped-for news—the prisoner was being sprung to a house in Greenwich, Connecticut, twenty miles away from Katonah. Though she did not have model roommates, Jean was thrilled to be out of the sanitarium. What she most desired, however, was denied her: to spend another summer in Dublin. Jean felt unable to insist upon Dublin in 1908 because she was living on her father's money. "I have been very much troubled lately and perfectly furious at my helplessness caused by my inability to earn my own living," she confided to a young Dublin friend. "You can't imagine how enraged I get, at times, at my stupidity and uselessness. It does seem as though I had the right to some means of doing *something* even with my illness. That doesn't need to prevent my working between times, especially now" (JC to Nancy Brush, 29 Mar. 1908, *UCCL* 07966).

On a trip to attend a memorial service at the end of June, while accompanied by a supportive sidekick in Albert Bigelow Paine, Clemens made a spontaneous detour to visit Jean who had been sent to Gloucester, Massachusetts instead of Dublin for the summer. Expecting the worst on the basis of information supplied by Lyon, both men discovered, to their shock, that Jean was healthy and vigorous in both mind and body. Clemens returned to his new home in Redding, Connecticut, which he had christened "Stormfield," and said "Dr. Peterson must cancel her exile and let her come home at once" (*AL-AMT3* 344). Though his visit did not end Jean's exile, both father and daughter were taking steps to advance their reunion. After moving from 21 Fifth Avenue in New York to the rural environment of Redding, Clemens now lived in a place that doctors deemed conducive to his daughter's health. Though a nearby farmhouse was rejected as uninhabitable, Jean thought Miss Lyon's newly renovated cottage looked like a promising alternative for the winter. Suddenly, "like a thunderbolt from a clear sky" as Jean characterized the news, she was being sent to Berlin to consult a German doctor (JC to Nancy Brush, 1 Aug. 1908, *UCCL* 08071). Jean loved Berlin, based on her childhood memories, but she remained conflicted about going to Germany. "Is it positively settled that I must go to Berlin?" she queried Lyon. "I have a dread of it. I did *so* want to be in Redding" (JC to IVL, 4 Aug. 1908, *UCCL* 08074).

Routinely treated as if she was eighteen rather than twenty-eight, Jean allowed herself to be ordered about and relied upon higher authority for direction. Her problems were not just the lack of an independent income (which was a huge barrier in itself) but a lack of self-confidence bred by the stigma of her disease. For Twain fitfully and for Lyon fully, Jean became her disease. With massive outside pressure to collapse herself into her illness, Jean was pushed to identify herself as a patient in search of a cure, an all-consuming role that put her fate in the hands of others. She fought heroically but sometimes lost the battle to keep her identity from wrapping itself around her epilepsy.

Jean sailed for Germany on September 26, 1908, with her maid Anna and her paid companion, Marguerite Schmitt. Though financially strapped, she was happy in Berlin and was shocked to receive peremptory orders to return home. Peterson disapproved of the medication she was receiving from the Berlin doctor, who had not been chosen by him but by Lyon, relying on the recommendation of family friends (*AL-AMT3* 342; JC to IVL, 5 Aug. 1908, *UCCL* 08075; Prof. Hofrath von Renvers to IVL, 16 Sept. 1908, *UCCL* 38034; JC to Marguerite Schmitt, 19 Oct. 1909, *UCCL* 08473, English typescript of French original). Sent to Babylon, Long Island, after returning from Berlin in early 1909, Jean was stunned by the contrast and appealed directly to her sister, which resulted in a happier situation at a small private care facility in Montclair, New Jersey (JC to SLC, 5 Mar. 1909, *UCCL* 08363).

Unlike Jean, Clara was a spendthrift who believed she was entitled to a share of her father's money. Decreasing infusions of cash in 1908 caused Clara to ask for an audit early the next year on the advice of the Clemens's family physician and old friend, Dr. Edward Quintard (*AL-AMT3* 331–32, 438). Lyon and Ralph Ashcroft, Twain's business manager, responded with a series of strategic maneuvers that involved formalizing their dealings with Clemens, who was asked to sign a series of contracts, one of which explicitly removed any housekeeping or letter writing responsibilities from Lyon's job description. As a result, Clemens wrote Clara on March 14, 1909, "The comradeship remains, but it is paid for; also the friendship. Stormfield was a home; it is a tavern, now, & I am the landlord" (SLC to CC, 14 Mar. postscript to 11 Mar. 1909 letter in *AL-AMT3* 399). Four days later, Lyon and Ashcroft were married.

Clara assumed the role of housekeeper at Stormfield, where conflict and crisis had embroiled everyone in a real-life melodrama of intrigue and lies. Ironically, the various maneuvers of Mr. and Mrs. Ashcroft forced Clara and her father to work together and, perhaps to their mutual surprise, their relationship was dramatically strengthened. On April 7, Clemens dropped by Clara's New York apartment for a family council. While the two were chatting, Jean happened to call and she sounded so strong and healthy that they both thought she was well enough to come home. Such conviction was not unprecedented, but Clara's next step was revolutionary. She made an appointment to meet with Dr. Peterson on her sister's behalf (SLC, Outline for "Ashcroft-Lyon Ms.," in *AL* file). Clara was astounded to hear Peterson say that it was her father's wish to keep Jean away. For three years, Lyon had been conducting a form of shuttle diplomacy between Jean's doctor and father, assuring Peterson that Clemens did not want his daughter at home while telling Clemens that the doctor thought Jean was too sick to return (*AL-AMT3* 358–59).

Always headstrong and now on a mission, Clara called in Dr. Quintard, but even a peer could not dissuade Peterson. Clara would have to send in the chief. After years of manipulation by Miss Lyon, Peterson's attitude was set in concrete. Twain wrote in amazement that Dr. Peterson "wouldn't believe *me* at first." As a result, the astonished father reported, "All I could get out of Peterson was permission to allow Jean to come home for one week" (*AL-AMT3* 359), and Outline for "*AL MS*"). On April 26, 1909, Jean was joyfully restored to her father, and the week of grace that Peterson had granted turned into a permanent stay.

"Jean is a surprise & wonder," Clemens wrote to Clara three months later, a surprise because he had not really troubled himself to understand her before she was exiled (SLC to CC, 18 July 1909, *UCCL* 08435). "I had never been acquainted with Jean before. I recognized that," he later admitted (SLC to CC, 29 Dec. 1909, *UCCL* 08527). And having had almost no communication with his daughter for three years that was not heavily manipulated or totally censored by his secretary, he was shocked to discover Jean's "character, courage, definiteness, decision; also goodness." While his judgment was no doubt affected by an upsurge of guilt at their reunion, he was also influenced by fresh observation and experience. He discovered she had "a humane spirit, charity, kindliness, pity; industry, perseverance, intelligence . . . dignity, honesty, truthfulness, high ideals, loyalty, faithfulness to duty" (SLC to CC, 18 July 1909, *UCCL* 08435). Conditioned to think of Jean only in negative terms, he was genuinely surprised by how much he liked her—and the stereotype of her "epileptic temperament" melted away. "Jean's—like her mother's—was a fine character; there is no finer," he concluded (*AMT3* 316).

One of Ashcroft's last authorized acts as Twain's business manager was the purchase of a local farm. Clemens gave this seventy-acre farm to Jean, who began immediately to turn it into a working unit. She repaired the house and barn, and bought chickens and ducks from the surrounding farmers. As usual, she gloried in spending time outdoors, tending to the farm, and riding for pleasure. She also begged to take over the role of Twain's secretary. The position was vacant as he had fired Mrs. Ashcroft before Jean returned home (*AL-AMT3* 345, 359–60).

Never a helpless invalid, Jean was now working like a day laborer and loving it. Finally allowed to live in her father's house, she rose before seven, ate a quick breakfast, and rode to get the mail at the post office. By nine she was giving her father his newspaper, exchanging pleasantries, and glancing at a few of his letters. Then she changed clothes and spent the rest of the morning at her farm, where her tasks included mixing chicken feed, feeding her brood, watering her plants, and doing some light carpentry. She usually returned to Stormfield around noon to work on her father's bankbooks and other accounts before returning to her farm for the afternoon. Back at Stormfield, she wrote checks and business letters and did bookkeeping for her father until dinner. After dinner, she played billiards with him until 9 p.m. and was asleep by 10 p.m. (JC to Marguerite Schmitt, 7 Nov. 1909, *UCCL* 08483, English TS of French original). Not every day was the same, but Jean was almost always occupied. How could Clemens not be swept off his feet by a daughter who played billiards? At age seventy-three, Twain suddenly had a family again.

Able to spend her first Christmas with her father in three years, Jean was in a flurry of Christmas preparations. Busily shopping for everyone and decorating a Christmas tree with silver foil and candles she intended to light at night, Jean was planning on giving her father a special gift: a globe of the world that he had long coveted (JC to Marguerite Schmitt, 21 Dec. 1909, *UCCL* 08513, English TS of French original; *MTB* 1548). Possessed by a deeply generous spirit, Jean could at last express her feelings materially. That Christmas Eve her father would write that

> last night Jean all flushed with splendid health, and I the same, strolled hand in hand from the dinner table and sat down in the library and chatted, and planned, and discussed, cheerily and happily (and how unsuspectingly!) until nine,—which is late for us—then went up stairs, Jean's friendly German dog following. At my door Jean said, "I can't kiss you good night, father: I have a cold, and you could catch it." I bent and kissed her hand. She was moved—I saw it in her eyes—and she impulsively kissed my hand in return. Then with the usual gay "Sleep well, dear!" from both, we parted.
>
> At half past seven this morning I woke, and heard voices outside my door. I said to myself, "Jean is starting on her usual horseback-flight to the station for the mail." Then Katy entered, stood quaking and gasping at my bedside a moment, then found her tongue:
>
> *"Miss Jean is dead!"*
>
> Possibly I know now what the soldier feels when a bullet crashes through his heart.
>
> In her bath-room there she lay, the fair young creature, stretched upon the floor and covered with a sheet. And looking so placid, so natural, and as if asleep. We knew what had happened. She was an epileptic: she had been seized with a convulsion and could not get out of the tub. There was no help near, and she was drowned. The doctor had to come several miles. His efforts, like our previous ones, failed to bring her back to life. (*AMT3* 311)

Jean had had a generalized convulsive seizure and drowned in her bath on the morning of Christmas Eve, 1909 (see CC to Julia Langdon, 23 Jan. 1910, *UCCL* 08545. Misinformation about Jean's death abounds, even in the scholarly literature). She was twenty-nine years old. Knowing that he had reclaimed his family, however briefly, Twain died less than four months after closing the valedictory for his youngest daughter with these words: *"End of the Autobiography."*

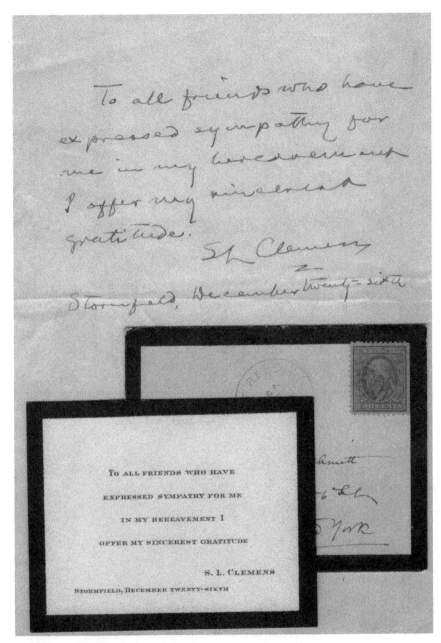

Two days after Jean's death early on Christmas Eve morning in 1909, her father drafted an acknowledgment card, the last thing he wrote that would be set in type during his lifetime. The card shown here was mailed to Jean's close friend, Marguerite Schmitt, who had arrived for a visit just hours after Jean's death.

Courtesy Kevin Mac Donnell, Austin, Texas

Part Three

Sam Clemens's Life Experiences

11

A Dialogue on Mark Twain's Autobiography

Victor Fischer and Benjamin Griffin

[Note: *The following dialogue between an Old Editor (O.E.) and a Young Editor (Y.E.) was overheard in an alcove of the Bancroft Library in Berkeley, California, and faithfully transcribed by the authors, both of them coincidentally editors as well. The opinions expressed do not necessarily correspond to those of the authors.*]

O.E. Mark Twain didn't intend his various autobiographical writings and dictations to adhere to a chronology or to present a consistent treatment or synthesized view of youth (or of any subject, for that matter). He aimed to follow whatever struck his fancy at the moment, with no commitment to stick with it, and with no particular agenda in mind:

> Start it at no particular time of your life; wander at your free will all over your life; talk only about the thing which interests you for the moment; drop it the moment its interest threatens to pale, and turn your talk upon the new and more interesting thing that has intruded itself into your mind meantime (*AMT1* 220).

Y.E. And yet he tells more than sixty stories from his childhood and youth. Do you seriously believe there are no common threads?

O.E. I believe there are several. One common thread in Clemens's writing about his youth in the *Autobiography* is moral education. For instance, after Clemens "went raging" to his mother to complain that Sandy, a young hired slave, had been singing ceaselessly for an hour without break, she answered in tears (a message that "went home" to him):

> Poor thing, when he sings, it shows that he is not remembering, and that comforts me; but when he is still, I am afraid he is thinking, and I cannot bear it. He will never see his mother again; if he can sing, I must not hinder it, but be thankful for it. If you were older, you would understand me; then that friendless child's noise would make you glad. (*AMT1* 212)

Y.E. It is beautifully told, and I see the lesson well enough: Be nice to people, especially to those who are suffering. But I am not sure I see any "learning." Clemens simply receives a preaching from his mother; and mother is always right. This command to be tolerant—is it of importance because it is the moral law, or because it comes from Jane Lampton Clemens?

O.E. It is important because the message "went home" to him, not simply because his mother told him how she felt, but because what she said enabled him to see the difference between his experience of childhood and that of Sandy and substitute understanding and sympathy for annoyance. He writes, "Sandy's noise was not a trouble to me any more." Although his mental process is not made explicit, it clearly took place and most readers would be expected to understand the process without having it explained. The larger unresolved issue here is of course his understanding of slavery. Clemens introduces the story—"one small incident of my boyhood days which touched this matter and it must have meant a good deal to me or it would not have stayed in my memory, clear and sharp, vivid and shadowless, all these slow-drifting years"—with the following words:

> In my schoolboy days I had no aversion to slavery. I was not aware that there was anything wrong about it. No one arraigned it in my hearing; the local papers said nothing against it; the local pulpit taught us that God approved it, that it was a holy thing, and that the doubter need only look in the Bible if he wished to settle his mind—and then the texts were read aloud to us to make the matter sure (*AMT1* 212).

In the same piece he writes, "All the negroes were friends of ours, and with those of our own age we were in effect comrades. . . . We were comrades, and yet not comrades; color and condition interposed a subtle line which both parties were conscious of, and which rendered complete fusion impossible." I would assert that the incident was an early step in his moral education, in which he later progressed far beyond his mother's teachings.

Y.E. But this early state of innocence as regards slavery—of never having heard anyone in Hannibal "arraign it"—this can't be true. Elsewhere in the *Autobiography* he says, about his brother Orion, "Born and reared among slaves and slave-holders, he was yet an abolitionist from his boyhood to his death" (*AMT1* 453). So Clemens had at least one vocal abolitionist near at hand.

O.E. Well, this is Mark Twain, and you must allow for exaggeration.

Y.E. The issue is, to what extent does exaggeration vitiate historical writing? But returning to "morality," let's take another anecdote of youth: "Jim Wolf and the Wasps." Clemens tricks Jim by brushing a "few hundred" wasps into

Jim's side of their shared bed. He makes his own side safe, and awakens to find Jim Wolf pounding him in the face. Very moral story! Every word a sermon in itself!

O.E. Don't be dense. The morality is in the commentary of the grown-up Mark Twain, about how he learned practical joking was wrong:

> In those extremely youthful days I was not aware that practical joking was a thing which, aside from being as a rule witless, is a base pastime and disreputable. In those early days I gave the matter no thought, but indulged freely in practical joking without stopping to consider its moral aspects. During three-fourths of my life I have held the practical joker in limitless contempt and detestation; I have despised him as I have despised no other criminal, and when I am delivering my opinion about him the reflection that I have been a practical joker myself seems to increase my bitterness rather than to modify it. . . . I played many practical jokes upon him [Jim Wolf], but they were all cruel and all barren of wit. Any brainless swindler could have invented them. When a person of mature age perpetrates a practical joke it is fair evidence, I think, that he is weak in the head and hasn't enough heart to signify. (*AMT2* 262–63)

Y.E. Excuse me, but once again the learning experience is absent. He liked practical jokes as a youth; now, having at some unspecified time "considered its moral aspects," he's against them. If these stories are supposed to show the process of a mind's development, they are failures; they are only before-and-after pictures.

O.E. Well, they certainly aren't failures; each is a good story well told. Although Mark Twain does not assert that his stories are there to demonstrate his moral education, surely you would admit that some of them do. I grant you that we don't in every case glimpse the mechanism that actually turns his innocence into experience. You're suggesting, I think, that the real catalyst is the maternal authority.

Y.E. I am. By the way, there is a scrap of manuscript, from around the time of the *Autobiography*, where he reveals that in his earliest schooldays God declined to grant his prayer for gingerbread. What he says about it is "I was as astonished as if I had caught my own mother breaking a promise to me" (*AMT2* 545). God's reputation is being tested—it is to be gauged against the mother's reputation, which is secure.

O.E. I'm glad you brought that up, because the *Autobiography* version of that incident is an instance where Clemens *does* recreate his learning process, and in doing so comes to reject the lessons of authority and question the lessons of the Bible, only turning to his mother for comfort in his disillusionment. Here are the steps: (1) His teacher, Mrs. Horr, who opened school each day with a prayer, a New Testament reading, and a talk, spoke on the text "Ask and ye shall receive," saying that "whosoever prayed for a thing with earnestness and strong desire need not doubt that his prayer would be answered." (2) Clemens, "so gratified by the opportunities which it offered," "believed in Mrs. Horr thoroughly" and had no doubt about the result (3). He prayed for gingerbread (4). The baker's daughter left her gingerbread sitting exposed on her desk. Clemens, deeply gratified, ate it when she looked away (5). He became a convert and did much praying, "sincere and earnest," for a repeat performance in succeeding days, but "like almost all the other dreams we indulge in in life—there was nothing in it" (6). He at last confessed to his mother, "with many tears," that he "had ceased to be a Christian." She was heart-broken," and asked him why. "I said it was because I had found out that I was a Christian for revenue only, and I could not bear the thought of that, it was so ignoble." This sentiment— perhaps crafted to please Jane Clemens, although it seems on reflection very sophisticated for a young child—provides the opportunity for the following zinger: "I gathered, from what she said, that if I would continue in that condition I would never be lonesome" (*AMT2* 177–78). Mrs. Horr's reputation is on the line here, not Mrs. Clemens's.

Y.E.   All zingers aside, you're overlooking what Jane Clemens is made to say here: that it's all right to be "a Christian for revenue only." And the reason it is all right is—that everybody is doing it. She is legitimizing religious hypocrisy—and conformism. A comfortable doctrine.

O.E.   Clemens is framing the moral insight that none of us is without sin. Really, don't you agree that youth, in the *Autobiography*, at least *offers* to be the progress of a moral education?

Y.E.   Youth, in the *Autobiography*, is a goldmine. The mature Mark Twain knows that his hottest property, his Big Bonanza, is his early life in Hannibal. It's telling that so many of these anecdotes are in the earlier dictations, made when he was expecting some of the material, at least, to be published imminently in the *North American Review*. Somehow we have to make our peace with this fact: The salability and re-salability of his tender years doesn't embarrass Mark Twain at all. About his story of "Jim Wolf and the Cats," he says,

> So that small tale was sold three times. I am selling it again, now. It is one of the best properties I have come across. (*AMT1* 163)

O.E. But that tale and that statement are not in the final form of the
Autobiography.

Y.E. Well, honestly, this book is impossible to talk about! If you say Mark Twain
wrote it, someone corrects you to "dictated"; if you say he left it unpublished,
they whisper "*partly* unpublished"; whenever Clemens recounts something,
editorial endnotes elaborately show that it never happened; and now you are
fussing about the "final form" of a book that wasn't finished.

O.E. Certainly some of these anecdotes are twice- and thrice-told tales—but
the *Autobiography*'s versions shed a new and different light on them.
Among the other common threads in the autobiographical stories Mark
Twain tells of his own youth are incidents in which the young Clemens is
humiliated because of his youth or ignorance or unfortunate circumstance.
Here are two of the humiliation stories: During his first visit to school at
the age of seven, a young girl of fifteen asked him if he chewed tobacco.
When he said no, she "reported him" to the crowd: "Here is a boy seven
years old who can't chaw tobacco," which made him realize he was "a
degraded object" and "cruelly ashamed of himself." In another incident,
when he was fourteen, he was asked to play the part of a bear in a "small
fairy-play" at his elder sister's party, to which he was not otherwise invited.
To practice, he "undressed in the flood of cruel moonlight" before putting
on his costume, doing "everything a bear could do, and many things which
no bear could ever do and no bear with any dignity would want to do,"
unaware of two girls behind a rickety screen full of holes, until after a
conversation with Sandy, the hired slave boy who was with him, he heard
"a burst of feminine snickers" that caused him to topple into the screen
bringing it down. He escaped, grabbing his clothes, and hid until very
late that night, "very heavy-hearted and full of a bitter sense of disgrace."
Returning home he found an anonymous note pinned to his pillow: "You
probably couldn't have played *bear*, but you played *bare* very well—oh very
very well!" Clemens wrote, "We think boys are rude unsensitive animals,
but it is not so in all cases. . . . I suffered miserably over that episode.
During several weeks I could not look any young lady in the face" (*AMT1*
155–57, 216).

Y.E. The stories about learning a lesson, those I can understand; it's a common
enough trope and Clemens, by his own admission, considers preaching his
vocation. Why does he tell these stories about being humiliated in youth?

O.E. I would think he tells them because they are good stories. The second one
even has a kicker. It ends with a meeting, forty-seven years later in Calcutta,

[handwritten marginal notes: "this dialogue inventively introduces how the Autobio. talks of youth"]

with one of the long unidentified "girls," who reminds him of the incident by quoting what Sandy said at the time that caused them to snicker.

Y.E. Could there be another reason he tells these stories?

O.E. If you're looking for psychological reasons—not really knowable, of course—one might suggest that perhaps he tells them in self-imposed penance for the relish he admittedly takes in humiliating other youths. When Clemens was twelve or thirteen, at work alone in the printshop and feeling very sorry for himself, he dropped a half watermelon rind on Henry from a third story window, "a thing which I have been trying to regret for fifty-five years." When Henry retaliated with a cobblestone to the head, Clemens got no sympathy from his mother: "She knew I deserved it" (*AMT1* 458–59).

Y.E. If youth, in the *Autobiography*, is structured around moral progress, how in the world are we to relate this to Clemens's habitual opposition to "the Moral Sense," as we encounter it in *What Is Man?* and the "Mysterious Stranger" manuscripts and a dozen other places?

O.E. Of the writings you just mentioned, *What Is Man?* was published anonymously for private circulation in a small edition, and the "Mysterious Stranger" manuscripts remained unpublished at the time of his death and were not published complete until the late 1960s—they are part of his esoterica.

Y.E. But I thought the *Autobiography* was part of this esoterica, too—that it was meant to serve as the repository of the truth, until such time as the remorseless truth could safely be told?—Well, never mind. Just confining myself to the *Autobiography*: Mark Twain says that Man is a machine, that individuals are constrained by "the law of their make" (*AMT3* 196). Under these circumstances, how comes it that the young machine has *any* "development," moral or otherwise?

O.E. I know what he says when he feels discouraged, but Clemens can't really have believed these things. There is no way we can read his tender, insightful accounts of his daughters' childhood and feel that he is describing the inevitable operation of a machine. He is so proud of their moral maturation. In the "Family Sketch"—

Y.E. Not *Autobiography*, not allowed.

O.E. All right, then, in the selections from "A Record of the Small Foolishnesses of Susie & 'Bay' Clemens (Infants)" that he includes in the *Autobiography*.

Y.E. It's true he refrains from calling Livy and the girls machines, but that is just patriarchal good manners. You happen to have seized upon a place where

Clemens's philosophical determinism smashes up against his Victorian feelings about females.

O.E. The lack of structure and accountability in the *Autobiography* allows Clemens to have it as many ways as strike him at the time, with no worries about consistency. In one instance, he lists major incidents of his life in an attempt to prove his positive belief that every event was an accident or circumstance stemming from a previous accident —"the first circumstance that ever happened in this world was the parent of every circumstance that has happened in this world since; that God ordered that first circumstance and has never ordered another one from that day to this." In another instance he suggests that it is character that prevails; he compares Murat Halstead's sixty years of "diligent, hard slaving at editorial work" with his own lifetime total of (by his count) ten years of working—"not diligently, not willingly, but fretfully, lazily, repiningly, complainingly, disgustedly, and always shirking the work when I was not watched," characterizing his piloting days and every subsequent occupation as "play—delightful play, vigorous play, adventurous play—and I loved it" (*AMT2* 236; *AMT3* 245).

Y.E. But that is not his life, it is his legend—the story of the bad little boy who, in defiance of all precept, doesn't come to grief. Is this character of his, this proud inclination to fool around in the face of the Moral Law, really him? . . . or really *his*?—for you know "the human machine gets all its inspirations from the outside, and is not capable of originating an idea of any kind in its own head" (*AMT3* 127).

O.E. He does say that, and gives examples, but in his examples it is the self that understands, rationalizes, redefines, and sometimes rejects those "inspirations." In "Scraps from My Autobiography" (which wasn't in the matured plan of the work, but which made it into the *North American Review* in 1906–07), he inventories some things that happened in Hannibal—external events that affected him. All violent deaths.

One of the most traumatic is the time he gave matches to a drunken tramp in the village jail, which caught on fire, burning the tramp to death. Afterward, tortured by guilt, he had months of "hideous dreams" in which the tramp, in hell, said that Clemens was responsible for his death. Clemens writes that only later did he understand that he "was *not* responsible for it, for [he] had meant him no harm, but only good" (he adds, in a rationalizing vein, that the tramp had suffered for only ten minutes, while *he* had suffered for months). Other incidents included witnessing the death of Smarr in the main street of Hannibal, the Bible on his chest adding "the torture of its leaden weight to the dying struggles," which led to nightmares in which Clemens "gasped and struggled for breath under the crush of that vast book for many a night"; seeing the slave man "struck down with a chunk of slag for some small offence" and watching him die; seeing the "red life gush" from the breast of a young "Californian emigrant who was stabbed with a bowie knife by a drunken comrade"; watching the two "rowdy young Hyde brothers" trying repeatedly to kill their "harmless" old uncle with a revolver that "wouldn't go off"; witnessing the death of another young Californian emigrant who proposed to raid "the Welshman's house" and was shot to death by the woman who lived there. Clemens writes, "My teaching and training enabled me to see deeper into these tragedies than an ignorant person could have done. I knew what they were for. . . . They were inventions of Providence to beguile me to a better life" (*AMT1* 157–59).

These violent episodes threw the young Clemens back upon solitude; they "went home to him," but he has escaped them, now. The events, and the Calvinist theology through which he interpreted them, came "from outside"; but his eventual liberation from providential thinking is the fruit of reflection, *his* reflection.

Y.E. Assuming it happened at all. Clemens admits the possibility that some of these memories are manufactured. He "remembers" his brother Henry walking into a fire when he, Henry, was one week old. Clemens introduces this memory solely in order to question it, reason over it, and brand it as a fake. He berates his so-called memory and memory in general, and he issues his famous dictum:

> When I was younger I could remember anything, whether it had happened or not; but my faculties are decaying, now, and soon I shall be so I cannot remember any but the latter (*AMT1* 209).

O.E. Perhaps he means to let that stand as a kind of stipulation—his memory is unreliable, so he's off the hook if any of his reports turns out to be untrue. It's a clever strategy, this disowning of his faculties—but of course he doesn't mean it.

Y.E. Doesn't he?

O.E. No. Everywhere in the book he expects us to trust his memory. Think of the celebrated piece of writing in "Random Extracts," where he describes his uncle's farm, that "heavenly place for a boy." He brings it alive by the use of his powerful sense-apparatus and his powerful memory. He catalogues the food, the smells, the physical experience of youth at the farm, and he mortises each item in place with the repeated phrases "I remember . . . I remember" (*AMT1* 217–18).

Y.E. In that passage, Mark Twain is an epic poet. He is invoking the muse, and his incantatory "I remember, I remember" is nothing more than "Sing, Goddess." Whether what he remembers really existed is a non-question; it doesn't matter at all whether these are accurate memories.

O.E. *You* think so, with the benefit of twentieth-century formalism behind you. But Mark Twain is trying to bring different times in his life into dialogue with each other, and if you decide it's all fantasy, you won't see what he is driving at. The anecdote about baby Henry walking into the fire—

Y.E. Now, Clemens himself brands this as a "screen memory."

O.E. Yes, but look what we learn from it when we bring it into dialogue with what actually happened. Henry can't have walked into a fire at one week of age. But what did happen? In 1858 the steamboat *Pennsylvania*, on which Henry was a clerk, exploded, and Henry was fatally burned.

Y.E. So in a way Henry *did* "walk into the fire," and Clemens's childhood memory is manufactured to stand in for an adult memory that he shies away from. But Clemens doesn't actually draw this connection for us, does he?

O.E. We don't know that he made the connection himself, it's true. But he did trust that *we* would make the connections, if he just pumped out his memories indiscriminately and heaped them together, so that they would react off of each other. Perhaps that's what he meant when he told Howells that, despite the autobiographer's "shirkings" and "extinctions" of the truth, "the remorseless truth *is* there, between the lines" (*AMT1* 21).

Y.E. It is like panning for gold—the autobiographical dictations are nuggets in the pan of the curious prospector, of varying value or no value at all, with any given passage glinting differently in the light of other passages.

O.E. Dynamic rather than static. It reminds me that when Mark Twain began the dictations Einstein had just published his papers on special relativity. . . .

[*Here the authors ceased to eavesdrop, because the conversation's pants were getting very fancy and it promised to falute at a correspondingly high level.*]

Sam's Boyhood Friends

Henry Sweets

As with Sam Clemens's siblings, deaths from accidents and disease stalked both his childhood friends and the adults of his boyhood town, and like his siblings, their joys and sorrows, adventures and mishaps, became the inspiration for the youthful incidents in Mark Twain's writings. Sam spent most of his youth along the Mississippi River in Hannibal, an environment in which most families struggled to make ends meet. As he commented in an essay he later wrote about his mother, "In the small town of Hannibal, Missouri, when I was a boy, everybody was poor but didn't know it; and everybody was comfortable and did know it" (*HF&TS* 85). The general poverty combined with disasters, both natural and man-made, making life full of fears for young people. Death for youngsters was common. In Hannibal's Mount Olivet Cemetery, the obelisk above the graves of Zachariah and Elen Draper enumerates six children, ranging in age from three months to nine years, who died between 1837 and 1852. The Robert and Rebecca Buchanan marker lists four infant deaths. Many families shared grief over the deaths of children—and of mothers dying in childbirth. Indeed, Elen Draper was Zachariah's second wife.

Deaths of men were frequent as well. Many were from accidents and diseases, and sometimes from murder. James McFarland, for example, was stabbed to death by Vincent Hudson in 1843, inspiring a story in Twain's *The Innocents Abroad* (1869). In 1845, Sam Smarr was gunned down by William Owsley—an incident resurrected as the killing of Boggs by Colonel Sherburn in *Adventures of Huckleberry Finn* (1885). Late in life Sam recalled how he, and probably some friends, passed matches through the jail window to an inmate who set fire to his cell and perished—a story he had put into print in 1883 in chapter 56 of *Life on the Mississippi* (*AMT1* 156). Tom Sawyer and Huck Finn also pass tobacco and matches to Muff Potter in his jail cell in chapter 23 of *The Adventures of Tom Sawyer* (1876)—but without the resulting fire.

Death visited children's play as well. Drownings were common. One of Sam's playmates, Clint Levering, drowned during a contest to see who could stay submerged the longest in a swimming hole (*HH&T* 36). Sam and his pals knew of a method believed to bring drowned bodies to the surface by firing cannons over the water or floating quicksilver in loaves of bread. When Tom and his friends are feared drowned in *Tom Sawyer*, that method is tried in chapter 14.

During the mid-nineteenth century, treating diseases was problematic because antibiotics and basic disease theory were still unknown. In spring 1844, a measles epidemic hit Hannibal "with uncommon virulence," killing nearly forty citizens (Holcombe 900). Unable to stand the suspense while seeing other children succumb, Sam figured he would not be spared anyway, so he sneaked into his friend Will Bowen's house and climbed into bed with him to contract the disease. "It was a good case of measles that resulted," he later recalled. "It brought me within a shade of death's door" (*AMT1* 420–21).

Fear substituted for medical knowledge, and Hannibal residents relied upon superstitions to explain unknown causes of death. Tom's fright at hearing a "death-watch" in the bedroom wall at night and his reaction to a baying dog foreshadowing death are examples of rampant fear and attempts to explain the unknown. Religious fervor was often high, boosting church attendance, and religious revivals were commonplace. Ministers were largely from the Calvinistic tradition and in an environment in which premature death, accident, and disaster were all too frequent companions, the themes of sin, the Last Judgment, and eternal punishment were frequently preached and sat heavily on the minds of youths. Sam recalled another playmate who had drowned three weeks before Levering did, after falling off a flatboat: "Being loaded with sin, he went to the bottom like an anvil. He was the only boy in the village who slept that night. We others all lay awake, repenting" (*LM* ch. 54).

For recreation, boys engaged in the usual childhood games of the day—marbles, high-spy, gully keeper, and tag. In addition to the arsenal of discarded objects that became boys' treasures—a lost key—a glass decanter stopper—blue bottle glass to look through—numerous toys are mentioned in *Tom Sawyer*. Undoubtedly remembered from Sam's own childhood, they included marbles, kites, India rubber balls, drums, wagons, tin soldiers, and spool cannons. Youngsters in Sam's village often turned to fantasy to escape the harsh realities of everyday life. The "book learning" that some of his gang possessed inspired activities based on fictional stories, complete with "rules" to be followed. *Tom Sawyer* provides a catalog of these diversions—Ben Rogers impersonating a steamboat; choosing sides to fight mock wars; playing pirates, Robin Hood, and Indians—all activities

that turned the mind to more pleasant thoughts. Even *Huckleberry Finn* starts
with Tom's unsuccessful gang of robbers. These childhood escapes from reality
no doubt influenced the adult Sam when he wrote about a fantastical balloon
escapade in *Tom Sawyer Abroad* (1894) and a perilous encounter with Indians in
his unfinished "Huck Finn and Tom Sawyer Among the Indians." They also likely
inspired nineteenth-century Hank Morgan's escape to sixth-century England in
A Connecticut Yankee in King Arthur's Court (1889).

Winters could be brutal in Missouri. Clapboard houses with no insulation
provided little barrier against the cold, and insufficient clothing made outdoor
activities dangerous. We know, nevertheless, that boys played outside in winter,
as Sam's friend Tom Nash "went deaf and dumb from breaking through the ice"
during an evening skating party on the frozen Mississippi River (*HH&T* 31). It
is noteworthy, however, that Sam documented few other winter activities. Twain
interesting the writer could have left readers shivering with goose bumps from reading what
might have been his masterful descriptions of the cold in Hannibal—but he
chose not to write such descriptions—at least not of Hannibal. In fact, he avoided
writing about many of the hardships and sorrows we know he experienced. *Tom
Sawyer* and *Huckleberry Finn* are set in summer times. *Life on the Mississippi*
does not emphasize winter navigation with the impediments of ice and cold on
the river. Twain the writer preferred writing about the balmy summer joys of
childhood when relating the experiences he shared with his Hannibal playmates,
but not without hints of death and disaster.

Most of Sam's playmates attended school. Sam himself was a pupil at schools
run by Elizabeth Horr, Samuel Cross, and J. D. Dawson. In those schools he and
his friends faced strict discipline and grueling memorization tasks as pupils. His
best friend, Will Bowen, was a fellow pupil and his cohort in many adventures. A
louse Will once brought to school became a plaything and later inspired a scene
in chapter 7 of *Tom Sawyer* in which Tom and Joe Harper take turns tormenting
a tick. Yellow-haired John Robards was another school chum and comrade-
in-arms whom Twain later described as "eternally and indestructibly amiable.
I may even say devilishly amiable; fiendishly amiable; exasperatingly amiable"
(*AMT1* 338). John usually wore the school's weekly Amiability Medal award,
and Sam its Spelling Medal. In a letter Sam wrote to Will on February 6, 1870, he
mentioned a school escapade. Addressing Will as his "First, & Oldest, & Dearest
Friend," he recalled how he, Will, and others

> got up a mutiny rebellion against Miss Newcomb, under Ed. Stevens' leadership,
> (to force her to let us all go over to Miss Torry's side of the schoolroom,) &

gallantly "sassed" Laura Hawkins when she came out the third time to call us in, & then afterward marched in in threatening & bloodthirsty array, & meekly yielded, & took each his little thrashing, & resumed his old seat entirely "reconstructed." (*L4* 51)

That incident may have been the inspiration for Tom's being seated among the girls by his schoolmaster. Sam also later remembered Margaret Kooneman, the Hannibal baker's daughter whose gingerbread he pilfered during a prayer period in Mrs. Horr's school (*AMT2* 178).

Outside school, Hannibal afforded several choice playgrounds for children. Cardiff Hill—as it is now called—was just north of the village and above it. As described in *Tom Sawyer*, it "lay just far enough away to seem a Delectable Land, dreamy, reposeful and inviting" (*TS* ch. 2). Near the crest of the real Hannibal hill was the Holliday mansion. Ben Holliday went to California in the gold rush and died in the West. His widow loved to give parties for the young people in town, complete with ice cream. She inspired *Tom Sawyer*'s Widow Douglas. One day, Sam and several friends, including Will, climbed atop the hill and loosed a large boulder that tore down the hillside and crashed into a cooper's shop. The boys spent many days fighting mock wars using swords made from wood lathes or reenacting scenes from Robin Hood.

The Mississippi River was the center of activity for the town. Steamboats discharged a wide assortment of visitors and brought goods to fill the stores. The river itself became part of the boys' playground. Barnett Farthing described an afternoon when he, Sam, and John Briggs "borrowed" a skiff and set across the river to an island. In the middle of the river, they discovered the skiff was leaky and it began to sink. Their cries for help were heard and they were ingloriously towed back to shore. Sam recalled several incidents when he was saved from drowning by both adults and other playmates. After one such episode, Jane Clemens stated, "People born to be hanged are safe in water" (*MTB* 35). On another occasion, Sam, John, and Will and Sam Bowen crossed the river to Bird Slough on Sny Island, where they discovered the mutilated body of a runaway slave.

The great cave south of town was familiar to the youngsters. Its constant 52-degree temperature would have made it a summer paradise. *Tom Sawyer* tells about children exploring the cave "holding their candles aloft and reading the tangled web-work of names, dates, post-office addresses and mottos with which the rocky walls had been frescoed" (*TS* ch. 31). Today it is estimated that 250,000 names adorn the real cave's walls. Among these one finds many of Sam's playmates—Thomas Nash and his sister Ellen, Samuel Honeyman, Norval Brady, John, and Artimissa Briggs—a seemingly endless list of the youth of the day. However, to date the name of Samuel Clemens has never been found among the candle-smoked signatures.

Hannibal offered other activities to youths. The Cadets of Temperance was formed in April 1850 to instill abstinence from alcohol and tobacco. Sam is the first name recorded on its membership roster, followed by the names of fifty boys, aged eleven through eighteen. They include Sam's younger brother, Henry, along with Thomas Nash, Samuel Honeyman, and John Meredith. Sam's real-life experience in the cadets is mirrored in *Tom Sawyer*, in which Tom joins the cadets and later resigns. Similarly, on the cadet roster—now held in Hannibal's Mark Twain Museum collection—Sam's name is followed by the notation "withd," indicating his voluntarily withdrawal. One wonders, however, what vice overcame Jimmy McDaniel, the son of a candy maker; his name is followed by "expelled."

Sam's cohorts in play and scheming also included slave children. A young family slave named Sandy, who lived in the Clemens household, came from Maryland. His constant singing initially so annoyed Sam that he complained to his mother. She responded by lecturing him, noting that Sandy would never see his own family again and that singing was one of his ways of forgetting (*AMT1* 212). On another occasion, Sam was rehearsing his part as a bear for a play Pamela was staging. Sam and Sandy thought they were in an empty room and Sam practiced his part in the nude. The practice came to a quick end when two girls' voices were heard and the boys fled. In Calcutta, India, about fifty years later, Sam learned the identity of one of those girls, Mary Wilson, when she greeted him with one of the lines he had uttered that embarrassing night (*AMT1* 155–57).

Sandy is sometimes suggested to have been the model for the slave boy Jim in *Tom Sawyer*. Sam never identified other slave children he had known by name, but their presence and impact on him were real. Speaking about Hannibal, but alluding to his visits to Florida, Missouri, as well, Sam remarked, "I was playmate to all the niggers, preferring their society to that of the elect, I being a person of low-down taste from the street, notwithstanding my high birth, and was ever ready to forsake the communion of high souls if I could strike anything nearer my grade" (*HH&T* 51–52).

Jane took Sam and his siblings to visit her sister, Patsy, and brother-in-law, John Quarles on the Quarles farm at Florida during several summers. The Quarles family included eight children, of whom Tabitha, nicknamed "Puss," was a favorite of Sam's. She recalled Sam as a mischievous boy with "spindly legs and thin body and curly hair that wouldn't be combed straight" ("Mark Twain's Cousin"). Later in life, Sam started sending regular stipends to Tabitha to help support her and once to start a business. At the Quarles farm white and slave children played by day and in the evening sat around fires and listened to older slaves tell stories. But Twain qualified these playmates:

> All the negroes were friends of ours, and with those of our own age we were in effect comrades. I say in effect, using the phrase as a modification. We were comrades, and not yet comrades; color and condition interposed a subtle line which both parties were conscious of, and which rendered complete fusion impossible. (*AMT1* 211)

The experience with the slaves' speech and superstitions at Florida and in Hannibal engrained itself in Sam's mind to be used many times in his writings, notable in *Huckleberry Finn* and *Pudd'nhead Wilson* (1894).

In his preface to *Tom Sawyer*, Sam wrote,

> Most of the adventures recorded in this book really occurred; one or two were experiences of my own, the rest those of boys who were schoolmates of mine. Huck Finn is drawn from life; Tom Sawyer also, but not from an individual—he is a combination of the characteristics of three boys whom I knew, and therefore belongs to the composite order of architecture.

Various boys have been suggested as the "three boys" alluded to in the preface. Will Bowen, John Briggs, John Garth, and Joe Buchanan are mentioned most often, but others are suggested as well. The adventures in the book are highly reminiscent of Sam's real life, and Tom himself is a composite of Sam's vast memory and probably not as easily identifiable as many wish. The model for one major character, however, Sam later positively identified: Tom Blankenship— the son of a town drunk and ne'er-do-well. He inspired Huckleberry Finn, the "juvenile pariah" of the fictional St. Petersburg. "In 'Huckleberry Finn,'" Sam later wrote, "I have drawn Tom Blankenship exactly as he was. He was ignorant, unwashed, insufficiently fed; but he had as good a heart as ever any boy had" (*AMT1* 397). Four years older than Sam, Tom Blankenship was eager to participate in the boys' activities. Another Hannibal denizen, Barney Farthing, told how one day several boys played hooky from school to explore the cave. Blankenship was at his father's fishing boat but quickly forgot work to join Farthing, George Butler, John Meredith, Norval "Gulliver" Brady, Bob Bodine, Tom and Frank Pitts, and Sam on an expedition that ended up with the boys becoming lost and spending more than twenty-four hours inside the cave (Farthing). One of the boys lost in the cave, Norval "Gull" Brady, linked Blankenship to a childhood prank of taking cats and skunks to the Western Star Tavern to disrupt a wedding party. Tom was apparently the one who conjured up the escapade:

> While the boys were in the alley on the night previous to the reception discussing plans, Tom Blankenship said somewhat abruptly, "Boys, a bright idea has just struck me!" For an instant the boys were dumfounded, almost speechless with surprise. In Tom's whole career they had never known such a thing to happen to him before. "One boy inquired, 'Did it hurt much, Tom?'" "Before he could frame a suitable reply, Sam Clemens said, 'Couldn't hurt nothing: had too soft a place to strike.'" ("Prank")

Huck must have borne a strong resemblance to Blankenship because Pamela Clemens Moffett's daughter later remembered how her mother "had only read a few pages of *Tom Sawyer* to her mother [Jane Clemens] when Pamela said 'Why, that's Tom Blankenship!'" (*MTBM* 265). However, the real Tom Blankenship had seven siblings and both living parents while he was in Hannibal; he was not the homeless waif portrayed as Huck in Sam's stories. Following Hannibal's 1850 census, there is little trace of the Blankenships. Perhaps fittingly, the family simply fades into obscurity while Huckleberry Finn continues to receive accolades as one of literature's preeminent figures.

We may never know how flirtatious Sam was as a youth. In later years, he named quite a number of Hannibal girls as having been his sweethearts. The names of Mary Miller, Artimissa Briggs, Mary Lacy, Jennie Brady, Lavinia Honeyman, Mary Moss, Julia and Sally Willis, and Kitty Shoot all appear as having been objects of Sam's affection at one time, but at least two of these girls he named were nine or ten years older than him and thus too old even to have been his playmates (*AMT1* 417–18; Sanborn; *SCOH* 183–84).

In 1908, Sam wrote to Margaret Blackmer,

> About next Tuesday or Wednesday a Missouri sweetheart of mine is coming here from Missouri to visit me—the very first sweetheart I ever had. It was 68 years ago. She was 5 years old, and I the same. I had an apple, and fell in love with her and gave her the core. I remember it perfectly well, and exactly the place where it happened, and what kind of a day it was. She figures in "Tom Sawyer" as "Becky Thatcher." Or maybe in "Huck Finn"—anyway it's in one of those books. She is bringing one of her granddaughters with her—a grown-up lady, I guess." (*UCCL* 08123)

That childhood sweetheart was Laura Hawkins, a girl two years younger than Sam who lived across Hill Street from the Clemens family and attended school with Sam. Sam identified her as the model for Becky Thatcher. Laura herself verified that several incidents in *Tom Sawyer* really happened. For example, Tom's showing off with gymnastics was Sam in real life turning handsprings. She also confirmed that Sam and Tom Blankenship played hooky from school. However, her memory of Sam from childhood did not predict his future greatness:

> As children we considered him humorous, not that what he said or the stories he told were particularly so, but he had a drawling, appealing voice, which made his talk impress his hearers, and the same stories told by others fell flat. In those days he certainly gave no indication, however, of being the great writer that he was in later life. ("Mark Twain's Playmates")

Sam never again lived in Hannibal after leaving the town in 1853, so direct connections with his boyhood friends were sporadic thereafter. Like Sam, his good friend Will Bowen and two of his brothers, Sam and Bart, also became steamboat pilots and occasionally worked with Sam on the river. In 1861, after leaving the river, Sam revisited Hannibal and had a brief experience in a local militia group composed of local boys that is fictionalized in "A Private History of a Campaign That Failed" (1885). Upon reading of Sam's marriage in 1870, Will wrote to him, provoking this reply: "The fountains of my great deep are broken up & I have rained reminiscences for four & twenty hours. The old life has swept before me like a panorama; the old days have trooped by in their glory, again; the old faces have looked out of the mists of the past" (*L4* 50). The wellspring of Sam's memory could be opened at any time with remarkable clarity and detail.

Other former playmates also had roles in Sam's adult life. Robards remained in Hannibal but always stayed in touch with him. As cofounder of Mount Olivet Cemetery, Robards contacted him and arranged to have the remains of his father and his brother Henry moved to the new cemetery in 1876. Laura married Dr. James Frazer in 1858 and remained in the Hannibal area. The next time she and Sam saw each other again was in 1902, during Sam's last visit to Hannibal. On that occasion, they dined with Helen Kercheval Garth, another childhood friend and the widow of John Garth, still another of Sam's old gang. Shortly after building his last home, Stormfield, in Redding, Connecticut, Sam made Laura one of his first house guests. In addition to having inspired Becky Thatcher in *Tom Sawyer*, Laura also lent her name to the femme fatale in *The Gilded Age* (1873). On his last visit to Hannibal in 1902, Sam and John Briggs rode around

Hannibal together and stopped atop Cardiff Hill to view the town and reminisce about their childhood memories. Sam also saw his old friend Tom Nash.

That 1902 visit brought attention to his childhood friends still living. In later life, Laura was frequently celebrated as Becky Thatcher. She poured tea in the Clemens household to celebrate Twain's birthday in 1915, attended early film productions of his works, and spoke of her experiences for reporters and in radio broadcasts, and when she died, her tombstone was carved with the name "Becky Thatcher" prominently displayed.

The childhood friends of Sam left impressions deep in his memory, ever ready to be called forth at a moment's notice to provide inspiration for his characters. These youthful friends became idealized with the passage of time, which tended to spread a happy mist over his memories. Hannibal itself became heaven when he named it "St. Petersburg" in *Tom Sawyer*. Twain's fondness for his childhood was summarized when he wrote to Will's widow in the summer of 1900: "I should like to call back Will Bowen and John Garth and the others, and live the life, and be as we were, and make holiday until 15, then all drown together" (*UCCL* 05814).

13

Health, Disease, and Children

K. Patrick Ober

*Disease! That is the force, the diligent force, the devastating force! It attacks
the infant the moment it is born; it furnishes it one malady after another:
croup, measles, mumps, bowel troubles, teething pains, scarlet fever, and other
childhood specialties. It chases the child into youth and furnishes it some
specialties for that time of life. It chases the youth into maturity, maturity into
age, and age into the grave.—Mark Twain* ("Letters from the Earth" 427)

In 1847, when Samuel Langhorne Clemens was in his twelfth year of life, his
hometown Hannibal *Gazette* reported a sobering statistic: Half the children born
in that era were expected to die before reaching their twenty-first birthday. The
Gazette's observation was a bleak one, but it would not have come as a surprise to
Samuel Clemens. Sam was the sixth of seven children born of the union of John
Marshall Clemens and Jane Lampton Clemens. He never met his parents' third
child, a boy named Pleasant who died in infancy. He had brief acquaintance with
an older sister, Margaret, who died of "bilious fever" when he was only four, and
only a slightly longer time to share with an older brother, Benjamin, who died
after a brief illness when he was six. Sam's younger brother, Henry, was destined
to die in a steamboat explosion at the age of twenty. It appears that the *Gazette*
had its facts straight. A child in nineteenth-century Hannibal was never far from
disease and early death.

Sam learned all about disease and death at an early age. Disease gave no
special dispensations. Anyone could get sick. Anyone could die. Preventatives
never prevented. Curatives rarely cured. The deadliest diseases preferentially
attacked the young. Mostly, though, Sam learned that there was almost nothing
a person could do when disease came to town, except to fret and worry about
how many children were going to die. "In 1845, when I was ten years old, there

was an epidemic of measles in the town and it made a most alarming slaughter among the little people," he later remembered. "There was a funeral almost daily, and the mothers of the town were nearly demented with fright" (*AMT1* 420).

When Clemens was a boy, the causes of most diseases were still unknown. Numerous explanations were invented, most of them unfettered by facts. In 1843, an article in the British medical journal *Lancet* proposed a new system for classifying causes of death. Some deaths were, it said, attributable to encounters with environmental hazards such as "arsenic, sulphuric acid, the bite of a mad dog, or a locomotive engine." The causes of most other deaths were less certain, though, and *The Lancet* suggested the term "miasm" to explain such deaths. All-purpose pathogens, miasms were invisible forces that worked in mysterious ways. They came from nowhere and could "steal insensibly into the system." Within hours of their arrival, miasms could "deprive the strongest man of all power, and even of *life* itself" (Gregory). Miasmatic diseases seemed to come from tainted air, and some experts proposed that the impure air and the disease were the same thing. The reasoning was circular, but it provided an explanation of sorts. Bad air was *mal aria*, and "malaria" was a disease. Malarial diseases were thus miasmatic diseases: They came from nowhere, they gave little warning, and they brought death. That was about all that anyone really knew about disease.

Cholera was chief among the miasmatic diseases that visited the Mississippi River Valley during Sam's childhood. It came in waves. Cholera originated on the Indian subcontinent, traveled the world's waterways, and caused global epidemics. The "great epidemic of the world" struck the Atlantic seaboard in 1832, worked its way along the coastline, and traveled up the Mississippi River in 1835. As the cholera moved northward by waterway traffic toward St. Louis, John Clemens and Jane Clemens were traveling westward by land in order to settle their family in the same region. Cholera made it to St. Louis first. The Clemens family heard the news and shifted directions. They veered clear of the river and headed to the upland village of Florida in time for Sam's birth in April 1835.

Another major cholera epidemic came up the Mississippi River in 1849. By then, the Clemens family lived in Hannibal, squarely in the epidemic's pathway. A steamboat passenger arriving in April became Hannibal's first cholera case of the new epidemic. Hannibal then had six cholera deaths between June 15 and June 19. Three people died of cholera on a single day in July. One of the summer's cholera victims was the father of one of Sam's playmates. There was only one effective strategy for dealing with the dreaded miasmatic cholera— avoidance. The facts were simple. Cholera killed. Doctors had no idea of what caused cholera, so they had no rational therapy to offer. *The Lancet* of 1853 scoffed at all the conflicting theories concocted to explain the nature of cholera: "Is it a fungus, an insect, a miasm, an electrical disturbance, a deficiency of ozone, a morbid offscouring from the intestinal canal?" Any explanation seemed as likely as any other, and the truth was anyone's guess, *The Lancet* admitted. "We know nothing; we are at sea, in a whirlpool of conjecture" (Wakley 393). It was a confusing time for medical science and a worrisome time for public health.

Clemens never forgot Hannibal's "cholera days of '49" and the panic they created. "The people along the Mississippi were paralyzed with fright. Those who could run away, did it," he remembered. "And many died of fright in the flight. Fright killed three persons where the cholera killed one." Not everyone ran away. The Clemens family stayed put, but Jane Clemens was not about to let its members become passive victims. She was a woman of action. "Those who couldn't flee kept themselves drenched with cholera preventives," Sam recalled, "and my mother chose Perry Davis's Pain-Killer for me" (*AMT1* 352). Jane Clemens had already seen three of her children die, and now she feared for Sam's life. In her desperation, she dosed him with an alcohol-heavy preventative patent medicine by the name of Perry Davis's Pain-Killer. Davis claimed it was effective for almost anything imaginable, including the prevention of cholera. As far as Jane Clemens was concerned, Davis was correct. The Pain-Killer worked. She had undeniable proof. She gave Sam the Pain-Killer. Sam never got cholera.

Sam was less certain about his mother's conclusion. For one thing, he did not take the full dose as prescribed. The Pain-Killer was an intolerably foul beverage, and Sam poured some of his share down the cracks between the floorboards whenever he could. He also dosed the family cat with the vile concoction for his own amusement when no one was watching. If his mother took credit for saving Sam from cholera with the Pain-Killer, he was equally certain that he had saved both the floor and the cat from the disease. "The floor was not carpeted. It had cracks in it and I fed the Pain-Killer to the cracks with very good results—no cholera occurred down below" (*AMT1* 353). He immortalized the event in *The Adventures of Tom Sawyer* (1876) by having Tom pour Pain-Killer down the throat of Aunt Polly's cat Peter. The cat immediately jumped into the air, "rose on his hind feet," and raced around the room in frenetic circles as it squealed, flipped "double summersets," and destroyed everything in its path (*TS* ch. 12).

Cholera was not the only miasmatic disease that created panic among the mothers of Hannibal. Scarlet fever was also highly stationed on the list of frightening diseases that went after the young. That disease killed some children and permanently injured others. Sam's friend Tom Nash was infected with scarlet fever and survived, but he "came out of it stone deaf" (*AMT1* 353). Clemens never forgot the impact of Nash's scarlet fever. In later years, he imported the disease into *Adventures of Huckleberry Finn* (1885), in which it attacked Jim's four-year-old daughter, Elizabeth, rendering her as deaf as Nash. Before Jim was aware his daughter had lost her sense of hearing, he gave her an order. When she failed to obey his unheard words, Jim slapped her to punish her disobedience. After learning that Elizabeth was deaf and had not heard his command, Jim became overwhelmed with guilt for striking the innocent child:

> Oh, Huck, I bust out a-cryin' en grab her up in my arms, en say, "Oh, de po' little thing! De Lord God Amighty fogive po' ole Jim, kaze he never gwyne to fogive hisself as long's he live!" Oh, she was plumb deef en dumb, Huck, plumb deef en dumb—en I'd ben a-treat'n her so! (*HF* ch. 23)

Through Jim's guilt-ridden confession, Huckleberry Finn discovered his humanity: "I do believe he cared just as much for his people as white folks does for theirn," Huck observed. "It don't seem natural, but I reckon it's so" (*HF* ch. 23).

Clemens eventually moved away from the miasmatic Mississippi Valley of his childhood. He married Olivia Langdon from Elmira, New York; settled in the East; and became a father. Despite the considerable changes in his surroundings and circumstances since his Hannibal days, one thing remained the same: Children continued to be easy victims of serious illnesses. Clemens's first child and only son, Langdon, died in 1872 at the age of nineteen months. Clemens blamed himself for the infant's death, as he confessed in an autobiographical dictation in 1906:

> I was the cause of the child's illness. His mother trusted him to my care and I took him a long drive in an open barouche for an airing. It was a raw, cold morning, but he was well wrapped about with furs and, in the hands of a careful person, no harm would have come to him.

Clemens was inattentive, however, and lapsed into daydreaming. Langdon's wraps fell off, and his bare legs were exposed to the cold. By the time the problem was discovered, "it was too late. The child was almost frozen. I hurried home with him. I was aghast at what I had done, and I feared the consequences" (*AMT1* 433).

There is no evidence that Clemens's distraction caused the boy's death. Indeed, there is suspicion that the boy died from diphtheria. Nevertheless, Clemens never stopped feeling responsible. When it came to Langdon's death, "Mr Clemens was often inclined to blame himself unjustly," his sister-in-law Susan Crane observed (*L5* 100–01). After Langdon's death, Sam and Livy Clemens would find plenty of reasons to worry about the health of their daughters. As the Clemens family was getting settled in their Hartford home during the mid-1870s, the rate of childhood illnesses appeared to be increasing in general, and particularly among America's most affluent families. Impure air remained the touchstone explanation, and so the increased rate of illness in affluent families seemed counterintuitive. Modern homes were built to be snug and free of drafts in order to prevent miasmatic air from entering. A new thought arose: Perhaps the disease-producing bad air did not come from outdoors but instead was produced inside the house. Two internal sources of foul air seemed likely—pipes and people. The newly installed pipes and drains of what was then modern plumbing seemed ideal places for fluids to stagnate and ferment and create new kinds of miasms. The emanations of the human body were coming under blame as additional contributors to the unhealthiness of indoor air. Exhaled breath was identified as a waste product, a type of "effluvial matter" much like the miasms of the swamps ("Quarantine and Hygiene" 468). The bodily waste from the lungs was as "truly excrement" as the material that was "ejected from the bowel," experts claimed (Beecher and Stowe 57). Despite this, Americans cooped themselves up in airtight buildings with their entrapped respiratory waste and went on "breathing it, and sucking it in, as if it were a confection or a luxury!" (Henry Ward Beecher 174). The progress of the Gilded Age thus seemed to turn human beings into perpetrators of pestilence, and miasmatic diseases had evolved into "diseases of filth."

In January 1875, four months after the Clemens family had moved into its new Hartford home, Susy Clemens, whose name was also spelled "Susie" within the family, was sick. It looked like she had membranous croup. "It kills somebody's child every day," Clemens wrote, "& all the mothers are in a state of fright which nobody can realize who hasn't seen it." Livy was terrified. Sam promised to stay home until the "epidemical & dreadful membranous croup" had "quitted the atmosphere" of Hartford. The household was in an uproar. "Our small Susie was threatened last night," Sam reported, "& I never have seen Mrs. Clemens so scared before . . . it is a wonderfully sudden disease & *incurable*" (*L6* 349–51). The panic from membranous croup in Hartford likely awakened Sam's memories of the cholera scares of Hannibal and reminded him of old times on the Mississippi.

"Membranous croup and diphtheria have much in common," the New Haven Department of Health reported in 1875 (*Third Annual Report* 21). The two diseases are now known to be the same disease (which is why "membranous croup" is nowhere to be found in today's medical vernacular), but in 1875 they were considered separate but similar diseases. Diphtheria is a bacterial infection of the upper airways of the most malevolent kind. Diphtheria germs create a grayish-white, shaggy "pseudo-membrane" in the throat, forming a thick obstruction that blocks the air passages, stops the flow of air, and strangulates and suffocates the sufferer.

"Membranous croup" is not the only pseudonym that diphtheria has used. It was labeled *morbus suffocans,* or *garrotillo,* when it was epidemic in sixteenth-century Spain; it went by the name *morbus strangulatorius* in 1758, when it terrified the families of England. Diphtheria has been called the "Strangling Angel of Children" in reference to the wing-shaped patches of whitish pseudo-membrane that built up on children's tonsils prior to suffocating them. It is a fearful disease that has attacked and killed children for centuries. No matter the name, it has always been a horrible way to die. None of the afflicted and distraught families of Sam's era, or of preceding centuries, could prevent it or treat it. There was only one thing a frightened world could do about this horrific disease, and even that was a cynical gesture; "if they could not cope with it intelligently," sanitary reformer Harriette Plunkett observed in 1885, "they could fit choking names to it which vividly indicate its chief point of attack." Championing the health benefits of sanitary living to quell diphtheria's severity, Plunkett warned how "unsanitary conditions have the power to push it into malignant virulence" (Plunkett 188).

The 1875 episode at the Clemens's household turned out to be a false alarm. Susy had a less serious disease, not membranous croup. "Susie is croupy," Clemens reported a couple of days later to William Dean Howells, "but today we believe it isn't going to be serious" (*L6* 349–51). Considering the degree of Livy's distress at the time, Sam's publication of a semifictional account of the episode later the same year may seem a bit surprising. "Experience of the McWilliamses with Membranous Croup" was one of three stories about the McWilliams family he based on incidents in his own family's life. Even though Susy's illness was not membranous croup, that disease had been the initial worry, and Livy was frightened as Sam had never seen her before. Sam turned the misdiagnosis and Livy's associated anxiety into a story of humor.

When Clemens wrote the McWilliams story, the Clemens household included Sam and Livy, three-year-old Susy, and the baby Clara (or "Bay," as she was called, due to Susy's inability to articulate both syllables of "Baby"). The fictional Mrs. McWilliams (representing Livy) has "a face as white as a sheet" as she tells her husband (the stand-in for Sam) of her fear that daughter Penelope (Susy) and "the Baby" ("Bay") will become victims of the epidemic of membranous croup ravaging the area.

The fictional Mr. McWilliams remains calm but becomes so exhausted by his wife's frenetic activities to save Penelope from the nonexistent "membranous croup" that he falls asleep and begins to snore "as only a man can whose strength is all gone and whose soul is worn out." The doctor then arrives and announces that there is no membranous croup. Mrs. McWilliams has overreacted. Penelope has been coughing on a pine sliver she was chewing. The sliver is finally coughed up and the child is well. However, the experience proves awkward to Mr. McWilliams. In order to maintain the "deep and untroubled serenity" of his marital relationship, the event has to become the "one episode in our life which we never refer to," according to Mortimer McWilliams. In his *Atlantic Monthly* review of the story, Howells suggested Clemens had crossed the line of propriety in sharing the details of his home life: "The Experiences of the McWilliamses with the Membranous Croup is a bit of *genre* romance, which must read like an abuse of confidence to every husband and father" (reprinted in *L6* 657).

The Clemens's medical worries returned in 1876, when Susy was diagnosed with diphtheria. Clemens told a visitor, Annie Fields, that he had an extremely sick child on his hands. Fields wrote that "the little girl did not really seem very sick," and she thought the family was unnecessarily excited. "The effect on them, however," Fields observed, "was just as bad as if the child were really very ill" (*MTDP* 00225). After Langdon's death, worry about the health of their children was an ongoing concern for Sam and Livy.

In 1889, fourteen years after writing the burlesque account of Susy's membranous croup scare in his McWilliams story, Sam recast the episode in *A Connecticut Yankee in King Arthur's Court* (1889). His tone was substantially different in the revised telling. While the McWilliams story had been satirical, the Yankee's story was romantic. Mortimer's McWilliams's nonchalant sarcasm toward his wife's behavior was replaced by the Yankee's compassion and empathy. In *Connecticut Yankee*, Sam's role was given to Hank Morgan, the Yankee, and Livy's role went to Hank's wife, Sandy. The story was essentially the same as both the 1875 McWilliams family story and the real Clemens family experience—at least on the surface. In each version a child is sick, apparently with membranous croup, and a mother is "wild with terror." In the third telling, however, Hank is not flippant as Mortimer is, but is instead attentive and concerned about the baby girl's condition: He "took her in [his] arms, and lavished caresses upon her." This time, it is Hank/Sam/Mortimer, not Sandy/Livy/Caroline, who is the first to recognize the seriousness of the child's illness and takes "in the situation almost at a glance—membranous croup!" In this revisionist history, Hank/Sam/Mortimer gets it right by identifying the urgency of the situation that was made a joking matter in 1875. This time around, there is no suggestion that a distraught mother might be overreacting to a trifle. A child is sick, a mother is worried, and a devoted father needs to take charge. "'Quick' . . . telephone the king's homeopath to come!"

This retelling of the membranous croup episode in *Connecticut Yankee* allows Hank to trumpet the sterling maternal qualities of Sandy: "Ah, Sandy, what a right heart she had, how simple, and genuine, and good she was!" Hank's tribute can be read as an apology for Mortimer's derision of Caroline McWilliams's instincts under identical circumstances, if not an opportunity for Sam to acknowledge Livy's exemplary motherly characteristics. "She was a flawless wife and mother," Hank Morgan proclaims in tribute, perhaps on behalf of all three husbands. "I didn't know I was drawing a prize, yet that was what I did draw" (*CY* ch. 41). As the nineteenth century ended, the bacteriological causes for many contagious illnesses were becoming established. Microbes replaced "miasms" as the explanation for numerous diseases. Sam kept up with the scientific and medical advances of his time. In 1905, he wrote "Three Thousand Years Among the Microbes" and told the story of a cholera germ named Huck, who lives in the body of a tramp. Cholera, the mysterious miasmatic disease of his youth that sent his mother for Davis's Pain-Killer preventative, had by then been found to be a bacterium.

In his later years, Clemens grappled with the metaphysical implications of the life-threatening illnesses of children. The existence of such diseases seemed incompatible with the actions of a beneficent deity. In 1908, he pursued the topic through the story of "Little Bessie" (*CTSS2* 864–74). Almost three years old, Bessie is "a good child, and not shallow, not frivolous, but meditative and thoughtful, and much given to thinking out the reasons of things." Bessie asks about the causes of the "pain and sorrow and suffering" in the world. Her mother explains they are gifts of God. "He alone sends them, and always out of love for us, and to make us better." Like Sam, Bessie is troubled by the idea that a loving God would do such things. She cannot understand why "billions of little creatures are sent into us to give us cholera, and typhoid, and lockjaw, and more than a thousand other sicknesses." Her opinion is succinct: "It's awful cruel, mama! And silly!"

A sacrilegious and sarcastic man named Mr. Hollister tells Bessie that "all troubles and pains and miseries and rotten diseases and horrors and villainies are sent to us in mercy and kindness to discipline us." He explains that "Providence's invention for disciplining us and the animals is the very brightest idea that ever was, and not even an idiot could get up anything shinier." Bessie's mother disapproves of Mr. Hollister's attitude. Bessie does not argue further with her mother but instead makes a suggestion to reveal the absurdity of her mother's way of thinking: "Mamma, brother Eddie needs disciplining right away; and I know where you can get the smallpox for him, and the itch, and the diphtheria, and bone-rot, and heart disease, and consumption, and—*Dear* mamma, have you fainted?"

As astute as she is, precocious Little Bessie can never understand why the Almighty shows his love by sending cholera and scarlet fever and diphtheria to afflict innocent children. And, as astute as he was, Sam never understood it, either.

14

Mark Twain's Angelfish

Barbara Schmidt

Samuel Clemens's autobiographical dictation of April 17, 1908, contains one of the most candid admissions he ever made:

> After my wife's death, June 5, 1904, I experienced a long period of unrest and loneliness. Clara and Jean were busy with their studies and their labors, and I was washing about on a forlorn sea of banquets and speech-making in high and holy causes—industries which furnished me intellectual cheer and entertainments, but got at my heart for an evening only, then left it dry and dusty. I had reached the grandpapa stage of life; and what I lacked and what I needed, was grandchildren, but I didn't know it. (*AMT3* 219)

At that time, Clemens was one of the most famous men in America, but adjusting to life as a widower had brought him self-doubt. Where and how should he live out the remainder of his life? Separated from his two surviving daughters, Clara and Jean, by circumstances beyond his control, he ultimately embarked on behavior characterized by collecting surrogate granddaughters from wealthy families. He called the girls his "angelfish" and the roots of his behavior were complex and ran deep.

For a man born in 1835, Clemens had married late in life. He spent his bachelor years as a steamboat pilot on the Mississippi River and as a newspaper reporter in Nevada and California. He also traveled to the Sandwich Islands and to Europe, writing travel dispatches for American readers. He was thirty-four years old when he wed Olivia "Livy" Langdon, ten years younger than him, on February 2, 1870. Their first child, a son named Langdon, was born prematurely on November 7 that same year. Their first daughter, Susy, was born on March 19, 1872. Langdon died from diphtheria almost three months later. Clemens harbored guilt over the boy's death and blamed himself for having allowed Langdon's blanket to slip off during a carriage ride in cold weather.

In July 1873, the Clemens family visited Edinburgh, Scotland. While there Livy became ill and Clemens sought medical help from Dr. John Brown based on Brown's literary reputation as author of the famous children's book *Rab and His Friends* (1859). Clemens found a kindred spirit in Brown, a man who had a profound respect for the innate intelligence of children. Livy recovered under the care of Brown, who gave her a copy of an essay he had published ten years earlier about a local child prodigy named Marjorie Fleming. Fleming, who died from meningitis in 1811, had kept a diary of innocent but worldly observations some critics believed revealed the development of a human conscience. When Brown told Clemens he considered Fleming his own dream grandchild he sparked in Clemens an awareness of wisdom that could be found in children's behaviors.

Clemens's second daughter, Clara, was born in 1874; his third, Jean, in 1880. From 1876 to 1885, he kept a record of their conversations in "A Record of the Small Foolishnesses of Susie & 'Bay' Clemens (Infants)" and took delight in observing their verbal and moral development (see *FSk*). When it came to his daughters telling lies, he compared his own observations of their behavior to those published by naturalist Charles Darwin (*AMT2* 223–24). He transplanted echoes of his children's conversations and behavior into his ongoing manuscript *Adventures of Huckleberry Finn* (1885). As the girls matured and mastered correct pronunciations, he felt "something that was precious has gone from us to return no more; a subtle, elusive, but nevertheless *real sense of loss*" (SLC to Mollie Fairbanks, 9 Feb. 1876, *UCCL* 01306).

In 1896, Susy died suddenly of meningitis at the age of twenty-four. Afterward, Clemens stated, "Whenever I think of Susy I think of Marjorie Fleming" (*AMT1* 328). Shortly after Susy's death, Jean was diagnosed with epilepsy, a disease that meant she would probably never marry. Meanwhile, Clara struggled to gain independence and build a career in music with a talent that was adequate but not stellar. In 1903, when Livy's health was beginning a slow decline, the family went abroad in search of healthy climates. A year later, Livy died in Florence, Italy. During her final days, Clemens sent her love notes, one of which quoted passages from Fleming's writings.

Livy's death left Clemens a widower at sixty-eight—an age at which many men had grown children ready to assume the roles of caretakers for their elderly parents. Clemens, however, had only a few paid employees to look after him. When he settled in a New York City brownstone apartment at 21 Fifth Avenue, his household was managed by Isabel Lyon, a former governess who had been Livy's secretary. His daughter Clara preferred living apart from him, and Jean was cared for in sanitariums because Lyon felt Jean's epilepsy would be an unmanageable burden. After Albert Bigelow Paine received permission to write Clemens's biography in 1906, he became a daily visitor. Clemens then hired a stenographer to take down his dictations as he rambled through stories about his life to Paine. Clemens meanwhile maintained a circle of famous and influential friends, who included young actresses and female correspondents. However, in 1907, when newspapers printed rumors that Clemens might remarry, he issued a statement, "I have not known, and shall never know anyone who could fill the place of the wife I have lost. I shall not marry again" (*AMT2* 565).

In late December 1905, Clemens had a chance encounter at Carnegie Hall with fifteen-year-old Gertrude Natkin. Toward the end of the month, she wrote a letter to him, signing it, "I am the little girl who loves you" (*MTAq* 8). Clemens then began a playful correspondence with her. Just before Valentine's Day the following February, he sent her a copy of a book about Fleming. Six weeks later, he wrote to her that he considered her his own "dream grandchild," just as Fleming had been for Dr. Brown (*MTAq* 22–23). Entries in Natkin's personal diary indicate she enjoyed public displays of affection with Clemens. After she turned sixteen in April 1906, Clemens felt that their relationship was bordering on improper. He wrote her on April 8, "Now back you go to 14!—then there's no impropriety" (*MTAq* 25). Again on April 27 he admonished her, "Cling to your blessed youth—the valuable time of life—don't part with it till you must" (*MTAq* 27). On June 30, 1906 he sent her his book *Eve's Diary* and on November 30, his birthday, she sent him a leather case. In February 1907, he gave her a copy of *Christian Science* and in May 1907, he visited with her at least twice at the Actor's Fair fundraiser in New York.

A photo of Natkin in the Mark Twain Papers at Berkeley shows a smiling young girl dressed in white with head tilted to one side and one hand pulling back her long hair. Natkin's beauty and pose is comparable to photos of famous showgirl Evelyn Nesbitt, who was involved in a notorious sex scandal throughout 1907 and 1908. The young childlike wife of millionaire Harry Thaw, Nesbitt had been seduced in her teens by prominent architect Stanford White. When Thaw murdered White in an insane rage in June 1906, Clemens followed the highly publicized case through two trials in 1907 and 1908. He felt that "Stanford White was a shameless and pitiless wild beast disguised as a human being" (*MTA2* 454). Clemens viewed himself as a defender of female purity, and any hint of something more than friendship with Natkin made him uncomfortable. He subsequently minimized his contact with her.

In late summer 1906, thirteen-year-old Dorothy Butes and her mother Janet visited Clemens. Her father, Alfred Butes, was a British journalist and personal secretary to publishing magnate Joseph Pulitzer. According to Clemens, Dorothy "wanted to come and look at me. Her mother brought her" (*MTAq* 138). Dorothy visited him every few weeks. When Butes resigned his position with Pulitzer and returned to London in July 1907, Isabel Lyon described Clemens as "heart sick" (*MTAq* 188). He would later claim that his acquisition of surrogate granddaughters began with Dorothy Butes and he made no mention of Gertrude Natkin.

In 1906, George Harvey, the editor of the *North American Review*, began publishing portions of Clemens's ongoing autobiographical dictations. Twenty-five installments ran in the *Review* from September 1906 through December 1907. With the proceeds, Clemens planned to build a home on his property near Redding, Connecticut. Albert Bigelow Paine's home was within walking distance of Clemens's property, where Clara and Isabel Lyon took on the task of designing the new house that would have more than 7,600 square feet and ten bedrooms—all for a man who then had no family to occupy all the spaces (see Mac Donnell, "Stormfield"). Lyon suggested the house be named "Autobiography House" (Shelden 89). On November 5, 1906, Clemens confided to his friend Emilie Rogers that he was building a country home for his daughter Jean, who was residing in a "pathetic exile and captivity" at a sanitarium. "I must have a country home for her" (*HHR* 620).

Clemens originally estimated the cost for his home would be about $25,000. By comparison, Paine's own farmhouse and thirty-acre farm had cost only $900. Clemens's only requirements were space for his billiard table and orchestrelle. He otherwise refused to be involved in the planning. However, Clara's revisions pushed the cost to over $45,000. Paying for it required additional proceeds from the sale of "Extract from Captain Stormfield's Visit to Heaven," a story that appeared in the December 1907 and January 1908 issues of *Harper's Magazine*.

Construction of the home began in May 1907. On June 8, Clemens departed for England to accept an honorary degree from Oxford University, sailing on the SS *Minneapolis*. Onboard he met sixteen-year-old Frances Nunnally and her mother who were embarking on a tour of Europe. Frances was the daughter of James Nunnally, a candy manufacturer from Atlanta, Georgia. She and her mother, along with Clemens and his traveling companion, Ralph Ashcroft, stayed at Brown's Hotel in London, and Clemens invited Frances to accompany him around London on social calls. When the Nunnallys returned home in September 1907, they accepted Clemens's invitation to visit him at his summer retreat in Tuxedo Park, New York. Clemens and Nunnally corresponded for the next several years. He fondly referred to her as "Francesca" and wrote letters frequently asking her for more visits.

Just as Clemens had met Nunnally on the trip to England, he met eleven-year-old Dorothy Quick on his return voyage home to New York on the SS *Minnetonka* in July 1907. Dorothy was traveling with her mother Emma Gertrude Quick and her grandparents Charles Aaron and his wife of Plainfield, New Jersey. Aaron was president of a large leather manufacturing establishment in New York. Dorothy, an avid young reader, impressed Clemens with her familiarity of his books and for the duration of the voyage they were close companions. A few weeks later Dorothy and her mother visited Clemens at Tuxedo Park, and Dorothy subsequently began to spend extended time with him there and later at his Fifth Avenue home that winter. In addition to her love of reading, Dorothy knew how to play billiards, one of Clemens's favorite pastimes. Dorothy also liked to wear white dresses when she was with him in order to match the color of his white suits. Taking great delight in her adoration of him and her interest in becoming an author, Clemens tutored her and they formed an "Authors' League" of two. After Dorothy's first visit, Clemens wrote her on August 9, 1907 describing a feeling of overwhelming emptiness after her departure:

> For five hours this has been a dreary place, a sober & solemn place, a hushed & brooding & lifeless place, for the blessed Spirit of Youth has gone out of it, & left nothing that's worth while. Aren't you sorry for me, you fresh breeze blown from fragrant fields of flowers? I thought this was a home. It was a superstition. What is a home without a child? Particularly a home that's had such a child as you in it. It isn't a home at all, it's merely a wreck. (*MTAq* 49)

In Quick's memoir *Enchantment: A Little Girl's Friendship with Mark Twain* (1961), published only a year prior to her own death at age sixty-six, she wrote, "Loving few outside my family, I had given my heart to Mr. Clemens in a combination of hero worship and the deep affection that it is only possible for a child to hold" (Quick 36).

While developing his friendship with Quick, Clemens began having second thoughts about building a house in Redding. Dorothy Quick could easily visit Fifth Avenue on weekends but trips to visit him in Connecticut would be more difficult to manage. On August 5, 1907, Lyon noted Clemens had been troubled about the possibility of "having to live alone out there for [Clara] cannot be with him now, and he mustn't be with Jean" (*MTGF* 182). However, architect John Howells told him that stopping the construction would make him liable for between ten and fifteen thousand dollars. His move-in date was expected to be in mid-June 1908.

The self-doubt that came from building an extravagant mansion with no family to occupy it triggered Clemens's drive to enlarge his circle of surrogate granddaughters. Between January and April 1908, as his mansion neared completion, he made two trips to Bermuda, spending a total of fifty-four days on the island—a getaway paradise for the wealthy. Isabel Lyon and Henry H. Rogers, a wealthy industrialist and a close friend, accompanied Clemens on his second trip in 1908. A visit to a Bermuda aquarium helped set in motion his idea for an "Angelfish Club"—a name inspired by small colorful fish. Isabel Lyon recorded in her journal that Clemens had acquired an "aquarium of little girls" whom he called his "angelfish" and had purchased a flying angelfish scarf pin for himself. In a tone of near disgust she wrote, "Off he goes with a flash when he sees a new pair of slim little legs appear, and if the little girl wears butterfly bows of ribbon on the back of her head his delirium is complete" (*MTGF* 195).

Elizabeth Wallace, a dean at the University of Chicago, was wintering in Bermuda at the same time and often joined Clemens for sailing and donkey cart rides with the girls. In 1913, she published a memoir, *Mark Twain and the Happy Island*. In it, she described Clemens's personality: "This wonderful comprehension that he had of children, and his perfect sympathy for them, helped us to understand better the simplicity of his own character. When we were with him, we, too, felt like little children" (Wallace 44).

In April 1908, Clemens returned to New York rejuvenated. In his April 17 dictation, he described his first meeting with Dorothy and claimed she had inspired his quest for grandchildren. He also recounted meeting Frances Nunnally and Dorothy Quick and listed his Bermuda acquisitions:

- Margaret Blackmer, daughter of wealthy oilman Henry Myron Blackmer
- Irene Gerken, daughter of real estate magnate Frederick Gerken
- Hellen Martin, daughter of Canadian grain dealer Robert Martin
- Jean Spurr, daughter of Edwin Spurr, a wealthy stone contractor
- Loraine Allen, daughter of George Allen, who had incorporated the Bermuda Electronic Light, Power and Traction Company
- Helen Allen, daughter of William Henry Allen, American Vice-Consul to Bermuda
- Dorothy Sturgis, daughter of Boston architect Richard Sturgis

The girls ranged in age from nine to sixteen. A few months earlier on February 12, 1908, Clemens had described the girls as "pretty and sweet and naïve and innocent—dear young creatures to whom life is a perfect joy and to whom it has brought no wounds, no bitterness, and few tears. My collection consists of gems of the finest water" (*MTAq* xvii). The girls constituted his "Aquarium." He believed that children took great pride in being a member of something exclusive and he gave each girl an enamel lapel pin in the shape of an angelfish to signify her membership.

Clemens took an unprecedented interest in the building of his mansion.

> The billiard-room will have the legend "The Aquarium" over its door, for it is to be the Club's official headquarters. I have good photographs of all my fishes, and these will be framed and hung around the walls. There is an angel-fish bedroom—double-bedded and I expect to have a fish and her mother in it as often as Providence will permit. (*MTAq* 141)

By June 1908, he had added to his club Louise Paine, the daughter of his biographer Albert Bigelow Paine; Dorothy Harvey, the daughter of his publisher George Harvey; and Marjorie Breckenridge, the stepdaughter of attorney Henry Dater, who owned a summer home in Redding. That same month, he wrote Clara to tell her he had decided to rename his house "Innocence at Home." He liked the twist on the title of his book *The Innocents Abroad* (1869), and thought it implied an image of eternal youth and purity, but he jokingly told Clara, "Many populations will think it describes me" (Shelden 234).

Clemens moved into his new house on June 18 amid local public fanfare. Prior to the move, he had stated, "I am quite sure everything will be as I want it. I'd only like to see Dorothy Quick's face when I open the front door" (Quick 181). Quick, however, was ill and unable to attend his move-in day. Clemens wrote to Clara, who was in England, needling her that her suite might not be available if she stayed away too long. "No, I will lodge angel-fishes in it" (Shelden 243).

Clemens had built it and they came. Throughout the summer, most of the girls and their parents visited. On July 7, 1908, Clemens confided in a letter to Margaret Blackmer, "My house is named 'Innocence at Home' & it is the angel-fish that are to furnish the innocence, though the public don't know that. It isn't the public's affair." He further told Blackmer that days with the angelfish were spent playing card games out on the loggia and "I think I will call it the Fish-Market, for I built it for the fishes" (*MTAq* 186). Clemens did not like being alone in the big house and his guest book recorded 180 visitors the first year he lived there. In her later years, Paine's daughter Louise recalled,

> I could walk there easily, but other "Members of the Aquarium" came with their parents or governesses to stay for weekends or longer, and he taught us all to play Hearts and, with infinite patience, to manage billiards cues. He never made

us feel that he was an elderly man whose good manners included being kind to children. On the contrary, he seemed to be having such a genuinely good time himself that age differences were forgotten. (Shelden 247)

Clemens wrote a manuscript titled "The Aquarium" for the girls' amusement; it was a parody of club rules and restrictions. With a note of special emphasis, he wrote, "I have built this house largely, indeed almost chiefly, for the comfort & accommodation of the Aquarium. Its members will always be welcome under its roof" (*MTAq* 191). Throughout 1908, Clemens and the girls exchanged several letters a week. Many of the angelfish letters are filled with his fanciful illustrations and flashes of Clemens's famous wit indicative of the joy he found in corresponding with young readers.

After Clara came home in September 1908, things changed, and Clemens described the new situation as "gone to hell" (*MTGF* 227). Always protective of her father's reputation, Clara was uncomfortable with his attention to young girls, and she would ultimately object to publication of photos of him in affectionate poses with the girls. At her suggestion, Clemens renamed his house "Stormfield." Meanwhile, an ongoing state of discord erupted between her and Isabel Lyon that could not be repaired after she accused Lyon and her new husband, Ralph Ashcroft, of mismanaging Clemens's assets. By mid-April 1909, Clara had persuaded her father to dismiss Lyon and bring Jean home to a house she had never previously been allowed to visit.

Letters and visits from angelfish then declined, along with Clemens's health. Lyon had been the facilitator for the girls' visits and no one took her place after she was fired. On October 6, 1909, Clara married musician Ossip Gabrilowitsch at Stormfield and then left again to live in Europe. In the December 1909 issue of *Harper's Bazaar*, Clemens published "Marjorie Fleming, the Wonder Child." It was his final tribute to Dr. John Brown and the little dream granddaughter whose writings Clemens believed revealed "the human race in little" (*E&E* 358).

Jean died in her bathtub at Stormfield on Christmas Eve 1909. Clemens worked through his sorrow as he wrote "The Death of Jean," which he called the last chapter of his autobiography. In it, he chastised himself, asking, "Why did I build this house, two years ago? To shelter this vast emptiness? How foolish I was!" (*AMT3* 315). He then went on to disclose how painfully he had needed a real family:

When Clara went away two weeks ago to live in Europe, it was hard, but I could bear it, for I had Jean left. I said *we* would be a family. We said we would be close comrades and happy— just we two. . . . We were together; *we were a family!* the dream had come true—oh, preciously true, contentedly true, satisfyingly true! and remained true two whole days. (*AMT3* 319)

After Jean's death, Clemens's heart condition worsened. Paine acted the role of a protective son and arranged for Clemens to return to Bermuda for an extended stay with William and Marion Allen, the parents of angelfish Helen. For over three months, Clemens lived with the Allens and watched them struggle to manage a maturing daughter. Some of Clemens's last writings focus on Helen. He described her temper and arguments with her parents. As if writing from personal experience, he added, "In a year or two from now they will be as courteous to her as they are to the servants" (*MTAq* 274). He complained that Helen had "a prodigious interest in any & all members of the male sex, under 45 married or single" (*MTAq* 276). One manuscript is more disturbing and contains passages that can be interpreted as threats against Helen's boyfriend Arthur: "If I catch him around these premises again, I will carve him up with his own Excalibur" (*MTAq* 278).

Biographer Hamlin Hill has suggested Clemens may have acted improperly with Helen Allen. However, there is no evidence to indicate Clemens acted inappropriately with any young girl. The angst found in the Helen Allen manuscripts reflects the same anxiety Clemens felt with his own daughter Clara when she was sexually mature. On May 2, 1903, when Clara was twenty-nine and still single, Clemens published in *Harper's Weekly* "Why Not Abolish It?"— the "it" being a law that established a legal age of consent for sexual activity outside of marriage:

> There is *no* age at which the good name of a member of a family ceases to be a part of the *property* of that family—an asset, and worth more than all its bonds and money. . . . There is *no* age at which consent shall in the least degree modify the seducer's crime or mitigate its punishment. (*CTSS2* 551–52)

In early April 1910, Paine traveled to Bermuda and brought Clemens back to Stormfield, where he died on April 21. Clara and her husband Ossip had returned from Europe to be with him during his final days. It is unclear whether he knew Clara was pregnant with his only granddaughter at the time.

The motivations behind Clemens's Angelfish Club were multifaceted. The question might be asked why Clemens did not also create a circle of young boys around him during his final years. He had a close bond with Harry, the young son of Henry H. Rogers and had dedicated *Following the Equator* (1897) to him. However, young boys may have served as a painful reminder of his lost firstborn son, and what might have been. Some of the photos of Clemens with the girls suggest he had a need to receive and give affection—poses rarely seen in other photos taken earlier in his life. The angelfish were a means to reconnect with something undefined and again see the world through the eyes of a child.

Mark Twain with Dorothy Quick, one of the earliest and most loyal of his "angelfish" girls, on his return voyage from England in 1907. Many years later, Quick published a memoir about her friendship with Mark Twain.

Courtesy Kevin Mac Donnell, Austin, Texas

Part Four

Mark Twain's Writings

15

Early Stories and Sketches

David E. E. Sloane

Although Mark Twain's major "boy" novels attract the most critical attention, a modest handful of his early sketches on the ethics of children deserve a closer look for their startling representations of his pessimism. Four sketches published around the period 1864–65, when he was reporting in San Francisco, and a later return to the setting in an 1870 *Galaxy* sketch, "Disgraceful Persecution of a Boy," show a dark view of how human behavior is shaped, all in terms of the social training of youth. "King Leopold's Soliloquy" and similar pieces may suggest that Twain's pessimism was a "late" occurrence, but the children he portrays in the San Francisco sketches of the middle 1860s are as deeply corrupted by greed and hypocrisy as any later imperialist. The vision of social abuse, focused on the Chinese immigrant population, and even the mechanics of Twain's presentation implicate adults and children alike in the corrupt education of youth as they take their place in the corrupt political world of adulthood.

Twain's radical rejection of childhood ethics is a direct result of his role as a literary comedian as practiced in the 1860s. He begins from a comic perspective that is seemingly radical libertarian as was the case with his fellow comedians, but then advances directly to his most pungent social satire. In that, his comic writings on youth and moral action vary markedly from the sentimental tone and apparent acceptance of conventional Victorian American beliefs expressed in his own personal family writing. Egalitarian cynicism trumps didactic morality; his contrarian ethical reversals parallel the pessimistic proclamations that are often characterized as typical of the "later" Twain, and his "later" sardonic Calvinism is very much present in his earliest views of youth in many early comic short sketches. The cynicism of the omniscient advisor and commentator provides the comic fulcrum on which the curdled sardonic humor balances. The ultimate conclusion, however, is that Twain's only interest in children is that they are a vehicle for the social vision that pervades his canon, at its best in *Adventures of Huckleberry Finn* (1885), but at its worst everywhere else in the pervasive inhumanity of mankind toward man.

Twain's description of his own family, and especially his admiration of his wife Livy as a mother and trainer of children with her gentle morality is, of course, touching. He describes Livy's way with Susy, the model child, to be direct, moral, and modestly rigid without being harsh and Susy's responses to be positive and sincere. The perfect Victorian family is displayed in "A Family Sketch" and in parts of "A Record of the Small Foolishness of Susie and 'Bay' Clemens (Infants)," especially where noted as "sweet, gentle, tractable, and lovable creatures" (*FSk* 76). Little suggests anything other than a rather conventional, even blandly idealistic, upbringing, surrounded by tutors, lulled to sleep by an obedient father delivering numerous stories. An occasional irony slips into other narratives beyond this source, such as his telling his daughters that Uncle Remus (Joel Chandler Harris) was late to a Farmington Avenue visit because he had to be white-washed to come in their front door, but by and large, the narrative is a tame one. Regrettably, an article in the *New York Times* quotes him, during a speech to Congress defending extended copyrights, as saying, "I know a lot of trades. But that [income royalty] goes to my daughters, who can't get along as well as I can because I have carefully trained them as young ladies, who don't know anything and can't do anything" ("Mark Twain in White Amuses Congressmen"). If his advice to youth seems retrograde, perhaps it was not retrograde enough fully to reflect his chauvinism, and he could very likely have felt the truth of what he was saying.

Understandably, the deaths of Susy and Jean broke his heart twice, and his wondering how a human being can withstand such a thunderclap of grief as their deaths can easily be understood in their innocent conformity of natures to his own needs as a father. It is hard to think that the youth defined in his early sketches would have attracted such an attachment. Twain's real children have nothing in common with the literary children who preceded them. In fact, Twain's sentiments as a father chafed against the popular humorist Josh Billings, who opined, "To bring up a child in the way he should go, travel that way yourself." Billings bolstered that sentiment with an even more maudlin Victorianism: "A child's heart: a sweet little vault where God has locked up creation's destiny." Both sentiments are embalmed in *Josh Billings on Ice* (1868). The first is in "Hartes" section 38; the second in "Josh Epistolates" section 70. Twain's own notorious lifestyle, featuring cheap cigars, egregious admiration for profanity, and a determination never to have the toothache if two scotches a day could prevent it, disallows the first possibility of leading a childish heart by example. The second is deconstructed in "The Story of a Bad Little Boy Who Didn't Come to Grief." Its protagonist, "Jim," specified as not "James in your Sunday-school books," doesn't have a sick consumptive mother; instead, his mother is fat and abusive and declares that if Jim "were to break his neck it wouldn't be much loss." When Jim steals apples, he does not get a dog-bite. Instead, he "knocked [the dog] endwise with a brick when he came to tear him." When he steals a penknife, no "white-haired improbable justice of the peace" redeems, but rather the guilt is transferred to "the model boy George," who gets Jim's deserved thrashing. Those children inherit the corrupt anti-Calvinism of Twain's darker social philosophy: The agents of authority are mindless instruments of enforcement, able to punish but setting nothing to rights. Twain even varies his diction into the vernacular— "This Jim bore a charmed life—that must have been the way of it"—to introduce a veritable cascade of supposed one-line moralistic plots crescendoing in his running off to sea and coming home not to a tumble-down cottage and lost family but "drunk as a piper, and got into the station-house the first thing." In fact, the paragraph that follows is frequently quoted as a set piece:

> And he grew up and married, and raised a large family, and brained them all with an axe one night, and got wealthy by all manner of cheating and rascality; and now he is the infernalist wickedest scoundrel in his native village, and is universally respected, and belongs to the Legislature. (Rasmussen, *Mark Twain's Book* 94)

Twain would naturally place Jim in the Legislature, with a capital *L*, because as the center of authority and power, the Legislature is also the center of corruption and hypocrisy—natural accompaniments of Jim's vicious nature and violation of moral expectations. Adult criminality is the natural outcome of early behavior— all the sages have said it. Twain portrays it as part of a natural train of events through petty civil crimes to larger criminal authority.

In general, Twain's comic depiction of advice to youth establishes ironically that no ethical basis exists that meaningfully governs behavior along the lines to which his own family seems to have adhered. His fictional youth are preeminently actors on a social stage, representatives of social viewpoints of the 1860s and 1870s. Those viewpoints, as the literary comedians satirized them, were selfishly egocentric, opportunistic, and often intolerant of the weak. Twain's addresses to youth were, in fact, a platform on which to address unwilling readers about their arbitrary social hypocrisy, among other lapses in ethics, including the treatment of the defenseless minorities of California. A useful variety of writings that suggest Twain on youth in the early period is conveniently deployed in R. Kent Rasmussen's *Mark Twain's Book for Bad Boys and Girls* (1995) and my discussion is naturally located in those texts. My conclusion, however, stretches to 1870 and beyond in "The Disgraceful Persecution of a Boy," which like "Goldsmith's Friend Abroad" raises the issue of the flagrant mistreatment of Chinese immigrants on the West Coast reaching from the 1860s beyond the 1880s. The social corruption of youth finally matures into fictional vision when Huck Finn escapes his corrupted nature—obviously with much difficulty, including a pledge to go to Hell—and how the ambiguous nature and distorted nurture of Tom Driscoll and Chambers, contorted by their swapping in the cradle, is resolved by continuing social and economic injustice.

"Advice to Parents on Curing Their Children," published as "Those Blasted Children" in the New York *Sunday Mercury* on February 21, 1864 (Rasmussen, *Mark Twain's Book* 169–73) is typical of Twain's early ranting fulminations, easily read superficially as a comic set piece rather than as a serious statement. The sketch's particular savages, worthy of scalping or having bootjacks thrown at them, are to be treated with arsenic, have the brains taken out (referring for precedent to William Shakespeare), swallow catfish to catch worms (be quiet, the fish won't bite if disturbed), and mutilation. Parboiling is prescribed for cramps. The pronoun used for the child is "it," consistently, and other tendencies to make visually apparent the comic distance of the author abound in the choice of language and elaboration of details. For example, he quotes in closing a burlesque letter, from "Zeb Leavenworth," a Mississippi River crony who was also called in to do comic duty in 1867 burlesque newspaper pieces on female suffrage. Such devices are Twain's stairway to surprise, the epistolary tool in the hands of the comic contriver. Translated, this comic rant is an exercise in the expression of annoyance. It is literary humor; the real message is that children should be seen and not heard, tricked out with a secondary theme that fake medical advice is a means of flirting with young mothers. Twain the persona is closer to the "Veritable Squibob" John Phoenix than to a real parent. Children, in fantasy if not in fact, are brutalized, unregulated, and subhuman.

The paired pieces "Advice for Good Little Boys" (from *California Youth's Companion* of June 3, 1865) and "Advice for Good Little Girls" (*California Youth's Companion* of June 24, 1865) take the form of mock-homilies directly addressed to boys and girls, as their publication site suggests, although nothing else about them seems other than tongue-in-cheek. The underlying assumptions of the comic bits composing each piece, however, are that the actors are inclined to harmful behavior, and their primary need is not a reform of character but rather a physical defense against a punitive world: "You should never do anything wicked and then lay it on your brother, when it is just as convenient to lay it on some other boy." On the girls' side, the admonishment is "not to attempt to make a forcible swap" of your sawdust-stuffed rag doll for a costly china one "unless your conscience would justify you in it, and you know you are able to do it" (Rasmussen, *Mark Twain's Book* 2). Since the "more fortunate little playmate" will be the victim of this forcible swap, we understand that the deadpan irony is directed at the human situation of envy and selfishness, a basic motivator of small children . . . and Gilded Age capitalists, as well as modern Wall Street. Artemus Ward, in his London letters to *Punch*, mused at the end of his seventh letter that he was putting down his pen, which he asserted was mightier than the sword, perhaps, but would stand a rather slim chance against the needle gun. Twain admonishes little girls never to sass old people unless the old people " 'sass' you first." In this child world, might makes right. As Twain casually reels through his inventory of childhood pranks, the lessons reverberate. Ethics are strictly nominal attributes in the world of negative action. Only a literary comedian of Twain's caliber could have contrived to make this viciousness into a comic vision and get away with it.

"The Story of the Good Little Boy Who Did Not Prosper" (Rasmussen, *Mark Twain's Book* 72) in the 1870 *Galaxy* carries on the program. The dripping sarcasm of the deadpan naïf that played the central role in the persona of literary comedians of this period flowers in this sketch. Nevertheless, the ultimate outcome is pure Twain. For openers, the good little boy, Jacob Blivens, even has an awkward-sounding name, and the front phrase is a tagline for a literary burlesque: "Once there was a good little boy named Jacob Blivens." The mock fable is already a study in opposition, and the second sentence builds this out in the sentence format followed in the paired pieces advising good boys and girls: "He always obeyed his parents, no matter how unreasonable and absurd their demands were; and he always learned his book, and was never late for Sabbath-school" (Rasmussen, *Mark Twain's Book* 77). Forcing "unreasonable and absurd" into the middle of the sentence as a qualifier sufficiently undermines not only the opening of obedience but also the closing set pieces covering learning and Sunday-school attendance. In short, there really is no part of the process that escapes ironic reversal and the discrediting power of the burlesque exaggeration of tone. As a good burlesque must, the one-liners expand to anecdotes, including the boys in a sailboat who do not drown, the faithful cabin boy who is not given a chance, the kindly boy who rescues dogs. In this final ultimate case, the would-be "good boy" is struck by no less than an alderman, symbolizing the intrusion of government authority in persona, and boy, dogs and alderman are every one of them blown to bits across five counties because Jacob was sitting on a nitroglycerine can. To make sure we get the point, Twain specifies that the torso is found in one county and four inquests have to be held over fragments in four other counties, thereby drawing government into our consciousness. It is perfect Twain in the lawlessness of the closure as much as it is of the type of literary comedy that masterfully builds from exaggerated cliché to exaggerated cliché. True also to literary comedy, alderman and counties are present by inclusion to flavor our sense of this cosmos with political overtones.

"Disgraceful Persecution of a Boy" is the clearest of all the youth pieces, and, although published in the Twain's "Memoranda" column in the May 1870 *Galaxy*, it takes us back in its closure specifically to Twain's misadventure with the San Francisco *Call* in 1864. The persecution of Chinese in San Francisco has lately been the subject of a study by Hsuan L. Hsu's *Sitting in Darkness: Mark Twain's Asia and Comparative Radicalization* (2015), which provides a telling analysis of "Disgraceful Persecution of a Boy" in the context of the neglected racial play *Ah, Sin!* (1877) that Twain coauthored with Bret Harte. Without reconstructing Hsu's complete discussion, it can simply be pointed out that the lines of the story are controlled by the atrocious legal deformities that California imposed in special mining taxes on Chinese, while depriving Chinese of the right to testify in a court of law and offering no civil protection against violence due to the loss of a voice in any court proceeding. The state also ignored frequent lynchings for minor offenses. For Twain, the item he wrote, recalling his piece in 1864, uses the third-person voice but employs the device that made his writings the most powerful moral presentations in America—the deadpan naive voice. In each of his points, the voice expresses confusion about how and why a boy might be punished for doing what he has been taught. The catalog builds quickly:

> In San Francisco, the other day, "a well-dressed boy, on his way to Sunday school, was arrested and thrown into the city prison for stoning Chinamen." What a commentary is this upon human justice! What sad prominence it gives to our human disposition to tyrannize over the weak! San Francisco has little right to take credit to herself for her treatment of this poor boy. What had the child's education been? How should he suppose it was wrong to stone a Chinaman? . . . The chances are that his parents were intelligent, well-to-do people, with just enough natural villainy in their compositions to make them yearn after the daily papers, and enjoy them; and so this boy had opportunities to learn all through the week how to do right, as well as on Sunday. It was in this way that he found out that the great commonwealth of California imposes an unlawful mining

tax upon John the foreigner, and allows Patrick the foreigner to dig gold for nothing—probably because the degraded Mongol is at no expense for whiskey, and the refined Celt cannot exist without it. It was in this way that he found out that a respectable number of the tax-gatherers—it would be unkind to say all of them—collect the tax twice, instead of once; and that, inasmuch as they do it solely to discourage Chinese immigration into the mines, it is a thing that is much applauded, and likewise regarded as being singularly facetious. It was in this way that he found out that when a white man robs a sluice-box (by the term white man is meant Spaniards, Mexicans, Portuguese, Irish, Hondurans, Peruvians, Chileans, etc., etc.), they make him leave the camp; and when a Chinaman does that thing, they hang him. It was in this way that he found out that in many districts of the vast Pacific coast, so strong is the wild, free love of justice in the hearts of the people, that whenever any secret and mysterious crime is committed, they say, "Let justice be done, though the heavens fall," and go straightway and swing a Chinaman. . . . And, therefore, what could have been more natural than for this sunny-hearted boy, tripping along to Sunday school, with his mind teeming with freshly learned incentives to high and virtuous action, to say to himself:

"'Ah, there goes a Chinaman! God will not love me if I do not stone him.' And for this he was arrested and put in the city jail. Everything conspired to teach him that it was a high and holy thing to stone a Chinaman."

Boys, the astonished author now concludes, will be arrested and the pious aldermen of San Francisco will be comfortable in their position, because it costs them nothing and leaves the lazy police to carry on their cowardly business with a hypocrisy that serves the white population. In case we missed the point, which we could not possibly have missed, Twain adds an asterisked footnote:

*I have many such memories in my mind, but am thinking just at present of one particular one, where the Brannan street butchers set their dogs on a Chinaman who was quietly passing with a basket of clothes on his head; and while the dogs mutilated his flesh, a butcher increased the hilarity of the occasion by knocking some of the Chinaman's teeth down his throat with half a brick. This incident sticks in my memory with a more malevolent tenacity, perhaps, on account of the fact that I was in the employ of a San Francisco journal at the time, and was not allowed to publish it because it might offend some of the peculiar element that subscribed for the paper. —EDITOR MEMORANDA (*CTSS1* 379–81)

Considering the fury with which Twain infuses a piece on boy-behavior with sardonic social protest, it hardly seems surprising that his choice to become a writer and sermonizer of low humor brought him to the brink of suicide during the period in which these sketches of youth were written, for only at that brink could a writer of this level of conviction fuse fantastic reality with literary comedy to bring about social protest.

The issue was not one that would go away easily. G. A. Sala, in "American Revisited" in 1882, offered a handful of cartoons, several attributed to *Harper's Weekly*, that developed the mistreatment of Chinese as a parallel to discrimination against Freed Negroes. Various cartoons showed the two targets in the same frame, and among them is a separate cartoon depicting a young boy kicking a Chinaman while tough guys from a saloon look on. Sala, in fact, brought Twain's writings to England in the 1860s in his collections of *Yankee Drolleries*, featuring Artemus Ward, Billings, Twain, and others as well. It is interesting to note racism and violence toward minorities at the center of attention even for a non-native observer of American humor. The fact that it pushes into Twain's tales of youth seems very reasonable, however unexpected, and even more reasonable to see how it could invest itself in him so deeply and jar so discordantly against his own recollections of his and Livy's parenting.

One final addition to the discussion also bears on Twain's depiction of ethics through stories of youth. Yuko Yamamoto proposes that Huck's interests are at risk as much or more as Jim's due to prevailing law governing the rights of children, and suggests that Huck is a legal outcast; rather than being merely a "free" boy, his situation is that of a "vagrant" (Yamamoto 23–36). He is an undesirable and a legal misfit. Yamamoto makes this subtle point clearly evident in two very minor points in *The Adventures of Tom Sawyer* (1876), first where the Welshman responds to Huck's frantic knock with the comment that Huck "ain't a name to open many doors." Later, the man welcomes Huck into his home with words that "were strange words to the vagabond boy's ears and the pleasantest he had ever heard." Huck has proven in action, without being bound into any Sunday-school definition or legal framework, that he values humanity. He is the counter-statement to Twain's earlier visions of youth, as Yamamoto brings out. Legal situations bear on him and his actions, and he is outside our approval, but he is a natural phenomenon whose morality outdistances the constraints of our Native American social hypocrisy. In our understanding of Twain's treatment of youth, Huck's status might lead us to understand that the moral homilies delivered as deadpan comedy are, in fact, more condemning than the mere froth that we could dismiss as a comic writer's playful rascality. Twain's humor has bite. We might extrapolate from this discussion to the depictions of the 1860s, that the moral status of youth is highly ambiguous in terms of personal freedom, rights, physical safety, and social action. To extrapolate from

Yamamoto's interpretation, Twain's angry distortion of ethics reflects his realism about the practical status of children in a society that damns itself.

In summary, Twain's advisories to youth are really sketches of a corrupt society subject to the irony of a pragmatic reporter. Ethics are conditional because they are conditioned by prevailing social practice in regard to the legal status of children and in regard to the tortured legal status of any dependent person as reflected in the vulnerability of minorities like Negroes and Chinese, completely reversing in criminal practice the rhetoric of freedom and equality under the law. Twain's career from his early comedy through the *Galaxy* years, and *Huckleberry Finn*, and on to the end of his life in *A Dog's Tale* (1904) and other tales of moral outrage is consistent after all. The real moral lesson for children is that in a society that tells lies to itself at its very base of instruction, justice is tortured, and anything other than an absurdist position is a lie.

16

The Adventures of Tom Sawyer

Peter Messent

In Mark Twain's own words, *The Adventures of Tom Sawyer* (1876) is "simply a hymn put into prose form to give it a worldly air" (*MTL2* 476). Youth itself, in the depictions of Tom, and the antebellum American world through which he moves are equally celebrated in the novel. The representation of the boy, the time, and the place combine to make the book an iconic text—one that has had the most extraordinary effect on the national cultural consciousness. There is little need to look far for evidence of the way the book has passed into common memory. One sign of this lies in a shared knowledge of scenes like the whitewashing of Aunt Polly's fence. Another is in the continuing recycling of Twain's characters and settings in a present-day context, nowhere more obviously than in Tom Sawyer's Island at Disneyland. As Stephen Railton puts it on his University of Virginia website, *Mark Twain in His Times*,

> In *Tom Sawyer* generations of readers have found access not just to childhood as a realm of summertime adventures, but to a mythic "once upon a time" in the national past, a place before the disruptions of industrialization, urbanization and immigration that were already beginning to transform the face of America even when M[ark] T[wain]'s novel first appeared.

Such a nostalgic view of the novel, as will later be shown, tends to obscure some of the book's more disturbing and ambiguous aspects. But it is clear just how important the subject of youth is to the book: Samuel Clemens's own youth and that of his protagonist, as well as that of the still-young and developing nation, to which both are symbiotically tied. Twain clearly based the novel on his own boyhood experience in Hannibal, Missouri (the St. Petersburg of the text) where he lived from 1839 to 1853. In the novel's preface, he speaks of Tom as being "a combination of the characteristics of three boys whom I knew," but also says that "one or two . . . of the adventures recorded . . . were experiences of my own." Tom Sawyer is not a million miles away from the boy Twain himself once was. Twain's version of his past self can never be entirely trusted but he does generally seem—to paraphrase Huck Finn—to have "mainly . . . told the truth"—though with a few stretchers. So, in *Life on the Mississippi* (1883), he recalls a "whisky-sodden tramp" burnt to death in the local jail in a fire started by matches he himself had provided: "I saw that face . . . every night for a long time afterward; and I believed myself . . . guilty of the man's death" (*LM* 549). This incident is not exactly replicated in *Tom Sawyer*, but Tom does smuggle "small comforts" to the town drunk, Muff Potter, when he is jailed for the murder of Dr. Robinson (ch. 11). And, in the manuscript of the novel, the words "burnt up the old sot" are written, suggesting such a plot turn as a possible intention and confirming the autobiographical link (Hill, "Composition," 94).

Twain refers back to his Hannibal boyhood on numerous occasions in the first two volumes of the recently published and authoritative version of the autobiography. Here, further links between his own youth and Tom's become apparent. To focus on just one: Just after the scene in which Tom resigns from the Cadets of Temperance, thus missing his chance to parade in his regalia at old Judge Frazer's funeral, the novel adds a throwaway line about "a phrenologist and a mesmerizer" visiting the village, leaving it, when they went, "duller and drearier than ever" (ch. 22). This recalls Twain's own boyhood love of performance, of taking center stage even if—as is sometimes the case with Tom—an element of fraud is involved. He remembered the "burning desire" in his mid-teens to be put under the influence of a visiting "mesmerizer," so he could "be conspicuous and show off before the public." Pretending to be hypnotized, he acted out his directed roles, "fled from snakes; passed buckets at a fire . . . made love to imaginary girls and kissed them," and so forth. He even put up with the pins members of the audience were invited to stick into him to test the depth of his hypnosis—"suffering agonies of pain" as a "conceited boy" looking "to keep up his 'reputation.'" That reputation is confirmed when the young Twain—seeing "the majestic Dr. Peake," a local celebrity, join the audience—repeated a story Peake had told of the great 1811 theater fire in Richmond, Virginia. While it is assumed he recreates this history under genuine mesmeric influence, in fact he has overheard Peake's recounting of it, as a silent and unnoticed presence, some years before (*AMT2* 297–304). This circus-side to the young Twain's nature was one that recurred at times in his later life, a liking for the taking of center stage and of melodramatic performance that is Tom Sawyer-like in the extreme, as in the Lizzie Wills affair (see Messent, *Male Friendship*, 42–45).

In *Tom Sawyer* itself, youthfulness itself constitutes a major theme. The tension between adulthood and boyhood is marked from the start of the novel's first chapter. Here, Tom takes "flight" from Aunt Polly, scrambling over the "high board fence" to "play hookey" in the spaces beyond. She, in response, muses over her "duty" and the disciplinary methods necessary to bring Tom into line: her consequent obligation to make him work the next day (Saturday) despite her knowledge that he "hates work more than he hates anything else." The adult/boy opposition is already marked here by a series of related pairings that will run through the entire book: authority versus evasion, work versus play, social confinement versus a freer space beyond, punishment and duty versus self-indulgent irresponsibility, and school-time versus holiday. Already, too, Tom's subversive potential is made clear. For not only is he generally associated with the latter term in each pairing, he also possesses the ability in some cases to transform what is defined as "adult" into its opposite.

So, in chapter 2, Tom converts the punishment of whitewashing his aunt's fence ("captivity at hard labor") into a form of "skylarking." Adopting a nonchalant pose and emphasizing the positive rather than negative aspects of his task ("Does a boy get a chance to whitewash a fence very day?"), he lures other boys into doing his work for him. Meanwhile, he "sat on a barrel in the shade close by, dangled his legs, munched his apple"—one conned from Ben Rogers in exchange for the opportunity to help in this task. Twain intrudes as narrator here to name the principle that Tom exploits: "Work consists of whatever a body is *obliged* to do, and . . . Play consists of whatever a body is not obliged to do." The fact that work and play here can be applied to the same activity suggests both Tom's ability to transform one into the other and also the general instability of the oppositions Twain sets up in the novel (something later explored). For now, it is Tom's commitment to the play principle on which the focus lies.

Tom's subversive ability to convert the routines of the adult world to the province of play is clear throughout the text. At school, the "vindictive" and sadistic "lashings" of Mr. Dobbins, the schoolteacher, metaphorically bounce off Tom in chapter 21 (see also Messent, "Discipline" and Brodhead). He pursues his own agenda in the classroom, whether making his innocent romantic advances toward Becky Thatcher or playing a desktop game with Joe Harper as they manipulate a tick—to "exercise the prisoner"—Tom has released from the percussion-cap box in his pocket (ch. 7). Later in the book, Tom and the other boys undermine Dobbins's disciplinary authority and sense of self-importance by way of a practical joke. As Dobbins performs before his village audience on "'Examination' day," drawing a map of America on a blackboard to test his geography class, a cat lowered from the garret above claws off his wig, revealing his bald head has been gilded by the sign-painter's boy, in whose home the teacher lodges. The boys thereby achieve "a dazzling victory," with the teacher this time in the role of suffering victim (ch. 21).

Tom acts similarly in regard to that other mainstay of village institutional life: the church. Church and Sunday are synonymous here. So too—for Tom Sawyer anyway, and, the assumption is, for any boy with spirit—are Church and Confined Restriction. Tom is "uncomfortable" in the more formal clothes dedicated to Sunday wear, finding "a restraint about the whole clothes and cleanliness that galled him." He hates Sunday-school "with his whole heart." While the "high-backed uncushioned" nature of the pews in which he is forced to listen to the minister's sermon symbolizes the sense of puritanical stiffness associated with the Sunday experience in general (ch. 4). Just as the "dreary time" of school-life is contrasted with Tom's playful adventuring on Cardiff Hill, "its soft green sides" bathed in "flaming sunshine" (ch. 7), so church going here is contrasted with "the seductive outside summer scenes." Bored by the sermon, Tom makes his own amusement, releasing a large "pinch-bug" (beetle). The consequent diversion caused by the yelps of the "vagrant poodle dog" that sits on the bug causes "smothered bursts of unholy mirth" in the whole congregation. It also lightens Tom's own mood, "divine service" being much improved by the "bit of variety" he has brought to it (ch. 5). Later, he takes the most solemn ritual of the church, the funeral service, and converts it to his own playful and dramatic ends, when he, Huck, and Joe Harper (all presumed drowned) stage their own resurrection—"marching up the aisle" as the congregation mourns (ch. 17). Official rites and rituals in all their forms, then, are turned upside down by Tom's boyish games.

It is, however, beyond the windows and fences of this ordered social world that youth (in Tom's guise) looks for the fullest self-expression. Cardiff Hill, Jackson's Island, the space beyond Aunt Polly's fence, even McDougal's cave, all act as territory where Tom's love of adventure, mystery, and romance can be played out to their fullest. In these places, the "captivity and fetters" of school and its like can be swapped for that sense of freedom Tom associates most strongly with Huck Finn, who "came and went, at his own free will," who did not "have to call any being master or obey anybody," who had (in Tom's eyes) "everything that goes to make life precious" (ch. 6). Boyhood play and an idyllic natural world with which it is (at best) associated come together on the summit of Cardiff Hill and on Jackson's Island. On Cardiff Hill, where "nature lay in a trance," Tom and Joe play at Robin Hood, convinced that "they would rather be outlaws a year in Sherwood Forest than President of the United States forever" (ch. 7). On Jackson's Island, the two boys, along with Huck, fry bacon, thinking it "glorious sport to be feasting in that wild free way in the virgin forest of an unexplored and uninhabited island, far from the haunts of men." Here, too, they go "whooping and prancing," frolicking naked "in the shallow limpid water of the white sand-bar," their behavior the very epitome of unrestricted boyish delight (chs. 18–20). And though Huck and Tom's hunt for the Murrell gang's buried treasure is fraught with fear and peril—for boyhood is not without its deep anxieties too—Tom's dramatic public revelation of their eventual find, "pour[ing] the mass of yellow coin upon the table," provides a fitting climax to the narrative of youthful adventure the book tells (ch. 34).

This representation of Tom Sawyer and his playful exploration of the spaces apparently beyond the boundaries of the disciplinary reach of Aunt Polly, Mr. Dobbins and their like, crucially connects with changing attitudes to youthful play in the period as a whole. In post-Civil War America industrialization and mechanization were rapidly advancing as the nation developed a modern economy. As labor (for many) became less fulfilling in their lives, so play accordingly was more valued. Michael Oriard shows how what was, in fact, an uneasy tension between labor and leisure was disguised in the popular books of boyhood (and girlhood) of the time—books that (in line with the larger needs of the emergent capitalist system) constructed a binary system, with "work and play as two halves of the ideal life," and childhood seen as "the time for play" before the serious business of living was underway (Oriard 399). This new concept of a youth/manhood divide was, according to Oriard, already current in the prewar time of the novel's setting but was firmly established by the 1870s when Twain wrote *Tom Sawyer*.

In his boy protagonist, Twain taps into the same kind of cultural understanding. For he creates—in words Oriard uses in the wider context of the boy book as a then-popular genre—an "idealized figur[e] on whom middle-class America projected its desires and fantasies, but without jeopardizing its ultimate commitment to work" (Oriard 398). Indeed, the ongoing currency of such ideas of boyhood helps to explain the book's continued appeal. For Twain shows how, even at this stage of his life, and despite all his apparent rebelliousness, Tom is a deeply conventional protagonist, already committed to the system of values of the adult world. If he is associated with "boyhood's free spirit" and with adventure and imagination, an escape from adult duty and responsibility, he is also linked to proto-capitalist attitudes and practices, depicted as an entrepreneur, an emergent businessman, rewarded at the text's end by the status, praise, and financial good fortune that symbolize conventional social acceptance and success.

Youthful play and grown-up responsibility and work are, then, categorized as separate spheres in a developing capitalist economy and, at the same time, deeply connected in their underlying assumptions. So as Twain looks back to the antebellum period in which such divisions were starting to become apparent, he illustrates how the same set of social values are finally shared by both children and adults. Tom ends the novel both a successful member of the community and a businessman and entrepreneur in chrysalis form. The whitewash scene presents him in this light, making a profit from limited resources through what might be seen as astute business practice. He tends to be duplicitous in his dealings, effectively conning the other boys into handing over their treasures, "a wily fraud" (ch. 4) in his acquisition of bible tickets, but ends up making substantial profits in each case.

Enterprise and an eye for the main chance were part and parcel of business life in Jacksonian America and even more so in the postbellum period. Tom ends up the novel with a fortune and the fact that this is most likely stolen money made from the criminal activities of John A. Murrell's notorious bandit gang seems matter for little concern. We might, retrospectively, even see an implied connection here between Tom's actions and those of a later generation of American "robber barons," Gilded Age capitalists and entrepreneurs whose excess profits, in the popular imagination, were associated with unscrupulous means. The fact that Tom gains a "simply prodigious . . . income" merely by having his money invested at "six per cent" suggests this connection, for his gain, too, is entirely dependent on the labor of others. Tom, accordingly, ends up as the hero in a traditional American success story, deeply imbued with the hegemonic values of his time and place, with a future mapped out at "the National military academy" and "the best law school in the country" (ch. 35).

The narrative ends up, then, as deeply conventional, Tom's rebellious boyhood behavior is revealed as *nothing more than play*, merely a stage in a larger trajectory of social assimilation and success. The deep attraction of the figure of Huck Finn to Twain, both in this book and his later novel, would be his status as an outsider rather than the "sanctioned rebel" that Tom reveals himself to be (Fetterley). And this is why, we can assume, Twain would write famously to William Dean Howells, on July 5, 1875, that Tom's story could, for him, go no further: "I have finished the story & didn't take the chap beyond boyhood. . . . If I went on, now, & took him into manhood, he would just be like all the one-horse men in literature" (*L6* 503).

There are, as shown above, clear connections between the 1830s and the 1840s setting of this novel and the period during which Twain wrote. If this is so, there are also vast differences. The novel, accordingly, celebrates America's own youth but can still point to certain less attractive traits there that have affected its later development. In its nostalgic recall for an earlier time, we might compare it to Henry Adams's autobiography. For Adams, looking back on his boyhood self from the vantage point of a time fifty years later, comments that "in essentials like religion, ethics, philosophy; in history, literature, art; in the concepts of all science, except perhaps mathematics, the American boy of 1854 stood nearer the year 1 than to the year 1900" (Adams 53). This comparison poses the risk of oversimplification, but it is clear that Adams's equation of the Civil War with a type of historical rupture was widely shared. Indeed, the war was the landmark event in this transition, perhaps *the* major watershed in the entire history of America, separating what were essentially small and mostly premodern frontier towns—like this fictional St. Petersburg—from the booming and expansionist modernized America of the post-Civil War period.

Twain, then, connects up *Tom Sawyer* with a sense of lost innocence and nostalgia for a simpler American time and place. So, the representation of his boy protagonist, in many ways, merges into the depiction of a particular antebellum environment. Twain was writing the novel at a time of considerable social change and tension. The 1873 financial panic triggered by the collapse of the Northern Pacific railroad had begun a five-year depression in the United States, with six thousand businesses closing in 1874 alone. The period was also one of growing industrial unrest, capped by an 1877 railroad strike with mass interclass violence on a nationwide scale that spurred fears of a second civil war. Marcia Jacobson accordingly sees the popularity of the boy book in this period as speaking "to the persistent and apparently insoluble needs" of its American audience at a time of "massive, disruptive social change"—as offering a "vicarious escape from . . . the culture that produced it" (Jacobson 4, 7, 13). The appeal of *Tom Sawyer*, both then and now, can clearly be seen in such a move to an earlier and simpler world—to a rural setting often presented in idyllic terms, to the more relaxed and intimate social patternings of an antebellum time, shifting away from adulthood and a growing contemporary sense of conditioned and regimented behavior to childhood and its romantic adventuring.

But, again, Twain's representation of more youthful American times is never that simple, containing resonant ambiguities and paradoxes. We might approach some of the book's complexities via the work of Cynthia Griffin Wolff, whose focus is not so much on the nostalgic sense of authenticity, innocence, wholeness, and security recreated in the text (and certainly responsible for one part of its readerly effect) but rather on the "darker side" of the novel, the "ominous air of violence" suffusing it (Wolff 99). This violence is mainly associated with Injun Joe, the "murderin' half-breed" who kills Dr. Robinson in the graveyard (ch. 9), threatens to "slit" the nostrils of the Widow Douglas and "notch her ears like a sow" (ch. 29), and is associated with the extremes of antisocial behavior, terror, and violent mayhem throughout the book. The spaces on the edge of the village and beyond its disciplinary borders turn, with Joe, into a nightmare realm, an area of social upset and uncontrollable violence, rather than one where the free expression of the playful self can be realized.

As Wolff and other critics have pointed out, Tom and Injun Joe are curiously twinned: in their crossing of symbolic boundaries (Joe leaps through the courthouse window in the trial scene); in their anti-authoritarian and rebellious tendencies; and in their joint presence in the (symbolic) depths of McDougal's cave, with the virginal and helpless Becky Thatcher caught between them (or, at least, so the underground symbolic triangle formed by the three characters implies). On the one side is Tom's book-led romantic adventuring; on the other, a move beyond social regulation associated with savage, unregenerate, and dangerous individualism. It is no coincidence then that Joe ends up dead, caught behind an iron door (symbolic of an encroaching industrial age) erected on the orders of Judge Thatcher, the most powerful representative of legal and social authority in the novel.

What this suggests is that the nostalgic efficacy of Twain's St. Petersburg and the idyllic youthful American world it represents depend on a good deal of literary whitewash. First, the whole matter of slavery, the black stain at the heart of antebellum southwestern culture, and one that Twain would clinically expose in later works, is covered over in this book. When Tom, dressing for Sunday school, is given a thorough washing by Mary, we are told that "when she was done with him he was a man and a brother, without distinction of color" (ch. 4). The reference here is to Josiah Wedgwood's powerfully effective antislavery medallion, "Am I not a man and a brother?" But Wedgwood's abolitionist question is converted here only to a passing joke. Moreover, the only slave playing any real part in the novel, and that a small one, is Jim—a "small colored boy" (not the adult Jim of *Huckleberry Finn* (ch. 1). Moreover, we merely assume Jim to be a slave, for his status is not explained. The institution on which the social hierarchies, even the economies, of such southwestern villages as St. Petersburg were largely based is notable then by its virtual absence, creating a view of a younger America flawed in its very essence. This is no criticism of the author. For such a picture is crucial to his purposes in a boy book, in which romance rather than realism rules the day, and where an attractive and nostalgic version of small-town life is the projected intent.

This representation—or rather, the lack of it—of slavery ties in with the depiction of "Injun Joe." If slavery gets barely a mention in an odd footnote in chapter 10, then Joe, the racial other of this text, has projected onto him, in his melodramatic representation, all the darker aspects of community life: its deepest fears and anxieties concerning renegade behavior, the antisocial denial of normative rules and regulations. Joe is an "Injun devil" whose violence, cruelty, and implied sexual threat are an implied product of his racial difference (ch. 10). For Wolff, the death of this "ruthless predator" is "an ending with no resolution at all," as Joe is simply banished from sight, mind, and text as "all too dangerous to traffic with" (Wolff 99–104). Tom's resurrection from the cave, with its symbolic connotations, is consequently presented as the prelude to the start of his useful adult career, any anxiety about his own antisocial impulses carefully put below ground with Joe's dead body. Joe then, to use Robert Tracy's words, is another spurned version of a "man and a brother," a racially other member of this developing society who is given presence only to be cast from view:

> In [Walt] Whitman's phrase "dusky demon and brother," whose brotherhood is denied and whose demonhood is exaggerated. . . . [At the end] the Indian dies and the treasure disappears into a bank—a neat and accurate symbol of the fate of the trans-Mississippi frontier. Civilization's progress exorcizes the devils, exterminates the Indians, and banks the proceeds. (Tracy, "Myth & Reality in *Tom Sawyer*," in Scharnhorst *Critical Essays* 110)

But to call this ending "no resolution at all" is incorrect. Again, Twain is not writing a realistic novel here and exactly such obfuscatory tactics are necessary if his version of a more youthful (and white) America is to retain its romantic and nostalgic effect.

As a final footnote to my essay, it is worth mentioning what happens to Tom Sawyer, or, rather, a close version of him, in Twain's later career, when his view of human and social possibility has soured. In the unfinished "Which Was the Dream?" (1897), another Tom, Thomas X, recalls another small-town rural boyhood, in Kentucky. This Tom differs from Tom Sawyer in being from a "quality" family, but like his namesake he, too, resists matriarchal discipline. Once spring comes and "all the common boys had been barefoot for as much as a week already," the eleven-year-old Tom X—in part to prove he is not under his "mother's thumb"—himself goes "barefoot, the first 'quality' boy in the town to be 'out'" (*CTSS2* 222). The context for this information, too, is significant, for Tom X is describing the start of his relationship with the then-five-year-old Alice, conducted along lines very similar to those of Tom Sawyer's boyhood romance with Becky.

In Twain's later story, however, childhood incidents are part of a more extended narrative. Tom X grows up to see distinguished service in the Mexican War of 1846–48 and becomes both an army general at a very young age and the youngest-ever elected US senator. Indeed, he would have been US president had his extreme youth not constitutionally barred him from the office. Again, we see parallels here with Tom Sawyer, though this later Tom rises even further than the earlier Tom and the glittering career Judge Thatcher foresees for him. By this later date in Twain's life, however, the idea of worldly success is blighted, transformed—partly because of his own circumstances—into a narrative of ruin and disaster. A number of details in "Which Was the Dream?" echo those in Twain's own life (Messent, *Male Friendship* 138–39). Now married and with a loving family, Tom X sees his house burn down and his wealth squandered through the misplaced trust he places in an old family friend. He then has a complete breakdown, recovering consciousness eighteen months later in a town called "Hell's Delight" in California. His family's life is transformed into one of poverty and drab anonymity.

The playful humor of Twain's 1876 novel dissipates here in the face of Twain's later pessimism both about human nature and about America, and his growing sense of the fragility of individual identity and agency. Such a re-visioning could never, however, then or later, obliterate the power and influence of his earlier book. The nostalgic glow of *Tom Sawyer* had already become, and remains, too deeply embedded in the national and transnational consciousness for that ever to happen.

Courtland P. Morris, who had been the model for Huck Finn fifty-three years earlier, looks on from the stands in Atlantic City, New Jersey, as dozens of boys fitted out with straw hats, fishing poles, and pipes compete for the role of Huck in the 1938 film adaptation of *Tom Sawyer*. Nation-wide searches for boys to portray Mark Twain's most famous characters drew out thousands of hopeful applicants, demonstrating the great popularity of Tom and Huck.

Scrapbook of Courtland P. Morris, Courtesy Kevin Mac Donnell, Austin, Texas

17

The Prince and the Pauper

Hugh H. Davis

[handwritten: basically focuses on university of novel.]

Mark Twain's *The Prince and the Pauper* (1881) proclaims in its subtitle that it is "A Tale for Young People of all Ages," suggesting the author saw the novel as being both about and for young people, with a universal appeal. Obviously, the historical tale of lookalike children features young people at its narrative center. Moreover, given the enduring popularity of the novel, both in its original form and in the many adaptations produced in the more than 130 years since its initial publication, it has remained a favorite story of many, presumably matching the author's announced audience of the young and young-at-heart. This novel of confused identities and youthful claimants that Twain published between *The Adventures of Tom Sawyer* (1876) and *Adventures of Huckleberry Finn* (1885), his two most famous novels about and for children, has been a popular story for readers. It offers a timeless tale of characters searching for understanding and place in society and provides a commentary on the nineteenth century as seen through the sixteenth century.

The dual youthful protagonists of *The Prince and the Pauper* obviously drive the story, and part of the power of this "democratic fable" comes from the fact that its condemnation of social injustice comes mostly from Edward Tudor, the yet-to-be-crowned boy king (Cox 154). As Edward walks in the pauper's footsteps, the royal's reactions to life and society provide one-half of the commentary on the nature of society, just as his doppelgänger Tom Canty's tedium and fatigue from the life at the court provide the other half. While these youthful characters serve as each other's proxies, they also serve as proxies for the readers, allowing them to see up-close the Tudor world as Twain depicts it, replete with its injustices. With children at its center, *The Prince and the Pauper* is a youth-driven take on issues of humanity, filtered through a Tudor lens.

Throughout his works, Twain writes many youth-driven stories featuring youthful characters, and, through these young protagonists, he reaches and communicates with young readers of all ages. Tom Canty and Edward Tudor easily stand alongside the likes of Huck Finn, Tom Sawyer, Joan of Arc, and even No. 44 as well-defined and strong leading characters. The use of these youthful heroes connects the novel, which is otherwise set apart from many of the works in Twain's canon by its historical and geographical setting, to the broader traditions of the author's works. Like *Pudd'nhead Wilson* (1894), *The Prince and the Pauper* is a tale of confused identity with lookalikes in swapped roles. Several of Twain's works, in fact, involve the confusion of identities, with characters assuming each other's roles, often as part of elaborate deception, and sometimes as part of youthful play. In *Huckleberry Finn*, for example, Huck fakes multiple identities throughout the novel, including pretending in the book's final section to be Tom, while Tom takes the role of his own younger half-brother, Sid. Like *Huckleberry Finn*, *The Prince and the Pauper* shows its youthful characters in a world that is stark and dangerous at times. The titular characters, who parallel Twain's most famous boy heroes, traverse this perilous world in which few adults support them.

Edward Tudor and Tom Canty are amalgamations of Huck and Tom (Blair 190). The two Toms, Huck, and Edward inhabit worlds with few adults to help them. Edward, like Huck, must navigate a strange and difficult land with only one adult companion/surrogate parent at his side. Just as Huck relies upon Jim, Edward relies upon Miles Hendon. In both cases, the adult provides protection and safety, but both youths also offer aid to their adult companions. As a slave, Jim needs the white Huck at times, and Huck's decision to save Jim from captivity drives the conclusion of that work. Miles aids and protects Edward throughout the novel, beginning by saving him from a mob. At the novel's conclusion, he is granted the rewards of an earldom and the right to sit in the presence of the king, when the child—now King Edward VI—returns the many favors that Miles extended him.

Both Huck and Tom Canty have abusive fathers; both Toms succeed through their wits and use books as a means for escape (Levy 85). Like *Tom Sawyer*, *The Prince and the Pauper* shows "an irresponsible boy moving toward responsible maturity" (Blair 49). All three novels spotlight and highlight children and show that these youths can succeed in many ways and amid a variety of circumstances, some more dire than others. All three works present boys as on educational journeys through disillusionments and initiations (Blair 49). The educational journeying marks the maturation of the boy characters. As Levy notes, while the Tudor novel might appear and even read differently from *Huckleberry Finn* and *Tom Sawyer*, *The Prince and the Pauper* "still shared the same gene pool of ideas about children" (Levy 84). All three novels depict children who learn the world and mature over the course of their adventures amid commentaries on and critiques of society, using their young protagonists as a means to deliver their social messages. Their subject matter marks their depth and potential for universal reading, particularly as these works comment on children facing a challenging world. *Tom Sawyer* is a classic story for children that can be enjoyed by readers of all ages, and in *The Prince and the Pauper* Twain crafts a novel that can be enjoyed by a similarly wide range of readers, thanks to its carefully constructed narrative revealing the idealistic aspirations of a pair of children.

Critics read *The Prince and the Pauper* as brimming with "Twain's idealism of childhood," a basic allure they see throughout his best works (Einfeld 12). They find the novel features an "appeal to the natural goodness of children" (Salomon 108) and displays Twain's belief in instinctive goodness, with a kindness of heart seen as an attribute of childhood (Blair 192). That kind instinct is especially evident in Tom Canty and Huck. However, the novel provides multiple scenes that challenge characters to maintain that natural kindness. Tom Canty struggles with the concept that the prince has a whipping boy; Prince Edward is repeatedly mistreated after leaving the castle, regularly needing Miles's protection; the Prince later learns that Miles has been dispossessed by his own brother; Edward further sees the injustice of the world in which he will ascend the throne, should his educational journeying return him properly to his rightful place. Both boys are continually ignored and mistreated for proclaiming the truth. However, Twain suggests that both, despite these events, retain their kindness and idealism, with the real King Edward's short reign particularly marked by his benevolence.

Twain's novel depicts a cruel England whose citizens suffer through and from injustice and imbalance. While both *1601* (1880) and *A Connecticut Yankee in King Arthur's Court* (1889) are set in historical (or perhaps mythic) England, these European-set works are obviously in the minority of Twain's works. However, the England of *The Prince and the Pauper* is a device through which he weaves his tale. Having visited England, he was prompted to make comparisons between it and America. He was comparing the two countries and making notes about them as he prepared the novel; Edward and Tom's world comes from this comparison (Blair 188). Though set in the sixteenth century, *The Prince and the Pauper* is a commentary on Twain's own time and the people of it. Just as *Connecticut Yankee* is less about medieval England and more about Twain's America (Cunliffe 75), so too is *The Prince and the Pauper* less about the sixteenth century and more about the nineteenth century. While some see the novel's failings in the fact that it "was about a foreign land" and not Twain's own, a larger view of the work reveals that Twain uses England as the site for his youthful protagonists' training just as he uses the Mississippi River as the site for Huck's educational journeying (Cummings 97). Europe and the United States shared a continuity in Twain's imagination when he was writing these novels (Einfield 166), and he used his settings, no matter how superficially familiar or foreign, to provide commentaries on his own contemporary society. He may have worked to write in a language evoking a sixteenth-century English milieu (or at least an artificial approximation thereof), but his consideration of Tom and Edward's challenges as claimants is voiced "in a characteristically American way" (Einfield 170); despite his painstaking research to provide authentic details for both story and setting, the novel's perspective remains "distinctly American" (Einfield 165).

Even as he recounts the fictional adventures of his Tudor-based English youthful characters, Twain is writing about his own contemporary America, just as he does throughout his works. Given that he worked on *The Prince and the Pauper* and *Huckleberry Finn* alternately, with both novels concerning related issues for children (particularly those growing up in the absence of fathers and of characters making claims on independence and growth), the presentation of Prince Edward and Tom Canty as boys who would fit into the world of Tom Sawyer and Huck Finn is not surprising. Though the anachronistic dialogue and detailed descriptions of the landscape and castles of *The Prince and the Pauper* continually remind readers that the novel is placed in a world removed from the author's nineteenth century, the crises for the English boys are not alien to the readers, particularly those familiar with Twain's other books about children.

The worlds depicted in *Tom Sawyer* and *Huckleberry Finn* are also artificial constructs. St. Petersburg is a town crafted through a lens of nostalgia and literary artisanship, and the many locations visited by Huck and Jim on their raft, while rooted in reality, are also fictional approximations of river towns. Though they are not as far removed from Twain's present as the England in *The Prince and the Pauper* (also rooted in reality and Twain's historical research), the locations in the American-set novels are also fictional inventions. When he writes about Huck and Tom, with their respective novels occurring closer to his own present time, the setting (both place and time) are clearly meant to evoke the author's views of America and its citizenry. Though he goes to great lengths to give the double leads of *The Prince and the Pauper* their historical place (and, through his preface and its talk of whether the events may have happened, granting them a type of pseudo-mythic/legendary status), they are also products of their time of composition. On first glance, the boy-king Edward and his impoverished lookalike may seem odd representatives of Twain's age, but his use of them in their roles as young men who aspire to happiness makes them sort of everymen (or perhaps "every children") for their readers.

Though they may seem odd candidates to represent the average young reader, Prince Edward and Tom Canty are presented as universal characters to the reader. Their dichotomous relationship—the formally trained Prince and the imaginatively driven pauper—evokes the similar pairing of the obviously different characters of Tom Sawyer and Huck Finn, a pair often read as representative of children and as presumably unprejudiced observers of—and commentators upon—the world around them (Carpenter and Prichard 4–5). Huck and Tom are distinct characters, but readers can relate in some way to one or both of them. Similarly, Tom Canty and Prince Edward are distinct, and readers can find ways to relate to either or both of that pair. The universality of the characters is partly created through Twain's adjustment of their ages. In *Tom Sawyer*, neither Tom's nor Huck's age is directly stated, allowing the boys to fit the imaginative ages of the readers. Similarly, in *The Prince and the Pauper*, Twain avoids mentioning dates that remind readers that the boys should be under ten years old (Blair 398), allowing them to remain relatable to all readers. Though Twain increases Edward's age by three years to enhance the drama and adventure of his story (*CCMT* 375), the author is careful not to dwell upon this point. The result is that both Edward, England's boy king, and Tom, his poor double, are, in effect, ageless in a story for young people of all ages. Their mutability in the hands of Twain makes Edward and Tom, like Tom and Huck, dual characters with universal appeal who represent vibrant childhood in general.

One effect of this universality, perhaps in spite of the novel's seemingly highly specific setting and background, is that the text is one of the author's most often retold tales, with many retellings changing the location and time of the tale. Shortly after its publication, *The Prince and the Pauper* was quickly transformed into a theatrical production, and Twain even performed an amateur play of the text with his daughters at home (*MTEncy* 591). Since first becoming a theatrical production, the novel has been transformed into children's books, records, comic books, and, perhaps most significantly, film and television adaptations. The story is one of Twain's most frequently adapted works. To date, more than fifty adaptations of the novel have been produced for film and television. The first, a two-reel silent abridgement of the text made in 1909, even featured Twain on film for one of the only times in his life (*MTEncy* 500). It began the long cinematic history for *The Prince and the Pauper*. The history of these retellings is an odd assortment of productions. Many, such as Alexander Korda's full-length silent film (1920) and William Keighley's sound film (1937), are traditional presentations of the novel. Keighley's film, the first major Hollywood studio version, is a lavish, big-budget rendition, casting its story in the swashbuckling tradition of adventure films and highlighting the heroics of Miles Hendon (Errol Flynn). Though this film tweaks the plot, making Hertford a menace to the pretending Tom Canty and the captain of the palace guard a threat to Edward, it presents the story of its title characters (played by real-life twins Bobby and Billy Mauch) earnestly. Marketed as a film for audiences of all ages and perhaps ignoring the sixteenth-century English setting, this film, like many from Warner Bros. in the 1930s, takes a populist stance and defends the proletariat, as the prince learns the plight of the working class, just as the pauper sees the flaws of royalty. Twain's novel, already an anthem for the needs of the underdog, finds in its cinematic incarnation a strong case for compassionate rule and understanding.

Several of the cinematic incarnations continue the tradition of a straightforward adaptation set in Tudor England, with perhaps the most notable example coming with the swashbuckling comedy *Crossed Swords* (1977), which ages the title characters considerably by casting nineteen-year-old Mark Lester as the doppelgängers, allowing an enhanced romantic angle and a seemingly more-adult story that also highlights slapstick-style comedy. However, there have also been several more radical reinterpretations of the novel, as well as many re-fittings of the text, which shoehorn the story to fit into the framework of a preexisting series, but the effect with both is one of maintained prevalence for the novel. With each new version, a new audience is found, and the novel finds new readers. As many versions simplify the plot into a variation of Aesop's "Town Mouse & Country Mouse," the story can be warped, offering a new conclusion (one that ignores almost completely the resolution for Canty and often for Miles Hendon) and perhaps misrepresenting the novel's social commentary. These simplifications of *The Prince and the Pauper* often occur in youth-oriented retellings. The re-fittings of the novel are often somewhat gimmick-driven, offering a previously unknown lookalike for an established character and then switching identities as chaos ensues. However, each version does keep the story alive in its own way, and, as many of the re-fittings connect the story to children's series, young viewers are introduced to the novel.

It is tempting to declare the reshaping of the text to be an invention of more recent years, concocted as the text neared its century mark, but cinematic history suggests otherwise, showing that filmmakers have long looked to adopt and adapt. In 1940, MGM produced "Alfalfa's Double" as part of the *Our Gang* series of short comedies, the first of many times that *The Prince and the Pauper* was adapted in a bare-bones way. Since this film short, Twain's novel has surfaced many times as a vehicle for pop-culture icons, appearing as installments featuring such television series and characters as the *Monkees*, *The Rocky and Bullwinkle Show*, the *Simpsons*, *Johnny Bravo*, *Garfield*, *Wishbone*, *Phineas and Ferb*, *Veggie Tales*, Mickey Mouse, *Fame*, Barbie, and even Ringo Starr. Some of these appropriations of the text reveal and even influence the perception of the novel, such as versions broadcast as episodes of *Shirley Temple Theatre* and *Happily Ever After: Fairy Tales for Every Child*—both programs devoted to adaptations of fairy tales—as they take to heart the novel's preface and present the story as a timeless legend. These episodes, especially, mark the story as belonging to children, or, at least, viewers of all ages.

[handwritten margin note: popular adaptations]

Like its twin titular characters, who recognize each other because of their common looks and despite their disparate upbringings, *The Prince and the Pauper* is, at once, familiar to viewers and readers. Whereas the first images conjured by the name "Mark Twain" might be of Huck floating on a raft or of Tom's not whitewashing a fence, the best-known story details may very well belong to this text. Mark Twain's novel involves discovering the reality of a mistaken identity, so readers continue to come to the novel, and many both recognize elements of the story and discover new ideas within its pages. This novel of two boys and their educational journeying is well remembered by readers as a tale of identity and growth. The continued legacy of *The Prince and the Pauper* is one of a familiar children's tale, both a story of and for young people, one that might—in the words of the book's preface—find "fathers transmitting it to the sons and so preserving it." The legacy of this "Tale for Young People of All Ages" is one of repeated retellings and re-readings, and fans of all ages can feel comfortable and confident they are turning to a story they have known since childhood, know well, and will know for ages to come.

[handwritten margin note: again universality]

18

Adventures of Huckleberry Finn

Andrew Levy

To best comprehend the relationship between Mark Twain's *Adventures of Huckleberry Finn* (1885) and youth, one must think like Edgar Allan Poe's detective C. Auguste Dupin—another memorable nineteenth-century original—does in "The Purloined Letter" by looking for the answer in plain sight. One cannot say the topic of childhood and *Huckleberry Finn* is something new, as that is among the most ridiculous things one could possibly say about the book. For much of the twentieth century, *Huckleberry Finn* was arguably *the* book for American children, and Huck was "America's child" (Lane 3). It was read by tens of millions of people and was arguably the most often-taught American book in postwar American schools (Applebee 27–32). It was translated into numerous film, radio, and television productions often starring iconic boy actors such as Mickey Rooney and Elijah Wood. It was adapted into numerous abridged editions, and cartoon after cartoon, all over the world. And references to a "Huck Finn childhood" still appear on editorial pages, and in the promotional materials of summer camps. It is, invariably, an "innocent," outdoor childhood, free from school and grown-ups, and as such largely resistant to interpretation.

At the same time, the idea that *Huckleberry Finn* might be something more—a serious book, a great book, a turbulent, controversial book—did, obviously, take hold. That discussion simply avoided the issue of children. As critics and biographers praised the novel as a stylistic and moral masterpiece, they also labeled Twain as "arrested" (Brooks 14). His ability to transcend "meaningless conventions" (Shelden 215) when speaking with children, lauded in his day, was defined after his death as a tragic failing. Similarly, as the book became a civic artifact, celebrated by politicians internationally and then reconstituted as a site of controversy, the book's conflicted vision of race occupied the foreground of most discussions. That there might be a politically interesting book about children—or that the "controversial" book about race, and the "innocent" one about children might share some cultural DNA—was a marginal consideration.

To claim that *Huckleberry Finn* is a serious book about childhood, then—a book as ambitious about childhood as about race, at least—does not require any discovery. It only requires turning the *letter* inside out. In fact, the prevalence of the idea that *Huckleberry Finn* was a "celebration" of "innocent" childhood should have told us that this was just the place to look for buried treasure. Drifting amid the corpses (thirteen, by most counts), the suicidal ideation ("as a general thing," Huck tells us, "it makes a body wish *he* was dead . . ."), the child abuse ("I used to be scared of him all the time," Huck says of Pap, "he tanned me so much"), the "deadly dull" schools and churches, as well as the genuine lightness, and the deep, deep empathy, we should have guessed long ago that *Huckleberry Finn* was no simple portrait of American childhood (chs. 1, 5, 22).

Over the past two decades, however, there have been three shifts in intellectual sentiment, and in resources, that have reshaped how *Huckleberry Finn*'s approach to childhood can be regarded. First has been the rise of the field of childhood studies, within which the idea of "youth" as a cultural construction is as vital as the notion in other fields that race and gender are like constructions. In this view, *Huck*'s moment, the mid-Victorian, was a watershed when modern views on parenting came into focus—and Huck, far from living an ideal childhood, was experiencing the kinds of social anomie that modern social scientists regard (and acclaim Twain for identifying with such clarity) as the markers of abused children, children of alcoholics, even children likely to have criminal adulthoods.[1]

Second has been the recent, rapid evolution of the young-adult fiction marketplace, which has helped blur the century-old distinction between children's and "serious" fiction—recreating, to some extent, the publishing milieu of the mid-Victorian, when authors like Twain faced the same issues that modern authors such as Michael Chabon and Isabel Allende do as they move between "adult" and "young adult" genres. And third has been the happy issue by the University of California Press, in 2014, of significant previously unpublished Twain materials in *A Family Sketch and other Private Writings*— which reveal a curious father recording the thoughts and language of his children with a scholar's care, and reflecting upon parenthood in ways that overlapped, inevitably, with his published work.

The net effect of these developments has been to bring our time and Twain's closer to one another: to make legible a personal and public history set in the

Victorian era, not the antebellum, wherein an inventive author might think deeply about children and might write something designed to reach both those children and their parents in rich ways. Twain had an epic memory and drew wonderfully upon his past, but the notion that was *all* he did became so canonical—Franklin D. Roosevelt called Hannibal, Twain's hometown, the "cradle of the chronicles of buoyant boyhood" (*AHF* cxxxviii)—that it obscured the fact he was also thinking about childhood in non-nostalgic terms and creating something genuinely new in the history of childhood and literature.

What, then, might a reading of *Huckleberry Finn* attuned to these concerns look and feel like? One might start with the thing hiding in plain sight by considering if—amid all the creative impulses that inspired *Huckleberry Finn*— what Twain wanted most was to bring a child's voice to life. He told William Dean Howells this, the summer in 1876 when he began writing—that his main regret about *The Adventures of Tom Sawyer* (1876) was that it was not written in the first person (*MTHL* 91). Also, Twain devoted much of "A Record of the Small Foolishnesses of Susie and 'Bay' Clemens (Infants)"—composed, intriguingly, over the same time span he wrote *Huckleberry Finn*, 1876 to 1884— to a verbal record of his three daughters, Susy, Clara, and Jean. And he did not merely find their language "cute." Instead, he described their literally childish variants of standard English as self-aware, even possessing a "discriminating *exactness*" (*FSk* 78). It is the same bedrock belief in the conscious artistry of a child's voice that would make *Huckleberry Finn* possible.

Equally important, Twain's affinity in *Huckleberry Finn* for a child's voice overlapped with his affinity for a child's perspective, which he intuitively felt was undervalued. Much has been written about the relationship between *Huckleberry Finn* and slavery, the failure of Reconstruction and the rise of Jim Crow. The degree and clarity of Twain's commitment on race remains a vital topic for anyone who loves (or hates) the book. At the same time, a quick review of newspapers in Twain's era reveals that the issue of childhood occupied almost as many front pages as did race matters. Child mortality, labor, homelessness, and illiteracy were the flashpoints of other reform debates—debates that Twain would later enter with passion. That children were not well heard in the nation's capitals—and that the literature addressed to children was sanctimonious and echoed adult interests—were driving inspirations for many of Twain's humorous sketches in the 1860s and 1870s. The titles alone attest to his yearning for subversion on the issue of children and moral education: "The Story of the Bad Little Boy That Bore a Charmed Life," for instance; or "The Story of the Good Little Boy Who Did Not Prosper."

But *Huckleberry Finn* was new. Rather than acting as "ambassador," as he once called himself, between adults and children (Shelden 161), he gave up the pen to the child. In so doing, he expanded his artistic and political ambitions. Start with those opening words, "You don't know about me." Reading the entire opening sentence at normal reading speed, this lead phrase might be missed, its challenge to the reader—implicitly, an adult, as what child would address another child this way—blunted. Chapter 1 of *The Adventures of Tom Sawyer* opens with a similar callout: Aunt Polly cannot find Tom while wearing her "state pair," the glasses she wears for "style," and which cannot be "looked *through*" to locate something as "small . . . as a boy." The same impulse catalyzes both books: a belief that children are waiting to be discovered, but that our favored lenses are inadequate to the task.

From that point forward, the first pages of *Huckleberry Finn* unfold remarkably. Twain's efforts are restless and polyglot, as always—but there are many, many passages in which he adopts a child's sensibility with extraordinary results. Note, for instance, the scene in chapter 1 in which Huck is scolded for being "fidgety," a scene cited by modern scholars such as David Nylund comparing Huck's restlessness to that found in present-day children diagnosed with attention deficit disorders: "Miss Watson would say, 'Don't put your feet up there, Huckleberry,' and 'Don't scrunch up like that, Huckleberry—set up straight.'"

We are placed so thoroughly within Huck's perspective that we do not see the fidgeting that creates the scolding—it is as normal to us as it is to him. As a result, the scolding of adults seems as arbitrary to us as it does to him. These moments, these spaces, are everywhere: When Huck sees Boggs shot by Colonel Sherburn in chapter 21, and scrambles to get "a good place by the window" to watch him die, Huck does not think twice about his voyeurism and violence: it, too, is intuitive for him.

It is these gaps—the creation of a child's perspective through the absence of signifiers, those absences providing a detailed roadmap of the alienation between children and adults—that makes a "serious" reading of *Huckleberry Finn* on youth sometimes as hard to find as a "serious" reading of *Huckleberry Finn* on race proved for earlier generations, yet equally as available. In fact, a fresh reading of *Huckleberry Finn* attuned to youth would pause often where most readings do not now pause. For example, at the way Huck feels "like I would die" when Mary Jane Wilks places her hand over his (ch. 28). Or, conversely, Tom's shaming of Aunt Sally by kissing her on the lips and saying that "everybody" told him to (ch. 33). Another possible pause might be at the way Huck intuitively uses the

*pause
to
read
as youth
import*

same language to describe his feelings about institutions like school and actual physical abuse. Contrarily, such a reading would also pause where Twain calls out to parents: When an adult casually contemplates an empathic approach to children ("spos'n *I* was a boy," one mother observes in chapter 41), for instance, or sees (rightly) conspiracy in youthful efforts to overturn the grown-up world— "So it was you," Aunt Sally exclaims to Huck and Tom, at novel's end, "that's been making all this trouble" (ch. 42).

In addition, familiarity with the history of childhood reveals a satire on childrearing as sharp and relevant as familiarity with Reconstruction reveals an allegory on race relations. As Twain composed *Huckleberry Finn*, the idea of "childhood" in America was undergoing a significant transformation. On a variety of stages, childhood was becoming standardized and professionalized. This was the age when the number of doctors specializing in children exploded, when shared spaces like public parks altered the face of cities and towns, when compulsory education laws were approved nationwide, and when legislators for the first time argued over funding a federal education system that would reach children of all races, religions, and classes.

Simultaneously, this was also when certain anxieties about children entered the foreground of American life. We think we are the first generation to raise children obsessed with violent popular culture or to witness children as agents of violence themselves. But the Victorians were inured to stories of children committing crimes inspired by popular "dime novels"; newspapers printed jailhouse interviews with teenage killers. Victorian academics argued that a period of wildness was a normal part of growing up. But newspapers cried about a "bad boy" crisis, on the one hand and lamented, on the other, that those children in those new schools were losing touch with nature, with their families, and with some ineffable innocence that marked the childrearing of earlier generations (see *IE*; Mailloux).

In turn, *Huckleberry Finn* reverberated wildly amid these Victorian debates—a fact largely lost on modern readers. Tobacco was considered a huge threat to the health and morals of American children. Wasting no time whatsoever, Twain makes Huck a defiant smoker on the book's third page. Truancy was considered as the most punishable of teenage sins, and Huck, too, makes his preference clear on this topic. That said, the newspapers (such as the *New York World*) that dismissed Huck as "Mark Twain's Bad Boy" missed half the point (*World*, 2 Mar. 1885). Huck is also attuned to nature, and resists the one major character in the book (Tom, of course) who cannot tell the difference between real life and pop life. Half the time, Huck is the kind of child for whom compulsory education laws were passed and for whom work farms were built. And half the time, he is the model that education reformers (then and now) aspired to have all children emulate (see Levy).

In this contradiction, of course, lies Twain's brilliance on the subject—in his refusal to vote a "straight ticket" (*AMT2* 319), as he often said of himself. *Huckleberry Finn* was not intended to placate any agenda on how to raise children. Twain himself was deeply ambivalent. He respected his wife Olivia's well-organized childrearing style, for instance. But he undermined it often: "Mamma loves morals," Susy reportedly said, "papa loves cats" (*AMT2* 224). And when expected to practice discipline himself—corporal punishment, in particular—he was mortified. Instead of spanking Jean, he "fraternized with the enemy" (*AMT2* 223). *Huckleberry Finn* recognizes the dualism implied in those words: that children and parents were enemies in generational conflict. However, the conflict was often as false as that between black and white. For Twain, the gains Victorians made in the humane treatment of children—which shape our consensus today—were marred by the paternalistic philosophy that treated children like inferior adults to be molded alike into the same mass-produced shape.

Longstanding efforts to universalize Huck as "America's child" miss some of the beauty of Twain's nonconforming vision. All American childhoods were not and are not alike. On the semi-autobiographical level, Huck was based on neither African-American children from the South nor laboring immigrant children in the cities, nor middle-class children in those newly organized public schools. He was based on the frontier children of the mid-nineteenth century, whom observers saw as nomadic, profane, and numb to violence: "At two o'clock in the morning a highway Robber was hung on a large pine tree. After breakfast we went to see him. At ten o'clock preaching ... at two o'clock Sunday school. At three o'clock a foot race," wrote one such girl from Montana in 1865, in a tone as deadpan as anything Huck manages (Graff 379).

Simultaneously, however, Twain was channeling his own children, home-schooled in Europe and in New England, surrounded by family and servants—a most un-Huck-like upbringing, seemingly. Line up "Small Foolishnesses" with *Huckleberry Finn*, read them side by side (as Twain wrote them side by side), and the echoes are unmistakable. Repeatedly, Twain marks Clara and Susy's dark humor, their bluesiness. "Mamma, what is it all for?" Susy asks in several variants (*FSk* 77). These traits emerge in Huck's voice, of course, especially when his loneliness and dissonant spirituality rise to the book's surface: "If a breeze fans along and quivers the leaves, it makes you feel mournful, because you feel like it's spirits whispering—spirits that's been dead ever so many years—and you always think they're talking about *you*" (ch. 32). Twain even admires Clara's use of the adjectives "weary" and "lonesome" to describe a baby's cry (*FSk* 82). He has Huck meditate upon the right sound to call "lonesomest" as well (and settle upon "the dim hum of a spinning wheel" (ch. 32).

In fact, if one reads "Small Foolishnesses" alongside *Huckleberry Finn*, one will see how clearly Twain viewed unconventional religiosity and idiosyncratic self-expression as signs of a healthy child. Just as Susy spends much of "Small Foolishnesses" finding her own way to talk to God—finally telling her mother that "you would not approve of the way I pray now" (*FSk* 81)—so, too, does Huck's moral development famously peak when he ironically asks God for the courage to turn in Jim, and discovers instead that "You can't pray a lie" (ch. 31). And just as Huck chooses truancy over school, Susy and Clara teach themselves to read English against the wishes of their parents who wanted them to learn German first. Twain raved about their independence in so doing: "Nobody has given her an instant's assistance," he exulted of Clara (*FSk* 80). That tells us just how strongly he believed that childrearing was a complex, sometimes passive, and often shapeless act.

Seen through this prism, in fact, many of the flaws conventionally ascribed to *Huckleberry Finn* take on new light. They reflect efforts to give form to this formless and intersectional vision of childhood. Twain wrote in "A Family Sketch" that children grew up haphazardly: "Mamma, or the school or the pulpit" might get the "credit . . . if it be of a creditable nature," he added, but "countless outside unconscious and unintentional trainers do the real work" (*FSk* 29). And he wrote *Huckleberry Finn* like a bildungsroman whose very form reflected not the false linearity of conventional views of parenting, but this excited, atomized vision of how children really grow up.

In this context, the book's haphazard plot is the point: It demonstrates how a child raises himself via contrasts and contexts that flirt just behind the surface and rarely make themselves available (in the book, as in real life, as Twain notes) for analysis and reproduction. That Miss Watson refused to let Huck smoke while she herself takes snuff galls Huck; "that was all right," he sneers, "because she done it herself" (ch. 1). It signals to him that she might be a hypocrite in other ways, too—such as respecting family in the abstract but planning to sell Jim away from his wife and daughter. Likewise, as Myra Jehlen has observed, Huck appears to take Judith Loftus's lessons about how the difference between a boy and a girl is a matter of how one throws a lead lump or threads a needle—that is, all performance—and apply it to his relationship with Jim (see Jehlen). Such a reading has been used to illustrate Twain's integrative vision: What applies to gender applies to race (ch. 11). But such a vision also aligns with what some modern educational theorists describe as the dynamic, unpredictable reality of children and growth: We learn by accident, but we learn.

Similarly, the closing section of the book, the "evasion," has been excoriated for decades by those who believe that Twain subverts the moral arc on race he created in earlier chapters. After having vowed to free Jim or "*go to hell*" in chapter 31—the book's high point, in many readings, Huck does not prevent Tom from soon afterward turning Jim's escape into a burlesque wherein the slave is entrapped by a boy's fantasy. A fresh reading of that section, however, might acknowledge its many pages devoted to the destruction of a middle-class slaveholding household by children, twinned with its critique of corporal punishment (Aunt Sally "sluicing out coffee with one hand and cracking the handiest child's head" with the other, for instance [ch. 37]). The debate on race in those closing sections does not recede by recognizing this material on youth but is illuminated by it. A story about the failure of American adults to raise their children humanely and wisely is being told *inextricably* from a second story about endemic and cyclical racism. It is not that one story is "serious" and one is "innocent." It is the shared and complicated outrage we should feel about both that matters.

In fact, the achievement of *Huckleberry Finn* is that it offers us the opportunity to see where our childrearing practices interact with our national politics—a conversation we rarely have, and one we defy having by maintaining that *Huckleberry Finn* was a light-hearted book about children and a deep one elsewhere. It is the same Twain who flirts with race-blind structures—Huck and Jim "free and easy" (ch. 18) on the raft—that flirts with a holistic vision of childhood as a fluid, autodidactic realm. And it is the same Twain who displaces Jim from that raft into the pseudo-slavery of Tom's imaginings that also morosely recognizes the likelihood that official institutions will tightly control childhood, whether or not they have earned the right to do so. When Huck says he will "light out for the Territory" rather than be "sivilized," he means many things: But he means, first and foremost, that an older generation cannot teach him anything (ch. The Last). It is a line written by a parent to parents, and it is meant to sting.

Note

1 See, for instance Elizabeth Prioleau, "'That Abused Child of Mine': Huck Finn as the Child of an Alcoholic," *Essays on Arts and Sciences* 22 (Oct. 1993): 85–98; Maureen Donohue Smith, "Failed Families and the Crisis of Connectedness in *Huckleberry Finn*," in *Huck Finn: The Complete Buffalo & Erie County Public Library Manuscript—Teaching and Research Digital Edition* (Buffalo, NY: Buffalo & Erie County Public Library, 2002); Michael J. Kiskis, "Huckleberry Finn and Family Values," *This Is Just to Say: NCTE Assembly on American Literature* 12, no. 1 (Winter 2001): 1–7. Other important books and articles that explore *Huckleberry Finn* using a childhood studies approach include Beverley Lyon Clark, *Kiddie Lit: The Cultural Construction of Children's Literature in America* (Baltimore: Johns Hopkins University Press, 2003); Kenneth B. Kidd, *Making American Boys: Boyology and the Feral Tale* (Minneapolis: University of Minnesota Press, 2004); Keith M. Opdahl, "You'll Be Sorry When I'm Dead: Child-Adult Relations in *Huck Finn*," *Modern Fiction Studies* 25, no. 4 (Winter 1979–80): 613–24.

19

Pudd'nhead Wilson

Debra Ann MacComb

Mark Twain's novel *Pudd'nhead Wilson* (1894) chronicles the far-reaching effects passionate mother-love has on the history of a small but prosperous Mississippi riverfront town, Dawson's Landing, and its black and white, slave and free, inhabitants. In 1830, Roxy, a virtually white slave woman, bears a son, Chambers, fathered by a member of the local "First Family of Virginia" aristocracy. According to the legal norms of the times, that one-thirty-second part African-American boy, like his mother, is a slave. Remarkably, on the same day and in the same household, another boy, Tom Driscoll, is born to Roxy's masters, the socially prominent Percy Driscolls. Although the babies share a birthday and almost indistinguishably similar blond, blue-eyed looks, Tom's future is filled with promise while Chambers can anticipate only servitude. As caretaker of both babies after Tom's mother dies, Roxy seizes the opportunity to switch them in their cradles, rewriting their identities and fates to ensure that her own beloved son—now the false Tom Driscoll and destined to become her master—will never have to endure "being sold down the river."

Trained to assume their new social places, the changelings would live out the fates Roxy's action has determined for them with no one the wiser, if it were not for unexpected circumstances that intervene. A gruesome murder, ostensibly meaningless fingerprint impressions, and the savvy detective work of David "Pudd'nhead" Wilson changes the boys' destinies. Although the story unfolds in early nineteenth-century antebellum South, the novel critiques the prevailing late-nineteenth-century essentialist view of race that credited nature rather than nurture for the social, intellectual, and moral development of youth.

In the decade before the publication of *Pudd'nhead Wilson*, well-respected physiognomist Joseph Simms urged parents to "train up a child in the way he should go," announcing an educational theory that would seem to match that found in *Pudd'nhead Wilson's Calendar*. If "training is everything" (*PW* ch. 5), influences of nurture outweigh any other factors on the child's way to "virtue, wealth, and honour" (Simms 276). Ironically, however, the "highly popular" (Burrows 10) Simms contends in *Physiognomy Illustrated* (1887), a work that saw eight editions, that nature—biological makeup and socio-historical condition— in fact trumps nurture for individuals belonging to those races whose "ancestors . . . have been in the path of progress only a few years." Indeed, such individuals "are not susceptible of more than small attainments" (Simms 281). To underline his point, Simms includes an arresting illustration comparing the faces of two school-age children, a "White Boy" and a "Negro Boy" (Simms 282). Beneath the white child's picture, representing for Simms the very image of "Young America," a lengthy caption details prodigious feats of memory and recitation at a mere three-and-one-half years of age.

The space beneath the picture of the "Negro Boy" is blank. Orison J. Stone of Boston—for such is the "White Boy's" name and place of residence—meets the reader's gaze directly, while the "Negro Boy," lacking those signal attributes of personhood, looks away. He is as generalized a being as the Stone boy is individualized, a type rather than an actual child, a type that draws a blank. And true to type, the "Negro Boy" looms large if not menacingly next to Orison; he is the product of "forefathers . . . who cultivated only their animal passions" and

White Boy.   Orison J. Stone, of Boston, who   Negro Boy.
learned his letters at three years of age,
and could repeat a large book from memory
when three years and six months old.

Joseph Simms, Physiognomy Illustrated (1887)

who lack therefore "the capacity for civilization" (Simms 281). When in 1892, Homer Plessy, a white "Negro," boarded an interstate train in Louisiana, took a seat in the whites-only car, and announced to the conductor that he was colored, he intentionally challenged a state's right to label one citizen "white" and another "colored." Buttressed by the authority theories like Simms's assumed, the US Supreme Court articulated the separate-but-equal principle in *Plessy v. Ferguson* (1896) with the argument that law could not "eradicate racial instincts or abolish distinctions based on physical difference."

Pudd'nhead Wilson, like other Twain novels that take up "the matter of Hannibal," links the author's present to his past experience and tenders the always present if implicit question about the civility and humanity of so-called American "civilization." In the case of *Pudd'nhead Wilson*, the dehumanizing theories of racial inferiority developed to disenfranchise blacks from the social and political life of post-reconstruction America recall his boyhood experience of men, women, and children who, as human property, lived precarious existences dependent on the will or whim of a white master. In this last respect, slaves and children have their tremendous vulnerability in common: Both are helpless in the face of adult and institutional power that is remote, frequently frightening, self-serving, and absolute.

Children will, with any luck, grow into the relative safety of adulthood, not so slaves. Although Clemens recalled, "In my schoolboy days I had no aversion to slavery. I was not aware that there was anything wrong about it" (*AMT1* 212), slavery nevertheless left deep impressions in him that suggest pain, confusion, and the child's sense of powerlessness. Unable to recall ever seeing a slave auction in Hannibal, he believed, in retrospect, that its absence in his memory was due to the fact that such events were "a commonplace spectacle, and not an uncommon or impressive one." The sight, however, of "a dozen black men and women chained together lying in a group on the pavement, waiting shipment to a Southern slave-market" remained vivid, no doubt because they "had the saddest faces I ever saw" (*MTB* 48). Another incident that stayed in his memory, "clear and sharp, vivid and shadowless" concerns a young boy named Sandy, who had been brought from Maryland, "away from family and friends," and sold in Missouri (*AMT1* 212). John Clemens hired the child from his owner to do household chores, but Sandy's "trifling little blunders and awkwardnesses" frequently provoked his father into "cuffing" him (*SCOH* 75). Although Sandy was ever "a cheery spirit, innocent and gentle, and the noisiest creature that ever was," Sam once angrily petitioned his mother to stop Sandy's loud, inveterate singing. His mother's reply humanized the slave boy for the "out of temper"

used
often

youth: "When he sings, it shows that he is not remembering . . . but when he is still, I am afraid he is thinking. . . . He will never see his mother again. . . . If you were older, you would understand me; then that friendless child's noise would make you glad." His mother's words "went home, and Sandy's noise was not a trouble to me anymore" (*AMT1* 212).

Earlier in Sam's boyhood, the Clemens family had owned a slave woman named Jenny—"the only slave we ever owned in my time" (*AMT1* 471). She traveled with the family from Tennessee to Missouri and, as Ron Powers notes, undoubtedly nursed Sam through his sickly infancy and young childhood "and likely saved him from drowning once in Bear Creek" (Powers, *Dangerous Water* 122). Despite her long service to the family, the implacable John Clemens sold her in 1840 to a speculator who had a reputation for cruelty; whether he did so because Jenny had taken a whip from Jane Clemens's hands (Levy 22) or to repair the family's desperate financial situation (Powers, *Dangerous Water* 122), she was taken south, "down the river," the worst possible fate for a slave. That Jenny's sale had made an impression on the five-year-old Sam is evident in notes in "Villagers of 1840-3," which states that she "was seen years later, a [chambermaid] on a steamboat" (Powers, *Dangerous Water* 122), thus establishing a link between her and the fictional Roxy, prime mover of the *Pudd'nhead Wilson* plot. Roxy, too, works as a chambermaid on a Mississippi River steamboat. Clemens's horror at the individual tragedies created by the slave trade resonates when he recalls an experience that devastated John Briggs, a childhood friend whose father sold a young slave down the river for striking his son; in fact, the reverse was true: Briggs had hit the slave child. Traumatized by his complicity in the slave boy's fate, he "could never bring himself to confess" the truth of "something so shameful" to his father (*AMT1* 627–28). It is the terrible helplessness and hopelessness at the threat of being "sold down the river" that generates the plot of *Pudd'nhead Wilson*, galvanizing Roxy, a biracial slave, to take desperate measures to preserve her son from ever realizing that fate.

Pudd'nhead Wilson combines a detective plot with a changeling plot to question the reliability of our sensory perceptions in a world constructed by social, scientific and legal fictions. The detective plot features David Wilson, a lawyer who is pronounced a "pudd'nhead" because of an unfortunate remark he once made; his odd hobby of collecting fingerprints confirms that title. Wilson's hobby nevertheless provides the evidence to solve a murder case and restore to their "proper" social positions two individuals switched in their infant cradles. In *Pudd'nhead Wilson*, Hannibal becomes Dawson's Landing, a Missouri town that turns its quaint, flower-bedecked, and self-satisfied face to the Mississippi, and owes its existence to the "rich, slave-worked grain and pork country back of it" (*PW* ch. 1). The careful division in the town between front and back is, of course, also the division between "white" and "black," a line that the town's foremost citizens officially police to maintain racial boundaries.

Roxy is "of majestic form and stature . . . very fair, with the rosy glow of vigorous health in her cheeks" and, indeed, "as white as anybody." This description undermines the idea of "black" slavery, embodying as Roxy does the unofficial and unacknowledged truth that generations of miscegenation undergird the town's slave economy. "Only one-sixteenth of her was black," but it "outvoted the other fifteen parts and made her a Negro." When she has a son who is "thirty-one parts white" and endowed with "blue eyes and flaxen curls," it is clear that the color line has been breached once again. Coincidentally, Roxy's son Chambers ("no surname—slaves hadn't the privilege") is born on the same day as his master's blue-eyed, golden-haired son. That boy, Thomas à Becket Driscoll, the long-awaited son of Percy Northumberland Driscoll and nephew of Dawson's Landing's "chief citizen," Judge York Leister Driscoll, is ushered into the world only to lose his mother a week after his birth (*PW* ch. 1–2). Roxy thus becomes "mother" to both.

a little too much p. sum

The confusion caused by the faux twins' remarkable physical resemblance is dispelled only by the clothing each infant wears. As befitting a Driscoll, heir to an "old Virginian ancestry" (*PW* ch. 1), Tom wears "ruffled soft muslin and a coral necklace, while [Chambers] wore merely a coarse tow-linen shirt which barely reached to its knees, and no jewelry." Clothed, "even the father of the white child could tell them apart," but only Roxy can make the call when they are free of their distinguishing habiliment (*PW* ch. 2). The salient difference between the infants is driven home to Roxy with "profound terror" when petty thefts plague Driscoll, and he threatens to sell his slaves to a trader: "Her child could grow up and be sold down the river!" (*PW* ch. 3). Perceiving the threat that countless other slave mothers had faced, and thinking as those mothers must have thought, Roxy seizes upon the saving agency of killing her son and herself by jumping into the river. Her choice balances a few moments of fear in an immediate death against the prolonged suffering that being sold down the river all but guaranteed.

If Roxy's ability to effect escape is severely limited, she controls the staging of her tragedy. Determined not to be "fished out" of the river wearing her "miserable ole linsey-woolsey," she changes into her new Sunday gown, dresses her hair "like white folks," and is ready to go out in a blaze of glory. At that moment, the contrast between her own "splendors" and Chambers' "pauper shabbiness" touches Roxy's "mother-heart" and she exchanges her son's inadequate shirt for "one of Thomas a Becket's snowy long baby gowns." The change wrought on the lowly slave baby surprises his own mother, and she recalls that the day before when bathing both boys, Tom's "own pappy asked [her] which of 'em was his'n" (*PW* ch. 3). Thus, Roxy hatches a new plan: She puts the heir in slave's garb and places the distinctive coral necklace on her own son's neck, and the transformation is complete. Tom is stripped "of everything"—his clothing, his family, his white privilege and personhood. Nevertheless, *Pudd'nhead Wilson's* consideration of the slave mother's relation to her children demonstrates that even a strong, independent woman's resistance to chattel slavery's dehumanizing operations is doomed: Chambers is "saved," but at the cost of the innocent Tom's freedom. By "trying to address the wrongs of slavery regarding her children within the slave system itself" (Chadwick, "Forbidden Thoughts" 87), Roxy merely replicates it, finding justification for the baby switch within her oppressors' own actions: "Tain't no sin—white folks has done it!" (*PW* ch. 3). While her statement literally points to a changeling plot in which king and commoner are taken for each other, it also implies that by making slave children mere things, "white folks" have not only doomed them to perpetual captivity but have deprived them of their humanity as well.

When, as an adult, the false Tom Driscoll learns his true identity, he asks, "Why were niggers and whites made?" Chapter 4 provides an extended narrative on *how* they are made, and shaped to fill the socially constructed role they are apparently "born" for. Roxy's awareness that her beloved son is also her master means that there is no demand he can make that she won't try instantly to answer: "Indulged in all his caprices, howsoever troublesome and exasperating they might be," the young Tom learns his own importance and privilege within the household and exploits it at every opportunity. Crying, screaming, and holding his breath beget immediate attention; clawing and pounding servants or breaking windows earn no punishment: Tom is allowed whatever he commands, even "things that would give him a stomach-ache."

Paralleling Simms's illustration of the white and negro children, the false Chambers's boyhood is a relative blank. Tom's training and development receive uninterrupted attention for pages, and Chambers merely supplies the contrast, the polarized image of Tom. "Tom got all the petting, Chambers got none. Tom got all the delicacies, Chambers got mush and milk, and clabber without sugar. In consequence . . . Tom was 'fractious,' as Roxy called it, and overbearing; Chambers was meek and docile." One might expect that Chambers would at least receive Roxy's tender ministrations, if only to keep up appearances she has created; however, this single comfort is denied him. His supposed mother, although she never goes beyond scolding him or boxing his ears for "forgitt'n' who his young marster was," is blind to anything but Tom, "her darling, her master, her deity."

In her introduction to the Oxford University Press edition of *Pudd'nhead Wilson*, Sherley Anne Williams writes of the "unmothering of black people." This term has resonance for the false Chambers, who is in fact twice "unmothered," first by the death of his biological mother and then by Roxy's single-minded love for Tom. Although Williams refers to the separation of slave mothers and their children, Chambers suffers what other slave children surely did when a master's child took precedence over all else in a black nurse's life (*PW 1996* xxxix). After acting as the necessary foil to underline Tom's nasty character, Chambers vanishes from the novel like an inconsequential pawn until its conclusion requires his service. After he is restored as the true heir, he is expected to snap back into the social role his birth confers, but he lacks the innate qualities his heritage would seem to predict. He feels "at home and at peace nowhere but in the kitchen" for which his training has formed him (*PW* Conclusion).

Exuberant play is a hallmark of youth and, as Anthony Rotundo has convincingly argued, the energy, noise, self-assertion, and violence constructs a "boy culture" in opposition to social and moral authority signified by the home. Indeed, the boy-constituted realm of scuffle and play, a cultural space "with its own rituals, and its own symbols and values," provides a necessary—if temporary—escape from the limits imposed by both public and private spheres (Rotundo 15). But if Tom's play is filled with self-assertion and violence, it bears little resemblance to the adventure and camaraderie suggested by Rotundo's model or embodied in a novel like *The Adventures of Tom Sawyer* (1876). The false Tom Driscoll has no real friends, white or black, and his play reinstates rather than resists the social order, as Tom insists upon the differences between himself and Chambers that "the fiction of law and custom" asserts (*PW* ch. 2). Subject to his young master's mean-spirited authority, Chambers acts as Tom's proxy when boisterous boy culture gets too rough or dangerous. If the slave is allowed a turn at marbles, his master confiscates all his winnings. Should Chambers be admired for his athleticism by other boys, Tom turns him into a tool for a joke, as when he pushes a rowboat under Chambers's downward-arcing dive and knocks him unconscious.

Because Tom's authority is buttressed by the threat of physical violence from both Percy Driscoll and Roxy, Chambers rarely demurs when his master commands except when he is asked to defend his tormenter against overwhelming odds, and even then he is roundly punished. However, if Chambers's training at home and abroad makes him a slave, Tom's upbringing infantilizes him. Never knowing a being more important than himself, his uncorrected youthful selfishness, laziness, and cruelty make him lacking in all self-discipline. With no reason to reform, he maintains these traits into young manhood and becomes a gambler, liar, and, eventually, a murderer.

According to James M. and Dorothy Dennen Volo, child rearing became a conscious process in the nineteenth century (Volo and Volo 256), and one that changed in form from corporeal correction to psychological influence (Messent, "Discipline and Punishment" 225). Relying on emotional discipline, reason and love, parents were told they could raise a child of good character. As Richard Broadhead explains, "Early parental love initiates the child into a world of other-directedness and in that sense begins the socialization of identity." Self-monitoring, or "correction by interiority," begins when a child internalizes parental values by sensing an omnipresent, omniscient parent (quoted in Messent, "Discipline and Punishment" 228). For Twain, however, physical punishment had an occasional role. Although his letter "On Training Children," an 1885 rejoinder to "What Ought He to Have Done" appearing in the *Christian Union*, received mixed responses, he maintained that "a whipping"—one delivered without "temper" or "revenge" and strictly on the "business principles" underlying a well-ordered family—could remind a child who resists reason and love of the respect he owes his family (*DMT* 116).

Such parenting in *Pudd'nhead Wilson*, however, is utterly absent. In addition to Roxy's dangerously indulgent treatment of her son/master, Percy Driscoll is a preoccupied and distant father. Although croup, measles, and scarlet fever carried off his children one by one before the birth of Thomas à Becket, when this last child and heir is born he "soon absorbed himself in his speculations" and leaves the boy's care entirely to Roxy. As has already been noted, he is so inattentive to his son that he cannot recognize him without the telltale dress of status and privilege. When Percy Driscoll dies, "the bliss-business" of raising the idol Tom continues under the auspices of Judge Driscoll and his sister, Mrs. Pratt, who pet, indulge, and spoil Tom (*PW* ch. 5). The only sort of brake the judge ever attempts to apply to his nephew's behavior is coercive—the threat of disinheritance—and thus all Tom's guile is driven underground. Despite Roxy's later attribution of her son's "low down ornery" behavior to "de nigger in [him]" (*PW* ch. 14), Twain's insistence that training creates social identity pointedly counters notions of innate black inferiority, indicting thereby "both the patriarchy and slavocracy" (*PW 1996* xl) for turning persons into unreflective tyrants and unresisting slaves.

The well-ordered domestic space is the conventional site of childrearing. In noting the contrast between the lavishly detailed description of Dawson's Landing's exterior facades and the lack of representation afforded its domestic interiors, Paula Harrington examines the meaning of the house as signifier in *Pudd'nhead Wilson* (Harrington 92-93). While this discrepancy certainly provides an index of the town's concern for "perfect" outward appearances ("laid on so thick as to raise suspicion," she writes), it also emphasizes the emptiness at the center of the home, the domestic hearth—the nineteenth century's preeminent symbol of familial nurturance. Indeed, both boys' childhood experiences bear this out. Family relations are dysfunctional at best and, if one is a slave, all but obliterated. Tellingly, when Roxy wishes to meet Tom to reveal their kinship and secure a small income from the generous allowance he receives, she names Dawson's Landing's haunted house, the interior of which, Harrington notes, is the only such place described in the novel. Sparsely furnished with clean straw and packing crates, "a tin lantern freckling the floor with little spots of light," Roxy has created the inverse of the town's "empty" interiors in a dilapidated building where no home would seem possible (*PW* ch. 9).

For Harrington, "the disappearance of domestic description" in Dawson's Landing's cookie-cutter houses "serves to underscore that there can be no true home or family under a system in which white patriarchs do not acknowledge their children by slave women, nor in which black slaves who do the work of domestic life are not recognized as fully human, let alone family" (Harrington 94-95). It is also important to assert that Dawson's Landing exists not only as an antebellum setting, but also as one that resonates with the postwar and postreconstruction violence against black Americans. Despite its "little spots of light," the haunted house exists as a reminder that in Jim Crow America there was no safe or adequate space for black mothers and their children when gothic theories of racial inferiority reinstated an unofficial slave state and thereby sanctioned their treatment as lesser beings.

Wilson's comment about killing his half of the barking "general" dog suggests that violence done to a part of the body politic is experienced by the whole. Thus, if black children are at risk, all children are. Although the nineteenth-century experts described childhood "as a period of guardianship" (Volo and Volo 256), *Pudd'nhead Wilson*, like *Tom Sawyer* and *Huckleberry Finn*, is at its heart a novel that examines childhood vulnerability to the dangerous influences of the adult world. The issues of childhood and servitude—independent of the South's chattel slavery—reappear in the subplot concerning Angelo and Luigi Capello, Italian twins who make an unlikely visit to Dawson's Landing. Divulging their past to Judge

Driscoll and Wilson, the twins bitterly report that their parents died insolvent, but neither their "Florentine nobility" nor their extreme youth protects them from "being seized for . . . debts and placed among the attractions of a cheap museum in Berlin to earn the liquidation money. It took us two years to get out of that slavery" (*PW* ch. 6). Even when the youths arrive in Dawson's Landing, it is clear they have not entirely shed their object status: Their unique otherness causes Aunt Patsy Cooper and her daughter Rowena to regard them as social capital that will create a "grand stir" (*PW* ch. 4). Of course, the twins' experience of "slavery" differs in both kind and degree from the chattel slavery of the American South; for them, there is an end game, a point at which they will have paid the price of their freedom. In the case of young Sam Clemens, stirred by the sad faces of the slaves in the Hannibal street, chastened by an understanding of Sandy's plight, powerless to affect his remote and implacable father on Jenny's behalf, there is a point where he, too, outdistances the impotence of childhood and, as Twain, indicts a social system that reinforces the dominance of the powerful over the powerless.

20

Personal Recollections of Joan of Arc

Ronald Jenn

From its conception to its reception, Mark Twain's 1896 novel *Personal Recollections of Joan of Arc* is strongly linked to questions of childhood, youth, and gender. Because the historical Joan died at the age of nineteen, she could hardly be regarded as anything other than a youth, even by medieval standards, and Twain's book consistently refers to her as either a "child" or a "girl." Indeed, his book most frequently calls her a "child," thereby grounding his pet character in the indeterminacy of childhood. This observation is confirmed by marginalia in one of the French sources he used while writing his novel. Next to a passage depicting a distressed Joan pressed with questions by her English jailers in his copy of Monseigneur Ricard's *Jeanne d'Arc la vénérable* (1894), he wrote, "Poor hunted child." Also, when his historical romance was being anonymously serialized in *Harper's Monthly Magazine*, beginning in April 1895, and he was being repeatedly asked if he was its author, he declared, "I am always willing to adopt any literary orphan that is knocking about looking for a father, but I want to wait until I'm sure that nobody else is going to claim it" (*CI* 155).

Samuel Clemens claimed his first encounter with Joan of Arc occurred in Hannibal when he was a youth in 1849, after his father had died. One day, as he crossed a street on his way home from the print shop where he was an apprentice, he supposedly saw a page from a history of Joan wafting down the street. The stray page had a passage describing Joan "in the cage at Rouen, in the fortress, and two ruffian soldiers had stolen her clothes" (*MTB* 81–82).

There is a tradition of disbelief in this story among critics. Accepting that Joan blew into Twain's life so early on encourages us to think that before he wrote his novel about her, she had been on his mind since his own youth, and, therefore, to believe, along with Twain himself, in a world "wholly determined from the beginning" (Stone 1). Part of the reluctance in accepting the floating-page anecdote stems from its having been told by Twain's biographer Albert Bigelow Paine after Twain's death, combined with the fact that Twain himself had failed to mention the incident where it would have fitted best—in his 1910 essay "The Turning-Point of My Life."

Even though Twain's first encounter with Joan probably did not happen in such a dramatic fashion, there are reasons to believe that young Sam may have run across some material related to Joan while working as a printer. Remarks in his September 15, 1899, letter to British publisher T. Douglas Murray help us retrace the overall evolution of popular and scholarly interest in Joan:

> In a bookshop window in Rouen I saw a bibliography of their [the French] contributions to her literature containing 3,000 titles, 99 hundredths of that must have been written since 1848; five centuries hence they will find something to be vain about in their treatment of [Alfred] Dreyfus. (*UCCL* 12412)

This dating makes perfect sense in the context of the post-1848 Atlantic world. Because Joan was a patriotic figure condemned by the Church and not yet canonized at the time Twain was writing, she aroused the interest of freethinkers and historians looking for figures who could become emblematic of a country torn among a monarchist tradition, a recent imperial episode, and republican intervals following violent revolutionary outbursts. As a Roman Catholic figure supporting a French king, Joan could, as a matter of fact, bring grist to the mill of virtually every political faction in France. After the Revolution of 1848, she increasingly became the center of attention. Given the remarkable fluidity of the transatlantic book and newspaper trade through that period, it would not be surprising if a history of Joan reached Hannibal a year after the 1848 revolution. Moreover, because Twain's novel *Joan of Arc* seems to be such an oddity in the Twainian canon, we tend to forget that the rise of Joan's popularity—which would culminate in her 1920 canonization—nearly coincided with Sam's own lifespan and that he was just one of the many who wrote about her around the same time.

Joan of Arc's youthful and adult readers

None of the early editions of *Joan of Arc* targeted young readers, but there are many indications that Twain intended his historical romance for readers of all ages. Following observations by Twain's friend William Dean Howells, Albert Stone pointed out in 1959 that "children especially (though not exclusively) seem to be the audience Twain had in mind" (*MMT* 151; Stone 1959, 8). As we learn from his notebooks, Twain routinely read his works in progress to his wife and children, his "household critics," as this passage from his unpublished 1897 notebook (no. 31), quoted by Stone, shows:

> Every book from Huck Finn & Prince & Pauper on, was read to the household critics chapter by chapter nightly as it was written. Joan was thus read: the first half at the Villa Viviana [sic, properly Viviani] winter of 92–3; the third quarter at Etretat [France] Aug. & Sept. '94-("wait till I get a handkerchief, papa")-the final chapter in Paris Nov. Dec. 94 finished in the next month (Jan. '95) I think. (Stone 2)

This writing and reading process may account for structural parallels between *Joan of Arc* and *Adventures of Huckleberry Finn* (1885). John Seelye has pointed out that both novels feature a treacherous Dauphin and that the final third of each book is distinctly different from what precedes it. He also noticed that Joan's entry into Orleans resembles Tom Sawyer's several heroic returns to his hometown (*JA 1980*).

Support for believing that Twain regarded *Joan of Arc* as a perfect read for the family circle appears in a letter he wrote to his friend Mary Mason Fairbanks in 1893: "That is private & not for print, it's written for love & not for lucre, & to entertain the family with, around the lamp by the fire" (*MTMF* 269). In nineteenth-century literature for children, the device of a storyteller spinning yarns by the fireside, the campfire, or on a porch, was a very common feature that is echoed in *Joan of Arc*'s narrator, the Sieur Louis de Conte, dedicating his text to his "Great-Great-Grand Nephews and Nieces." This device places the readers themselves in the situation of nephews or nieces listening to an old uncle's story about his youth. As Andrew Tadie says in his introduction to a modern edition of *Joan of Arc*, "Our appreciation of Twain's story is dependent on our ability to imagine ourselves as de Conte's young relatives" (*JA 1989* 21). In this perspective, the dislike and disuse into which *Joan of Arc* has fallen could thus stem from an evolution of our own reading habits.

De Conte's dedication also conjures up the idea of a childless uncle passing down the story to a much younger generation and marks de Conte as an uncle figure. Here, there is a parallel with Twain's personal life. During his later years, he would often "adopt" intelligent and lively young people as honorary nieces and nephews, as Lewis Leary has noted (*MTLM* 3). One of Twain's favorite young people was his close friend Henry H. Rogers's daughter-in-law, Mary Benjamin Rogers. In a 1906 letter to Mary, Twain, the uncle figure, expatiated on the qualities of his youthful symbolic niece: "Ho, you miraculous combination of quicksilver, watchsprings and sunshine, how you do dance out from your pen and light up this solemn solitude and set things amoving! No matter how long you live you'll never get old." (*MTLM* 42).

Twain's fascination with youth could be a sign of his modernity. Remaining young and keeping in touch with youth could be a necessity and a response to an ever-shifting environment linked to technological advances and improvements. From this perspective, *Joan of Arc* can be construed as a harbinger of Twain's growing interest in youth.

There is another indication that Twain intended his book for younger people and women in particular. *Joan of Arc* was the book he gave to young women more often than any of his other books. He did this to the end of his life and obviously thought it a good gift for women. Twain himself gave copies to a friend of his daughter Clara, a female relative of his biographer Paine, and others. He also gave a book about Joan to an angelfish (Mac Donnell email).

An allegory with manly features

In *The Ordeal of Mark Twain* (1920), Van Wyck Brooks argued that Twain himself could be seen as a child and considered most of his books, *Joan of Arc* included, as meant for younger readers (Brooks 176). Although the astute essays penned by Mentor L. Williams (1947) and Albert Stone focused on Joan as a child, the allegorical dimension of a character who stands for democracy and patriotism was always another major concern of critics. Williams challenges the notion that Joan should be construed as the epitome of the Victorian woman and instead champions the idea that she is more of a "Missouri girl" (Williams 247).

As early as 1951, Philip Foner overlooked the gender and age questions to focus on class and power-related issues. To him, *Joan of Arc* is primarily a statement against monarchy, but childhood and youth still operate as metaphors in his politically minded discourse. Foner reminds us that Twain blamed France's predicament on "'the gilded children of privilege' [who] had long been divorced from the 'mighty underlying force' of the people." Here, Joan's youth is perceived as a rejuvenating force that revitalizes France, literally bringing the nation back to life: "The 'marvelous child' of Domrémy rose to check the degradation of France. Through her, the exhausted nation drew strength, and 'dead France woke suddenly to life.'" In an approach that subsumes gender lines, Foner states that *Joan of Arc* stands for "the common man" (Foner 152–53).

In his insightful introduction to the 1980 Stowe-Day edition of *Joan of Arc*, John Seelye also strikes a subtle balance between the perception of Joan as a child and that of Joan as a woman. He remarks that Twain's Joan is the epitome of the Victorian ideas and aesthetics of womanhood and that she is "sister to that monumental virgin with the profile of Michelangelo's David who even yet guards the portals of the New World—a gift, like Saint Joan, from the people of France" (*JA 1980*). He then draws a parallel with another major French and virgin-like figure in nineteenth-century literature—Evangéline: "Mark Twain's Joan is a heroine in the line direct from [Henry Wadsworth] Longfellow's Evangéline (also French, also martyred) connected pele-mele to Ben Franklin and Andrew Jackson." In these lines, Joan cuts a monumental womanly figure, but her allegorical status leads to a comparison with men (*JA 1980*).

In his introduction to the 1996 Oxford University Press edition of *Joan of Arc*, Justin Kaplan would later insist on that allegorical dimension of Joan: "Mark Twain's Joan is more a character out of a school pageant than she is a flesh-and-blood historical figure who led armies into battle and endured imprisonment and martyrdom" (*JA 1996* xxxvii–xxxviii). This parallel then allows Kaplan to initiate a comparison between Joan and the American general Ulysses S. Grant. This comparison was later taken up by Forrest Robinson: "So numerous and close are the similarities between the paired portraits that, to an informed eye, *Personal Recollections* has the quality of a palimpsest in which Grant's life is everywhere discernible beneath Joan's" (Robinson 75). The manly traits of Grant seem to be piercing through the shallow mask of *Joan of Arc*, and it is her allegorical dimension that made it possible for a masculine reading of her character to emerge.

Joan among the feminists: Childhood and motherhood

Back on the Twain scholar's shelves in hardcover and annotated editions in the 1990s and retrieved from a dusty oblivion, *Joan of Arc* is lending itself to increased reading and criticism. The novel's comeback and greater availability has coincided with the rise of gender studies, which, understandably, have provided a suitable frame of analysis for a novel featuring a cross-dresser. Mostly unnoticed until recent years, Joan's transgression of clothing conventions became a prominent concern of the 1990s (see, e.g., Knoper).

As early as 1982, Susan K. Harris pioneered a shift of focus from childhood to gender. Assuming that de Conte's narrative agenda consistently overrides that of Joan to the point of overshadowing it, Harris paved the way for analysis in which the questions of adulthood, manhood, and womanhood would prevail. In his introduction to the Ignatius edition of *Joan of Arc*, Tadie views de Conte as a narrative device that helped Twain tackle the power of Joan's personality. As the critical discourse of the 1990s would later confirm, the gender-oriented approach requires a more mature Joan in order to function properly, and that inevitably entails some erasure of childhood and youth. Harris's essay foreshadows this coming of age when she draws the reader's attention to Joan's childlessness, construed as connected to the youthful continuum in which some of the novel's characters seem to be living. Forever young, the children of de Conte's and Joan's generation never really grow up: "Either they die young, like Joan, or they live to old age, like de Conte, but they never marry, never take their place within the community and continuity of human life" (Harris 51).

Although it has been impossible for the critical discourse totally to erase or jettison the child dimension of Joan, there has been an increasing focus on gender roles and their transgression. Justin Kaplan is probably the one critic who did not so easily yield to the gender trend. In his introduction to the Oxford edition, he underlines the fact that Twain perceived Joan as a "'wise little child' . . . abstracted beyond any recognition that she could ever become a mature woman" and that he "saw Joan as a paragon of purity and selflessness who would never have to meet the confounding test of sexuality." However, Kaplan also acknowledges the fact that Joan could have been Twain's response to the growing social, political, and sexual empowerment of late-nineteenth-century women: "This 'little woman' would never grow up to be the much heralded but also dreaded 'New Woman' of Mark Twain's era" (*JA 1996* xxxviii).

The foregrounding of the theme of transvestitism has meant that Joan is starting to be approached in terms of male-female relationships rather than adult-child. One of the first to synthesize the newly available book with the latest of feminist criticism was J. D. Stahl, who relied on a strong characterization of Joan as a woman and of de Conte as a man in 1994, following the assumption that "woman is represented only in relation to the male self in Twain's work" (Stahl 145). According to Stahl, and in a stand that fairly encapsulates the rest of critical discourse, Twain places overpowering emphasis on "the association between motherhood and martyrdom, womanliness and self-sacrifice. Womanhood, nurture, womanly love and virtue are equated with victimization" and "Twain's ideal of womanhood is the woman who sacrifices herself—for her virtue; for her beliefs; for her children; her husband, or her nation" (Stahl 16). Joan is turned into a mother figure, the virgin and childless character is endowed with the attributes of a mother. This approach is taken up and further developed by Susan K. Harris in her afterword to the Oxford *Joan of Arc*.

In Twain's reading, Joan's most womanly act lies precisely in the self-sacrifice she makes when she assumes masculine prerogatives, from dress to military power; in her heart, he claims, she would rather be home with her mother. In addition to stressing her youth, emotional vulnerability, and selflessness, Twain partially resolves Joan's gender contradictions by suggesting her maternalism; in this context, Charles VII and France are Joan's children, whom her nurturing instincts compel her to protect. Emotionally the devoted daughter and mother, Twain's Joan balances her masculine behavior with her feminine sensibility (*JA 1996* 3).

Indeed, two female figures, Twain's wife Olivia and his daughter Susy, seem to have been hovering in his mind as he was writing his novel. In his August 30, 1906, autobiographical dictation, Twain recalled that the very framing of the story was the result of intense research and that he had tried six different patterns before reaching one on which Olivia finally agreed:

> In the story of "Joan of Arc" I made six wrong starts, and each time that I offered the result to Mrs. Clemens she responded with the same deadly criticism— silence. She didn't say a word, but her silence spoke with the voice of thunder. When at last I found the right form I recognized at once that it was the right one, and I knew what she would say. She said it, without doubt or hesitation. (*AMT2* 197)

It is not surprising then, that Samuel dedicated the book to his wife. He had, after all, very early on compared her to Joan in his letters: "In your sphere you are as great, & as noble, & as efficient as any Joan of Arc that ever lived" (*L3* 63). Only Susy would later compete in Twain's mind for comparison with Joan. Linda Morris gives the gender-based approach a new twist when she demonstrates how Susy's relationship with her college friend Louise Brownell influenced Twain as he was writing *Joan of Arc*. Morris insists on the vexed nature of the relationship between father and daughter because of Susy's relationship with Brownell, and notices that the connection between Susy and the historical character "could only have been strengthened" by Susy's illness while the family was staying in Rouen during the final stage of writing (Morris 120). From this perspective, it could be added that the description of Susy's fever reaching the 100s and the comparison of the family's stay in Rouen to a form of captivity strongly echo Joan's imprisonment and martyrdom at the stake in the same French city. In his letter of October 5, 1894, to his friend Henry Huttleston Rogers, he wrote, "Susy was not well. . . . Temperature during three days, 104, 103, then 101. Necessarily we were a good deal alarmed, but she is ever so much better now. We shall be captives here indefinitely, of course" (*HHR* 80).

In the wake of more than two decades of gender-inspired readings, how can the critical approach to *Joan of Arc* be expanded and rejuvenated? It seems that the book has not yet revealed all of its transnational and translational potential. Written almost entirely overseas and partly in France from a number of French sources, the novel sheds light on Twain both as a translator and a cosmopolitan traveler. *Joan of Arc* can be seen as the climax of Twain's long-time and paradoxical relationship with France, the French, and the French language. From this perspective the book can be construed as another episode in the writer's protracted tug-of-war with French critic and translator Thérèse Bentzon, whom he had accused of mangling his jumping frog story. Because *Joan of Arc* poses as a translation, it can be viewed as another form of literary experiment carried out on language(s) connected to a number of other minor and major texts. From his hilarious franglais in *A Tramp Abroad* (1880); literal or interlinear translation in "The Jumping Frog in English, Then in French, Then Clawed Back into a Civilized Language Once More by Patient, Unremunerated Toil" (1875); imagined translation in "At a Dinner for Monsieur Fréchette of Québec" (1882); and pseudo-translation tinged with real translation in *Joan of Arc*, Twain demonstrated a will to explore the range of possibilities offered by linguistic exchange with a view to both literary fame and financial reward (Jenn 40–56).

An avenue of research could lie in a revaluation of French sources, as whole chunks of the novel are actual translations of the books Twain used for historical reference. Because *Joan of Arc* was a saintly figure even before she became canonized, the French authorities Twain read, heavily annotated and in many instances translated, looked at Joan as neither a child, a youth, nor a woman but as the saintly figure she was to become. As early as October 1894, ten years before publication of the essay "Saint Joan of Arc," Twain wrote a letter to Lloyd S. Bryce, the owner and editor of the *North American Review*, from Rouen insisting that Joan was nothing other than a saint: "And now that Church is threatening her with a tinsel saintship—a girl who was born a saint & never was anything else till she died" (*UCCL* 04797).

21

Gender Bending as Child's Play

Linda A. Morris

"Gender bending," a term for gender-role reversals and twisting, is an expression Mark Twain himself would never have used. Indeed, the term did not even come into existence until the late twentieth century. Applied to the works of Twain, it has a very contemporary ring to it, but in fact the issues to which it points are of long standing. For example, how much does one's biological sex dictate one's behavior; what happens when someone does not easily fit into the role proscribed by society for proper gender behavior; how much room is there in a given society for breaking the rules; what happens when one "switches" gender; what are the roles of "nature" and "nurture"?

What words might Twain and his contemporaries have used to describe a young person who did not conform to gender norms? Two terms he did use in stories featuring children who do not conform are "tomboy" for a girl and "milksop" for a boy. The first he used with some affection; the latter was clearly derisive. As I argue in *Gender Play in Mark Twain: Cross-Dressing and Transgression* (2007), Twain plays with gender in nearly a dozen stories and tales written over the full span of his career. He did challenge gender stereotypes in his work, he understood and exposed, at times, the notion that gender is a social construct, not a "natural" order. He also demonstrated vividly that there is no essential relationship between appearance and reality. In the end, however, even as he challenged and played with the notions of gender norms, his work also tended to reinforce conventional gender roles.

Girls tend to have considerably more latitude in breaking out of gender roles than do male characters. In part this is because historically girls have been more restricted, so taking on more male-identified roles almost automatically means they gain more freedom. By contrast, boys—as iconic characters such as Tom Sawyer and Huckleberry Finn exemplify—already have considerable physical freedom. In Twain's imagined world, girls play with dolls and are physically timid and restricted, while boys can literally travel the world—consider, for example, *Tom Sawyer Abroad* (1894). By looking carefully at stories, novels, and tales by Twain involving various degrees of "gender bending" and characters who either overtly or covertly challenge gender norms, we can gain new insight into just how far Twain could go in allowing himself to create characters who crossed into territory that otherwise seemed forbidden. That he did so at all is remarkable. What is even more remarkable is that he came back repeatedly to variations on this larger theme in nearly every decade of his writing career. He was clearly fascinated with making gender a challenging topic for his fiction, but no matter how often he approached it, he ultimately could not come to a satisfactory resolution of the problems he posed for himself and his characters in his stories. To see how youths fare when they challenge gender norms for whatever reasons, it is useful first to understand the fates of the adults who do so in his fiction.

The first gender-altering story Twain wrote was "An Awful—Terrible Medieval Romance" (1870), which he wrote for the *Buffalo Express*. It opens with a woman who has cross-dressed as a man all twenty-eight years of her life. Identified only by her male name, she has been raised as a male by her father, the king, so she can inherit his kingdom upon his death. The tale involves complex rules of inheritance, but the fundamental one dictates that she cannot inherit the kingdom as a woman but can as a man. A further complication involves a prohibition: If a woman ever sits on the royal throne while the king remains alive, she will be put to death. Despite that rule, the king turns over his power to Conrad while he is alive, placing her at risk of being executed for violating the prohibition. Even as the story begins to unfold, certain burlesque-like absurdities are evident, such as an ongoing confusion of gender-appropriate pronouns. For instance, the king calls the fully adult Conrad—dressed in male armor—into his presence to reveal the truth about the mystery of his son's upbringing, and calling him "my daughter."

Conrad befriends a young woman who is subsequently seduced and impregnated by a villainous young man who skips town. Ironically named "Constance," the young woman then publicly accuses Conrad of fathering her child. In Twain's writings, accusations of paternity appear to leave the accused—male or female—helpless to deny them. Consequently, the only way Conrad can prove his innocence is to reveal *he* is actually a *she*, thereby risking execution for sitting in the ducal throne as a female while the king, her father, still lives. Conrad is thus in a double bind, as she also knows she will be put to death for fathering Constance's child if she does not reveal her "true" gender. It appears, therefore, that Conrad must die no matter what she does. At that point, Twain gives up on resolving the story, adding, in a bracketed postscript:

> [The remainder of this thrilling and eventful story will NOT be found in the WEEKLY BUFFALO EXPRESS.
>
> The truth is, I have got my hero (or heroine) into such a particularly close place that I do not see how I am ever going to get him (or her) out of it again—and therefore I will wash my hands of the whole business and leave that person to get out the best way that offers—or else stay there. I thought it was going to be easy enough to straighten out that little difficulty, but it looks different now.] (*CTSS* 339)

This was not the last time Twain was unable to finish one of his cross-gender tales, but it contains the most overt and frank admission that he cannot get his hero, or heroine, out of the dilemma into which he got him (or her). Nor is it the last such tale to end with a female cross-gendered person fathering a child. Susan Gillman was the first scholar to describe a series of Twain stories as "transvestite tales." Her reading of these tales in *Dark Twins: Imposture and Identity in Mark Twain's America* (1989) remains seminal. A story that Twain wrote in 1902, toward the end of his career, "How Nancy Jackson Married Kate Wilson" (originally titled "The Feud Story and the Girl Who Was Ostensibly a Man"), is one of his darkest tales involving full-blown transvestitism. The protagonist, a young woman named Nancy Jackson, is the victim of a sadistic man's revenge against her mother. At the story's beginning, Nancy is being hunted by the townspeople for having shot a man who had just killed her brother. She flees from a lynch mob to the one house in the village where no one would ever expect her to hide because it is the home of a sworn enemy of her family—Thomas Furlong. Furlong agrees not to turn her in if she will leave their town and live out the rest of her life *as a man*. Otherwise facing certain death, Nancy reluctantly agrees and is immediately forced by Furlong to put on the clothing of "a young negro" who was himself lynched three years before. Then Furlong sends her off into the world.

This anti-fairy-tale beginning sets in motion one improbable scene after another. Now renamed Robert Finlay and graced by Twain with a masculine pronoun, Nancy travels to another village, and is taken in by the Wilson family. Their young daughter, Kate, who has been seduced, impregnated, and abandoned by another stranger to the village, flirts shamelessly with Nancy/Robert, who does not respond. In part to save face, Kate tells her parents that Robert is the father of her yet unborn child. Robert is then "commanded" by Mother Wilson to marry her daughter. He does so, but much to everyone's dismay, he refuses to live with his wife after they are married. The only person who receives any satisfaction from the arrangement is the villain Furlong, who learns what is happening through a letter Nancy writes to her mother that Furlong intercepts. Furlong's response is worth citing in full, for it is an instance of demonic and explosive physical laughter in Twain's writing:

> Furlong put down pipe and letter and threw back his head and delivered himself of crash after crash, gust after gust of delighted laughter; then, mid-aged man as he was, got up, mopping the happy tears from his leathery cheeks, and expended the remaining remnant of his strength in a breakdown of scandalous violence, and finally sank into his chair, heaving and panting, limp and exhausted, and said with what wind he had left—
> "Lord, it's just good to be alive!" (Cooley 121)

Meanwhile, the townsfolk notice how estranged Kate and Robert are and gossip about it freely. The story ends abruptly with these words: "At last the child was born—a boy" (Cooley 123). As in "A Medieval Romance," Twain apparently does not know what to do with the situation he has created of a female-to-male transvestite who will not play his/her part fully but who is implicated in what Gillman calls "female fatherhood" (Gillman 108). Everyone is stuck and has nowhere to go. In some ways, the situation reads like a frame tale of the old Southwest. The same-sex marriage that is forced upon the protagonist is framed by the power and villainy of Furlong. While we can read this story as an attempt by Twain to imagine the life of a female-to-male transvestite, even a reluctant one, he seems only able to imagine it through the lens of a vengeful frame narrator. The territory of transvestitism that has been forced upon Nancy/Robert—potentially a site for good comedy—in this story contains only one paragraph with a comic thrust. It occurs when the story makes fun of the way Kate flirts with Robert and is angered when he does not respond to her wiles. Otherwise, it is a dark story for everyone—Nancy herself, her mother who will never see her daughter again, and Kate and her parents—and there is no resolution.

Twain also wrote a story featuring two adult men—one a biological male and the other a male-to-female transvestite. Called "Wapping Alice," the story was written and rewritten over a number of years but was rejected for publication during Twain's lifetime. It was finally published in a limited Bancroft Library edition in 1981. It, too, was written as a frame tale with a "Mark Twain" as its outside frame narrator, passing along the main story as told to him on an

Indian Ocean voyage by a man named Jackson. The fictional story drew many details from an actual event that took place in the Clemenses' Hartford house that deeply involved Sam Clemens, so Twain shifted it to another time and location and created another narrator. In actuality, Clemens learned that a female member of his staff, Alice, was likely having an affair with one of the workmen there. When confronted with the charge, Alice claimed to have been seduced by the workman. In the space of only one day, Clemens engineered a forced marriage between the serving woman and the workman and then congratulated himself on his fine work.

In the final version of the tale, Clemens distanced himself from the possible scandal of a clandestine heterosexual affair that was taking place in his household by creating the frame tale and having the main story narrated by someone named Jackson. Remarkably, he changed one other detail: After the wedding takes place in the story, the narrator is shocked to learn that Alice is a male-to-female transvestite. Why Twain changed the facts of the case, substituting a homosexual relationship for a heterosexual one, remains mysterious. The explanation he gives in his autobiographical dictation for April 10, 1907, states that the one "fact" he changed, Alice's gender, is a "considerable detail . . . but it is non-essential." He goes on to say he changed Alice into a man "for delicacy's sake." That explanation is simply not persuasive. More likely, this was as close as Twain could come to imagining in print a male homosexual relationship, although he genuinely wanted to try to do so. Ironically, in the story he created, the laugh is on the narrator for "forcing" a marriage on two people who have tricked him into believing they are something they are not.

Children who cross gender boundaries in Twain's writings have a better time of it than adults. In "The 1002d Arabian Night" (written in 1883) two babies, one a boy and the other a girl, are each mistakenly assigned opposite-sex genders. They live out their childhoods and young adulthoods as though they were the gender assigned to them. This is a story Twain wrote the same summer he was completing *Adventures of Huckleberry Finn* (1885), so it should be considered a work of his mature imagination. He was very fond of the story, although his friend William Dean Howells did not share his opinion and discouraged him from publishing it (*S&B* 89). The story of the children, Fatima and Selim, is embedded in a long drawn-out tale invented by the narrator, Scherezade, to fend off her execution after coming to the end of her 1001 stories. Her immediate listener, King Shahriyar, tells her repeatedly that her details are tedious and of no interest, and indeed he is correct. But the central story, when Scherezade gets to it, reveals that the long-awaited son of the sultan of the Indies is assigned a female identity at birth because a witch parted his hair the wrong way. Likewise, a daughter of the Grand Vizier whose fate is destined to be intertwined with the sultan's son is assigned a male gender because of the same trickery of the witch.

As with "A Medieval Romance," "1002d Arabian Night" involves complex laws of succession associated with the gender of the ruling leader. In short, the reign of the sultan will end if he does not produce a son; if he produces a daughter, and that daughter gives birth, both mother and child "must be beheaded." Against these "laws," the children play out their lives. Remarkably, "nurture" seems to have no effect on either child—the boy raised as the girl Fatima dislikes everything a girl apparently should like—such as playing with dolls, singing birds, cats, and fairy tales—and always "detested his feminine costume, without knowing why" (*S&B* 108). When no one is watching, Fatima "throws handsprings" and stands on his head.

Fatima's counterpart, Selim, who is born a girl and raised as a boy, likes to wheel around a baby carriage and do other "girlish" things and is temperamentally shy and timid. "Verily," we are told, "he is a milksop" (*S&B* 107). As a young woman encountering a serpent in a garden, Selim screams in terror, only to be rescued by Fatima, who slays the dragon. They then fall in love, persuade their parents to let them marry, and give birth to a child. Miraculously, the "father" Selim gives birth, not the "mother" Fatima. The sultan's destiny is secure, and his "daughter" is saved from execution because she did not bear the child.

Several things are especially interesting in "1002d Arabian Night," in addition to the ways Twain burlesques the original *Thousand and One Nights*. Throughout the tale, he tends to use the pronoun for each child that corresponds to the child's biological sex. Fatima is thus "he" and Selim "she," no matter how they are perceived by those around them. This creates a gender confusion—not for the characters within the story, but for readers, who must continually remind themselves that "he" is represented throughout as "she" and vice versa. Of interest, too, are the stereotypes and essentialist notions behind the representation of each gender. The biological boy likes physical activity and detests fancy clothing; he is energetic and courageous. The biological girl is timid physically; and she is terrorized by swinging on the palace gate. Moreover, she likes playing with dolls ("how despicable is this, in a boy"). When they reach the age of maturity—thirteen—"Fatima still showed interest in none but matters proper to the manly sex, and Selim cared for nothing but matters proper to the womanly sex" (*S&B* 107).

In brief, in this story, "nature" not "nurture" rules the day. Finally, and it is difficult to know what to make of this fact, biological sex seems to be invisible in this tale. When the babies play together in the bath, no one notices their "true" sex, and when Selim becomes pregnant, no one notices that she is about to give birth. Thus, it is with great surprise to all that Fatima proclaims, "for lo, *not I but my husband is the child's mother*" (*S&B* 131). This is a remarkable and delightfully absurd statement, one toward which the whole story seems to move from the beginning. It is quintessential Twain.

In 1906, Twain published a novella in *Harper's Magazine*, which he entitled "A Horse's Tale." It features a young orphan girl named Cathy Alison, who was born in Spain. She comes to the American West at the age of nine to live with her uncle, a general commanding an army fort that also houses Buffalo Bill and his horse, Soldier Boy. The beautiful Cathy soon becomes the favorite of the whole fort, especially Buffalo Bill, who teaches her how to ride a horse, blow a bugle, and command troops. She becomes an accomplished rider, better than any other young person in the fort and develops a special affinity for Soldier Boy. Of all the young people in Twain's writing who break with traditional gender-role expectations, Cathy has the best time of it, until the end of the story, which will be addressed below. Cathy seems the least restricted by other people's expectations, perhaps because she is a foreign-born girl who is transported to the American Wild West. The only female adult figure in the story who might try to restrict her activities is Mammy Dorcas, a former slave and now a member of the family. She adores Cathy and makes no attempt to make her conform to gender norms. In fact, she offers the most imaginative explanation in all of Twain's work for why a character such as Cathy can be both a sweet and loving young girl and a fiery, athletic child. In doing so, Dorcas both articulates traditional sex-defined traits as she understands them and explains Cathy's androgyny:

> Dorcas is satisfied that there has never been a more wonderful child than Cathy. She has conceived the curious idea that Cathy is twins, and that one of them is a boy-twin and failed to get segregated—got submerged, is the idea. To argue with her that this is nonsense is a waste of breath—her mind is made up, and arguments do not affect it. She says:
>
> > "Look at her; she loves dolls, and girl-plays, and everything a girl loves, and she's gentle and sweet, and ain't cruel to dumb brutes—now that's the girl-twin, but she loves boy-plays, and drums and fifes and soldiering, and rough-riding, and ain't afraid of anybody or anything—that's the boy-twin; 'deed you needn't tell me she's only one child; no, sir, she's twins, and one of them got shet up out of sight. Out of sight, but that don't make any difference, that boy is in there, and you can see him look out of her eyes when her temper is up'" (*HT* 41–43).

At the same time that Dorcas reinforces notions of proper and expected male and female behavior, especially among young children, she makes the presence of both male and female characteristics in one person seem to be the most natural and acceptable order of things.

As for the ending of the story—unexpectedly and unaccountably—Cathy is taken back to Spain by the general to be with her aunt. He also takes Dorcas and Soldier Boy. Soldier Boy is stolen and turns up as a broken-down nag at a bullfight; Cathy recognizes him from the stands. As he is eviscerated by a bull she rushes to his side, where she too is killed. While it has been argued that Twain wrote the story primarily to expose the cruelty of bullfighting, nothing in the story justifies the way it is concluded. In *Mark Twain and the Feminine Aesthetic* (1992), Peter Stoneley calls Cathy a "conspicuously feminine maiden" and argues that Twain's main reason for the bullfight is to "allow for the tragic and bloody demise of his dainty heroine" (113). The larger question is whether Twain can envision an adult life for a character as gender-balanced as Cathy. The answer is that he clearly cannot. There seems to be no place in his imagination for such a girl to mature into a grown woman.

An unfinished Twain story that envisions the greatest cross-gender freedom and identification in a young girl is "Hellfire Hotchkiss" (1897). Like Cathy, Hellfire (Rachel) is an excellent horse person who rides astride at great speeds. Moreover, She has even more freedoms:

> Before the next four and a half years were out she had learned many masculine arts, and was more competent in them than any boy of her age in the town. All alone she learned how to swim, and with the boys she learned to skate. She was the only person of her sex in the country who had these accomplishments—they were taboo. She fished, boated, hunted, trapped, played "shinny" on the ice and ball on the land, and ran foot races. She broke horses for pastime, and for the risk there was in it. At fifteen she ranked as the strongest "boy" in the town, the smartest boxer, a willing and fearless fighter, and good to win any fight that her heart was in. (*S&B* 195)

If there is a "girl" twin in Hellfire's life, it is her male counterpart, Thug Carpenter. Ironically named, he is actually cowardly and indecisive. He is rescued by Hellfire from drowning in a river whose ice breaks underneath him and he is too afraid to try swimming ashore. According to one of the townspeople, "There's a considerable difference betwixt them two—Thug and her. Pudd'nhead Wilson says Hellfire Hotchkiss is the only genuwyne male man in this town and Thug Carpenter's the only genuwyne female girl, if you leave out sex and just consider the business facts" (*S&B* 187).

Hellfire comes close to reaching adulthood, still true to her own "nature," for by the age of sixteen she is still able to assert herself, coming upon a mugging by the Stover brothers, knocking one brother out with her baseball bat and knocking the other one "senseless." It is her undoing, however, for the next day she is visited by "Aunt" Betsy Davis, who takes it upon herself to represent the gossips in the town and to try to reform Hellfire Rachel. "Aunt Betsy" hints that Rachel is being talked about in terms that are never articulated, and that have never before been spoken in their town. The gossip is clearly not about Hellfire's male-identified activities, for they have long ago been recognized and accepted by the town folks—this is something different.

The silence that surrounds this discussion suggests that Hellfire is suspected of being sexually deviant, which is the real "taboo" in the story. The term that cannot be named brings a blush to her face, and she swears to try to reform. It remains ambiguous, however, whether she ever can go against her nature and conform to society's expectations, for she makes a series of promises to herself that she is unlikely to keep: "'Withdraw from the boys. The Stovers. Church. That makes three. Three in three days. It is enough to begin with; I suppose I have never done three in three weeks before—just as duties.' And being refreshed and contented by this wholesale purification, she went to bed" (*S&B* 200).

Once again Twain leaves a gender-troubling tale unfinished, this time, however, in a different and more positive way. Hellfire is too strong a person for us to imagine that the town gossips can ultimately contain her. In fact, of all the cross-gendered characters Twain created, Hellfire is the most fully realized person who cannot conform to the town's limitations. No wonder Twain could not project her further into the future and does not finish the tale.

All told, Twain was fascinated by what happens when characters' gender expressions did not match their biological sex. He created situations in which young people were arbitrarily assigned to an opposite gender, forcing characters to cross dress as members of their nonbiological sexes. Male transvestites successfully pass as women, and spirited young girls risk being seen as masculine when they claim male-defined territory as their own. He situated his "gender bending" characters in remote medieval times, in the Wild West, and in a town that for all intents and purposes is his native Hannibal. No matter how he came at it, however, he ran up against his own deeply held notions of biological essentialism. Female children could stray from gender-defined characteristics, but he ultimately could not imagine adult lives for them that defied gender norms. He could not resolve the issue of gender definition, and he could not leave it alone.

22

Orphans and Adoption

Wendelinus Wurth

"I've been an orphan myself for twenty-five years," Mark Twain claimed in a lecture for the Cleveland Protestant Orphan Asylum on January 22, 1869. His claim was not quite accurate, as he had lost his father in 1847; however, he was merely joking (*MTSpk* 38). Throughout his life, he referred to orphanhood in his speeches, stories, and novels. When addressing the New England Sons in Philadelphia in 1881, for example, he used "orphan" as a metaphor, portraying himself as an American without ancestors: "My first American ancestor . . . was an Indian—an early Indian. Your ancestors skinned him alive, and I am an orphan. Not one drop of my blood flows in that Indian's veins today. I stand here, lone and forlorn, without an ancestor" (*MTSpk* 163). Here, he describes the typical orphan situation combining the term with the adjective "forlorn," as he often does, pointing to the orphan's isolation, his special situation.

Strictly speaking, Twain was only a half-orphan from his twelfth year on, since his mother did not die until 1890, shortly before Twain turned fifty-five. When talking or writing, however, he did not distinguish between orphans who had lost one parent from those who had lost two. That view is in accord with dictionary definitions of "orphan."

According to Dr. Selina Schryver, orphans behave differently from other children: "Children, as well as adults, who realize that they are in any way different from others in their society suffer from a feeling of loneliness and usually of inadequacy." Schryver goes on to explain that their basic trauma is the loss of the parent, who should have been the guide to maturity. The one characteristic to be found in nearly all orphans is insecurity. Children who have lost the support of their parents behave in several possible ways, depending on temperament and inherent reaction patterns. The main trends fall into two groups: Reactions may be in the direction of too early and too strong striving for independence and self-sufficiency. In contrast to this, there may be a tendency to seek love by attention-getting mechanisms and increased egoism. Striving for independence is an overcompensation, so that independent children often become introverted and withdrawing, trying to convince themselves that life without the help of adults is quite possible. These children appear to be stubborn, ungrateful, and egoistic. They may also shrink from accepting affection and, in a vicious circle, become even lonelier. The attention-demanding personality results from the fact that the orphan can never feel secure of love because the first love relation has come to an end (Schryver 257–64).

Among Twain's fictional orphans, Huckleberry Finn and Tom Sawyer come immediately to mind. Twain came remarkably close to portraying real-life orphans in describing their behavior. Broadly speaking, Tom and Huck fall into the two categories Schryver found: On the one hand, there are attention-demanding protagonists like Tom Sawyer and Laura Hawkins of *The Gilded Age* (1873), who manipulate their audiences and hardly stop from hurting other people. We might even count Hank Morgan, the time-traveling Connecticut Yankee, in this category, if we consider him an "orphan in time." On the other hand, there are those who rather withdraw into the background and act unobtrusively like Laura Hawkins's adopted brother Clay Hawkins and Huckleberry Finn.

Short stories allow little space to develop protagonists, so they cannot really be representative for orphans. Most often Twain mentions orphans only in passing, as in "How the Author Was Sold in Newark" (1872), "The Case of George Fisher" (1872), and "A Ghost Story" (1870), which were collected in *Sketches New and Old* (1875). However, even when making orphans the main actors in stories, as in "Edward Mills and George Benton: A Tale" (1880), their orphanhood is not at the center of the stories. Twain calls "Edward Mills" a "tale," but it is rather a parable, if not a satiric fable exploding beliefs about the possibilities of education on the one side and the effects of a life formula on the other. The names alone tell the story: George Benton is "bent on" following, he cannot act against his innermost drives. Edward Mills "mills," but he is not worth more than a mill—which had the value of one-tenth of a cent. The name of the family that adopts Edward and George, Brant, also speaks: It is related to the German "Brand." The well-meaning childless Brant couple literally burns its fingers in adopting the two boys. The tale does not take a position on whether orphan behavior is inherited or is a result of upbringing. Most of the tale deals with the part of life when both boys are grown-ups, so orphan psychology does not really apply to them.

Twain often uses orphans when seeking readers' sympathy, as in *Life on the Mississippi* (1883), in which the cub pilot exclaims, after a practical joke played at his expense: "It was a fine trick to play on an orphan, *wasn't* it?" (ch. 13) In *The Innocents Abroad* (1869), his narrator appeals to a guide in the Azores, "Sir, I am a helpless orphan in a foreign land. Have pity on me" (ch. 7). Here, it is insecurity to which the speaker points. Twain often alludes to orphanhood in a humorous manner.

In his novels, Twain explores the orphan theme in several different ways. However, he does not simply follow a literary trend in the nineteenth century, when orphans were often used as protagonists. Examples with which Twain was probably familiar include Charles Dickens's *Oliver Twist* (1839) and *Great Expectations* (1861) and the Brontë sisters' novels. Moreover, life on the frontier along which he grew up was rough and "Indian massacres, natural disasters or epidemics created homeless orphans in large numbers," as historian Robert Bremner writes (Bremner 99).

Twain's first novel, *The Gilded Age*, written in collaboration with neighbor and fellow author Charles Dudley Warner, opens with the Hawkins family moving from Tennessee to the Missouri frontier. They pass a log cabin in which a ten-year-old boy is crying. An old women explains the situation:

> His mother, po' thing. Died of the fever, last night. . . . Husband and the other two children died in the spring. . . . She's ben sick three weeks; and . . . that child has worked . . . and sot up nights and nussed her, and tried to keep up her sperits, the same as a grown-up person . . . . And Clay, he—Oh, the po' motherless thing— (*GA* ch. 2)

This scene depicts a situation that frequently occurred on the frontier. Although the scene is not free of sentimentality, it shows the intimate bond between the mother and son and Clay's devotion to his mother. Despite already having a large family, when Laura Hawkins's adoptive father Squire Hawkins learns that Clay has no parents he does not hesitate to adopt the boy: "I would not put my back on a homeless orphan. If he will go with me I will give him a home, and loving regard—I will do for him as I would have another do for a child of my own in misfortune" (*GA* ch. 2). Clay then becomes a member of the Hawkins family and recedes into the background. Later, the Hawkinses adopt yet another orphan, a "girl of five years, frightened and crying bitterly . . . . Something in the face of Mr. Hawkins attracted her and she came and looked up at him; was satisfied, and took refuge with him" (*GA* ch. 5). Since the girl's parents cannot be found, the Hawkinses quite naturally adopt her into their family. Soon afterward, Hawkins says to his wife that the adopted children are worth all the trouble and Mrs. Hawkins says that they pet and spoil her even more than the other children do (*GA* ch. 5). A guide through life that the orphans need has been provided; they are integrated into a functioning family and feel comfortable there. Not even a controversy about her real father can estrange Laura from her family. She continues accepting Mrs. Hawkins as her mother and vows that this shall always be (*GA* ch. 10). After going to Washington, DC, Laura supports her mother and brother Washington with money earned by using her beauty and intellect as a lobbyist for the corrupt Senator Dilworthy, who calls her "my daughter" (*GA* chs. 32, 34). Laura and Clay show their gratitude for having been taken into the family. In the end, it is the two adopted children who keep the Hawkins family alive.

In his second novel, *The Adventures of Tom Sawyer* (1876), Twain makes Tom the titular hero. Aunt Polly calls him "my own dead sister's boy, poor thing" (*TS* ch. 1). Tom lives with his half-brother, Sid, and cousin Mary in his aunt's house, which has no other male figure with whom to identify. Initially, Sid is used as a foil to Tom, and Mary plays the role of the encouraging, understanding parent. Tom is a more fully developed character than either Laura or Clay Hawkins. Very resourceful and energetic, he likes to out-trick others. Although he is often active, he has a quiet side, too, especially when he feels unjustly treated, then he shows a rather morbid vein. He seeks the solitude of nature, "wishing . . . that he could only be drowned . . . without undergoing the uncomfortable routine devised by nature." This thought is immediately countered, however, with the memory of his new love interest, Becky Thatcher, and the pansy she has thrown to him. He wonders if she would pity him if she knew his sadness. He would like to be comforted by her but fears that she would turn coldly away (*TS* ch. 3). The orphan's dilemma is that, on the one hand, he can be obsessed with death because being set back always reminds him of the parents he has been deprived of. On the other hand, he is always looking for the feelings that the missing parents can no longer give. The death wish recurs when Tom is rejected and seeks "comfort" in nature ending his musings with the wish to die . . . temporarily (*TS* ch. 8).

Soon afterward, Tom leads the boys to their own funeral, thus exhibiting another typical trait of his: his attention-seeking behavior, ranging from attempting to show off by winning a Bible in Sunday school to revealing the fabulous gold treasure at the end of the book. The adopted Tom is emotionally well integrated and a full member of St. Petersburg's society.

In many ways, Tom's sidekick, Huckleberry Finn, is the opposite of Tom. The difference between the two may be neatly summed up in the formula

"Tom urged—Huck held back" (*TS* ch. 26). Huck's mother is dead; his father, the town drunkard, does not care for him. Having no real home, Huck lives withdrawn in a hogshead and does "not have to go to school or to church, or call any being master or obey anybody" (*TS* ch. 6). The emotional contrast between him and Tom is especially evident when the two boys, along with their playmate Joe Harper, are welcomed when they appear at their own funeral service after having been presumed drowned in the Mississippi River. Huck stands alone uncomfortably, not knowing what to do or where to hide and eventually withdraws (*TS* ch. 17). Not only does Huck feel uncomfortable because no one rushes to hug him, he also knows that as the town pariah he is unwanted. Used to relying on himself alone, he strives to avoid uncomfortable situations.

By the end of *Tom Sawyer*, Huck seems to have found a way into St. Petersburg society. He helps save the Widow Douglas from Injun Joe's violence, and he and Tom share the gold treasure. The widow then takes him into her home. However, "whithersoever he turned, the bars and shackles of civilization shut him in and bound him hand and foot. He bravely bore his miseries three weeks, and then one day turned up missing." Huck's discomfort with the widow's lifestyle outweighs the comfort of regular meals and her company. Tom's efforts to persuade Huck to return cannot really tempt him. Huck tells Tom that being rich is not what he had expected: "It's just worry and worry, and sweat and sweat, and a-wishing you was dead all the time" (*TS* ch. 35). Huck's discomfort is so intense that he wishes he were dead—a common feeling with Twain's orphans. Only blackmail helps; if Huck remains at the widow's, he can become respectable and may be a member of Tom's gang. Huck reluctantly agrees; the price for Tom's company is for Huck to be adopted by the widow.

In *Tom Sawyer*, Twain discovered a principle of structuring his novel. Most of the book's action has Tom at its center. Tom—as the title suggests—is the thread that holds the plot together. After finishing *Tom Sawyer*, Twain immediately started writing a new novel, refining the principle he had discovered in the previous one—but it took him seven years to finish: *Adventures of Huckleberry Finn*. In the meantime, he wrote other books, including another with orphan protagonists: *The Prince and the Pauper* (1881). Several orphans figure in that novel but they do not constitute a structural pattern similar to that in *Tom Sawyer*. Its plot revolves around Edward Tudor, the Prince of Wales, and Tom Canty, a pauper boy. Both are born on the same day, but whereas Edward loses his mother soon after being born, Canty's parents both live. After they have an accidental meeting and exchange their clothes, the prince observes that Tom Canty has "the same hair, the same eyes, the same voice and manner, the same form and stature, the same face and countenance, that I bear" (*P&P* ch. 3). When the prince is mistaken for the pauper, he is expelled from the palace, leaving Canty in his place. While struggling to get back into the palace, Edward learns that his father, King Henry VIII, has died: "He realized the greatness of his loss, and was filled with a bitter grief; for the grim tyrant who had been such a terror to others had always been gentle with him." Although further realizing he should be the new king, he yet feels "the most forlorn, outcast and forsaken of God's creatures" (*P&P* ch. 12).

Despite their similar looks, Edward and Canty are different. Before being displaced, Edward had to follow court etiquette strictly and be restrained in his behavior. Canty worked to get out of his impoverished environment, learned to read Latin, and organized a mock royal court. "He was the prince; his special comrades were guards, chamberlains, equerries, lords and ladies in waiting, and the royal family. Daily the mock prince was received with elaborate ceremonials borrowed by Tom from his romantic readings" (*P&P* ch. 2).

Edward is lucky to find a protector in Miles Hendon, a grown-up orphan who treats him like an "adopted child" (*P&P* ch. 12) and behaves toward him like a true father would: caring and protecting him and teaching him as well. Instinctively, it seems, Hendon takes to the prince, who has suffered the same fate Hendon once did. In the end, the prince's and pauper's true identities are established, the prince is crowned king, and Canty becomes the king's ward.

With *Huckleberry Finn*, Twain created another plot that centers on its title character. This time, it is Huck himself who tells his story. An intricate web of themes and motifs accompany the protagonist—all connected with his orphan state. Most of these are touched on in the novel's first chapter. The Widow Douglas adopts Huck and allows "she would sivilize" him, Huck announces. However, Huck finds "it was rough living in the house all the time, considering how dismal regular and decent the widow was in all her ways; and so when I couldn't stand it no longer I lit out." He thereby follows a typical orphan pattern: As soon as he feels the slightest discomfort, he tries to escape from its source as best he can. Despite the presence of other people in the widow's home, Huck feels lonesome. The strict regimen and insensitive teaching of the widow's sister, Miss Watson, do not alleviate his lonesomeness. Connected with isolation and loneliness is superstition. When the world is quiet and dark, emotionally insecure orphans are especially susceptible to signs and omens. No wonder, then, that the whoo-whooing of an owl, a dog's barking, and a whippoorwill's crying announce someone's death. When a spider is accidentally killed in Huck's candle, Huck believes it will bring him bad luck.

From this feeling of fear, it is only a small step for the orphan to wish he were dead (*HF* ch. 1).

Luckily, Tom saves Huck from his desolate mood. The contrast between the two orphans is again apparent: Whereas Huck wants to leave the widow's house without causing a stir, Tom has to put on a show. This basic contrast is also kept up in the evasion sequence at the end of the novel. Tom acts out his imagination because he is after attention and adventure, Huck prefers to stay in the background and wants to get things done in a down-to-earth manner. However, Huck is not secure enough to oppose Tom's schemes and gives in to Tom's "authorities," as he earlier gives in to Miss Watson's and the widow's "authority" until the moment his father appears.

Huck's father, Pap, kidnaps Huck and takes him to a remote cabin. Huck soon likes the "rule-free" life with his father—except for his father's cow-hidings and his feelings of lonesomeness when he is locked in the cabin drive him to escape. Being on his own makes him lonesome again, but discovering Jim on Jackson's Island relieves that feeling: "I warn't lonesome, now" (*HF* ch. 8). As long as he and Jim are together, Huck rarely feels lonesome. However, the feeling overcomes him once again later when he reaches the Phelpses' farm, where the atmosphere seems "lonesome and like everybody's dead and gone" (*HF* ch. 32). The feeling becomes even more intense when Huck hears the dim hum of a spinning-wheel wailing and "then knowed for certain I wished I was dead—for that *is* the lonesomest sound in the whole world" (*HF* ch. 32).

Another theme running through *Huckleberry Finn* is lying. Huck lies occasionally, especially in inventing fictional family stories about himself. In these stories, he is always orphaned. He tells the kindly woman he attempts to deceive, Judith Loftus, for example, that "my father and mother was dead, and the law had bound me out to a mean old farmer in the country thirty mile back from the river, and he treated me so bad I couldn't stand it no longer" (*HF* ch. 11). This is an allusion to the common nineteenth-century practice of hiring out unadopted orphans as indentured laborers. Such orphans often had hard lives.

At the end of the novel, when Jim is finally told he is a free man, he tells Huck that the dead man he had earlier seen in the floating house near Jackson's Island was Huck's own father. Jim has held back that information. Huck is a full orphan now—deprived of both Pap and his surrogate father, Jim. He now feels he is back where he started: "Aunt Sally she's going to adopt me and sivilize me and I can't stand it. I been there before" (*HF* ch. 43). He wants to flee from the discomfort of civilization to the Indian Territory. The structural pattern Twain had discovered in writing *Tom Sawyer* works even better in Huck's first-person narrative.

In *Pudd'nhead Wilson* (1894) Twain has a white and a slave baby boy come into the world on the same day. The latter, Valet de Chambre, is only one-thirty-second part black and looks almost identical to the white baby, Tom Driscoll. Tom's mother dies within a week after his birth and Chambers's white father, Colonel Cecil Burleigh Essex, is absent as a parent, so both boys are half-orphans from the start. Roxana, Chambers's mother, switches the babies, making the slave boy into a master and the master into a slave. The false Tom turns out badly, terrorizing the false Chambers. Soon the false Chambers disappears from the scene and action focuses on the false Tom. After both his supposed and real fathers die, he is adopted by his supposed father's brother, Judge Driscoll and his wife, who had been childless. Even though they see that Tom is no good, their joy over having a son makes them tolerate more than they should, showing that adoption does not always yield the expected results.

The novel eventually abandons the orphan theme because Twain is more interested in the effects of training and heredity in the grown-up Tom and Chambers. In a murder trial the novel's titular hero, David Wilson, reveals the decades-old swapping of the babies and the real Chambers is sold down the river. Freed from his slave status, the real Tom suddenly becomes rich, but he can neither read nor write, and his speech is that of a slave, as are his manners. Not even money and fine clothes can change this (*PW* Conclusion).

In the posthumously published story *No. 44, the Mysterious Stranger* (1982), which Twain wrote during the last decade of his life, he returned to an orphan narrator whose parents are not even mentioned. Sixteen-year-old August Feldner is an apprentice in a medieval Austrian printshop. The very setting of the tale itself suggests orphanhood: "Austria was far from the world . . . and our village was in the middle . . . of Austria" (ch. 1). The castle in which the action takes place could house a thousand people, but the handful of persons actually living there were virtually lost in it (ch. 2). The printing shop, in which the narrator works, is hidden away in a round tower of the castle (ch. 3).

One day a stranger appears in this castle, "a most forlorn looking youth," sixteen or seventeen years old and friendless, who calls himself No. 44 (ch. 3). The narrator and Katrina, the housekeeper, are impressed by the stranger's looks and feel drawn to him, but the castle's other inhabitants meet No. 44 with hostility. August, a Huck-like orphan, does not dare to befriend the boy openly but secretly seeks to. Only Katrina does, she "was a mother at last, with a child to love,—a child who returned her love in full measure, and to whom she was the salt of the earth" (ch. 5). No. 44 accepts being adopted and calls Katrina "mother" (ch. 13). He has supernatural powers and overcomes all animosities, behaving like an attention-seeking Tom Sawyer. August and No. 44 become friends and the latter becomes the teacher of the former. In the final chapter, No. 44 reveals to August

> there is no God, no universe, no human race, no earthly life, no heaven, no hell. It is all a Dream, a grotesque and foolish dream. Nothing exists but You. And You are but a *Thought*—a vagrant Thought, a useless Thought, a homeless Thought, wandering forlorn among the empty eternities! (ch. 34)

No. 44 turns August not only into an orphan, but into a mere orphan thought. This may be Twain reflecting on his own situation at the time of writing: Except for his daughters Jean and Clara, all his family members had died one by one. He had reason to feel orphaned—even by God, with whom he quarreled in "Letters from the Earth." There is no Indian Territory to escape to anymore. Worse yet there is nothing, existence itself is reduced to a thought. And one may speculate if the "You" in *No. 44*'s conclusion is not Twain himself, since he ends the story with "I knew, and realized, that all he said was true." Perhaps this is a fitting finale to his lifelong fascination with orphans.

Part Five

Modern Perspectives

23

Black and White Youth in
Mark Twain's Hannibal

Shelley Fisher Fishkin

In the Hannibal in which Sam Clemens was raised, black and white children often lived together and played together, but the ways in which they experienced childhood were profoundly shaped by the color of their skin. This chapter will explore the lived experience of black and white children in Hannibal during Sam's childhood there and after he left against the backdrop of actions that an adult Sam took involving education and black youth. It will tell this story in part by tracking the experiences of two children born in 1835 in northeastern Missouri—one white and free (Clemens) and one black and enslaved (Henry Dant)—whose legacies and descendants would help shape the education of black and white children in Hannibal in the twenty-first century.[1]

In *Huck's Raft: A History of American Childhood* (2006) Steven Mintz observes, "Our cherished myth about childhood as a bucolic time of freedom, untainted innocence, and self-discovery comes to life" in Hannibal, Missouri. But, as Mintz notes, this idealized view of Hannibal, comes at the expense of denying the terror and insecurity that figured prominently in the Hannibal childhood of Clemens himself and in his novels set there (Mintz 1–2). Before his twelfth birthday, Sam had seen a classmate drown, watched a man burn to death, and seen another man killed by a lump of iron ore thrown at his head. Nights in Hannibal gave cover to murderous gangs of fugitives as well as drunken sociopaths with revolvers. Ron Powers put it aptly, "Hannibal was 'a heavenly place for a boy,' and a hellish one as well" (Powers, *Dangerous Waters* 57, 97–117).

Black children faced the same terrors of childhood that white children did, but also had to deal with the possibility of being separated from those they loved on a master's whim and of having masters who would subject them to neglect or overwork. One Hannibal master who wanted to buy something for his house put his slave Emma Knight's father up on the auction block. Knight later recalled, "We went barefoot until it got real cold. Our feet would crack open from de cold and bleed. We would sit down and bawl and cry because it hurt so" (Knight). As a child, William Henry Dant spent nearly every waking moment driving hogs, looking after horses and mules, making brooms and baskets, cradling wheat, and plowing corn "till midnight" (H. Dant).

Clemens may have joined the world of work at age eleven, but many black children in Hannibal had already been working for years when they reached that age. In *Searching for Jim: Slavery in Sam Clemens's World* (2003), Terrell Dempsey notes that black children as young as nine "were sought as household servants in Hannibal and Palmyra—taken from their mothers and put to work emptying bedpans, bringing in firewood, tending fires, and doing other unpleasant tasks around the house" (Dempsey 80). Clemens's memory of Sandy, a child his father hired, was fresh in his mind decades later—"a little slave boy whom we had hired from some one, there in Hannibal" from the eastern shore of Maryland, who had been brought away from his family and his friends halfway across the American continent, and sold. He was a cheery spirit, innocent and gentle, and the noisiest creature that ever was, perhaps. All day long he was singing, whistling, yelling, whooping, laughing—it was maddening, devastating, unendurable.

One day Sam begged his mother to "shut him up." Tearfully she responded,

> *[margin note: often repeated]* Poor thing, when he sings, it shows that he is not remembering, and that comforts me; but when he is still, I am afraid he is thinking, and I cannot bear it. He will never see his mother again; if he can sing I must not hinder it, but be thankful for it. If you were older you would understand me; then that friendless child's noise would make you glad. (*AMT1* 212)

Twain "used Sandy once"—in *The Adventures of Tom Sawyer* (1876), in which he appears as Jim, "the small colored boy" (*AMT1* 212). Tom envies Jim's freedom to fetch water while he must whitewash the fence and tries to persuade him to switch chores with him because the pump is a place where "white, mulatto, and negro boys and girls were always there waiting their turns, resting, trading playthings, quarreling, fighting, skylarking" (*TS* ch. 2).

Slave children like Sandy took their pleasure where they could, singing and shouting as they did chores, lingering longer than necessary at the pump to enjoy the lively socializing there. Others were happy to serve as companions to their masters' children. John Ayres, a contemporary of Clemens's, recalled chasing rabbits "with 'Black John,' a half-grown negro, belonging to my grandmother, and Tom Blankenship." Ayres noted that "Black John and Tom Blankenship were naturally leading spirits and they led us younger 'weaker' ones through all our sports. Both were 'talented,' bold, kind, and just and we all 'liked' them both and were easily led by them." (Ayres). As Clemens put it in his autobiography,

> All the negroes were friends of ours, and with those of our own age we were in effect comrades. I say in effect, using the phrase as a modification. We were comrades, and yet not comrades; color and condition interposed a subtle line which both parties were conscious of, and which rendered complete fusion impossible. (*AMT1* 211)

If the lives of black and white children intersected on a daily basis within the household, in the yard, in the woods, and at the water pump, there was one place where they never intersected at all: the schoolroom. In 1847, the Missouri legislature passed an ordinance forbidding anyone from teaching a black or mulatto child to read. The penalty for violations was a $500 fine and six months in jail (Missouri State Archives).

Sam Clemens was born in Florida, Missouri, in 1835. During that same year, Henry Dant was born south of Monroe City, Missouri, on the farm of Judge Daniel Buford Kendrick (H. Dant). The two births occurred about fifteen miles apart, and both boys would spend significant portions of their childhood in or near Hannibal. Both men—through their descendants or their writing—would shape Hannibal's future in intersecting ways.

There were some curious resonances between the households in which the boys grew up. The paterfamilias in each—Sam's father and Henry's master—were county judges in adjacent counties: John Marshall Clemens in Monroe County and Daniel Kendrick in Ralls County. During the boys' early years, both men were deeply invested in transportation schemes they thought would help their home regions prosper (Ralls; *SCOH* 105, 291–92; Scroggins 253). Meanwhile, the two boys developed skills that earned them money doing things they found interesting. Sam learned the printer's trade and wrote squibs for various papers, while Henry learned how to play the fiddle for dances, a skill that was a ready source of pocket money.

The two boys may have crossed paths at Bear Creek: Sam and his friends often played there, and the mouth of the creek was the final destination of the hogs Henry drove. Whether or not the boys ever crossed paths, each would play an important role in how the other would be remembered in their shared hometown after their deaths.

As a child in Hannibal, Sam attended four schools, in which he excelled at spelling and did poorly in deportment. Henry never attended school. Although two of his master's sons were schoolteachers, neither seems to have offered to teach him to read. During the time when Sam attended school, there was no school for black children in the region. In 1853, the year Sam left Hannibal to work as a journeyman printer in other cities, black children were beginning to be taught to read and write in a room at the rear of the Baptist Church at Eighth and Center streets (Hagood, *Hannibal* 73). Blanche Kelso Bruce, who taught there from 1864 to 1865, would later become the first ex-slave to serve a full term in the US Senate (representing Mississippi), where he became an outspoken advocate of human rights who argued for more equitable treatment of Native Americans and against the exclusion of the Chinese (Christensen 128).

The Missouri state constitution ratified in 1865 mandated that cities "establish and maintain one or more separate schools for the colored children of school age" (H. Williams 138). As a result, in 1870, the town of Hannibal opened a new three-room school for black children at 924 Rock Street, between Ninth and Tenth streets, called the Douglasville School, after the neighborhood in which it was located (Hagood, *Hannibal* 73–74). All its teachers were white. One teacher recruited during the school's early years was a young woman named Roxanne (Annie) Delaney, who was hired despite having no experience, training, or qualifications. Her diary reveals that she "could not control the children," and whipped a child named Amos and another named William Chills nearly every day in an attempt to maintain discipline. Black parents complained and petitioned the school board to hire black teachers (Hagood "Douglasville;" *Hannibal* 74). In 1874, the board hired the first black teachers, among whom was twenty-six-year-old Joseph Pelham. Hired as principal, he would remain in Hannibal for over four decades, during which the Douglasville School was renamed the Douglass School in honor of Frederick Douglass and became a place where local black students could get an excellent education (Hagood, "Douglass School;" *Hannibal* 75–76). In 1875, Pelham's sister-in-law, Fannie Barrier, a twenty-year-old woman from Brockport, New York, started teaching at the school (Hendricks 29, 184n4; Hagood, *Hannibal* 80).

Barrier had grown up in an integrated, interracial community, in which she was fully welcomed in the homes of her white friends. After receiving a first-rate education at a New York normal school and collegiate institute, she decided to follow the lead of several of her white girlfriends and become a teacher in a black school in the South (Hendricks 10, 21–27; F. B. Williams 5–6). She went south with the idealistic goal of helping to educate black children. However, Hannibal gave *her* an education she had not expected. In 1904, Barrier wrote that until she went to Hannibal, "I had never been reminded that I belonged to an 'inferior' race. . . . It was here for the first time that I began life as a colored person, in all that term implies" (F. B. Williams 6). She recalled the impact her stay in Hannibal had on her:

> No one but a colored woman, reared and educated as I was can ever know what it means to be brought face to face with conditions that fairly overwhelm you with the ugly reminder that a certain penalty must be suffered by those who, not being able to select their own parentage, must be born of a dark complexion. What a shattering of cherished ideals! (F. B. Williams 6)

Barrier left Hannibal after two years, but her encounter with racism and discrimination in Hannibal prompted her to embark on a lifelong fight for civil rights that would make her one of the most prominent civil rights leaders in the country—a cofounder of both the National Association for the Advancement of Colored People and the National Association of Colored Women (Deegan xiii–lx).

By 1888, nearly one out of five students in Hannibal public schools was black (M. Powers). The Douglass School had such high enrollments that a second branch was opened during that year along with Douglass School, built on the corner of Willow and Barton streets. Joseph Pelham was named the school's superintendent.

The five children of Henry and his wife, Mary, did not have the opportunity to take advantage of the Douglass School—but some of their grandchildren and great-grandchildren did. Their two sons and three daughters attended a rural school near where the family farmed for a few years, but they left school before they were twelve to begin working, probably as farm hands and domestics in Hannibal or the surrounding countryside. Many of their grandchildren attended the elementary school, but only Ella Belle would graduate from the Douglass School and later attend Lincoln University in Jefferson City, Missouri.

Henry's son Charles Alexander, born a slave in 1857, when his parents were still enslaved, grew up, married, and began raising his own growing family in South River Township, Marion County, where they farmed. Like all of their neighbors, Charles and his wife and their twelve children were very poor. Melvin (1909–96), their youngest son shared memories of snow coming through holes in the roof of their shack. Holidays were prominent in his memories. He recalled that for Christmas he would usually get "an old sock filled with an orange and some nuts." He also remembered the family "tradition of saying 'Christmas Gift' upon entering someone's house on Christmas morning, as a substitute for exchanging gifts." Melvin married Roxie Virginia Kelley in 1934, raised four children, and saved money to buy a sixty-acre farm in Hannibal. Their son Joel was born in 1948 when they purchased the farm. Joel and his older siblings Melvin, Jr. and Charlotte, Henry's great-grandchildren, attended Douglass School until the boys transferred to a one-room country schoolhouse near the family farm. Joel remembers his father encouraging all of his children to get a good education but he was also fond of saying that "no matter what your education, you ended up with a broom." He told his son to "get up out of Hannibal" (F. Dant, Emails).

When Sam returned to Hannibal in 1867 to deliver a lecture in Brittingham Hall, there was no evidence that he noticed the little school for black children that had recently opened at Eighth and Center streets, some eight blocks from where he spoke. He was not yet particularly interested in the education of black youth. When he returned to Hannibal again in 1882 to collect material for *Life on the Mississippi* (1883), he noted casually that "colored folks" were now living in his old house on Hill Street (*LM* ch. 54). But if he noticed the Douglass School some ten blocks away, he did not mention it. Within months, however, the education of black youth would increasingly claim his attention; checks and letters that he wrote, and lobbying he did in the 1880s, would make clear his growing belief in its importance.

On June 12, 1882, just weeks after his return from Hannibal and other places along the Mississippi to gather material for his book, Twain met a man named J. Chester, who was a financial agent for Pennsylvania's Lincoln University, the first degree-granting university for black students in the United States. The result was a check for $150 (the equivalent of about $3,500 in 2015 dollars) that Twain wrote to the university to support a then-undetermined student (SLC to JC, 16 Aug. 1882, *UCCL* 41181). Twain was informed in August that the beneficiary of his gift would be a young man named A. W. Jones, who was "among the first" in his class with an academic average of 96.8. Twain may also have supported other students at Lincoln University. He was disappointed when Jones decided to study theology rather than "some useful occupation" but sent additional checks before deciding unequivocally that Chester was a "humbug," a "clerical fraud" and a "bilk" (SLC notes on envelopes from J. Chester in CU-MARK; *N&J3* 255).

By autumn of 1885, the issue of the education of black youth would become the focus of Clemens's attention once again after he met Warner T. McGuinn, one of the first black law students at Yale. In his capacity as president of the Kent Club, McGuinn met Clemens at the railroad station and escorted him to the dean's house when he came to speak at Yale. While working as a part-time clerk, waiter, and bill collector, McGuinn, was having difficulty finding sufficient time for his studies (Fishkin, *Lighting Out* 100–08). Evidently he wrote requesting financial assistance sometime after they met. Soon after meeting and hearing from McGuinn, Twain wrote his friend Francis Wayland, dean of the law school, to learn whether it would be wise to assist McGuinn financially. Sent on Christmas Eve, 1885, the year that *Huckleberry Finn* was published, the letter included a succinct comment on racism's shameful legacies: "We have ground the manhood out of them," he wrote, referring to black people, "& the shame is ours, not theirs, & we should pay for it." He asked whether he should send six, twelve, or twenty-four months' board (SLC to Wayland, 24 Dec. 1885, *UCCL* 42826). Wayland responded positively and Twain paid McGuinn's board for the remainder of his time at Yale. He received interim reports from Wayland, like the October 1886 report calling McGuinn "the most promising colored youth we have ever had" (Wayland to SLC, 6 Oct. 1886, *UCCL* 43074). In the fall of 1887, Wayland wrote Twain that McGuinn had won one of the school's top prizes during his final term at Yale (Wayland to SLC, 1 Oct. 1887, *UCCL* 43789). Some influential friends of Twain's—like *Hartford Courant* editor Charles Dudley Warner—argued that higher education for African Americans encouraged idleness among them (Warner 384). Twain disagreed.

After practicing law in Kansas City, Kansas, and editing a black newspaper there, McGuinn moved to Baltimore, where he established a law practice and played a leading role in fighting segregation in the city (Bogen 723, 743; Koshy 17–22, 30–33, 59). In 1917, Baltimore's white establishment lined up against him in federal court, confident in their ability to maintain the status quo. However, McGuinn thoroughly bested his opponents and won a major civil rights victory that became a milestone in the effort to desegregate American cities (Koshy 73–76).

Future US Supreme Court justice Thurgood Marshall was born in Baltimore in 1908. During his Baltimore childhood, one of his father's "favorite pastimes was to listen to cases at the local courthouse before returning home to rehash the lawyers' arguments with his sons" ("Thurgood Marshall"). Marshall later recalled that it was those discussions that got him interested in law. In 1917, after McGuinn's victory in federal court, a *Baltimore Afro-American* headline trumpeted the news: "Segregation in Baltimore Gets Final Interment" (Koshy 76). The *Philadelphia Tribune* ran a front-page picture of McGuinn, identifying him as, "The Attorney Who Knocked Out the Segregation Ordinance" (McGuinn). McGuinn's legendary victory had to have been a topic of lively discussion around the Marshall dinner table, giving nine-year-old Thurgood a sense that it *was* possible to challenge segregation through the courts.

When Marshall returned to Baltimore to practice law after graduating from Howard Law School, McGuinn allowed him to operate out of an office next door, lent him a desk, shared a secretary with him, and occasionally sent him work (Koshy 32; H. Williams 61–70). Marshall told biographer Mark Tushnet that McGuinn "'bailed [him] out a couple of times' by keeping [him] from making mistakes in his lawyering" (Tushnet 19). When Marshall was asked about McGuinn by the *New York Times* in 1985, he said, "He was the greatest lawyer who ever lived," and added, "If he'd been white, he'd have been a judge" (McDowell).

During the autumn of 1885, Twain focused on the issue of education for black youth in another context, as well. In September 1885, a long article by William Lloyd Garrison's son in a *Century Magazine* series about his abolitionist father retold the story of Prudence Crandall's heroic efforts to create a high school for young black women in Canterbury, Connecticut, half a century earlier. In response to Crandall's efforts to open a high school for "young ladies and little misses of color" in 1833, the Connecticut General Assembly had passed a law specifically designed to close her school. Crandall ignored the law and continued to recruit students. She was arrested and briefly imprisoned, and went through three trials as the town's hostility mounted. Garrison wrote that doctors refused to treat her or her pupils; Crandall's "own family and friends were forbidden under penalty of heavy fines to visit her;" and the school's "well was filled with manure" (Garrison 783). In her last trial, charges were dismissed on a technicality by the state supreme court. When an angry mob torched Crandall's establishment on September 9, 1834, she realized that the safety of her students was at stake. She closed her school and moved to the Midwest. By 1885, when the Garrison article appeared, she was living in poverty in an isolated cabin outside of Elk Falls, Kansas. The article featured both a reproduction of the portrait of the idealistic young woman that the New England Anti-Slavery Society had commissioned in 1838 and an image of a haggard, elderly Crandall from a photograph taken of her by a visitor in 1882 (Garrison 781, 784). A campaign began to get the state of Connecticut to compensate her for the loss of her school.

Twain read the *Century* regularly (excerpts from *Huckleberry Finn* had appeared in it a few months earlier). It is highly likely that Garrison's September 1885 article, with its striking portraits of Crandall in her youth and as an impoverished, elderly widow, would have caught his eye. Twain supported Crandall's petition to the Connecticut legislature for a pension that was presented in January 1886. During hearings in January and February, Twain's close friend, the Reverend Joseph H. Twichell testified (D. Williams 316). The *Hartford Daily Courant* took up Crandall's cause, arguing "if real justice could be done, her old place in Canterbury might be purchased . . . and she [should] be allowed and invited to spend her last days among the New England hills where she was born, instead of on a lonesome farm in the far west" (D. Williams 317). Crandall declined the invitation to return to the East but was delighted to learn later that none other than Twain had been her secret benefactor, offering through his friends at the *Courant*, to purchase her old home. Twain had also exerted his personal influence to lobby Connecticut legislators to vote for Crandall's pension (Buchanan 32; Commire 188). A resolution giving Crandall a modest annual pension of four hundred dollars was passed in both houses by April. Only after all was resolved did Crandall and the public learn about Twain's efforts behind the scenes on Crandall's behalf. Crandall wrote a letter of thanks to "Mark Twain My very Dear Friend," which read, "God bless your dear heart is my prayer for you. It is only lately that I ascertained that you were the person that offered to reinstate me in my home that I bought in the long ago in the town of Canterbury Conn" (Prudence Crandall Philleo to SLC 14, Apr. 1886, *UCCL* 42921). She confessed that she had once borrowed *The Innocents Abroad* (1869) from a friend, but had to return it before she could finish it. She asked him to send her a copy—as well his photograph. Twain sent her his picture and also wrote his publisher to send her not just *The Innocents Abroad*, but five other books, as well. In his letter he referred to Crandall as "Connecticut's heroine, of old days" (SLC to Charles L. Webster 22 Apr. 1886, *UCCL* 03385). Twain kept a photograph of Crandall in his billiard room in Hartford; it still hangs on the wall there today.

Crandall, as well as Warner McGuinn, would play a role in the case that set in motion the desegregation of the nation's schools—including schools in Hannibal, Missouri. Marshall incorporated arguments Crandall's lawyers had made appealing her conviction into the brief he wrote for *Brown v. Board of Education* (D. Williams 340–41). That argument, Marshall and his attorneys wrote in their brief to the court, was "one of the classic statements of the social and ethical case for equality of opportunity irrespective of race" (D. Williams 340–341).

In addition to supporting the education of black students from the 1880s on, Twain increasingly took aim at the arrogance of white privilege and the absurdity of assumptions of white superiority. For example, sometime between 1883 and 1889, he penned a plot summary for "Man with Negro Blood," a sympathetic novel about "passing" set in the North after the Civil War. Its protagonist, a young man who has no desire to deny being black, finds that "even the best educated negro is at a disadvantage, besides being always insulted," and therefore decides to pass for white (Fishkin, "False Starts" 18).

After witnessing the devastation of indigenous populations by white settler-colonists in Australia and New Zealand during the mid-1890s, he wrote in *Following the Equator* (1897) "There are many humorous things in the world; among them, the white man's notion that he is less savage than the other savages" (*FE* ch. 21). In "The Stupendous Procession" (1901), Twain rewrote familiar texts inserting references to the implied but unstated racial ideology that lay behind them, imagining a phantasmagoric parade that featured banners saying things like, "'All white men are born free and equal.' *Declaration of Independence*" and "'Governments derive their just powers from the consent of the governed white men.' *Declaration of Independence*" (*SP* 56).

A Mark Twain for whom the arrogance of white privilege was becoming increasingly salient in his final years would have been proud of the achievements of Warner McGuinn and his protégé, Thurgood Marshall. And he would also have been pleased that 109 years after he lobbied the Connecticut legislature to give Crandall a pension and offered to buy her home; Crandall, whom he had called "Connecticut's Heroine," would be *officially* designated "Connecticut State Heroine" by an act of the Connecticut assembly on October 1, 1995 (*Register* 836).

When Twain returned to Hannibal for the last time in 1902, he attended a reception for the 1901 graduating class of Hannibal High School. That school would remain all-white until it was desegregated by law in 1955. When the Douglass School closed, students bemoaned the fact that the talented black teachers who had taught them, their parents, and even grandparents there, lost their jobs (Darr; Anon. "Education"). Joel Dant and Gloria Faye Green (who became known as Faye Dant) both received their earliest schooling at the segregated Douglass elementary school. But long after *Brown v. Board of Education* (1954) led to integration of the town's schools, Faye recalled,

> Jim Crow was alive and well in Hannibal. Before and after the schools were integrated blacks still had to use the back door for take-out in Hannibal restaurants. The local movie theater welcomed blacks—Balcony seating only. Black kids had to take their own skates to the local skating rink. In later years it changed—giving Blacks Tuesday night all to themselves.

The Ku Klux Klan was a visible presence, as well. Faye remembers Klan members flanking segregationist George Wallace at a rally in Hannibal's Central Park during her childhood. The only public reference to black people in "Mark Twain's town" during her childhood was a bizarre public marker that Dant remembers seeing often when she grew up here that referred to "Niggar Jim" (F. Dant, "Hannibal").

Black students at Hannibal High continued to face various forms of discrimination for decades. The school had been integrated for seven years by the time Larry Thompson graduated there in 1963. The bright young black man had been elected class president but was not allowed to attend the graduation parties, because they were held at the segregated country club (Baker). Undaunted, Thompson went on to become a deputy attorney general of the United States, a position that put him in charge of investigating cases of corporate fraud, including the investigations of Enron, WorldCom, and the Arthur Anderson accounting firm—just the beginning of his illustrious career in corporate America.

Young people attending school in Hannibal in the twentieth century never heard about Twain's active interest in the education of black youth, the role black people had played in shaping Twain's work as a writer, or his efforts to expose and undermine racism (Facen; F. Dant, Emails). It would have been good for them to know these things about the iconic author who was the engine driving the town's economy, particularly given the persistence of racism in their community and in the region (Ferguson, Missouri, after all, is only 109 miles southeast of Hannibal).

The fact that Hannibal had been a slaveholding town was ignored throughout the Mark Twain Historic District during the twentieth century (Fishkin, *Lighting Out* 17–69). In 2005, the Mark Twain Boyhood Home decided (over the objections of a board member) to place "several text panels addressing Twain's experience with slavery in Hannibal" in the home's Interpretive Center, costing the museum "the goodwill of its largest donor" (Faden 253, 255). But one would never know from the exhibit hall that racism persisted after slavery ended—or that racism (rather than slavery) was a target of Twain's criticism throughout much of his career, including in *Huckleberry Finn*, which was published two decades after slavery had been abolished.

The history of racism in "America's Hometown" (as Hannibal likes to call itself) was not taught in schools or mentioned in local museums—despite the key role it had played in shaping the life and work of the town's most famous native son. Also missing was any sense that Mark Twain had been a critic of the status quo in his hometown. It would take the descendants of Henry to bring this aspect of Twain to life in Hannibal; they would create an institution that would give Twain, the social critic, a presence in his hometown.

Back to the
Henry Dave Connection

Henry's great-grandson Donald L. Scott (son of Melvin's sister Beatrice) attended the segregated Douglass School in Hannibal for three years, commuting some thirty miles daily from Hunnewell, Missouri, where his family lived, and later attended Lincoln University, becoming the first member of his family to graduate from college. Scott went on to serve his country in a number of prominent roles: He rose to the rank of brigadier general in the US Army, was founder and director of AmeriCorps National Civilian Community Corps, and served as deputy librarian of Congress and first chief operating officer of the Library of Congress (Scott). Henry's great-grandson Joel Dant and all of his siblings followed their father's advice to get "out of Hannibal." After earning a graduate degree from Michigan State University, Joel had a successful career in human resources that included both domestic and international assignments. His wife, Faye, also a fifth-generation Hannibalian, who was descended from a Missouri slave named James Walker and whose mother had worked as a domestic in Hannibal, grew up in Douglasville and attended the segregated Douglass School and graduated from Hannibal High School. After earning an MA from the University of Michigan, she also worked for more than thirty years in human resources. Together, she and her husband raised three children. In 2011, they decided to move back to the family farm in Hannibal that Joel's father had purchased the year Joel was born and build a comfortable home for themselves on the family land (F. Dant, emails; J. Dant, emails).

Soon after returning to Hannibal, Faye observed that everything from her memories was gone; she sought and received donations of photographs, newspaper clippings, directories, furniture, clothing, and other artifacts depicting African-American life in Hannibal from slavery through the 1950s, for an exhibit on "Hannibal African American Life and History" at the Hannibal History Museum in downtown Hannibal that she curated. Over the next two years, she tirelessly gathered additional materials and also worked to gain support from the Marion County Historical Society, the Missouri Humanities Council, the Hannibal City Council, and the Hannibal's mayor. Her efforts culminated on September 21, 2013, with the grand opening of a new museum: "Jim's Journey: The Huck Finn Freedom Center" at 509 North Third Street. It is now the first building visitors encounter when they exit the highway to enter the Mark Twain Historic District.

The museum's grand opening was attended by the mayor, the superintendent of Hannibal schools, representatives of the Marion County Historical Society, and the local press. Members of Hannibal's black community who now live across the United States, came back for the event, which featured, in addition to tours

Faye Dant (third from the left) explaining an exhibit on slavery at *Jim's Journey: The Huck Finn Freedom Center* (jimsjourney.org), the history museum she founded in Hannibal, Missouri.

Photo by R. Kent Rasmussen

of the new museum, a lecture by Larry McCarty, a direct descendant of Daniel Quarles, the slave whose storytelling filled young Sam with awe and admiration, and upon whom the character of Jim in *Huckleberry Finn* was partially based. Henry's descendants played a central role. The opening was presided over by his great grandsons Brigadier General (Ret.) Donald L. Scott, who serves as board president of the new museum, and Joel, who serves as a board member, and of course, by a beaming Faye, its executive director.

The museum is housed in the "Old Welshman's House," a one-room stone structure thought to have been built by slaves in 1839 that Twain mentions in *Tom Sawyer*. The Marion County Historical Society saved it from demolition and moved it from its original location a few blocks away to its current address. Dant was determined that the new museum rescue and preserve for future generations the history that the town had ignored, along with important, neglected dimensions of Twain. She wanted to address Hannibal's failure to acknowledge its slave past and the town's erasure of those slaves' descendants—hard-working people who raised close-knit families, started businesses, and managed to thrive despite segregation and discrimination. She wanted to make people aware the key roles African Americans had played in shaping Twain's work. And she wanted them to know about Twain's efforts to oppose racism through his writing and his actions. The museum she worked hard to establish reconnects the history of African Americans in Hannibal with the life and work of the writer who learned much of his art by listening appreciatively to the voices of a gifted storyteller and a brilliant satirist who also happened to be slaves.

Visitors to the museum can see a photograph of Henry and read his story. They can learn that when he was set free, all he and his family were given was "a side of meat and a bushel of meal" (H. Dant). They can also see photos of the segregated Hannibal in which Henry lived for six decades after freedom came. Dant lived to be 105, dying in Hannibal in 1939. Jim-Crow-Era signs, such as "Colored Waiting Room," nestle against the museum's medals and citations testifying to what the town's black residents achieved despite the obstacles thrown in their way. The museum tells the story of the black-owned barbershops, beauty shops, fraternal organizations, night clubs, and funeral homes; the seven black-owned grocery stores, and the two black newspapers —all now gone. "Local African Americans developed, defined and created this separate, resilient community, often hidden from the eyes of white residents," Faye Dant has written. "They depended on each other for survival and found strength in adversity, excelling despite numerous hurdles" (F. Dant, "Hannibal").

There are scores of photos of the small, proud segregated Douglass School that gave generations of Hannibal's black children the skills to make their way in a white-run world that assumed they would never amount to much. The medals, honors and clippings about their achievements that line the display shelves attest to the foolishness of white Hannibal's low expectations of its black children. Students who attended Douglass became dedicated teachers, doctors, dentists, and lawyers; talented musicians and athletes; successful businessmen; and committed public servants like Joe Miller, who would serve as the only black member of the Hannibal Board of Education. Miller spent his senior year of high school integrating Hannibal High (Miller). A teacher told him later that more than two hundred white students boycotted the first day of school to protest the admission of black students (Darr).

The framed sign that greets visitors when they enter the museum reads, "In order to live in the present and prepare for the future, we must first understand the past. Welcome!!" The comment is reminiscent of James Baldwin's comment, "The great force of history comes from the fact that we carry it within us, are unconsciously controlled by it in many ways, and history is literally present in all that we do" (Baldwin 47).

Despite the fact that the new museum is fewer than four blocks from the Mark Twain Boyhood Home, staff at the Boyhood Home did not mention it when teachers from across the country arrived for a workshop on teaching *Huckleberry Finn* in the fall of 2014 (Chadwick). And despite numerous pleas, the sightseeing tours of historic Hannibal that the Hannibal Trolley Company offers visitors every day during the tourist season drive past the museum without mentioning it. Nonetheless, young people find their way to the museum—some from the tri-state region and some from as far away as Connecticut and Sweden; some with their families, and some on class field trips. About a thousand young people have visited the Museum (F. Dant, Emails).

The white child named Sam, born in 1835, would leave an indelible mark on his hometown through his writings. The black child named Henry, also born in 1835, would leave an indelible mark on his hometown through the work of his descendants. Youth in Hannibal today—both black and white—are indebted to the legacies of both men. The intersecting, interlocking stories of their legacies and their lives, will shape how black and white youth in Hannibal in the twenty-first century understand their community's past, and how they choose to craft its future.

Note

1   Although this chapter involves substantial new research conducted between 2013 and 2015, it also reprises some material presented in my previous books *Was Huck Black? Mark Twain and African American Voices* (1993) and *Lighting Out for the Territory: Mark Twain and American Culture* (1997), and in my most recent book, *Writing America: Literary Landmarks from Walden Pond to Wounded Knee* (2015). I would especially like to thank Faye and Joel Dant for sharing their time with me as generously as they have, both during my most recent visit to Hannibal and in responding to my endless questions about their family and the museum they created.

24

Mark Twain and the Movies

Mark Dawidziak

Nobody would recommend the 1944 Warner Bros. film *The Adventures of Mark Twain* as a model of authenticity and reliability. Indeed, Director Irving Rapper's sentimental biopic plays so fast and loose with the details of its subject's life that any reports of its being an actual biography should win the movie a GE rating—for greatly exaggerated. This is not to say that the film is without merit, however. Despite the many stretchers and whoppers that ended up in Alan LeMay's screenplay, *The Adventures of Mark Twain* steams along as a slickly made piece of Hollywood entertainment. It features an undeniably heartfelt and engaging performance by Fredric March, and it also, at times, gets emotionally near the appeal of Mark Twain as America's premier family author. It does this with a handful of scenes that emphasize the writer's near-mystical standing as a kind of literary fountain of youth. This emphasis is never more noticeable than when Livy Clemens (played by Alexis Smith) consoles her husband after the death of their son, Langdon. March's Sam Clemens laments that their son will never see the Mississippi River and the Missouri haunts of his boyhood. Livy rallies his sagging spirit.

"Our little son will never see it, but, Mark, you must save those things you loved," she tells him. "You must save them for whole generations of little boys, of all ages, forever. You mustn't let those precious things be lost. . . . You're the only man in the world who still is that little barefoot boy."

Livy's words inspire Twain to sit down and write *The Adventures of Tom Sawyer* (1876). Never mind that there is no evidence that the real Livy ever said any such thing to her husband. Never mind that Livy did not call her husband by the first part of his famous pen name. For a moment, disregard all of that, because, with all of its misinformation, misstatements, and misrepresentations, *The Adventures of Mark Twain* is about to lay a heavy dose of truth on us: "You've captured youth," Livy says after reading Sam's manuscript of *Tom Sawyer*.

Scene from the 1944 motion picture *The Adventures of Mark Twain* showing Mark Twain with his daughters. One of the reasons Fredric March was chosen for the title role was his physical resemblance to Mark Twain.

Warner Bros. Courtesy R. Kent Rasmussen

"Youth. That's what you are. I'll never be able to think of you as anything else." Indeed, the real Livy's nickname for her husband was, in fact, "Youth."

There it is. It is a lovely moment that captures why Livy called Sam "Youth." "That was her name for him among their friends, and it fitted him as no other would," Sam's friend and fellow writer William Dean Howells wrote in *My Mark Twain* (1910). "He was a youth to the end of his days, the heart of a boy with the head of a sage" (*MMT* 5).

So, yes, on some level, Hollywood innately understood this profound and enduring connection between Twain and youth. This stirring moment leaves little doubt of that. And yet, even armed with this realization, filmmakers consistently have missed the mark when it comes to adaptations of Twain's works. It certainly has not been due to any lack of effort, however. There have been dozens upon dozens of adaptations since the first short films appeared in 1907. By and large, these screen versions make as much a mess of Twain's stories as March's *The Adventures of Mark Twain* makes of the story of his life. The reasons are similar. Like *The Adventures of Mark Twain*, these adaptations tend to be sanitized, sentimentalized, and badly compromised. They scrub the rough edges away until the surface gleams with the wholesomeness and bright cheer of a Norman Rockwell painting. They veer away from the dark and dangerous and challenging corners that made Twain's writing so emotionally and psychologically true to childhood—a real childhood, not the overly simplistic or overly sophisticated extremes Hollywood loves to embrace. Documentary filmmaker and unabashed Twain admirer Ken Burns is fond of quoting historian and novelist Shelby Foote's observation that the author of *Tom Sawyer* and *Adventures of Huckleberry Finn* "wrote with the bark on." Twain wrote American English, with all of its rough edges, embracing both lively vernacular and the spirit of a young nation. Typically, the first thing Hollywood does is remove the bark, polishing the surface until it is as smooth and safe as possible. The idea is to commercially package these stories, making them tenable and palatable to the widest possible audience. The irony is that, in doing so, they strip away the very dark and dangerous elements that Twain knew would fetch and captivate the teen and pre-teen set. Consider how much disturbingly dark and wonderfully dangerous storytelling fuels the *Harry Potter* books and films. Think how wondrously attractive those dark and dangerous elements are to young readers and filmgoers. Kids know when you are playing it for real. J. K. Rowling might have learned that lesson from Twain, but filmmakers and television producers have a difficult time applying the lesson to his stories.

Somewhat more egregiously, filmmakers tend to stray alarmingly far from the characters and themes in Twain's books. Disney's *The Adventures of Huck Finn* (1993), for instance, gives us a lead character that is something of a modernized cross between Tom Sawyer and Huckleberry Finn. His speech and actions also run contrary to Huck, taking the character in directions that violate the spirit of Twain's novel. If this is the only view a young filmgoer has of Huck, it is a dangerously distorted one. Somewhat symbolically, this Disney-fied misfire even serves up a mangled version of Twain's original title, *Adventures of Huckleberry Finn* (1885). The reworked title flaps over this egregious effort, more as a caution flag than some kind of proud banner. It's almost as if writer-director Stephen Sommers is warning us not to expect any fidelity to the writer and his most celebrated book.

"I like Stephen Sommers a great deal," film historian and critic Leonard Maltin said during a recent interview. "He went on to do some terrific things, but early in his career, he got on a Mark Twain kick, and I wish he hadn't. It wasn't a good thing."

No, it wasn't. A year after *The Adventures of Huck Finn*, Sommers was a writer and producer on the lackluster Disney Pictures production *Tom and Huck*, starring Jonathan Taylor Thomas and Brad Renfro in the title roles. After taking such monstrous missteps in the Twain realm, Sommers found blockbuster success by hunting monsters in such films as *The Mummy* (1999) and *Van Helsing* (2004). Still, Sommers does not lack for company when it comes to filmmakers hitting shallow water with adaptations of Twain works.

The road through Hollywood history is littered with disappointing adaptations of Twain's books and stories. Since the earliest known versions appeared while Twain still was alive, more than one hundred movies and television shows have been adapted from at least twenty-one of Twain's books and stories. Four works account for about sixty productions: *The Adventures of Tom Sawyer* (1876), *Adventures of Huckleberry Finn* (1885), *The Prince and the Pauper* (1881), and *A Connecticut Yankee in King Arthur's Court* (1889). Between the movies and television, there have also been multiple attempts to adapt *Roughing It* (1872) and *Pudd'nhead Wilson* (1894).

Overall, Twain adaptations have had a dismal track record, to put it charitably. First published in 1969, Maltin's standard reference work, his *Movie & Video Guide*, popularized the star system for ranking movies. Not one film based on a Twain work earns the august four-star status. Not one. "It certainly wasn't for any lack of trying," Maltin said. "Many consider him America's greatest author, and yet there are no truly great movies based on his works. I think one explanation is that the first thing Hollywood veers away from is the amazing satire in all of his works. It's so much a part of who Mark Twain was as a writer, but Hollywood has never been fond of satire. They're not comfortable with it."

That discomfort most obviously hurt the many adaptations of *A Connecticut Yankee in King Arthur's Court,* which have jettisoned the book's dark social commentary in favor of slapstick. Remove that, and we are left with a hollow shell of Twain's novel. That book gets smashed up at the intersection of Hollow and Hollywood with such adaptations as a 1931 version starring Will Rogers, a 1949 musical vehicle for Bing Crosby, a 1989 television movie for *Cosby Show* star Keshia Knight Pulliam, and a 1995 Disney stunt fest, *A Kid in King Arthur's Court,* featuring a roller-blading Thomas Ian Nicholas, among many other adaptations. The tendency to veer away from anything dark and dangerous in the stories mirrors what happened with Twain's reputation for more than fifty years after his death in 1910. Working with the writer's daughter, Clara, biographer Albert Bigelow Paine suppressed any works or viewpoints that threatened to damage the grandfatherly image of Twain as America's favorite family author, folksy humorist, and genial wit. When the fierce social critic was allowed to emerge, Twain's stature only grew. Had the social criticism been allowed in the films, one or two might have emerged as masterpieces. One might object that we're not talking kid's stuff here, but of course we are. Echoes of the dark Twain can be found in the three novels Hollywood rightly believes have the strongest kid appeal: *Tom Sawyer, Huckleberry Finn,* and *The Prince and the Pauper.*

Some might dismiss film and television's failure rate with Twain with a familiar pop-culture canard: Well, Hollywood always mangles great works of literature. Not true. Not even remotely true. One need only look at how many splendid films and TV productions have been based on the works of Charles Dickens, another towering literary figure known both for his boy heroes and for being a beloved family author. Maltin awards four stars to the 1935 versions of *David Copperfield* and *A Tale of Two Cities,* director David Lean's versions of *Great Expectations* (1946), and *Oliver Twist* (1948), and the 1951 version of *A Christmas Carol.* That's not even counting the 1968 musical *Oliver!,* which won the Academy Award for best picture or the countless acclaimed Dickens adaptations that have aired on PBS over the last forty years. All in all, in some celestial cinema, Dickens is sitting in the front row, looking pretty pleased with what ended up on the screen. How about an American author? Maltin assigns four stars to three film classics based on John Steinbeck novels: *Of Mice and Men* (1939), *The Grapes of Wrath* (1940), and *East of Eden* (1955). Clearly, certain authors and books have been incredibly well served by Hollywood: the 1941 version of Dashiell Hammett's *The Maltese Falcon,* the 1962 version of Harper Lee's *To Kill a Mockingbird,* the 1993 version of Thomas Keneally's *Schindler's List.* Such auspicious successes only magnify Hollywood's failures with Twain.

Another measure of failure is how few Twain scholars, researchers, biographers, and enthusiasts were inspired by youthful encounters with film adaptation of his works. About thirty Twain scholars responded to a survey taken for this chapter to determine the influence of these movie and TV versions, and an immediate and overwhelming consensus emerged from the responses. "None of the adaptations ever did anything for me," said Stanford University professor Shelley Fisher Fishkin. "It was always reading Twain in the original that did it for me."

It was a typical response. Kevin J. Bochynski, the list administrator for the *Mark Twain Forum,* put it even more strongly. He recalls actually being desensitized to the books through "viewings of the various cornball adaptations." A television production, however, did inspire a passion for Twain's writing. It was the 1967 CBS airing of the special featuring ninety minutes of material from Hal Holbrook's acclaimed one-man show, *Mark Twain Tonight!* Bochynski's response to excerpts from *Huckleberry Finn* echoes the countless teachers who have told Holbrook since the 1960s that they used first his *Mark Twain Tonight!* record albums, then the VHS and DVD releases of the CBS special, to make Mark Twain and his writing come alive for students in junior high school and high school. Many Twain scholars cited Holbrook's show as a profound inspiration, but not the films based on Twain's work.

So, are we talking a total waste of Twain time, particularly when it comes to films for a young audience? Not quite. There does seem to be one grand exception among the Hollywood productions. Only three of the Twain scholars responding to the survey said they were influenced by a youthful encounter with a film adaptation, but, intriguingly, they all named the same film. If not quite a four-star masterpiece, the 1938 version of *The Adventures of Tom Sawyer* receives universally high marks from film historians and some Twain scholars. Although the silent and often-overlooked 1917 version of *Tom Sawyer* with Jack Pickford may be more faithful to the book, it is the 1938 adaptation that comes closest to capturing the spirit of Twain and youth. It's also the closest we get to a classic Twain film.

"I grew up on the 1938 *Tom Sawyer* movie and always liked it," said Maltin, who gives the film three and a half stars in his *Movie & Video Guide*. "It's splendid proof that Mark Twain can work on screen, and work wonderfully well, in the right hands. It's too bad more filmmakers didn't follow its lead."

Produced by movie mogul David O. Selznick and released a year before *Gone with the Wind*, *The Adventures of Tom Sawyer* stars Tommy Kelly as Tom, Jackie Moran as Huckleberry Finn, and Ann Gillis as Becky Thatcher. It also features a delightful lineup of all-star supporting players: May Robson as Aunt Polly, three-time Oscar winner Walter Brennan as Muff Potter, Victor Jory as Injun Joe, Donald Meek as the Sunday-school superintendent, Margaret Hamilton as Mrs. Harper, and Spring Byington as the Widow Douglas. Norman Taurog, the director of record, must have seemed like the natural choice to helm the Technicolor production for Selznick. He had directed the 1931 film version of *Huckleberry Finn*. However, he was not the original director of *The Adventures of Tom Sawyer*. Broadway veteran H. C. Potter, a recent Hollywood arrival, was the first one in the director's chair. Although fired by Selznick, he would go on to direct several hit films, including *The Farmer's Daughter* (1947) and *Mr. Blandings Builds His Dream House* (1948).

Taurog had won the best director Oscar for *Skippy* (1931), but, as with *Gone with the Wind*, Selznick brought in other directors to do uncredited work on *The Adventures of Tom Sawyer*. They included two of Hollywood's greatest filmmakers, George Cukor and William Wellman. If there is a Twain film adaptation that gets more than just a passing grade from Twain scholars and researchers, it is this one.

"I loved this film as a child, and it imprinted Mark Twain in my consciousness," said Winthrop University professor John Bird. "I think it is an excellent film version, capturing the charm and terrors of youth. I count that film, the original airing of Hal Holbrook's *Mark Twain Tonight!* on television, and my fifth grade teacher reading *Tom Sawyer* aloud to us every Friday afternoon for my interest in Mark Twain."

Everything that goes cinematically right in *The Adventures of Tom Sawyer* underscores what goes so terribly wrong in most other film versions of Twain's work. First, it does not try to sanitize the book in order to make it more acceptable. There is an undeniable charm at work in every frame of this film, yet it does not cross the line to saccharine sweetness.

Second, it embraces not only the joys of childhood but also the fears. As Bird suggests, this film, like Twain's stories about children, are very much in touch with both the small and vast terrors of childhood. Maybe it's something as small as petty-tyrant schoolmaster handy with the hickory switch. Maybe it's something as big as witnessing a murder in the graveyard after sunset.

"I was seven or eight years old and it absolutely hooked me," Joseph Csicsila of Eastern Michigan University said of this film. "The graveyard and courtroom scenes, in particular, fascinated me. I went straight to the book after that."

The word "adventures" is part of the title, after all, and can there truly be adventure without risk? Without darkness? Without danger? And what does appreciation of light mean without the contrast of darkness? Twain supplied the answer in *Extract from Captain Stormfield's Visit to Heaven* (1909) when he wrote, "You see, happiness ain't a thing in itself—it's only a contrast with something that ain't pleasant." (*ECS* part 1)

Ron Powers, who grew up in Hannibal, Missouri, aptly titled his biographical work about Twain's boyhood years *Dangerous Waters* (1999). It brilliantly explores how many somethings weren't pleasant in Twain's childhood. Twain drew on these terrors when writing books for and about children, playing those fears for real in *Tom Sawyer*, *Huckleberry Finn*, and *The Prince and the Pauper*. In *Tom Sawyer*, Tom and Huck are haunted, even in their dreams, by what they witness in the graveyard, and readers are haunted by the images Twain serves up for children and those adults who remember what it's like to be a child coping with fears that cannot (must not) be shared with adults. And we're not done with the terrors brought to chilling realization in *The Adventures of Tom Sawyer*. For eerie instance, is there a more frightening concept than being lost in a cave and running out of light?

In *Huckleberry Finn*, Twain shapes horrific images that would do Edgar Allan Poe proud: the floating house with the naked body of a man shot in the back; the derelict and doomed *Walter Scott* steamboat (and the fate of those left on board); Huck seeing Buck and another boy killed, then pulling their bullet-riddled bodies from the river; and the exhumation of Peter Wilks's corpse. And as for *The Prince and the Pauper*, it turned more than once into a Disney-esque folk tale by, well, the Disney Company; it's essentially an ongoing nightmare for both title characters. The favorite Hollywood trick played on Twain is to shy away from this profoundly scary and unnerving stuff, watering it down until the original strong brew has lost most of its potency. We are left with the happy postcard approach typified by the well-scrubbed 1973 musical *Tom Sawyer* with Johnny Whitaker as Tom, Jeff East as Huck, and Jodie Foster as Becky. Produced by Reader's Digest, it featured a screenplay and music by Disney's favorite songwriting team, brothers Richard and Robert Sherman, best known, perhaps, for the score of *Mary Poppins* (1964).

Contrast the Reader's Digest musical *Tom Sawyer* with the 1938 adaptation, which, unlike so many attempts to adapt Twain's work, is not afraid of the dark. The climactic scene in the cave with Jory's Injun Joe menacing Tom and Becky adds some Hollywood flourishes, to be sure, but this remains a superbly suspenseful and haunting segment almost eighty years after it was first seen. A Universal horror film from the same decade could have done no better. It is not as if Selznick and his team did not wrestle with these choices. Comment cards from audience members at sneak previews raised concerns about the cave sequence being too disturbing and horrific for children. Thankfully, only minor editing was done on this part of the film (Selznick 125).

While it does take a few liberties with the original story, the 1938 *Adventures of Tom Sawyer* is a film that still can be used as an effective recruitment and educational tool for young children and teenagers. Indeed, John R. Pascal, a teacher at Seton Hall Preparatory School in New Jersey, does use it—and it works. "I first saw it when I was seven years old, and it stuck with me," Pascal said.

> And when Injun Joe dies in the cave, I had nightmares for weeks. It was scary and haunting, but in a wonderful way. Now I show that to my class, and the kids love it. They are totally entranced by it. They flinch when the schoolmaster is whipping Tom. They cringe when watching Injun Joe staring menacingly at Tom on the witness stand. They cheer at the end when Sid gets slapped by Aunt Polly. They love it because it's so faithful to the book. I showed them a few scenes from the Reader's Digest *Tom Sawyer* with Johnnie Whitaker, and they hated it.

One of them said it was actually sickening because they didn't seem anything like the characters in the book.

Pascal gets plenty of opportunities to test Twain adaptations with his students. He shows his ninth graders, fourteen and fifteen year olds, *The Adventures of Tom Sawyer*, as well as the 1980 PBS version of *Life on the Mississippi,* starring Robert Lansing as Horace Bixby and David Knell as young Sam Clemens. He also shows the ninth graders the "The Chronicle of Young Satan" segment from filmmaker Will Vinton's 1985 claymation movie, *The Adventures of Mark Twain.* His juniors, sixteen and seventeen years old, get the 1986 PBS miniseries version, *Adventures of Huckleberry Finn,* generally conceded to be the best of the many film and TV versions. Pascal also teaches Twain to students at the College of Saint Elizabeth, a women's college in Morristown, New Jersey.

"When it reaches the point where the leadsman sings out 'Mark Twain' for the first time and the orchestral music swells in *Life on the Mississippi*, there's always at least one student with tears in his or her eyes," Pascal said. "They find the moment from *The Adventures of Mark Twain* very disturbing to watch because it's so dark and it drives home this is a man who had it all and lost so much. It's very creepy and very effective, and they get it." Yes, Vinton's *The Adventures of Mark Twain* is another of those rare Twain films that embrace the darkness.

While generally disappointing, the movie and TV record with adaptations is hardly a total loss. But while Vinton's *The Adventures of Mark Twain,* Holbrook's *Mark Twain Tonight!* and the PBS versions of *Life on the Mississippi, Huckleberry Finn, The Private History of a Campaign That Failed,* and *The Mysterious Stranger* all prove useful for inspiring interest and discussion among teenagers and young adults, they're not geared for the pre-teen set. What about viewers the age of Tom and Becky, the prince and the pauper—or younger? Here is where the Twain film and television adaptations fall into a state of profound poverty. Here is where we're left with such Mickey Mouse efforts as Disney's 1990 *Prince and the Pauper* with Mickey Mouse himself or *A Kid in King Arthur's Court* (1995). The younger the viewer, the more vapid and safe and, well, juvenile the approach tends to be. This reached an inane prime-time level in 1968 with NBC's *The New Adventures of Huckleberry Finn,* a mercifully short-lived series that, a la *Mary Poppins,* combined live actors with animation, presenting a time-hopping Tom, Huck, and Becky pursued by Injun Joe (played by Ted Cassidy, better known as Lurch on *The Addams Family*). Indeed, about the only faithful film suitable for pre-teen is that 1938 version of *The Adventures of Tom Sawyer.*

Finally, we return to *The Adventures of Tom Sawyer* and *The Adventures of Mark Twain*. At the end of the 1944 film biography, seventy-four-year-old Mark Twain is shown propped up in bed at his last home, Stormfield.

"Sometimes I feel like a stalk of corn, left standing all alone . . . in a field," he says. "Nobody left for me to play with anymore."

His daughter Clara notices Halley's Comet blazing across the night sky over Stormfield. A frightening thought occurs to her. She looks back at the bed to see her father has slipped away. She breaks down in tears. Twain's ghost appears behind her. He moves to comfort his daughter, but he's distracted by two boys glimpsed on a hill.

"Sam! Sam! Come on," they shout. "Come on!" One carries a fishing pole. Presumably, they are Tom Sawyer and Huckleberry Finn. Sam goes with them, disappearing over a hill. This is the Hollywood version, after all—sweet, sentimental, and sappy. Yet it's also metaphorically perfect as a comment on most film and television adaptations of Twain's works. The real Twain is being hidden from view, led down a sunny path of eternal summer by caricature versions of his two most famous characters.

25

Mark Twain Meets Generation Z

Jocelyn A. Chadwick

Because the future of Mark Twain lies in the hands of today's youths, it is important to understand how modern young people perceive the man and his works and how their perceptions differ from those of somewhat earlier generations. During many years as an educator working closely with high school and college students across the United States, I've seen significant changes among the successive generations. Here, I will draw upon my experiences to compare and contrast members of the so-called Generation Z—students of the twenty-first century who were born during the mid- to late 1990s—with members of earlier generations. Quite often teachers, principals, or curriculum directors ask me to come to their schools to discuss with their students specific pieces of literature or literary-historical periods. I prepare by rereading the texts and gathering appropriate texts that complement the literature. My goal is *not* to lecture, but to engage students from an inquiry-based approach encouraging student input and interaction.

My focus on "Gen Z" high school students and their interaction with Mark Twain emanates from personal observations, conversations, and—somewhat surprisingly—ongoing conversations with them long after I left their schools. Over the years, I have never found students to be the same in their reading perspectives toward Twain, or in their critical inquiry, or in their contemporary relationship to the texts. In fact, as we discuss Twain's works, it is their own contemporary milieu that shapes how they respond to his works. In the last five years, we have discussed family structures, Twain's personal perspective on women, class structure (then and *most certainly* now), thematic elements of positive and negative risk, the nature of choice, and in lieu of the specificity of race, the contemporary and larger issue of difference. Gen Zs follow previous "generations," such as Generation X (students born around 1965 through about 1979) and Millennials, who are also known as Generation Y (those born between about 1980 and mid- to late 1990s). A still earlier generation, popularly known as postwar "Baby Boomers" were those born between 1946 and about 1964. Gen Z is often distinguished from those earlier generations because of its members' unique experiences of growing up amid the Great Recession of the late 1990s and seeing both lightning technological changes and the rise of social networking. These experiences have made its members appear more reflective, cautious, and precociously curious. What most concerns them about Twain is not the traditional elephants in the room of censorship and race but other issues, which I shall discuss here. This I have observed to be true across class, ethnicity, gender, and geographical region.

Race has long been an articulated issue for *Adventures of Huckleberry Finn* (1885), especially since the 1950s, when the National Association for the Advancement of Colored People (NAACP) was among the first organizations that publicly recommended banning the book because of its heavy use of the offensive word "nigger." Prior to that time, writers of color, such as Langston Hughes, Lorraine Hansberry, and Zora Neale Hurston, had praised the novel, particularly in contrast to Harriet Beecher Stowe's antislavery novel, *Uncle Tom's Cabin; Or, Life Among the Lowly* (1852). *Huckleberry Finn*'s nineteenth-century readers were divided among those experiencing nostalgia for "America the way it used to be," those who experienced an enlightening narrative of a positive interracial relationship, and those who experienced a jolting aversion to the book's seeming assault on the English language itself.

From the time Benjamin Franklin published *Proposals Relating to the Education of Youth in Pennsylvania* in 1749, through 1892, when the Committee of Ten recommended standardizing American education, and up to the present day, certain short stories and novels have become entrenched in grades six through twelve in public school curricula. In 1892, the National Educational Association appointed the Committee of Ten with the task to create a standardized curriculum for public school students who were *not* college-bound. The committee asserted that these students should receive the same rigorous instruction, even though many would never complete their full education. Led by Harvard University president Charles Eliot, along with five other university presidents, the commissioner of education, William T. Harris, two head masters, and one professor, the committee meticulously created a report in response to their assigned task, and James Baker, president of the University of Colorado, submitted the report to the National Council of Education in 1893. Within the larger committee resided nine smaller subcommittees, or conferences, each dedicated to a specific content area. The Committee of Ten provided each of the nine conferences what we would today describe as guiding questions, ten of them, to focus work and discussions. Of course, English was one of the nine conferences, made up of ten men—six professors, one teacher from Michigan State Normal School, two high school teachers, and one superintendent. While the report clearly focuses on a coalesced K-12 educational curriculum, its emphasis and specifications on English language arts emerges clearly, particularly the secondary curriculum. What also clearly emerges from this report is the identification and delineation and codification on the core content areas, its focus primarily on the primacy of secondary education, and the purpose of this coalesced curriculum on preparation for students (J. Baker). By the twentieth century, Twain's own works were being interwoven into English language arts education. This literary connection has continued with both state-mandated curricula and the Common Core State Standards (CCSS) copyrighted in 2009.

While Twain's works have been present in curricula throughout the United States—in various combinations of texts—their audiences have continuously changed, as have all generations, thanks to shifting economic trends, social and cultural currents, regional demographics, and technological revolutions. The result—for me at least—has been a firm realization that each generation differs significantly from its predecessors.

My personal connection with Twain began within my own family. Both my father, a World War II navy veteran, and an uncle who was a Korean War veteran, loved Twain. Wherever I make educational presentations, I'm often asked how I first came to read *Huckleberry Finn* and how and when I first realized I liked Twain. My replies to such questions have never changed: because of my father. The fact that my father and uncle, who both experienced racial upheaval, not only respected and enjoyed Twain's works but helped me experience Twain both as immediate narrative and as extended condensed metaphor in a way that would remain with me for the rest of my life, is something students understand. That my father and uncle were both veterans in wars the students study—wars that were fought during a time of racial segregation and Jim Crow—and yet made uncommon choices in these endeavors further demonstrates to students how I came to study this author and his times.

Whenever I work with students, I am as wonderfully challenged as they are. They are concerned with thematic threads, voice, identity, and collateral influences inside the texts framed by the literacy context of relevance—their personal relevance. I have found young students to be provocative and promising readers of Twain in important and profound ways that I do not consistently see in older graduate students. With the younger students, *The Adventures of Tom Sawyer* (1876), *Huckleberry Finn*, and Mark Twain's short stories, interviews, essays, speeches, journal entries, as well as works of his contemporaries naturally come into instructional and exploratory play, providing an excellent milieu for twenty-first century literacy learning.

Setting the scene

The Mark Twain Circle has sponsored several sessions on the continued relevance of Twain, exploring, among other issues, the efficacy of having high school students read *Huckleberry Finn*. Much has already been said about this subject, about Twain's other works, and about new directions in Twain studies. As these conversations and new publications have continued, so also have changes affecting secondary-school teachers and students. These changes have affected far-reaching policy issues, demographic issues, and technological advances.

Reflecting on these changes, the reading of *Huckleberry Finn* in high schools, and the thematic focus of this collection of essays, caused me to suddenly realize that many scholars and educators have been ignoring one of Aristotle's fundamental tenets of effective rhetoric: audience. As scholars, we have established frameworks for discussion and advanced our theories but have failed to acknowledge, and thereby, even *see* the real audience—high school students. Essentially, this audience, a critical component to the relevance of any author, often remained *invisible*.

Complementing this invisibility was what many of us who work with high school students would describe as "the perfect storm" for English language arts (ELA)—its curriculum, its teachers, and most of all, its students. State and federal policies, such as the No Child Left Behind Act of 2001, the Elementary and Secondary School Act of 1965, the Race to the Top program of 2009, and the Common Core State Standards instituted in 2010 paved the way for many voices to enter into the education conversation, particularly for ELA. In what seemed like a nanosecond, almost everyone had an opinion about what literature belonged in ELA classrooms and what literature did not. Within this frenetic context also emerged unprecedented levels of technological advance and social and economic upheavals. And out of this seeming maelstrom emerged the heretofore invisible high school students. I must admit here that since 2010,

I had begun to notice a difference in the tone of high school students, but I did not reflect on the cause of that difference until I began writing books on standards and on literacy learning. Working on those books made me consider the differences among the generations and why they developed as they have.

Mark Twain and the "Millennials"

During the 1980s and 1990s, classroom discussions of Twain were typically framed within the contexts of the assigned works themselves—their characters, plots, figures of speech, and style. Discussions of Twain in literary survey courses also covered nineteenth-century America. Core readings covered those facets, followed by essay assignments and tests. During that period, students read selected Twain works in grades six through twelve. A conflict arises, however, between this approach of reading "for the assignment" as the ultimate aim versus reading for cumulative literacy learning. The Brazilian educator Paulo Freire calls the former approach "banking" instruction. Freire characterized that kind of instruction as passive with regard to the teacher-student relationship, in which students function as quiet receptors and teachers as the active depositors of knowledge (*Pedagogy of the Oppressed* 208–20).

When I visited classrooms around the country (Texas, Oklahoma, California, Utah, Mississippi, Connecticut, Minneapolis, Washington State, Washington, DC, Pennsylvania, Virginia, and Florida)—during those years, students tended to be passive and polite, asking targeted questions carefully, such as: "So, why are the sentences so hard? Why do they talk like this?" "Did slaves *really* have their own language before they became slaves, for real?" "Tell me again, the definition of satire, please." "So, is Huck still a racist at the end of the novel?" During this period students responded to *Adventures of Huckleberry Finn*, *The Adventures of Tom Sawyer*, "The Man That Corrupted Hadleyburg," and "A True Story, Repeated Word for Word, As I Heard It" in this fashion because of Twain's realistic and visceral exploration of race, and his daunting thematic and dramatic moments. For the most part, the realm of discussion and exploration I experienced with these students focused on censorship, dialectical style, race and ethnicity, religion, family, and friendship. I have always found exploring and experiencing a text with students fascinating and informative, and I have also found it demanding to persuade them to interact and engage with the text. Yet, not until 2010 did I begin to notice a decided shift in how high school students were interacting with texts.

Mark Twain and Gen Z

Since the turn of the twenty-first century, events such as 9/11, the explosive growth of the Internet, the War on Terror, ever-changing demographics, the Great Recession, the Columbine shootings, and the invention of smartphones, iPods, iPads, and social media have sculpted Gen Z members and have continued to stir them. These young people are our first "true digital natives"—"screenagers," as *Daily Telegraph* writer Harry Wallop called them in 2014.

First, let me address why those of us who are educators at all levels should be, indeed, must be aware of and understand Gen Z as our literary and rhetorical audience. Gen Zs read books but not as Millennials did. If our purpose is to sustain interest in Twain and his works, we must understand and master the far less passive approach of Gen Z. This task lies not solely at the feet of secondary teachers. Both secondary and college educators have pivotal roles and responsibilities to play.

How do Gen Z students understand and interact with Twain texts? Their characteristics include being reflexive, inferential, activist, individualistic, less frivolous, tech savvy, keen to volunteer, resilient, and pragmatic. Moreover, these "digital immigrants"—as they have been described—exude a sense of social responsibility and an awareness of privilege—whether they themselves have it or not. They tend to champion choice, diversity, voice, and making a difference. The most interesting characteristic I have encountered among them is a positive and frequently aggressive curiosity: They ask challenging questions. Critical thinking, critical reading, critical listening, and speaking personify them, even though, if one were directly to ask them how often they use critical thinking, they would probably reply they don't know. Such a response, I have observed, is an honest one, for they do not consciously tell themselves, "Now, I am going to think critically." However, when we observe them texting, tweeting, blogging, or chatting, these traits are readily evident. Across the entire country, I have found many Gen Zs share these traits.

Many educators have read, researched, and taught *Tom Sawyer*, and some have even written about it. They know the novel's plot, its style, and Twain's personal influences in the work. They probably have not, however, read the novel from the perspective of a Gen Zer. For example, when educators reread that novel, they know that Twain inserts Huck into it early and that he positions Huck in such a way that readers can discover what a different kind of character he really is. Yes, he may be a boy "from the other side of the tracks," but he is also a boy who slips away and does tasks for the slave Uncle Jake in exchange for food, which he sometimes eats with the man. In chapter 28 of the novel, Tom asks Huck where he is going to sleep. Huck replies,

> In Ben Rogers's hayloft. He lets me, and so does his pap's nigger man, Uncle Jake. I tote water for Uncle Jake whenever he wants me to, and any time I ask him he gives me a little something to eat if he can spare it. That's a mighty good nigger, Tom. He likes me, becuz I don't ever act as if I was above him. Sometimes I've set right down and eat *with* him. But you needn't tell that. A body's got to do things when he's awful hungry he wouldn't want to do as a steady thing.

Huck's behavior with the slave and Twain's attention to it fascinates Gen Z students, who are curious about its import.

Another example that captures students' attention occurs in chapter 35, when Huck rejects the comforts and privileges of living with the Widow Douglas because he cannot stand having everything "so awful reglar." Tom explains that conformity is the way of everybody, but Huck responds in an unexpected fashion:

> Tom, it don't make no difference. I ain't everybody, and I can't *stand* it. Its awful to be tied up so. And grub comes too easy—I don't take no interest in vittles that way. I got to ask, to go a-fishing; I got to ask, to go in a-swimming—dern'd if I hain't got to ask to do everything. Well, I'd got to talk so nice it wasn't no comfort—I'd got to go up in the attic and rip out a while, every day, to git a taste in my mouth, or I'd a died, Tom.

Huck then goes on to reject his share of the gold treasure he and Tom have found:

> Lookyhere, Tom, being rich ain't what it's cracked up to be. It's just worry and worry, and sweat and sweat, and a-wishing you was dead all the time. . . . Now you just take my sheer of it along with yourn, and gimme a ten-center sometimes—not many times, becuz I don't give a dern for a thing 'thout it's tollable hard to git.

Huck's own code of behavior is indeed a sense of ethics. When I discuss this novel with Gen Zs, they resonate with Huck from this perspective and are more than willing to explore his rationale, Twain's stylistic rationale for developing the character in this fashion, and their seemingly insatiable curiosity drives them to drill more deeply into the text and into Twain's rhetorical motivations. For me, the most essential learning moments occur when these students then take their analyses and move into synthesis—exploring just how these ideas and thoughts relate to them and their world. For the Gen Zs and for me, there is no one interpretation, no right or wrong answer, for the exploration and discovery via critical reading and collaboration will yield far more than we could have ever imagined.

As a wonderful result of the students' aggressive curiosity and their penchant to broaden a text's thematic scope beyond the obvious, I have been able to utilize more of Twain's works, as well as works of his contemporaries, than I did with earlier student generations. As popular-culture researcher Emily Anatole says in her February 8, 2013 online *Forbes* article, "Generation Z: Rebels with a Cause," because of the context into which they were born and literally *cut their teeth*, Gen Zs interact with texts quite differently, and, consequently, their requirements and expectation from texts are also different from those of previous high school students:

> Going forward, Zs will be looking for products and messaging that reflect their reality, rather than that which depicts a perfect life. More serious storylines and documentaries that highlight complex situations will appeal to them. Entertainment has become darker, with dystopian and post-apocalyptic stories dominating the youth space. Zs are turning to these tales to make sense of their lives and cope with challenges. Their role models are young, everyday characters like *The Hunger Games'* Katniss Everdeen, who face seemingly inescapable scenarios but rise above them to create a better society. In these stories, relatable characters are empowered to defeat their circumstances—just like Zs, who feel a responsibility to change the status quo.

Within Twain's diverse writings, characters such as Huck, Jim, Aunt Rachel, the man who returns to Hadleyburg, Roxanna, David Wilson, Pap Finn, Aunt Sally, the Widow Douglas, Miss Watson, and many others provide illustrative, condensed, and extended metaphors that Gen Zs can tackle and wrestle with, while pondering the conundrums Twain poses.

Another boon from these students emerges with their curiosity about Twain, the man, Twain's America, other places outside the United States at the time, and how it all relates to the students' present. When I have collaborated with Gen Zs, our thematic conversations do not linger over censorship or race and ethnicity. Our conversations instead delve into social justice, parental abuse, social responsibility, choices, and potential consequences for one's actions and inactions. Gen Z students *feel* deeply, and they articulate their perspectives and feelings without hesitation within learning environments that foster collaboration and expression.

Not long ago, I was Skyping with classes of students in one school, and months later, I was physically in other classrooms of students—who were all young men. Our conversations focused on *Huckleberry Finn, A Narrative of the Life of Frederick Douglass, The Columbian Orator, Freedom's Journal,* "The Declaration of Sentiments," excerpts from Twain's journals and notebooks, interviews of Twain, and several of his speeches: "Our Children and Great Discoveries," "Votes for Women," "Woman—An Opinion," "Courage," and "Literature." The ensuing conversations and analyses surprised the students themselves and elated me. As Anatole and others have referenced, as these students read and interact, they also analyze and subsequently synthesize their relationships to the texts. From this relational position with the literary text, I can introduce them to Twain's letters, speeches, interviews, and journal entries, thereby creating yet another level of reading and comprehension and relevance.

Technology appeals to Gen Zs' sense of curiosity. It also piques their interest and exposes them to digitized primary sources. That fact touches on yet another trait of Gen Zs—their being global citizens without ever leaving their own country. This is possible because they are connected—*wired*—twenty-four hours a day. As I engage these students, my goal is to tap into their predilections and share Twain with them, so that the author, his time, and his works resonate beyond my time with them and beyond the walls of the physical classroom. Consequently, in contrast to the questions I received from Millennials, Gen Zs' questions are testing and forward thinking. For example, "I have read several of Twain's works, and I want to know more about the women around him and the role of women in general. What did he really think about women?" "The Mississippi River extends throughout many of Mark Twain's works. Is this a deliberate message to the reader, and if it is, is he trying to tell us that where we live sometimes affects who we are?" "What about Twain's message about parents? He gives us many examples of different combinations and actions/reactions. I think he is giving us his ideas about how the idea of 'parents' can differ." "I want to do some research on how Twain viewed his work and its impact after publication, you know, like in the interviews we explored. What I want to find out is just how much his own attitudes changed and how close his ideas are to ours." So far, the results I have recounted here span the country, apply to both female and male students, and comprise a broadening mixture of ethnicities and classes. And as I have attested to many of their teachers, the Gen Zs pose questions that are conundrums my graduate students have never posed.

Moving forward

As we move forward, what Gen Z is achieving without even knowing it, is the longevity and the necessity for Twain. I continue to witness how Twain's works, his time, and his life resonate not weakly but strongly with these young people. And rather than focus solely on the stylistics or censorship, or ethnicity in the amazing wealth of his works and life, Gen Zs peer more deeply into his texts. Each time I collaborate with these students, regardless of where they live and who they are, I feel at ease and confident that Samuel Clemens, Twain, and his works will not succumb to the nether regions of obscurity into which too many authors slip.

Decidedly not invisible, Gen Zs are indeed global. They embrace telling their own stories and listening to or reading others' stories in creative ways. Their passion and sense of what they will come to understand, as ethos, as they mature, is infectious. In addition to the Gen Zs themselves are the educational initiatives—both policy-driven and educator-driven—designed to incite this audience and its unique twenty-first-century learning pathways as well as the level of literacy that college and careers will later demand of them.

When I collaborate with students about particular historical periods or events, such as the Gilded Age, colonialism, Independence Day, women's rights, differences of any kind, or the future of literature, I find that students are keenly interested and engaged. This approach has piqued their unceasing curiosity because they have never actually blended history, science, politics, geography, and literature into a tapestry that relates to them. Their particular learning pathways—the visual, the active, the social component, the reflection, and challenges confronting both Sam and Twain—appeal to Gen Z in ways not applicable to their generational predecessors. These students focus deeper into social, cultural, and political issues. They are curious, and seek out definitions of not only race or racism but society's resistance to *difference* of any kind, and because of their perspective they find Twain's works particularly generative and substantive.

That Twain is among the writers who spark that positive precocious curiosity of Gen Zs is something that we, too, must recognize and nurture and encourage throughout their educational lives. After all, for the literature we teach to survive into the future—particularly Twain's stellar and provocative works—we must adjust to our ever-emerging new audiences so they will want the texts to *live* outside their classrooms, ultimately to permeate and inform their everyday lives. Twain's clear and defiant articulation of the requisite qualities for writing a "good novel," steeped in relevance, in so many ways foreshadowed this curious, challenging, and engaging Gen Z. The May 31, 1891 issues of the *New York World* published an interview in which Twain was asked, "How far, in your opinion, does culture, education, what you will, enter into the making of books?" Twain replied,

> My dear sir, they [literary critics] speak of book culture as being the end of all things. . . . Nine out of ten of the qualities required for the writing of a good novel are summed up in one thing—a knowledge of men and life, not books or university education. If I could write novels, I shouldn't lack capital, because I have had intimate acquaintanceship with many groups of men, many occupations, many varieties of life in widely separated regions. It would be impossible for me to use that capital, that culture, for that is really what it is, because I should never be able to acquire the novel-writing art.

26

A Secondary School Perspective

John R. Pascal

Mark Twain knew how to capture the American spirit, and it is discerning to see how he has affected our lives.

Even though Mark Twain was being corrosive, he always spoke against something that was truly wrong.

Mark Twain's love for storytelling still exists today through the work of Hal Holbrook!

To many, the above exchange may read like scholars exchanging ideas for a new paper on Mark Twain. The truth, however, is very different. The remarks are actually the thoughts of fourteen-year-old ninth graders. They are students at New Jersey's oldest Catholic boys school, Seton Hall Preparatory School, where I teach English. These boys know that Twain is something much more than a white-haired man in a white suit after whom a local diner is named.

It is always a pleasure to converse with lovers of Twain who come from all walks of life with new ideas. But what can be said about the great man's future in our nation's high schools? As a schoolteacher myself, it is my responsibility to help ensure that Samuel Clemens's life and writings inspire young students to want to book passage on his steamboat, ride shotgun on his stagecoach, and talk with him on the deck of an ocean steamer bound for Europe or the Holy Land. My hope is that when Halley's Comet returns in 2062, today's students will smile and think of the comet's earlier passages over Twain's 1835 birth in Florida, Missouri, and his 1910 death in Redding, Connecticut, as they share Twain with their future children and grandchildren.

I do not wish to suggest I am the best teacher on Twain. I do not know every best way to teach him. No one can. He is too big and complex a subject for any one person to understand completely. That makes him sound daunting, but it is part of what makes Twain such a joy, as there is no end to what we can learn about him. He is ever-present for all of us to convey our love for him and his books to the next generation. In this chapter, I shall discuss a number of different approaches to teaching Twain's life and literature to high school students. The result these approaches have consistently produced is the students' delighted response as to what Twain saw and how he lived. They love his imagination, his inventive language, his believable characters, and realistic storylines. They are also intrigued by the breadth of his travels throughout the United States and around the world.

In analyzing *The Adventures of Tom Sawyer* (1876) and *Adventures of Huckleberry Finn* (1885), students imaginatively experience unusual outdoor settings far different from what they know in their own time with its ever-present modern technology. Often topically significant, these texts help them to examine their own moral choices—from excusable everyday troubles to making tough moral decisions. In addition to the Tom and Huck novels, my students have also read "How I Edited an Agricultural Paper" and "The Celebrated Jumping Frog of Calaveras County," about which they have written essays explaining why they have enjoyed these stories. The students are happily surprised that Twain's writing stimulates their senses and emotions with the result they want to read much more of his work.

When I teach Twain, I cover his life in four-fifty-minute class periods and use the information accompanying the Mark Twain Home Foundation's 2011 CD *Mark Twain: Words & Music*. While learning the origin of his pen name, students watch the beginning of the 1980 television adaptation of *Life on the Mississippi*, which shows the young Sam Clemens trying to persuade steamboat pilot Mr. Bixby to take him on as a cub steamboat pilot in training. What is wonderful is that when Bixby finally relents and asks, "What's your name, son?" the only reply is simply, "Sam, sir." My students have always smiled in recognition at that moment. When the leadsman finally sings out his long cry of "mark twain!," accompanied by rising orchestral music, some of the students' eyes well up. I ask them why. Jack R. speaks for all of them, saying, "Sam is our American heritage."

Those held-back tears are also evident when the students discover how Sam lost his son, his wife, and two of his daughters. Initially, of course, the students had no idea of his personal heartbreaks. But as student Cole K. says, "Sam did have turbulent times in his life, like the loss of his loved ones, but it did not hold him back to strive for the best." Student Leo H. remarks that "Mark Twain can never be considered as a renegade to his life after numerous tragedies struck him; he still chose to go on." By the by, the words "turbulent" and "renegade" are part of the students' weekly vocabulary tests. They are required to write sentences in response to Clemens's life, and these are their impressions. It is particularly gratifying to watch them as they compose their thoughts while moving their heads in rhythm to L. A. Suess's *Riverboat Memories* on the CD I bought in Hannibal in 2011.

When my students viewed "The Mysterious Stranger" episode in Will Vinton's 1985 Claymation film, *The Adventures of Mark Twain*, Willem J. found it "extremely disturbing and creepy." Michael D. noticed that the shrinking appearance of Satan and his world forms a tear in Mark Twain's eye and began to understand why Clemens's later texts grew so dark.

Before we start on *Tom Sawyer*, I ask the boys if they are ready to meet Mark Twain. Their answer is an excited yes, and I proudly introduce Mr. Hal Holbrook performing *Mark Twain Tonight!* The boys applaud along with the production's 1967 audience, leaning forward to study Holbrook's moving figure and absorb his voice. Michael reacts, "I wish I could just talk to him; he would understand me."

In developing the students' writing abilities, we know the power of the written essay. At the very least, a teacher should stress the need to understand literature through the elements of plot, character, theme, point of view, descriptions, and figurative language. In the tsunami of today's technological video games, I had concerns about giving students a story about a jumping frog. Happily, I was wrong. Only introducing the story's full title was needed to necessarily show Twain's start of his meteoric rise to fame. Students today need a visual hook, so I have them study *The Oxford Mark Twain* edition, which includes a photographic facsimile of the 1867 American edition of *The Celebrated Jumping Frog of Calaveras County and Other Sketches*. Both the picture of the book's illustrated cover and the story's typeface caught and held the boys' attention.

When I ask them to write why they have enjoyed the story, I expect them to examine it through the lenses of plot, characterization, and descriptions at the very least. Furthermore, I ask them to discuss what aspects of life Clemens shows them with Jim Smiley and his most celebrated jumping frog, Dan'l Webster. Their answers have made me think that I have hit the Comstock Lode in Virginia City.

Teachers generally ask the students to use a hook in the first sentence of their essays to get their reader's attention. Justice S. commences his essay thus: "To discuss this story is a pleasure. The descriptions are mind-blowing." Brandon H. asks, "Have you ever fallen victim to a cheater? No doubt you have. Here our Jim Smiley was robbed of his money and dignity on a simple bet!" Anthony A.

poses: "There is not a bet that Jim Smiley can lose, or is there? I love the way this story is told, almost like an old campfire story."

Perhaps our enjoyment of the central story makes us almost forget how the story is framed. The students haven't considered that possibility. Dan G. thinks the frame-story technique is "intriguing and intelligent, allowing for two ironic and comical narratives to be in one famous work." Pierson R. holds that "what causes us to fall in love with this work is that Wheeler's story is called a 'monotonous narrative.' But this is so far from the truth that the word choice alone is hilarious. Twain is always one step ahead of us."

In speaking of Simon Wheeler, Brandon comments that "he was fat and bald-headed, and had on an expression of winning gentleness and simplicity upon his tranquil countenance." He continues, "Having always struggled writing descriptions myself, I have come to appreciate the art of using little to do a lot. To summarize a person in one sentence, particularly in this short story where there is no space for deep character development is truly a rare and unique skill." What is amazing, Brandon says, is how Twain went from a well-spoken man from the East to the slurring Old West dialect of Simon, in phrases such as "and it seemed as if they warn't going to save her" and "thank the Lord for his inf'nit mercy." Although "warn't" and "inf'nit" are in no modern dictionary, we barely notice and instead pronounce the words with the correct accent. This is how Simon would have sounded if you were having a conversation with him face-to-face.

Brandon is not alone in his view. Preston Y. can tell the character's personalities just by the way they talked: "Thish-yer Smiley had a mare—the boys called her the fifteen minute nag, but that was only in fun you know. Because, of course, she was faster than that." Preston concludes, "This encompasses the dialect of the time period while giving the character a personality that I thoroughly enjoyed."

Twain's other animals left their tracks, too. Will K. notes that the "physical description of the asthmatic mare racing with her legs flailing and her nose snorting are colorfully vibrant, and classic Mark Twain, so we can enjoy the story on a deeper level." Michael G. writes that while creating comedy is elusive, everyone can enjoy the "pinnacle of personification" of the "little ornery bull pup Andrew Jackson, considering today's cute and adorable puppy images, only the reader knows how smart and vicious he is." Matthew M. observes Twain's "ironic humor is ingenious. I have never met a 'modest' frog." Wheeler states, "You'd see that frog whirling in the air like a doughnut." Mark S. points out, "This is hilarious because while Twain is using the common personification technique, since when do doughnuts whirl in the air?"

What life observation does Clemens give to students through Jim Smiley's lost bet? Dan writes, "Jim's unfortunate experience may teach a reader to be prudent and refrain from letting a sense of superiority cloud one's judgment." Indeed, when the feller agrees to bet against him, "Jim gets all jacked up," according to Cole. K. He adds, "Dan'l Webster being filled with quail shot is a decisive and extraordinary trick that was not seen coming. Smiley, confident as the Seattle Seahawks in this year's Super Bowl, did not recognize the shot filled to the chin." Ronan H. says, "It is easy to anticipate Jim's loss, but you are excited to see it."

Maybe we take the frame story for granted. Daniel S. reminds us that "as a stable is to a farm horse, Twain's descriptions, characterization, and plot cause us to find ourselves wanting to learn more about that 'yaller one-eyed cow that didn't have no tail,'" Emmet B. joins him: "The narrator's impolite and hasty exit due to his distaste for the old man's story leaves the reader somewhat angry for not listening to the whole tale." Preston concurs, "One almost wishes that it had been longer." Yet, Ronan declares, "I would love to read this story to my children someday. And do you want to know the most hilarious part? The narrator never got the information he wanted on the Rev. Leonidas W. Smiley!!!!"

Sound bites, talking heads, diverse news channels giving you their own versions of "the truth." Trusted television journalists inexplicably misremembering and conflating facts in reporting news. What example is being set for our nation's youth "about the intelligence and accuracy behind what they read and see?" asks Jonathan Z. Fortunately, Sam has been in our youth's corner since the nineteenth century, as he gives his relevant remarks by humorously showing that one needs neither experience nor talent to be a successfully authoritative "expert" in his 1870 sketch "How I Edited an Agricultural Paper Once." It provides an excellent set of Twainian spectacles to see through the sometimes mind-numbing similarities of today's news shows.

Willem begins our "coverage" of Twain's manuscript with its distinctive title:

> It sounds like it is affiliated with a book so boring that it will make someone want to gouge their eyes out after reading it. But Mark Twain connects this title to an idea that is exactly the opposite. He conveys how ignorant we can be sometimes with his exquisite sense of humor.

The sketch's substitute editor says, "Turnips should never be pulled, it injures them. It is much better to send a boy up and let him shake the tree." Willem sees Clemens's "whimsical humor. This editor is almost as moronic as Tom Sawyer telling Becky Thatcher that he was engaged to Amy Lawrence."

Possibly overlooked is the reason why the narrator took the job. He needs the money. "The sensation of being at work again was luxurious, and I wrought all the week with unflagging pleasure." David F. regards Twain

> to help better understand what life is all about, not just moaning every morning to get out of your bed and living the rest of your day with complaints. His words show the love for working hard and getting up to do your job. Life is truly about living every minute 100 percent and giving it all you got.

Every generation has their exclusive, ever-changing expressions. When the narrator says, "*Tell* you, you cornstalk, you cabbage, you son of a cauliflower?," Stefano M. "found this absolutely hilarious . . . I even got my friends to say it, too!" James M. doesn't miss the ironic humor as our narrator "does not know anything about agriculture, and yet he is calling the editor several different types of crops." Who can forget "Shake your grandmother! Turnips don't grow on trees!"? This line "keeps one alive when they read this. Twain can make any young reader laugh with his timing and mood," according to David.

"Have you ever read something that enrages you so much that you burn your house down and beat people up? Neither did I!" Jorge L. calls our attention to the "long cadaverous creature" that is enraged concerning the next article. Robert L. takes a quieter view:

> With Mark Twain's literature, not one subject has been handled without taste. The same goes without saying for one of the strangest yet true occurrences ever put to paper, an ax-crippling arsonist spurred into action by a faulty paper. Twain does not poke fun at how crazy this man is, rather he presents the information as it is and lets the readers determine their own response.

Michael notes,

> The final great irony is that when Mark Twain was ending his conversation with the editor, he honestly did not hold back his opinion that "the less a man knows the bigger the noise he makes and the higher salary he commands." This foreshadows what a major portion of his later life's writing was going to be like: dark and very powerful in showing society's flaws. He's a real muckraker.

Michael O. wryly comments differently: "Mark Twain tells his audience that some editors take their papers too seriously. The regular editor sees the paper's reputation as ruined, even though circulation has increased as never before."

Erik B. reminds us that even though it was first published in 1870, this sketch proves that "not everything you see or read in print, electronic and social media is true. Learn how to question the legitimacy of a watermelon tree and a peach-vine." Willem should have the final "word": "This and many others of Twain's works are perfect proof that whenever he is given pen and paper, magic happens."

"How many times have your parents told you that your Saturday morning plans are cancelled because you will do chores that last forever?" All hands are raised, and elbows drop in disgust upon their desks.

"Has anyone ever been to a boring church sermon?" All hands are raised quickly.

"How many of you have hated a teacher who you feel has picked on you all year and you would relish one practical joke in retort?" All hands on deck.

"Will any of you forget your first love?" No.

"Anyone ever like to show off, Academy Award-style?" Indeed, everyone.

"How many of you have taken your parents' shovel and pick ax to hunt for buried treasure and have been punished for digging up that rose garden set for a first prize?" Laughter with accompanying sheepish hand gestures of recognition.

"With due respect to the power of technology in your hands, how many of you would like a haunted house in your neighborhood?" Amid all raised hands, one student actually put up both hands and vociferously asked, "How soon can I get it? I'm surrounded by new McMansions!"

Now they are ready to study *The Adventures of Tom Sawyer*, a triumph that has outsold all other Clemens's works, but can be easily forgotten in the efforts of keeping *Huckleberry Finn* from being banned in some public school curricula.

An unfair question: What one quality encompasses all that is Tom? Wenzhe T. writes, "Being free is Tom's spontaneous humanity, because Mark Twain was a man who wanted to be free, too." Chris P. goes further: "Tom hooks you back to your childhood, to remind you of everything you want to do and can be, but cannot today." In step with these students, what strikes Dante N. is our jealousy:

> Nowadays, you can't sneak out to a cemetery or run away and be pirates — the police would arrest our parents and us! All our boyhood experiences are rolled into Tom's spring and summer. Trying tobacco, playing with pocketknives, exploring haunted houses, these are things we all want to do but we can't because there is too much structure. With parents today, you can't do much of anything on your own.
>
> *Tom Sawyer* is an adventure that we want to have and can live it as we read it, unlike *Jurassic Park*, which no matter how imaginative, it is not real. Tom is! He makes sense! Pretending to be sick, who hasn't done that?

As to the famous whitewashing scene, it can be asked how relevant is it to today's youth? Chris enthusiastically says, "That scene? Today, I have homework, so now I can get someone to do it for me. All I have to say is that 'doing homework will make you smarter!'" Chris is at the junior level in school when he said this. Freshman Colin K. has a more visceral viewpoint: "The apple that Ben paid Tom sure was juicy, and I wish I had it."

R. Kent Rasmussen's introduction to the new Penguin Classics edition of *Tom Sawyer* argues that the book has a "decidedly antifeminist slant." Reading his words, Dante responds "That may be true, but it's Tom's story for guys. Becky is just eleven-years-old, how strong is she supposed to be in the 1840s? Do you want her in the graveyard with Tom and Huck? I sure don't!"

The graveyard scene, the drowning of Injun Joe's partner "the rusty, ragged looking devil," and certainly the descriptive meanings of the horrible death of Injun Joe show that this story has a matchless undercurrent of violence below the sun-filled adventures on the surface. But the relevance of this violence is not lost on the students. Dante N. writes, "The dark themes are absolutely needed, so Tom's story isn't campy and all happy."

The relationship of *Tom Sawyer* to modern technology and modern youths' way of life is noticed by Timothy M: "Back in Tom's day, they had parsimonious iPads that were just small chalkboards." In concurrence, Jack R. writes what he thinks is Twain's purpose in writing *Tom Sawyer*:

> It is still one of the best-selling books worldwide because it shows how cool the life of a young mischievous boy was back then. Now kids stay inside and play video games and watch TV. But back then they HAD to go play outside and have REAL FUN since they didn't have any of our technology. A child's life in that time was much more exciting than ours now. So who wouldn't want to read about a great adventure for a couple of boys just trying to have fun and getting into trouble?

A recurring question is whether *Tom Sawyer* is a book for children or adults. This question was posed to the classes. After a few seconds in thought, John O'H. broadly grinned and said, "His books are like water, they're for everybody!"

In the tidal surges of discourse surrounding *Huckleberry Finn* in the past decades, there is a danger of forgetting that its title character was introduced in *Tom Sawyer*. How the adults of St. Petersburg regard him is caught by Chris: "Huck Finn is not respected, but to shun him because he has no one to care for him, is that respectable behavior on anyone's part? What the town thinks of him isn't respectable, but he is, especially when you read of him in *Huckleberry Finn*."

Patrick G. studied *Huckleberry Finn* during his junior year and states the view of many readers: "The relationship between an uncivilized boy and a runaway slave is just unprecedented." However, the connection of Huck and Pap requires "special attention." Michael A. sees Huck's welts from Pap's hick'ry, "but Huck knows Pap is all he's got left. Ironically, Pap is jealous of Huck for knowing how to read, so he feels tenfold about anyone over whom he feels superior to being more educated."

Cliff N. says Pap's fury about the "free nigger" and Ohioan college professor is so sad because "he himself has no education; when signing a pledge of reform, he just drew a single line." Jason S. holds that Pap views this learned man as a "poisoning of his country because all blacks were meant to be slaves." Joseph D. reasons that "Pap doesn't hate the black professor so much because of his skin color and education, he hates him because he is too dumb to think of a reason to hate him. Mentally, Pap cannot accept a free 'nigger' with an education."

According to Don O'C, Pap's screaming rants are "miserably ironic because he doesn't have the morale to go out and educate himself." Additionally, Patrick G. shows Pap's deep ignorance in not "knowing that an educated black is more responsible and better for Huck than he is. One of these 'educated' blacks is Jim, and despite a lack of academics, he has insight and compassion."

When I teach *Huckleberry Finn* at the College of St. Elizabeth, I employ the same methods I use in my high school classes. They evoked this unique woman's perspective, that of Jamie D'A:

> I cried when Huck cried for Buck Grangerford. It is the first time Huck cries, and what makes it even more upsetting is that he never cries when Pap beats him, probably because in a tragic way, he would love for Pap to pay attention to him, unfortunately, this is the only way Pap knows.

The summation by Michael G. is succinct: "It is ironic how a boy from Hannibal, Missouri with a limited education could become the best writer in American history, if not the world." David says "Sadly for us, Mark Twain is not extant, but we still talk about him through each generation."

The thoughts expressed in this chapter represent a cross section of students from more than 130 towns and cities in ten counties across central and northern New Jersey. Do they speak for all youths in our country? Perhaps not. However, my faith in their analytically thoughtful and energetic insights on Sam and his works suggest that Twain has indeed booked passage for a new group of youths on his steamboat, their tickets for his stagecoach, and his ocean steamships.

Teacher John Pascal (left) and his wife, Patty (right), with students from his special Seton Hall Prep course on Mark Twain meeting with Hal Holbrook after his *Mark Twain Tonight!* performance in New Brunswick, New Jersey, in October, 2015.

Photo by Richard Costabile. Courtesy of John Pascal.

Works Cited

The works cited in this volume are divided below into two sections. Mark Twain's own writings are confined to the first section, while works about Mark Twain, locations (such as CU-MARK and MTPO), and other sources may be found in the second section. Mark Twain's writings are listed in alphabetical order by title. Works cited by title in the essays are listed by title; works cited by abbreviation are listed by their abbreviations. Many abbreviations are compromises between concision and clarity. For example, Oxford University Press and the University of California Press have been reduced to "OUP" and "UCP," and all Harper imprints (Harper & Brothers, HarperCollins, etc.) are reduced to "Harper." Other less frequently cited imprints have been left intact. Abbreviations of titles of Mark Twain's own writings generally follow those used by the Mark Twain Papers and Project (MTP), but some do not, and others have been added.

1. Mark Twain writings

AHF. The Annotated Huckleberry Finn. Ed. Michael Patrick Hearn. New York: W. W. Norton, 2001.

AL. Ashcroft-Lyon Manuscript. CU-MARK.

AL-AMT3. "Ashcroft-Lyon Manuscript." *Autobiography of Mark Twain, Volume 3.* Ed. MTP editors. Oakland: UCP, 2015. 329–440. Also online at MTPO.

AMT-N. The Autobiography of Mark Twain. Ed. Charles Neider. New York: Harper, 1959.

AMT1. Autobiography of Mark Twain, Volume 1. Ed. MTP editors. Berkeley: UCP, 2010. Also online at MTPO.

AMT2. Autobiography of Mark Twain, Volume 2. Ed. MTP editors. Berkeley: UCP, 2013. Also online at MTPO.

AMT3. Autobiography of Mark Twain, Volume 3. Ed. MTP editors. Oakland: UCP, 2015. Also online at MTPO.

CI. Mark Twain: The Complete Interviews. Ed. Gary Scharnhorst. Tuscaloosa: University of Alabama Press, 2006.

CJF 1996. The Celebrated Jumping Frog of Calaveras County, and Other Sketches. Intro. Roy Blount. Afterword Richard Bucci. New York: OUP, 1996.

Cooley, John, ed. *How Nancy Jackson Married Kate Wilson.* Lincoln: University of Nebraska Press, 2001.

CTSS1. Mark Twain: Collected Tales, Sketches, Speeches, & Essays, 1852–1890. Ed. Louis J. Budd. New York: Literary Classics of the United States, 1992.

CTSS2. Mark Twain: Collected Tales, Sketches, Speeches, & Essays, 1891–1910. Ed. Louis J. Budd. New York: Literary Classics of the United States, 1992.

CY 1979. A Connecticut Yankee in King Arthur's Court. Ed. Bernard L. Stein. Intro. Henry Nash Smith. Berkeley: UCP, 1979.

DeVoto, Bernard, ed. *The Portable Mark Twain.* New York: Viking Press, 1946.

"Disgraceful Persecution of a Boy." *The Galaxy Magazine* (May 1870) Reprinted at twain.lib.virginia.edu/onstage/playscripts/galaxy01/html

ECS. Extract from Captain Stormfield's Visit to Heaven. New York: Harper, 1909.

E&E. Europe and Elsewhere. Intro. Albert Bigelow Paine. New York: Harper, 1923.

ET&S1. Early Tales & Sketches, Volume 1 (1851–1864). Eds. Edgar Marquess Branch and Robert H. Hirst, and Harriet Elinor Smith. Berkeley: UCP, 1979.

ET&S2. Early Tales & Sketches, Volume 2 (1864–1865). Ed. Edgar Marquess Branch and Robert H. Hirst, with the assistance of Harriet Elinor Smith. Berkeley: UCP, 1981.

FE. Following the Equator: A Journey Around the World. Hartford: American Pub. Co., 1897.

FE 1996. Following the Equator, and Anti-Imperialist Essays. Intro. Gore Vidal. Afterword Fred Kaplan. New York: OUP, 1996.

FM. Mark Twain's Fables of Man. Eds. John S. Tuckey, Kenneth M. Sanderson, and Bernard L. Stein. Berkeley: UCP, 1972.

FSk. A Family Sketch, and Other Private Writings by Mark Twain, Livy Clemens, Susy Clemens. Ed. Benjamin Griffin. Oakland: UCP, 2014.

GA 1996. The Gilded Age: A Tale of To-day. Written with Charles Dudley Warner. Intro. Ward Just. Afterword Gregg Camfield. New York: OUP, 1996.

HF 1996. Adventures of Huckleberry Finn. Intro. Toni Morrison. Afterword Victor A. Doyno. New York: OUP, 1996.

HF 2001. Adventures of Huckleberry Finn. Eds. Vic Fischer and Lin Salamo. Berkeley: University of California, 2001.

HF 2003. Adventures of Huckleberry Finn. Eds. Victor Fischer, Lin Salamo, and Walter Blair. Berkeley: UCP, 2003. Also online at MTPO.

HF 2010. Adventures of Huckleberry Finn. Eds. Victor Fischer, Lin Salamo, Harriet Elinor Smith, and Walter Blair. Berkeley: UCP, 2010.

HF&TS. Huck Finn and Tom Sawyer Among the Indians, and Other Unfinished Stories. Eds. Dahlia Armon and Walter Blair. Berkeley: UCP, 1989. Also online at MTPO.

HH&T. Mark Twain's Hannibal, Huck & Tom. Ed. Walter Blair. Berkeley: UCP, 1969.

HT. A Horse's Tale. New York: Harper, 1907.

HHR. Mark Twain's Correspondence with Henry Huttleston Rogers. Ed. Lewis Leary. Berkeley: UCP, 1969.

HTTS. How to Tell a Story and Other Essays. New York: Harper, 1897.

IA 1996. The Innocents Abroad; or The New Pilgrims' Progress. Intro. Mordecai Richler. Afterword David E. E. Sloane. New York: OUP, 1996.

JA 1980. Personal Recollections of Joan of Arc. Ed. John Seelye. Hartford: Stowe-Day Foundation, 1980.

JA 1989. Personal Recollections of Joan of Arc. Ed. Andrew Tradie. San Francisco: Ignatius Press, 1989.

JA 1996. Personal Recollections of Joan of Arc. Intro. Justin Kaplan. Afterword Susan K. Harris. New York: OUP, 1996.

"Jean's Illness." MS, CU-MARK.

L1. Mark Twain's Letters, Volume 1: 1853–1866. Ed. MTP editors. Berkeley: UCP, 1988. Also online at *MTPO Letters.*

L2. Mark Twain's Letters, Volume 2: 1867–1868. Ed. MTP editors. Berkeley: UCP, 1990. Also online at *MTPO Letters.*

L3. Mark Twain's Letters, Volume 3: 1869. Ed. MTP editors. Berkeley: UCP, 1992. Also online at *MTPO Letters.*

L4. Mark Twain's Letters, Volume 4: 1870–1871. Ed. MTP editors. Berkeley: UCP, 1995. Also online at *MTPO Letters.*

L5. Mark Twain's Letters, Volume 5: 1872–1873. Ed. MTP editors. Berkeley: UCP, 1997. Also online at *MTPO Letters.*

L6. Mark Twain's Letters, Volume 6: 1874–1875. Ed. MTP editors. Berkeley: UCP, 2002. Also online at *MTPO Letters.*

Letters. Mark Twain's Letters, 1876–80. Ed. Victor Fischer, Michael B. Frank and Harriet Elinor Smith. Mark Twain Project Online. Berkeley: UCP, 2002, 2007. marktwainproject.org/xtf/view?docId=letters/MTDP00225.xml;style=letterletter;brand=mtp

"Letters from the Earth." *WIM? What Is Man? And Other Philosophical Writings.* Ed Paul Baender. Berkeley: UCP, 1973.

LL. The Love Letters of Mark Twain. Ed. Dixon Wecter. New York: Harper, 1949.

LM 1980. Life on the Mississippi. Dir. Peter H. Hunt. Perf. Robert Lansing, David Knell, James Keane, and John Pankow. Monterey Media, 1980. Television adaptation on DVD.

LM 1996. Life on the Mississippi. Intro. Willie Morris. Afterword Lawrence Howe. New York: OUP, 1996.

"The Man with Negro Blood" Ms. fragment. Box 37 DV 128 No.4. CU-MARK.

MTAq. Mark Twain's Aquarium: The Samuel Clemens Angelfish Correspondence, 1905-1910. Ed. John Cooley. Athens: University of Georgia Press, 1991.

MTA1-2. Mark Twain's Autobiography. Ed. Albert Bigelow Paine. 2 vols. New York: Harper, 1924.

MTHL. Mark Twain–Howells Letters. Eds. Henry Nash Smith, William M. Gibson, and Frederick Anderson. 2 vols. Cambridge, MA: Belknap Press of Harvard University Press, 1960.

MTL1-2. Mark Twain's Letters. Ed. Albert Bigelow Paine. 2 vols. New York: Harper, 1917.

MTLM. Mark Twain's Letters to Mary. Ed. Lewis Leary. New York: Columbia University Press, 1963.

MTLP. Mark Twain's Letters to His Publishers, 1867–1894. Ed. Hamlin Hill. Berkeley: UCP, 1967.

MTNB. Mark Twain's Unpublished Notebooks. CU-MARK.

MTMF. Mark Twain to Mrs. Fairbanks. Ed. Dixon Wecter. San Marino: Huntington Library, 1949.

MTPO Letters. Online at marktwainproject.org

MTR. Mark Twain's Rubáiyát. Intro. Alan Gribben. Textual Note Kevin Mac Donnell. Austin & Santa Barbara: Jenkins Pub. Co., 1983.

MTSpk. Mark Twain Speaking. Ed. Paul Fatout. Iowa City: University of Iowa Press, 1976.

✓ *N&J1. Mark Twain's Notebooks & Journals, Volume 1 (1855–1873).* Ed. MTP editors. Berkeley: UCP, 1975.

✓ *N&J2. Mark Twain's Notebooks & Journals, Volume 2 (1877–1883).* Ed. MTP editors. Berkeley: UCP, 1975.

✓ *N&J3. Mark Twain's Notebooks & Journals, Volume 3 (1884–1891).* Ed. MTP editors. Berkeley: UCP, 1979.

No. 44: The Mysterious Stranger. Ed. John S. Tuckey. Berkeley: UCP, 1982.

P&P 1996. The Prince and the Pauper. Intro. Judith Martin. Afterword Everett Emerson. New York: OUP, 1996.

PW 1980. Pudd'nhead Wilson and Those Extraordinary Twins. Ed. Sidney Berger. New York: W. W. Norton, 1980.

PW 1996. The Tragedy of Pudd'nhead Wilson and the Comedy Those Extraordinary Twins. Intro. Sherley Anne Williams. Afterword David Lionel Smith. New York: OUP, 1996.

RI 1993. Roughing It. Eds. Harriet Elinor Smith, Edgar Marquess Branch, Lin Salamo, and Robert Pack Browning. Berkeley: UCP, 1993.

S&B. Mark Twain's Satires & Burlesques. Ed. Franklin B. Rogers. Berkeley: UCP, 1967.

SkS 1927. Sketches of the Sixties. 2nd ed. San Francisco: John Howell, 1927.

SN&O. Sketches, New and Old. Hartford: American Pub. Co., 1875.

SN&O 1996. Sketches, New and Old. Intro. Lee Smith. Afterword Sherwood Cummings. New York: OUP, 1996.

SP. "The Stupendous Procession." *Mark Twain's Weapons of Satire: Anti-Imperialist Writings on the Philippine-American War.* Ed. Jim Zwick. Syracuse: Syracuse University Press, 1992. 43–56.

TS 1980. The Adventures of Tom Sawyer, Tom Sawyer Abroad, Tom Sawyer, Detective. Eds. John C. Gerber, Paul Baender, and Terry Firkins. Berkeley: UCP, 1980.

TS 1982. The Adventures of Tom Sawyer: A Facsimile of the Author's Holograph Manuscript. Washington, DC: Georgetown University Library, 1982.

TS 1996. The Adventures of Tom Sawyer. Intro. E. L. Doctorow. Afterword Albert E. Stone. New York: OUP, 1996.

TS 2001. The Adventures of Tom Sawyer. Intro. Frank Conroy. New York: Modern Library, 2001.

TS 2014. *The Adventures of Tom Sawyer*. Intro. R. Kent Rasmussen. New York: Penguin Books, 2014.

TSA 1996. *Tom Sawyer Abroad*. Intro. Nat Hentoff. Afterword M. Thomas Inge. New York: OUP, 1996.

UCCL. *Union Catalog of Clemens Letters*. Ed. Paul Machlis. Berkeley: UCP, 1986. Online at *MTPO Letters*.

WA. *Wapping Alice by Mark Twain*. Ed. Hamlin Hill. Berkeley: Friends of the Bancroft Library, 1981.

WIM? *What Is Man? And Other Philosophical Writings*. Ed. Paul Baender. Berkeley: UCP, 1973

2. Other works

This section includes books, articles, people, and locations cited in the essays, and is arranged in a single alphabetical list by authors and abbreviations used in citations. Abbreviations for frequently cited works about Mark Twain generally follow those used by the Mark Twain Papers, and new ones have been added. Abbreviations for libraries generally do not follow those used by the Library of Congress.

Adams, Henry. *The Education of Henry Adams*. 1918. New York: Modern Library, 1931.

Anatole, Emily. "Generation Z: Rebels with a Cause." *Forbes* (28 May 2014).

Andrews, Kenneth R. *Nook Farm: Mark Twain's Hartford Circle*. Seattle: University of Washington Press, 1969.

Anon. "The American Stationer." [n.p.:] Howard Lockwood, 1890. Google Books.

Anon. "Education." jimsjourney.org/hannibaled

Applebee, Arthur. "Stability and Change in the High School Canon." *English Journal* 81:5 (Sept. 1992): 27–32.

Avery, Gillian. *Behold the Child: American Children and Their Books, 1621-1922*. Baltimore: Johns Hopkins University Press, 1994.

Ayres, John W. "Recollections of Hannibal" Letter of 22 Aug. 1917 to the *Palmyra Spectator*. Undated clipping in Morris Anderson scrapbook, Mark Twain Museum, Hannibal, Mo. Photocopy in MTP.

Baetzhold, Howard G., and Joseph B. McCullough, eds. *The Bible According to Mark Twain: Writings on Heaven, Eden, and the Flood*. Athens: University of Georgia Press, 1995.

Bailey, Susan Madeline, and Deborah Lynn Gosselin. *The Twain Shall Meet: The Mysterious Legacy of Samuel L. Clemens' Granddaughter, Nina Clemens Gabrilowitsch*. Greenville: Susan Bailey, 2014.

Baker, James. *The National Council of Education: Report of the Committee of Ten*. 1892. archive.org/details/reportofcomtens00natirich

Baker, Ruth. Interview with Shelley Fisher Fishkin, Hannibal, Missouri, 22 June 1995.

Baldwin, James. "White Man's Guilt." *Ebony* 10 (Aug. 1965): 47–48.

Barak, Benny, and Leon G. Schiffman. "Cognitive Age: A Nonchronological Age Variable." *Advances in Consumer Research* 8:1 (1981): 602–06.

Beecher, Catharine E., and Harriet Beecher Stowe. *The American Woman's Home; Or, Principles of Domestic Science.* New York, J. B. Ford & Co., 1869.

Beecher, Henry Ward. "A Discourse to Medical Students." *Herald of Health* 42 (1867).

Berkove, Lawrence, and Joseph Csicsila. *Heretical Fictions: Religion in the Literature of Mark Twain.* Iowa City: University of Iowa Press, 2010.

Bierce, Ambrose. "What I Saw of Shiloh." *A Sole Survivor: Bits of Autobiography.* Eds. S. T. Joshi and David E. Schultz. Knoxville: University of Tennessee Press, 1998. 10–26.

Billings, Josh. *Josh Billings on Ice.* New York: G. W. Carleton, 1868.

Blair, Walter, see *MT&HF.*

Bogen, David S. "Precursors of Rosa Parks: Maryland Transportation Cases Between the Civil War and the Beginning of World War I." *Maryland Law Review* 63 (2004): 721–51.

Branch, Edgar Marquess. *The Literary Apprenticeship of Mark Twain.* Urbana: University of Illinois, 1950.

Brashear, Minnie M., see *MTSM.*

Bremner, Robert H., ed. *Children and Youth in America: A Documentary History, Volume I, 1600-1865.* Cambridge, MA: Harvard University Press, 1970.

Brodhead, Richard H. "Sparing the Rod: Discipline and Fiction in Antebellum America." *Representations* 21 (Winter 1988): 67–96.

Brooks, Patricia, and Vera Kempe. *Language Development.* BPS Textbooks, 2012.

Brooks, Van Wyck. *The Ordeal of Mark Twain.* New York: E. P. Dutton, 1920.

Buchanan, Paul. *American Women's Rights Movement: A Chronology of Events and of Opportunities from 1600 to 2008.* Wellesley: Branden Books, 2009.

Burrows, Stuart. *A Familiar Strangeness: American Fiction and Photography, 1839-1945.* Athens: University of Georgia Press, 2010.

Burrows, Stuart, and Edwin H. Cady, eds. *On Mark Twain: The Best from American Literature.* Durham: Duke University Press, 1987.

Bush, Robert. "Grace King and Mark Twain." *American Literature* 44 (Mar. 1972): 42–51.

Cady, Edwin H. "A Note on Howells and 'The Smiling Aspects of Life.'" *American Literature* 17:2 (May 1945): 175–78.

CA-Hunt. Henry E. Huntington Library, San Marino, California.

Canby, Henry Seidel. "The American Tradition in Literature." *Saturday Review* (31 Aug. 1940).

Cardwell, Guy. *The Man Who Was Mark Twain.* New Haven: Yale University Press, 1991.

Carpenter, Humphrey, and Mari Prichard. *The Oxford Companion to Children's Literature.* Oxford: Oxford, 1984.

CC. Clara Langdon Clemens (later Gabrilowitsch and Samossoud).

CCMT. Rasmussen, R. Kent. *Critical Companion to Mark Twain: A Literary Reference to His Life and Work.* 2 vols. New York: Facts on File, 2007.

Chadwick, Jocelyn. "Forbidden Thoughts: New Challenges of Teaching Twain's *The Tragedy of Pudd'nhead Wilson*." *Mark Twain Annual* (2003): 85–95.

Chadwick, Jocelyn. Interview with Shelley Fisher Fishkin, Cambridge, Massachusetts, 1 Nov. 2014.

Christensen, Lawrence O., William E. Foley and Gary Kremer. *Dictionary of Missouri Biography*. Columbia: University of Missouri Press, 1999.

Cole, Thomas R. *The Journey of Life: A Cultural History of Aging in America*. Cambridge and New York: Cambridge University Press, 1992.

Commire, Anne. *Women in World History*. Book 4. Farmington Hills: Gale, 1999.

Connecticut Secretary of the State. *Register and Manual of the State of Connecticut*. Hartford: Connecticut, 1997.

Courtney, Steve. *"The Loveliest Home That Ever Was": The Story of the Mark Twain House in Hartford*. Mineola, New York: Dover, 2011.

Covici, Pascal, Jr. " 'Dear Master Wattie': The Mark Twain–David Watt Bowser Letters." *Southwest Review* 45 (Spring 1960).

Covici, Pascal, Jr. *Mark Twain's Humor: The Image of a World*. Dallas: Southern Methodist University, 1962.

Cox, James M. *Mark Twain: The Fate of Humor*. Princeton: Princeton University Press, 1966.

CT-MTHM. Mark Twain House and Museum, Hartford, Conn.

CT-SDay. Stowe-Day Memorial Library and Historical Foundation, Hartford, Conn.

CT-Yale. Yale University, Beinecke Rare Book and Manuscript Library, New Haven, Conn.

CU-BANC. University of California, The Bancroft Library, Berkeley.

CU-MARK. University of California, Mark Twain Papers, The Bancroft Library, Berkeley.

Dant, Faye. Emails and telephone conversations with Shelley Fisher Fishkin, 2013–15.

Dant, Faye. "Hannibal African American Life History: Hannibal's Invisibles." *Missouri Passages: Missouri Humanities Council News* 10 (Mar. 2012).

Dant, Faye. Interview with Shelley Fisher Fishkin, Hannibal, Missouri, 21 Sept. 2013.

Dant, Henry. Interview with Henry Dant. WPA Slave Narratives. Volume X: Missouri. gutenberg.org/files/35379/35379.txt (6 Mar. 2015) [See Works Project Administration below]

Dant, Joel. Emails to Shelley Fisher Fishkin, 2013–14.

Dant, Joel. Interview with Shelley Fisher Fishkin, Hannibal, Missouri, 21 Sept. 2013.

Darr, Bev. "Hannibal Middle School Students Will Compete in National Contest." Hannibal *Courier-Post* (6 June 2008).

Deegan, Mary Jo. "Fannie Barrier Williams and Her Life as a New Woman of Color in Chicago, 1893-1918." *The New Woman of Color: The Collected Writings of Fannie Barrier Williams, 1893-1918*. Ed. Mary Jo Deegan. DeKalb: Northern Illinois University Press, 2002. Xiii–lx.

Dempsey, Terrell. *Searching for Jim: Slavery in Sam Clemens's World*. Columbia: University of Missouri Press, 2003.

DeVoto, Bernard. *Mark Twain's America*. Boston: Little, Brown, 1932.

Dickinson, Emily. *The Poems of Emily Dickinson*. Ed. R. W. Franklin. Cambridge, MA: Belknap Press of Harvard University Press, 1999.

DMT. Rasmussen, R. Kent, ed. *Dear Mark Twain, Letters from His Readers*. Berkeley: UCP, 2013.

Dwyer, Ellen. "Stigma and Epilepsy." *Transactions and Studies of the College of Physicians of Philadelphia* 13 (Dec. 1991): 387–410.

Einfeld, Jann, ed. *Readings on "The Prince and the Pauper."* San Diego: Greenhaven Press, 2001.

Facen, Rev. Anne. Interview with Shelley Fisher Fishkin, Hannibal, Missouri, 22 June 1995.

Faden, Regina. "Museums and the Story of Slavery: The Challenge of Language." *Politics of Memory: Making Slavery Visible in the Public Space*. Ed. Ana Lucia Araujo. New York: Routledge, 2012. 252–66.

Fanning, Philip Ashley. *Mark Twain and Orion Clemens: Brothers, Partners, Strangers*. Tuscaloosa: University of Alabama Press, 2003.

Farthing, B. M. Barnet C. "Reminiscences of 'Mark Twain Boyhood.'" [n. d.] MS at MO-MTM.

Favorite Fairy Tales: The Childhood Choice of Representative Men and Women. New York: Harper, 1907.

Fetterley, Judith. "The Sanctioned Rebel." *Studies in the Novel* 3 (Fall 1971).

Fiedler, Leslie. "The Dream of the New." *American Dreams, American Nightmares*. Ed. David Madden. Carbondale: Southern Illinois University Press, 1972. 19–27.

Fishkin, Shelley Fisher. "False Starts, Fragments and Fumbles: Mark Twain's Unpublished Writing on Race." *Essays in Arts and Sciences* 20 (Oct. 1991): 17–31.

Fishkin, Shelley Fisher. *Lighting Out for the Territory: Mark Twain and American Culture*. New York: OUP, 1997.

Fishkin, Shelley Fisher. "Race and the Politics of Memory: Mark Twain and Paul Laurence Dunbar." *Journal of American Studies* 40 (2006): 283–309.

Fishkin, Shelley Fisher. *Was Huck Black? Mark Twain and African American Voices*. New York: OUP, 1993.

Fishkin, Shelley Fisher. *Writing America: Literary Landmarks from Walden Pond to Wounded Knee*. New Brunswick, NJ: Rutgers University Press, 2015.

Foner, Philip S. *Mark Twain: Social Critic*. New York: International, 1958.

Frear, Walter Francis, see *MT&H*.

Freire, Pablo. *Pedagogy of the Oppressed: Thirtieth Anniversary Edition*. New York: Bloomsbury, 2001.

Friedman, Lawrence J. *Inventors of the Promised Land*. New York: Alfred A. Knopf, 1975.

Fulton, Joe B. *Mark Twain in the Margins: The Quarry Farm Marginalia and A Connecticut Yankee in King Arthur's Court*. Tuscaloosa: University of Alabama Press, 2000.

Garrison, Wendell Phillips. "William Lloyd Garrison: Connecticut in the Middle Ages." *Century Magazine* 30:5 (Sept. 1885): 780–86.

Gillman, Susan. *Dark Twins: Imposture and Identity in Mark Twain's America.* Chicago: University of Chicago Press, 1989.

Graff, Harvey J. *Growing Up in America: Historical Experiences.* Detroit: Wayne State University Press, 1987.

Green, Leon M. "Mark Twain's 'Marjorie.'" Unpublished, 1916.

Gregory, George. "Lecture on the Laws Which Govern the Mode and Rate of Decay in the Human Frame." *Lancet* 40:1022 (1 Apr. 1843).

Gribben, Alan. "'Bond Slave to FitzGerald's Omar': Mark Twain and *The Rubaiyat*." *Sufism and American Literary Masters.* Ed. Mehdi Aminrazavi. Albany: SUNY Press, 2014. 245–62.

Gribben, Alan. "How Tom Sawyer Played Robin Hood 'by the Book.'" *English Language* 13:3 (Mar. 1976): 201–04.

Gribben, Alan. "'It Is Unsatisfactory to Read to Oneself': Mark Twain's Informal Readings." *Quarterly Journal of Speech* 62 (Feb. 1976): 49–56.

Gribben, Alan. "'A Splendor of Stars & Suns': Twain as a Reader of Browning's Poems." *Browning Institute Studies* 6 (1978): 87–103.

Gribben, Alan, see *MTLR*.

Hagood, J. Hurley, and Hagood Roberta. "Douglass School: A First Class High School." Hannibal *Courier-Post* [n. d.] Digitized 15 Nov. 2004 by Hannibal Free Public Library. cdm16795.contentdm.oclc.org/cdm/singleitem/collection/aanemo/id/192/rec/1

Hagood, J. Hurley, and Hagood Roberta. "Douglasville: A Venerable School." Hannibal *Courier-Post* [n. d.] Digitized 15 Nov. 2004 by Hannibal Free Public Library. digital.hannibal.lib.mo.us/B7255.htm (6 Mar. 2015).

Hagood, J. Hurley, and Hagood Roberta. *Hannibal Yesterdays.* Marceline: Jostens, 1992.

Haines, Michael. "Fertility and Mortality in the United States." EH.net.eh.net/encyclopedia/fertility-and-mortality-in-the-united-states

Hall, G. Stanley. *Senescence: The Last Half of Life.* New York: D. Appleton, 1922.

Harrington, Paula. "Dawson's Landing: On the Disappearance of Domesticity in a Slave Holding Town." *Mark Twain Annual*, no. 3 (2005): 91–97.

Harris, Susan K. "Narrative Structure in Mark Twain's *Joan of Arc*." *Journal of Narrative Technique* 12:1 (Winter 1982): 48–56.

Henderson, Archibald. *Mark Twain.* New York: Frederick A. Stokes, 1910.

Hendricks, Wanda A. *Fannie Barrier Williams: Crossing the Borders of Region and Race.* Urbana: University of Illinois Press, 2014.

Hilen, Andrew R., ed. *The Letters of Henry Wadsworth Longfellow, Volume I.* Cambridge, MA: Harvard University Press, 1982.

Hill, Hamlin. "The Composition and Structure of Tom Sawyer." *On Mark Twain: The Best from American Literature.* Eds. Louis J. Budd and Edwin H. Cady. Durham, NC: Duke University Press, 1987. 91–104.

Hoffmann, Donald. *Mark Twain in Paradise: His Voyages to Bermuda*. Columbia: University of Missouri Press, 2006.

Holbrook, Hal. *Mark Twain Tonight!* Dir. Paul Bogart. Perf. Hal Holbrook. Kultur, 1967. DVD.

Holcombe, R. I. *History of Marion County, Missouri*. St. Louis: E. F. Perkins, 1884.

Holmes, Oliver Wendell. *The Autocrat at the Breakfast-Table*. Boston: Phillips, Sampson, 1858.

Howe, M. A. DeWolfe, ed. "Bret Harte and Mark Twain in the Seventies: Passages from the Diaries of Mrs. James T. Fields." *Atlantic Monthly* 130 (Sept. 1922).

Howells, William Dean. *Criticism and Fiction, and Other Essays*. Eds. Clara and Rudolph Kirk. New York: New York University Press, 1959.

Howells, William Dean, see *MMT*.

Howells, William Dean, see *WDH*.

Hsu, Hsuan L. *Sitting in Darkness/Mark Twain's Asia and Comparative Racialization*. New York: New York University Press, 2015.

Hufeland, Christopher W. *Hufeland's Art of Prolonging Life*. Ed. Erasmus Wilson. Philadelphia: Lindsay & Blakiston, 1880.

Hunt, Peter, ed. *Children's Literature: An Anthology, 1801-1902*. Oxford: Blackwell, 2001.

IE. Stone, Albert E. *The Innocent Eye: Childhood in Mark Twain's Imagination*. New Haven: Yale University Press, 1961.

IVL. Isabel V. Lyon.

IVL. MS journal of seventy-four pages, 7 Nov. 1903 to 14 Jan. 1906, CU-MARK.

IVL. Diary in *The Standard Daily Reminder: 1905*. MS notebook of 368 pages, CU-MARK. [Lyon kept two diaries for 1905; some entries appear in both, but each also includes entries not found in the other.]

IVL. Diary in *The Standard Daily Reminder: 1905*. MS notebook of 368 pages, photocopy in CU-MARK. [In 1971 the original diary was owned by Mr. and Mrs. Robert V. Antenne and Mr. and Mrs. James F. Dorrance, of Rice Lake, Wisconsin; its current location is unknown. Lyon kept two diaries for 1905; some entries appear in both, but each also includes entries not found in the other.]

IVL. Diary in *The Standard Daily Reminder: 1906*. MS notebook of 368 pages, CU-MARK.

IVL. Diary in *Date Book for 1907*. MS notebook of 368 pages, CU-MARK.

IVL. Stenographic Notebook #4, with entries dated 5 Oct. 1907 to 17 Feb. 1908, CU-MARK.

IVL. Diary in *The Standard Daily Reminder, 1908*. MS notebook of 368 pages, CU-MARK.

IVL. Diary, 1909, entries transcribed in Lyon to Howe, 6 Feb. 1936, NY-Berg.

Jacobson, Marcia. *Being a Boy Again: Autobiography and the American Boy Book*. Tuscaloosa: University of Alabama Press, 1994.

JC. Jean Lampton Clemens.

JCD. Clemens, Jean Lampton. *Diaries of Jean L. Clemens, 1900–1907*. 7 vols. MS, CA-Hunt.

JCED. Clemens, Jean Lampton. *Excelsior Diary of Jean L. Clemens, 1907*. MS, CA-Hunt.

Jehlen, Myra. "Reading Gender in 'Adventures of Huckleberry Finn.'" *The Adventures of Huckleberry Finn: A Case Study in Critical Controversy*. Eds. Gerald Graff and James Phelan. Boston: Bedford St. Martin's, 1995. 505–18.

Jenn, Ronald. "Samuel Langhorne Clemens Traducteur." *Personal Recollections of Joan of Arc* (1895–1896) et les Trasvestissements de la Langue." *Amérique Traduite* [*Translating America*] *Revue Francaise d'Etudes Americaine* 138:1 (2014): 40–56.

JLC. Jane Lampton Clemens.

Kaplan, Fred. *The Singular Mark Twain*. New York: Doubleday, 2003.

Kaplan, Justin. *Mr. Clemens and Mark Twain*. New York: Simon & Schuster, 1966.

Kersten, Holger. "'It Is Better to Be a Young June-bug than an Old Bird of Paradise': Aging from the Perspective of America's Greatest Humorist." [Forthcoming]

Kessler, David, and Elizabeth Kübler-Ross. *On Grief and Grieving*. New York: Simon & Schuster, 2005.

Kingston, Anne. "Get Ready for Generation Z: They Smarter than Boomers and Way More Ambitious than the Millennials." *Maclean's* (15 July 2014).

Kiskis, Michael, and Laura E. Skandera Trombley, eds. *Constructing Mark Twain: New Developments in Scholarship*. Columbia: University of Missouri Press, 2001.

Knight, Emma. Interview with Emma Knight. WPA Slave Narratives. Volume X: Missouri. gutenberg.org/files/35379/35379.txt

Knoper, Randall. *Acting Naturally: Mark Twain in the Culture of Performance*. Berkeley: UCP, 1995.

Koshy, Tanya. *Remodeling Resistance: Black Civil Society and the Battle Against Baltimore's Residential Segregation Ordinances (1910-1918)*. Honors Thesis, American Studies Program, Stanford University, May 2006.

Krause, Sydney J. *Mark Twain as Critic*. Baltimore: Johns Hopkins Press, 1967.

Kübler-Ross, Elizabeth. *On Death and Dying*. New York: Scribner, 1969.

Lane, Lauriat. "Why Huckleberry Finn Is a Great World Novel." *College English* 17 (Oct. 1955).

Lawrence, D. H. *Studies in Classic American Literature*. New York: Seltzer, 1923.

Leisy, Ernest E. "Mark Twain's Part in *The Gilded Age*." *American Literature* 8 (Jan. 1937).

Lessels, Jeanette Barnes, and Eric Sterling. "Overseeing Racism in Jacob Abbott's *Stories of Rainbow and Lucky* and in Antebellum America." *Enterprising Youth: Social Values and Acculturation in Nineteenth-Century American Children's Literature*. Ed. Monica Elbert. New York: Routledge, 2008.

Levy, Andrew. *Huck Finn's America: Mark Twain and the Era that Shaped His Masterpiece*. New York: Simon & Schuster, 2015.

Lippard, George. *Legends of the American Revolution; Or, Washington and His Generals*. Philadelphia: T. B. Peterson, 1847.

Lystra, Karen. *Dangerous Intimacy: The Untold Story of Mark Twain's Final Years*. Berkeley: UCP, 2004.

Mac Donnell, Kevin. Email to Ronald Jenn, 2015.

Mac Donnell, Kevin. "Stormfield: A Virtual Tour." *Mark Twain Journal* 44:1–2 (Spring/ Fall 2006): 1–68.

Madden, David, ed. *American Dreams, American Nightmares.* Carbondale: Southern Illinois University Press, 1972.

Mailloux, Steven. *Rhetorical Power.* Ithaca: Cornell University Press, 1989.

Mark Twain Encyclopedia, see *MTEncy.*

"Mark Twain in White Amuses Congressmen." *New York Times* (8 Dec. 1906).

Mark Twain Project, *see* CU-BANK, CU-MARK, MTP, and MTPO.

"Mark Twain's Bad Boy." *New York World* (2 Mar. 1885).

"Mark Twain's Cousin, His Favorite, Tabitha Quarles." *Twainian* (July–Aug. 1951).

"Mark Twain's Playmates on Radio." Hannibal *Courier-Post* (29 Jan. 1926).

Marten, James. *The Children's Civil War.* Chapel Hill: University of North Carolina Press, 1998.

Marx, Leo. "Mr. Eliot, Mr. Trilling, and *Huckleberry Finn.*" *American Scholar* 22:4 (Autumn 1953): 423–39.

McDermott, John Francis. "Mark Twain and the Bible." *Papers on Language & Literature* 4 (Spring 1968): 195–98.

McDowell, Edwin. "From Twain, a Letter on Debt to Blacks." *New York Times,* 14 Mar. 1885. nytimes.com/1985/03/14/books/from-twain-a-letter-on-debt-to-blacks.html (6 Mar. 2015).

McGuinn, Warner T. Scrapbook kept by Warner T. McGuinn. Yale University Archives.

McKeithan, D. M., ed. *Traveling with the Innocents Abroad.* Norman: University of Oklahoma Press, 1958.

MEC. Mary E. (Mollie) Clemens.

Mentor, William L. "Mark Twain's *Joan of Arc.*" *Quarterly Review: A Journal of University Perspectives* LIV:10 (Autumn 1947): 243–50.

Messent, Peter. "Discipline and Punishment in *The Adventures of Tom Sawyer.*" *Journal of American Studies* 32:2 (1998): 219–35.

Messent, Peter. *Mark Twain and Male Friendship.* New York: OUP, 2009.

MFMT. Clemens, Clara Langdon. *My Father, Mark Twain.* New York: Harper, 1931.

MI-DPL. Detroit Public Library, Detroit, Mich.

Miller, Joe. Interview with Shelley Fisher Fishkin, Hannibal, Missouri, 21 Sept. 2013.

Mintz, Steve. *Huck's Raft: A History of American Childhood.* Cambridge, MA: Harvard University Press, 2004.

Missouri State Archives. *Missouri's Early Slave Laws: A History in Documents.* sos. mo.gov/archives/education/aahi/earlyslavelaws/slavelaws.asp

Mjakij, Nina. *Organizing Black America: An Encyclopedia of African American Associations.* New York: Routledge, 2001.

MMT. Howells, William Dean. *My Mark Twain.* New York: Harper, 1910.

MO-MTH. Mark Twain Home Foundation, Hannibal, Mo.

MO-MTM. Mark Twain Museum, Hannibal, Mo.

Morris, Linda. *Gender Play in Mark Twain: Cross-Dressing and Transgression*. Columbia: University of Missouri Press, 2007.

MS. Manuscript.

MT&H. Frear, Walter Francis. *Mark Twain and Hawaii*. Chicago: Lakeside Press, 1947.

MT&HF. Blair, Walter. *Mark Twain & Huck Finn*. Berkeley: UCP, 1960.

MTAZ. Rasmussen, R. Kent. *Mark Twain A to Z*. New York: Facts on File, 1995.

MTB. Paine, Albert Bigelow. *Mark Twain: A Biography*. 3 vols. New York: Harper, 1912.

MTBM. Webster, Samuel C. *Mark Twain: Business Man*. Boston: Little, Brown, 1946.

MTDP. Mark Twain Digital Project. Berkeley, California.

MTEncy. LeMasters, J. R., and James Wilson, eds. *Mark Twain Encyclopedia*. New York: Garland, 1993.

MTFM. Harnsberger, Caroline. *Mark Twain: Family Man*. New York: Citadel Press, 1960.

MTGF. Hill, Hamlin. *Mark Twain: God's Fool*. New York: Harper, 1973.

MTLR. Gribben, Alan. *Mark Twain's Library: A Reconstruction*. 2 vols. Boston: G. K. Hall, 1980.

MTP. *Mark Twain Project*. Berkeley, California.

MTPO. *Mark Twain Project Online*. Ed. MTP editors. Berkeley: UCP. marktwainproject.org

MTSM. Brashear, Minnie M. *Mark Twain: Son of Missouri*. Chapel Hill: University of North Carolina, 1934.

New England Business Directory and Gazetteer. [n.p.:] Sampson & Murdock, 1854. Google Books.

Nylund, David. *Treating Huckleberry Finn: A New Narrative Approach to Working with Kids Diagnosed ADD/ADHD*. San Francisco: Jossey-Bass, 2000.

Ober, K. Patrick. *Mark Twain and Medicine: "Any Mummery Will Cure."* Columbia: University of Missouri Press, 2003.

OC. Orion Clemens.

OLC. *Diary*. CU-MARK.

OLC. Olivia (Livy) Langdon Clemens.

OLL. Olivia (Livy) Louise Langdon.

Oriard, Michael. *Sporting with the Gods: The Rhetoric of Play and Game in American Culture*. Cambridge, England: Cambridge University Press, 1991.

OSC. Notebook containing several plays. On loan indefinite from CU-MARK to CT-MTH, MS.Doc3606.77-79.

OSC. Olivia Susan [Susy] Clemens.

OSC. *Papa: An Intimate Biography of Mark Twain*. Ed. Charles Neider. New York: Doubleday, 1985.

OUP. Oxford University Press.

Paine, Albert Bigelow. *Papers*. CU-MARK.

Paine, Albert Bigelow, see *MTB*.

Paine, Harriet E. *Old People*. Boston, New York: Houghton Mifflin, 1910.

PAM. Pamela A. Moffett.

Plunkett, Harriette Merrick Hodge. *Women, Plumbers, and Doctors; Or, Household Sanitation*. New York, D. Appleton and Company, 1885.

Poletti, Mary. "Rediscovering the Past: Hannibal Woman Searches for Clues to Black History." *Quincy Herald-Whig* (15 Mar. 2011).

Powers, Marion D. "Pelham, Lewis Had Profound Influence at Douglas School." [1969] hannibal.net/article/20100219/News/302199838

Powers, Ron. *Dangerous Waters: A Biography of the Boy Who Would Become Mark Twain*. New York: Basic Books, 1999.

Powers, Ron. *Mark Twain: A Life*. New York: Free Press, 2005.

"Prank of Tom Sawyer's Gang Cause of Consternation for Hotel, Brady's Story Reveals." Hannibal *Courier-Post* (6 Mar. 1935).

"Quarantine and Hygiene." *North American Review* 91 (1860).

Quick, Dorothy. *Enchantment: A Little Girl's Friendship with Mark Twain*. Norman: University of Oklahoma Press, 1961.

Quirk, Tom. *Mark Twain and Human Nature*. Columbia: University of Missouri Press, 2007.

Railton, Stephen. "That Sleepy Little Village . . . Those Easy Days . . ." twain.lib.virginia. edu/tomsawye/nostalgia/nostalgiahp.html

Ralls County Missouri Historical Newsletter 1:4 (July 2002). rootsweb.ancestry. com/~morchs/july02.htm

Raphelson, Samantha. "From GIs to Gen Z (Or is it iGen?): How Generations Get Nicknames." *NPR* (6 Oct. 2014).

Rasmussen, R. Kent, ed. *Mark Twain's Book for Bad Boys and Girls*. Chicago: Contemporary Books, 1995.

Rasmussen, R. Kent, see *CCMT, DMT,* and *MTAZ*.

Reed, Robert. *Black Chicago's First Century, Volume I: 1833-1900*. Columbia: University of Missouri Press, 2005.

Register and Manual of the State of Connecticut. Hartford: Secretary of State, 1997.

Robinson, Forrest G. *The Author-Cat: Clemens's Life in Fiction*. New York: Fordham University Press, 2007.

Rosenberg, Charles E., and Jane Golden, eds. *Framing Disease: Studies in Cultural History*. New Brunswick: Rutgers University Press, 1992.

Rotundo, E. Anthony. *American Manhood: Transformations in Masculinity from the Revolution to the Modern Era*. New York: Basic Books, 1993.

Ryan, Ann M., and Joseph B. McCullough, eds. *Cosmopolitan Twain*. Columbia: University of Missouri Press, 2008.

Sala, George A. *America Revisited*. London: Vizitelli, 1883.

Saleeby, C. W. *Worry: The Disease of the Age*. New York: Stokes, 1907.

Salsbury, Edith Colgate. *Susy and Mark Twain: Family Dialogues*. New York: Harper, 1965.

Sanborn, Margaret. *Mark Twain: The Bachelor Years*. New York: Doubleday, 1990.

Scharnhorst, Gary, ed. *Critical Essays on "The Adventures of Tom Sawyer."* New York: G. K. Hall, 1993.

Scharnhorst, Gary, ed. *Twain in His Own Time.* Iowa City: University of Iowa Press, 2010.

Schmidt, Barbara. Twainquotes.com

Schmidt, Barbara. "Mark Twain's Angel-Fish Roster and Other Young Women of Interest." twainquotes.com/angelfish/angelfish.html

Schryver, Selina. "Problems of Orphanhood." *Journal of Nervous and Mental Disease* CI (1945).

SCOH. Wecter, Dixon. *Sam Clemens of Hannibal.* Boston: Houghton Mifflin, 1952.

Scott, Donald L. Interview with Shelley Fisher Fishkin, Hannibal, Missouri, 21 Sept. 2013.

Scott, Donald L. *Recipient of Grace: My Incredible Journey from Hunnewell, MO, to Deputy Librarian & Chief Operating Officer, Library of Congress.* Bloomington, IN: Xlibris, 2015.

Scroggins, William G. *Leaves of a Stunted Shrub: A Genealogy of the Scrogin-Scroggin-Scroggins Family, Volume 6.* Cockeysville: Nativa Books, 2009.

Selznick, David O. *Memo from David O. Selznick.* Ed. Rudy Behlmer. New York: Viking Press, 1972.

Sharlow, Gretchen. "Mark Twain Reads Browning Again: A Discovery in the Langdon-Crane Family Library at Quarry Farm." *Mark Twain Journal* 28:2 (Fall 1990): 24–29.

Shelden, Michael. *Mark Twain, Man in White: The Grand Adventure of His Final Years.* New York: Random House, 2010.

Simms, Joseph. "The Rearing of Youth." *Physiognomy Illustrated; Or, Nature's Revelation of Character.* New York: Murray Hill Publishing, 1887.

SLC. Samuel Langhorne Clemens.

Snedecor, Barbara E. " 'He Was So Rarely Beautiful': Langdon Clemens." *American Literary Realism* 45:1 (Fall 2012): 60–69.

Stahl, J. D. *Mark Twain, Culture and Gender. Envisioning America Through Europe.* Athens: University of Georgia Press, 1994.

Stearns, Peter L. *Anxious Parents: A History of Modern Childrearing in America.* New York: New York University Press, 2003.

Stone, Albert E. "Mark Twain's *Joan of Arc*: The Child as Goddess." *American Literature* 31:1 (Mar. 1959): 1–20.

Stone, Albert E., see *IE*.

Stoneley, Peter. *Mark Twain and the Feminine Aesthetic.* Cambridge, England: Cambridge University Press, 1992.

Sweets, Henry. *The Hannibal, Missouri, Presbyterian Church: A Sesquicentennial History.* Hannibal: Presbyterian Church of Hannibal, 1984.

Third Annual Report of the Board of Health of the City of New Haven, 1875. New Haven: Tuttle, Morehouse & Taylor, Printers. 1876.

Thomas, A. E. "Mark Twain: A Humorist's Confession." *New York Times* (26 Nov. 1905).

"Thurgood Marshall." *Biography,* A&E Television Networks, 2015.

Trombley, Laura E. Email to Joseph Csicsila, 10 Oct. 2014.

Trombley, Laura E. Skandera. *Mark Twain in the Company of Women*. Philadelphia: University of Pennsylvania Press, 1994.

Trombley, Laura E. Skandera. *Mark Twain's Other Woman: The Hidden Story of His Final Years*. New York: Alfred A. Knopf, 2010.

TS. Typescript.

Tulgan, Bruce. "Meet Generation Z: The Second Generation within the Giant 'Millennial' Cohort." Rainmakerthinking.com (6 Nov. 2013).

Tushnet, Mark V. *Making Civil Rights Law: Thurgood Marshall and the Supreme Court, 1936-1961*. New York: OUP, 1996.

UCP. University of California Press.

United States Supreme Court. *Plessy v. Ferguson*, 163 U.S. 537 (1896). ourdocuments.gov

Usher, Shuan, comp. "Letter No. 120: What Great Births You Have Witnessed! Mark Twain to Walt Whitman." *Letters of Note: An Eclectic Collection of Correspondence of a Wider Audience*. San Francisco: Chronicle Books, 2013.

Valentine, Mark. "Mark Twain's Novels and Ned Buntline's Wildcat Literature." *Mark Twain Journal* 48:1–2 (Spring/Fall 2010): 29–48.

VI-U. University of Virginia, Charlottesville.

Volo, James M., and Dorothy Dennen Volo. *Family Life in 19th-Century America*. Westport, CT: Greenwood Press, 2007.

Wakley, Thomas. "Government Cholera Commission." *The Lancet* 62:1573 (22 Oct. 1853).

Wallace, Elizabeth. *Mark Twain and the Happy Island*. Chicago: A. C. McClurg, 1913.

Wallace, Elizabeth. *The Unending Journey*. Minneapolis: University of Minnesota Press, 1952.

Wallop, Harry. "Gen A, Gen Y, Baby Boomers—A Guide to the Generations." *The Telegraph* (31 July 2014).

Ward, Artemus [Browne, Charles F.] *The Complete Works of Artemus Ward*. New York: G. W. Dillingham, 1897 [1875].

Warner, Charles Dudley. "The Education of the Negro." *Complete Writings of Charles Dudley Warner, Volume 14*. Hartford: American Pub. Co., 1904.

WDH. William Dean Howells.

Webster, Samuel C., see *MTBM*.

Wecter, Dixon, see *SCOH*.

Wheeler, Candice. *Yesterdays in a Busy Life*. New York: Harper, 1918.

Whitman, Steven, and Bruce P. Hermann, eds. *Psychopathology in Epilepsy: Social Dimensions*. New York: OUP, 1986.

Williams, Jr., Donald E. *Prudence Crandall's Legacy: The Fight for Equality in the 1830s, Dred Scott, and Brown v. Board of Education*. Middletown: Wesleyan University Press, 2014.

Williams, Fannie Barrier. "A Northern Negro's Autobiography." Reprinted in Mary Jo Deegan, ed. *The New Woman of Color: The Collected Writings of Fannie Barrier Williams, 1893-1918*. DeKalb: Northern Illinois University Press, 2002.

Williams, Henry Sullivan. "The Development of the Negro Public School System in Missouri." *Journal of Negro History* 5:2 (April 1920), jstor.org/stable/2713590

Williams, Mentor L. "Mark Twain's Joan of Arc." *Quarterly Review: A Journal of University Perspectives* 54:10 (Autumn 1947): 243–50.

Wolff, Cynthia Griffin. "*The Adventures of Tom Sawyer*: A Nightmare Vision of American Boyhood." *Massachusetts Review* 21:4 (Winter 1980): 637–52.

Works Progress Administration (WPA). *Slave Narratives: A Folk History of Slavery in the United States from Interview with Former Slaves¼ volume X: Missouri Narratives.* Washington, DC: WPA, 1941.

Yamamoto, Yuko. "Huck and Jim in Conspiracy: Drifting down the River Against the Court." *Kansai Mark Twain Journal* 1 (2009): 23–36.

Notes on Contributors

Dr. Lawrence I. Berkove, an emeritus professor of English at the University of Michigan-Dearborn and a past president of the Mark Twain Circle of America, specializes in nineteenth- and early twentieth-century American literature. He has had a particular interest in Mark Twain, Ambrose Bierce, Jack London, and writers of Nevada's Sagebrush School—on all of which he has published extensively. Among his nineteen books are the Modern Library edition of *The Best Short Stories of Mark Twain* (2004) and, with Joseph Csicsila, *Heretical Fictions: Religion in the Literature of Mark Twain* (2010). The most recent of his numerous honors is a Legacy Scholar profile in the *Mark Twain Journal* (2014).

Dr. John Bird is Margaret M. Bryant Professor of English and director of the Teaching and Learning Center at Winthrop University in Rock Hill, South Carolina. The winner of the top teaching awards at both institutions where he has taught; he was also founding editor of *The Mark Twain Annual* through its first five issues. He is currently the president of the Mark Twain Circle of America and associate editor of the University of Missouri Press's Mark Twain and His Circle series. His publications on Twain include *Mark Twain and Metaphor* (2007) and articles in *American Literary Realism*, *The Mark Twain Annual*, *Texas Studies in Literature and Language*, and *Studies in American Fiction*, along with chapters in five books, and he writes the annual roundup of new publications on Twain for *American Literary Scholarship*. He has also published widely on American humor, Henry David Thoreau, and pedagogy.

Dr. Jocelyn Chadwick has taught English for more than thirty years—from a Texas high school to the Harvard Graduate School of Education. A consultant for school districts throughout the United States and abroad, she assists English departments develop curricula to reflect diversity and cross-curricular content, and she helped construct NBC News Education Nation's *Parent Tool Kit*. She was recently elected vice president of the National Council of Teachers of English. Her publications include *The Jim Dilemma: Reading Race in Adventures of Huckleberry Finn* (1998) and *Common Core: Paradigmatic Shifts, Teaching Literature in the Context of Literacy Instruction* (2015). She is currently authoring a book on using literature to teach writing. Her honors include Harvard

University's Honor a Teacher award, the Hugh M. Hefner First Amendment Award, and the Intellectual Freedom Award. In 2001, she co-moderated the Mark Twain Symposium in the White House Salute to American Authors series.

Dr. Joseph Csicsila, a professor of English at Eastern Michigan University, has published essays on numerous nineteenth- and twentieth-century American writers. He is also the author of *Canons by Consensus: Critical Trends and American Literature Anthologies* (2004), coauthor (with Lawrence Berkove) of *Heretical Fictions: Religion in the Literature of Mark Twain* (2010), and coeditor (with Chad Rohman) of *Centenary Reflections on Mark Twain's* No. 44, the Mysterious Stranger (2009). He has been a member of the editorial team of the *Prentice Hall Anthology of American Literature* since 2007 and is currently editor of the Mark Twain Circular.

Hugh H. Davis teaches English at Winton, North Carolina's C. S. Brown High School, where he was 2014–2015 Teacher of the Year. A former president of the Popular Culture Association in the South, he frequently infuses his classes with aspects of popular culture to help bring texts to life for his students. He has published articles in *Studies in Popular Culture*, *Journal of American Culture*, *Edgar Allan Poe Review*, and *Literature/Film Quarterly* and has contributed chapters to *Shakespeare into Film* (2002), *Past Watchful Dragons* (2007), *Kermit Culture* (2009), *Undead in the West* (2012), *Dickens Adapted* (2012), *and Supernatural Youth* (2013).

Mark Dawidziak, the television critic for the *Cleveland Plain Dealer*, has been a theater, film, and television reviewer for more than thirty-five years. His many books include *Mark My Words: Mark Twain on Writing* (1996), *Horton Foote's The Shape of the River: The Lost Teleplay About Mark Twain* (2003), and *Mark Twain's Guide to Diet, Exercise, Beauty, Fashion, Investment, Romance, Health and Happiness* (2015). The cofounder and artistic director of northeast Ohio's Largely Literary Theater Company, he has been portraying Mark Twain on stage since 1979 (with his makeup-aging process growing less time-consuming each year). He also frequently performs Twain material with his wife, actress Sara Showman, in their two-person show, *Twain by Two*. His most recent book is *Mark Twain for Cat Lovers*. He and Kent Rasmussen are currently writing a book on Mark Twain movies.

Victor Fischer has been an editor at the Mark Twain Papers and Project of The Bancroft Library at the University of California, Berkeley, since the late 1960s. Among the University of California Press editions in which he has received title-page credit are *The Prince and the Pauper* (1979, 1983); volumes 3 and 4 of

Mark Twain's Letters (1992, 1995); *Adventures of Huckleberry Finn* (1985, 1989, and 2001, 2003—after the discovery of the first half of the manuscript); *Mark Twain's Helpful Hints for Good Living: A Handbook for the Damned Human Race* (2004); the three-volume *Autobiography of Mark Twain* (2010-2015); and the web edition of *Mark Twain's Letters, 1876–1880* (2007).

Dr. Shelley Fisher Fishkin is Joseph S. Atha Professor of Humanities, professor of English, and director of American Studies at Stanford University. The editor of the twenty-nine-volume *Oxford Mark Twain* edition (1996), she has also written, edited, or coedited a dozen other books and more than one hundred articles, essays, and reviews, many of which have focused on issues of race, gender, and ethnicity in America and on recovering previously silenced voices from the past. She is especially well known for her publications in Mark Twain studies, including *Was Huck Black? Mark Twain and African-American Voices* (1993), *Lighting Out for the Territory: Reflections on Mark Twain and American Culture* (1997), *A Historical Guide to Mark Twain* (2002), *"Is He Dead?" A New Comedy by Mark Twain* (2003), *Mark Twain's Book of Animals* (2010), and the Library of America's *Mark Twain Anthology: Great Writers on His Life and Works* (2010). Her most recent book is *Writing America: Literary Landmarks from Walden Pond to Wounded Knee* (2015).

Dr. James Joseph Golden received degrees in divinity and history from the University of Edinburgh before completing a doctorate in modern history at the University of Oxford. Formerly a postdoctoral researcher on a public humanities project at the University of Cambridge, he is now director of education at the Mark Twain House and Museum in Hartford, Connecticut. His writing has been published in such scholarly journals as the *English Historical Review* and the *Journal of Ecclesiastical History*.

Dr. Alan Gribben is a professor of English at Auburn University's Montgomery campus, where he served as head of the Department of English and Philosophy for two decades and has been honored with a Distinguished Research Professorship, the Nance Alumni Professorship, and the Alumni Association's Faculty Service Award. His other honors include a Henry Nash Smith Fellowship from the Center for Mark Twain Studies at Elmira College. A cofounder and former president of the Mark Twain Circle of America, he is presently editor of the *Mark Twain Journal* and a member of the editorial board of *American Literary Realism*. For fifteen years, he reviewed Mark Twain publications for the annual *American Literary Scholarship* and is the author of *Mark Twain's*

Library: A Reconstruction (1980), editor of New South Books' six-volume *Tom Sawyer* and *Huckleberry Finn* series (2011), coeditor (with Jeffrey Alan Melton) of *Mark Twain on the Move: A Travel Reader* (2009), biographer of the library founder Harry Ransom, and author of dozens of articles on Twain's intellectual background. He is currently working on an extensively revised and enlarged edition of *Mark Twain's Library*.

Dr. Benjamin Griffin was educated at the University of California at Berkeley, Cambridge University (M. Phil and PhD), and Catholic University of America (MLS) before becoming an editor at the Mark Twain Papers and Project of the University of California's Bancroft Library. His editorial credits at the project include the three volumes of *Autobiography of Mark Twain* (2010–2015) and the anthology *A Family Sketch and Other Private Writings* (2014). He has also published a book on English historical drama, *Playing the Past* (2001) and articles on Twain, Friedrich Nietzsche, William Shakespeare, and other subjects.

Hal Holbrook, a distinguished stage and screen actor, has played the role of Mark Twain even longer than Samuel L. Clemens did. Since creating the one-man show *Mark Twain Tonight!* in 1954, he has appeared as Twain more than two thousand times, while also finding time to appear in well over one hundred television and film productions. His numerous acting honors include five prime-time Emmy Awards and six additional nominations, including one for his 1967 CBS-TV performance of *Mark Twain Tonight!* He also received a Tony Award in 1966 for the first of his three Broadway runs of *Mark Twain Tonight!* In 2009, he was nominated for an Academy Award as best supporting actor for his role in *Into the Wild*. His 1959 book *Mark Twain Tonight! An Actor's Portrait* contains selections from his show and a lengthy memoir of his acting career up to that point. In 2011, he published *Harold: The Boy Who Became Mark Twain*, the first part of his projected two-volume autobiography. He also contributed an introduction to the 1996 Oxford edition of Mark Twain's *Speeches*.

Dr. Ronald Jenn, a professor of translation studies at France's Université de Lille, wrote his dissertation on French translations of *Tom Sawyer* and *Huckleberry Finn*. In addition to a number of articles on French translations of other nineteenth-century American literature, he wrote *La Pseudo-traduction de Cervantès à Mark Twain* (2013), which contains a chapter analyzing translation issues in Mark Twain's *Personal Recollections of Joan of Arc*. He is currently working with Dr. Paula Harrington on *Mark Twain and France: The Anxiety of Culture*, which will be published by the University of Missouri Press.

Dr. Holger Kersten is professor of American literature and culture at Germany's University of Magdeburg. His primary research interests include nineteenth-century American literature, environmental writing, humor studies, the use of nonstandard language in literature, and the study of national images. His publications include *Von Hannibal nach Heidelberg: Mark Twain und die Deutschen–Eine Studie zu literarischen und soziokulturellen Quellen eines Deutschlandbildes* (1993). He is a member of various national and international academic associations and has served on the executive and advisory boards of the German Association for American Studies.

Dr. Andrew Levy is Edna Cooper Professor of English at Butler University, where he also chairs the English department and recently directed the master of fine arts program. He is author of the critically acclaimed *Brain Wider Than the Sky* (2010), the award-winning biography *The First Emancipator: Slavery, Religion, and the Quiet Revolution of Robert Carter* (2005), and *Huck Finn's America: Mark Twain and the Era That Shaped His Masterpiece* (2014). His essays have appeared in *Harper's*, *American Scholar*, and *Best American Essays*, and his work has been reviewed in *Time*, the *New York Times*, National Public Radio, and other national venues.

Dr. Cindy Lovell is executive director of the Mark Twain House and Museum in Hartford, Connecticut, and previously served as executive director of the Mark Twain Boyhood Home and Museum in Hannibal, Missouri. While holding the latter position, she received the Missouri governor's Ambassador Award in Tourism, the Hannibal Area Chamber of Commerce Community Betterment Award, Hannibal Area Chamber of Commerce Civic Contributor of the Year Award, and the Hannibal NAACP Martin Luther King, Jr., Award. Before becoming a museum director she held tenured faculty positions at Stetson University and Quincy University and since then has conducted numerous teaching workshops. Her publications include two children's novels, dozens of articles, textbook chapters, and essays, and she is a contributing writer for *The Huffington Post*.

Dr. Karen Lystra is professor of American studies at California State University, Fullerton, and author of *Searching the Heart: Women, Men, and Romantic Love in Nineteenth-Century America* (1989) and *Dangerous Intimacy: The Untold Story of Mark Twain's Final Years* (2004). She is an Organization of American Historians Distinguished Lecturer and past president of the Western Association of Women Historians. Among recent awards she most treasures is her university's Outstanding Honors Professor of the Year.

Dr. Debra Ann MacComb received her doctorate from UCLA in 1995 and joined the faculty at the University of West Georgia the following year as a specialist in American realism and naturalism. She has published on Henry James, Edith Wharton, William Dean Howells, Kate Chopin, Abraham Cahan, and William Faulkner. Her first book, *Tales of Liberation/Strategies of Containment: Divorce and the Representation of Womanhood in American Fiction, 1880-1920* appeared in 2000. A relative newcomer to Mark Twain studies, she is currently working on a monograph on Twain and male domesticity, a project growing out of an article she published in the 2012 issue of *The Mark Twain Annual*. She shares a farm in Roopville, Georgia, with three horses, five dogs, five cats, and a very patient husband.

Kevin Mac Donnell earned his MLS at the University of Texas and serves on the editorial boards of the *Mark Twain Journal* and *Firsts Magazine*. The owner of Mac Donnell Rare Books since 1986, he has published numerous articles on librarianship and antiquarian bookselling, as well as bibliographical articles on Louis May Alcott, Richard Henry Dana, Charlotte Perkins Gilman, Nathaniel Hawthorne, James Russell Lowell, Herman Melville, and Henry David Thoreau. He coedited (with Alan Gribben) *Mark Twain's Rubaiyat* (1983), contributed articles to the *Mark Twain Encyclopedia* (1993), and has reviewed dozens of books for the *Mark Twain Forum*. One of his many published articles on Twain went viral on *Salon.com* and *The Huffington Post*, and was cited as "research of note" by *The Chronicle of Higher Education* in 2013. He was honored as a Legacy Scholar in the *Mark Twain Journal* in 2016. His collection of more than 8,000 Mark Twain items—first editions, archives, manuscripts, and artifacts—is the largest in private hands, and he frequently shares his materials with other scholars and museums.

Dr. Peter Messent, an emeritus professor of American and Canadian studies at England's University of Nottingham, has written widely on Mark Twain. His *Mark Twain and Male Friendship* (2009) won two major European academic awards. His other books include *Mark Twain* (1997), *The Short Works of Mark Twain* (2001), *The Cambridge Introduction to Mark Twain* (2009), and *A Companion to Mark Twain* (2005, coedited with Louis J. Budd). His books on narrative theory, Ernest Hemingway, and crime fiction include *The Crime Fiction Handbook* (2012). He is presently coediting (with Harold K. Bush and Steve Courtney) Mark Twain's correspondence with Joseph Twichell.

Dr. Linda Morris is a professor emerita at the University of California, Davis, where she served as director of writing, director of women's studies, and chair of the Department of English. Her honors include a Bancroft Library Fellowship, a University of California President's Fellowship, and the John Ben Snow Award from Syracuse University Press for her book *Women's Humor in the Age of Gentility: The Life and Works of Frances M. Whitcher* (1992). She is also the author of *Gender Play in Mark Twain: Cross-Dressing and Transgression* (2007) and editor of *American Women's Humor: Critical Essays* (1994) and *Women Vernacular Humorists in Nineteenth-Century America* (1988). Her many articles on Mark Twain and American humor have appeared in *Studies in American Fiction, Mark Twain Annual,* and *Studies in American Humor,* as well as such books as *A Companion to Mark Twain* (1999), *A Companion to Satire* (2007), and *Women and Comedy: History, Theory, Practice* (2013).

Dr. K. Patrick Ober is professor of internal medicine at the Wake Forest School of Medicine in Winston-Salem, North Carolina. He earned his BS in biochemistry at Michigan State University and his MD from the University of Florida. He completed a residency in internal medicine and a fellowship in endocrinology and metabolism at Wake Forest, where he has ever since been on the faculty. The recipient of twenty major teaching awards and five yearbook dedications, he has also been formally recognized as one of the "best doctors in America" on multiple occasions. His book *Mark Twain and Medicine: "Any Mummery Will Cure"* was published by the University of Missouri Press in 2003. Since then he has been a regular presenter at Mark Twain studies conferences. He is currently writing a book examining an unusual explanation offered by nineteenth-century physicians of the health problems in Mark Twain's Hartford home and the White House.

John R. Pascal, a cum laude graduate of Villanova University, earned his MA in English at Montclair State University and his MBA at Seton Hall University. He is now in his fifteenth year teaching English at Seton Hall Preparatory School in New Jersey, where he has also served as mock trial team moderator and moderator of numerous student clubs and the student council. Recognized as a generous teacher, counselor, and moderator, he received the school's Salvatore N. Caprio Award in 2010. He is the author of *Artemus Ward: The Gentle Humorist* (2008) and has presented papers on Mark Twain and Artemus Ward at Mark Twain conferences in Elmira and Hannibal and reviewed books for the *Mark Twain Forum.* In 2006, he received the Lawrence Conrad Memorial Scholarship for Excellence in the Study of American Literature awarded by Montclair State University.

Dr. R. Kent Rasmussen is a retired reference-book editor and former associate editor of the Marcus Garvey Papers at UCLA, where he had earlier earned a doctorate in history. In addition to editing scores of reference books on history, politics, literature, criminal law, and other fields, he has written extensively on African history and other subjects. He is best known, however, as author of the award-winning *Mark Twain A to Z* (1995; revised as *Critical Companion to Mark Twain*, 2007). His other books on Mark Twain include *The Quotable Mark Twain* (1997), *Mark Twain for Kids* (2004), *Bloom's How to Write About Mark Twain* (2008), *Critical Insights: Mark Twain* (2011), and *Dear Mark Twain: Letters from His Readers* (2013). He has also contributed introductions and notes to the Penguin Classics editions of *Tom Sawyer* (2014), *Huckleberry Finn* (2014), and *Mark Twain's Autobiographical Writings* (2012). The recipient of numerous awards for his reference books, he was honored with recognition as a Legacy Scholar in the *Mark Twain Journal* in 2015. His most recent books include *Mark Twain for Dog Lovers*. He and Mark Dawidziak are currently writing a book on Mark Twain movies.

Dr. Lucy Rollin is a professor emerita at Clemson University, where she taught English and children's and adolescent literature. She has published many essays and book reviews, most recently "*Pinocchio*: An American *Commedia*," for *Walt Disney, from Reader to Storyteller* (2015). She edited a teaching edition of *The Adventures of Tom Sawyer* for Broadview Press (2006), and an edition of *The Prince and the Pauper* for Oxford University Press's World's Classics series (1996). Her other books include *Cradle and All: A Cultural and Psychoanalytic Study of Nursery Rhymes* (1992), *Psychoanalytic Responses to Children's Literature* (1999, with Mark West), and *Twentieth-Century Teen Culture, by the Decades: A Reference Guide* (1999).

Barbara Schmidt, now living in the Texas Hill Country, holds a degree in criminal justice and psychology and is retired from Tarleton State University, where she worked with faculty and staff in developing instructional materials for both classrooms and the Internet. She now works as an independent researcher and publisher. In 1997, she launched twainquotes.com, one of the first Internet websites devoted to a single author. She created the frequently cited and information-packed site to publish original research and make available a wide range of reference tools for students, educators, and other researchers. The site contains many of her own research articles, and her writings have also appeared in the *Mark Twain Journal*. She currently serves as book review editor for the *Mark Twain Forum*, an Internet listserv discussion group.

Dr. David E. E. Sloane, a professor of English at Connecticut's University of New Haven and member of the board of trustees of nearby Hartford's Mark Twain House, received his doctorate from Duke University in 1970. A former president of both the Mark Twain Circle of America and the American Humor Studies Association, he has published *Mark Twain as a Literary Comedian* (1979), *The Literary Humor of the Urban Northeast, 1830-1890* (1983), *American Humor Magazines and Comic Periodicals* (1987), *Adventures of Huckleberry Finn: American Comic Vision* (1988), *Mark Twain's Humor: Critical Essays* (1993), and *Student Companion to Mark Twain* (2001). His many honors include being named first Henry Nash Smith Fellow of Elmira College's Center for Mark Twain Studies in 1989, Carnegie Foundation Connecticut College Teacher of the Year in 2001, and a Legacy Scholar profile in the *Mark Twain Journal* in 2014.

Henry H. Sweets III, the executive director of the Mark Twain Boyhood Home and Museum in Hannibal, Missouri, holds a bachelor's degree in chemistry and a master's in engineering from the University of Illinois and a master's in American history and museum studies from the University of Delaware. He became director of the Hannibal museum in 1978 and has ever since edited its bimonthly newsletter, *The Fence Painter*. He is also author of *A Sesquicentennial History of the Hannibal (Missouri) Presbyterian Church (1984)*. He initiated and ran Hannibal's Mark Twain Writers Conference (1985–94) and now directs the Mark Twain Teacher Workshop and the quadrennial Clemens Conference, which was launched in 2011. He served on Hannibal's Board of Education for eighteen years, including fifteen years as its president. He also serves on the Missouri Board on Geographic Names and the board of Great River Honor Flight.

Wendelinus Wurth teaches English and German at the Upper Secondary Vocational School of Economics in Hausach, Germany. To date he has written five volumes of dialect poems and stories. His 1997 translation of *Adventures of Huckleberry Finn* marked the first time Mark Twain's novel was translated into different German dialects that reflect the multiple dialects of Mark Twain's characters. He is currently completing his dissertation, presently titled *Discomfort with Huckleberry Finn.*

Acknowledgments

This book has truly been a labor of love for everyone involved. We sincerely thank the contributors who poured their time, expertise, and energy into the essays they wrote for it. We especially appreciate their good-natured patience with our requests for revisions and seemingly endless queries. We must also express our gratitude to Hal Holbrook for taking time from his busy schedule to read many of these essays and write a marvelously passionate personal foreword. Hal has been Mark Twain incarnate on stage for more years than Sam Clemens himself and knows better than anyone living today how audiences, young and old, respond to Twain. He carries in his head more memorized writings of Twain than any Twain scholar—probably even more than Twain himself ever knew by heart.

We also wish to thank the editors of the Mark Twain Papers and Project in Berkeley for the long years of diligent work they have put into preparing the meticulous editions of Twain's writings—especially his previously unpublished works. We are particularly grateful for their timely completion of the magnificent three-volume *Autobiography of Mark Twain*—all of which they made available to us in PDF format—and for Ben Griffin's editing of Mark Twain's invaluable *A Family Sketch and Other Private Writings*. The scholarly significance of the Project's publications will be abundantly clear to all readers of the present volume who pay close attention to the essay's citations.

From the moment we began planning this volume, we agreed that because it would be a collaborative work by and for the field of Mark Twain studies that the most appropriate beneficiary of royalties accruing from the book would be the field itself. To that end, the book's royalties are to be divided equally and without restrictions among the four major Mark Twain research centers to further the study of the life and writings of Mark Twain. These centers are the Center for Mark Twain Studies at Elmira College, Elmira, New York, where Twain spent his summers and composed his greatest works, and where the International Mark Twain Conference has been hosted every four years since 1994; The Mark Twain Boyhood Home & Museum of Hannibal, Missouri, where the boy Sam spent the youth that reverberated in his life and writings the rest of his days, and where the quadrennial Clemens Conference is now being hosted every four years, timed to alternate with the Elmira conferences; The Mark Twain House & Museum of Hartford, Connecticut, where the beautifully restored and artifact-filled home in which Twain raised his family during his most productive years is open for guided tours; and the Mark Twain Papers and Project of The Bancroft Library of the University of California at Berkeley, where the bulk of Twain's own papers are housed, and whose editors are responsible for the standard scholarly texts of Twain's writings. The staffs of all four institutions have, as always, been generous with their time, and have cordially shared their expertise and resources.

We must also, of course, thank Mark Richardson and Grishma Fredric, our friendly and patient editors at Bloomsbury Press, for their unstinting support and encouragement. Finally, we are grateful to our wives, Donna Mac Donnell, and Kathy Rasmussen, who suffer no fools, but fortunately make exceptions for their husbands.

Index

In this index the names of fictional characters in Mark Twain's writings are followed by the titles of the works in which they appear, with the exceptions of Tom Sawyer and Huck Finn. All quoted and italicized titles are writings by Mark Twain unless otherwise noted, and because some of his stories and essays also appeared as book titles, some titles will be found indexed both ways. Boldfaced page numbers indicate illustrations. People are indexed by their surnames when known, including Samuel L. Clemens, who is otherwise cited simply as SLC for the sake of brevity. Clemens's daughters—Susy, Clara, and Jean—are usually rendered without their surnames in subheadings.

Fairbanks, Mary Mason   38–40, 42, 66, 197
Family Sketch and Other Private Writings, A
    xxiv, 61, 84, 114, 150, 177, 182
Fanning, Philip   53
Farthing, Barnett   121, 123, 124
Fatima ("1002d Arabian Night"
    character)   207–9
Feldner, August (*No. 44* character)
    219, 220
Fiedler, Leslie   4
Fields, Annie   133
Fields, Mrs. James T.   36
Finn, Huck   19, 171, 173 182, 267
    as "America's child"   176, 181
    compared to Tom Sawyer   215, 216
    death wish   177, 216, 218
    escape from social corruption   152, 156
    orphanhood   213, 217, 218
    reading   36
    real-life model for   123, 124
    in *Tom Sawyer*   216, 253, 254, 266
Finn, Pap (*Huckleberry Finn* character)
    19, 36, 61, 218, 255, 267
    as a parent   62, 177
Fischer, Victor   xxiii, 287
Fisher, George (short story
    character)   213
Fishkin, Shelley Fisher   xvi, 25, 242, 288
"Five Boons of Life, The"   4, 19
Fleming, Marjorie   137, 138, 143
Florence, Italy   82, 92, 137
Florida, Missouri   47–9, 122, 225, 259
Following the Equator   82, 144, 232
Foner, Philip S.   xx, 198
Foote, Lily Gillette   57, 92
Foote, Shelby   240
Foster, Jodie   245
frame stories   206, 207, 262, 263
Franklin, Benjamin   32, 199, 249
Frazer, James   125
Fredonia, New York   51, 53
Freire, Paulo   252

Gabrilowitsch, Clara Clemens (SLC's
    daughter). *See* Clemens, Clara
Gabrilowitsch, Nina Clemens (SLC's
    granddaughter)   63, 94, 144
Gabrilowitsch, Ossip (SLC's son-in-
    law)   85, 92, 94, 143, 144

Galaxy (magazine)   149, 153, 154, 157
games   56, 60, 76, 90, 95, 97, 119
Garfield (comic strip)   175
Garrison, William Lloyd   230
Garth, John   123, 125, 126
Garth, Kercheval   125
gender bending   203–11
generational conflict   181
Generation Z   248–58
Gerken, Irene   141
German language   57, 76, 78, 82, 89, 182
Germany   29, 57, 78, 82, 89, 101
"Ghost Story, A"   213
Gilded Age, The   xviii, 33, 34, 52, 125,
    213, 214, 215
    writing of   71
Gillette, William   81
Gillis, Ann   243
Gillis, Jim and Steve   xvii
Gillman, Susan   205, 206
Gleason, Rachel Brooks   85, 86
Goethe, Johann Wolfgang von   41
"Golden Arm" story   79
Golden, James Joseph   xxiii, 288
gold rush, California   121
Goldsmith, Oliver   32, 36
"Goldsmith's Friend Abroad"   152
Gone with the Wind (film)   243
Goodrich, Samuel   24, 25
governesses   56, 57, 78, 92
Grant, Dr.   48
Grant, Ulysses S.   34, 199
Grapes of Wrath, The (film)   xiii, 242
Gray, Thomas   32
"Great Dark, The"   62
Great Expectations (Dickens)   13,
    214, 242
Green, Sarah P. McLean   42
Gribben, Alan   xv, 12, 23, 288
Griffin, Benjamin   xxiii, 289
Griffin, George   90
Gulliver's Travels (Swift)   34, 92

Hall, Abraham   71
Hall, Fred J.   40
Hall, G. Stanley   4, 27
Halley's Comet   247
Halstead, Murat   115
Hamilton, Margaret   243